HIS FINE WIT: A STUDY OF THOMAS LOVE PEACOCK

His Fine Wit

A Study of Thomas Love Peacock

CARL DAWSON

> his fine wit
> Makes such a wound, the knife is lost in it;
> A strain too learned for a shallow age,
> Too wise for selfish bigots; let his page,
> Which charms the chosen spirits of the time,
> Fold itself up for the serener clime
> Of years to come, and find its recompense
> In that just expectation.
>
> SHELLEY, 'Letter to Maria Gisborne'.

LONDON

ROUTLEDGE & KEGAN PAUL

First published 1970
by Routledge and Kegan Paul Ltd
Broadway House, 68–74 Carter Lane
London, E.C.4
Printed in Great Britain
by Ebenezer Baylis and Son, Limited
The Trinity Press, Worcester, and London
© Carl Dawson 1970
SBN 7100 6621 x

For Hanne

CONTENTS

PREFACE

I address this book to those readers of Peacock who either already share my assumptions or who can take the time to be persuaded. The assumptions are that Peacock plays a significant part in the literature of Regency England, not merely as critic or devil's advocate, but as a creator of brilliant fiction and, more generally, as a man of letters. A century after his death, it is both timely and appropriate to take another look at his works.

Usually Peacock is understood as a satirist, whether as a cantankerous nay-sayer, as Mario Praz judges him, or as 'the great satiric commentator on the age', in the words of Ian Jack. Unquestionably he was a satirist, and a satirist more nearly approximating Mr. Jack's than Mr. Praz's description. Yet he was much more than a witty observer whose ears caught the new modulations of an 'age of personality' or an 'age of talk'. He was first a literary craftsman, a writer as gifted and as scrupulous in his way as the great poets of the generation were in theirs. He was also a writer of comedy, a peer of Jane Austen, for whom satire remained subordinate to fiction with a larger purpose. What is needed and what I hope may be found in the pages to follow is a sympathetic but critical account of Peacock's diverse achievement.

My emphasis here is on Peacock's fiction, or, more exactly, on his comedy, which includes related pieces like 'The Four Ages of Poetry'. I have not, however, restricted the discussion to these works alone, and the approach calls for some explanation. Peacock is largely and properly remembered for his novels, but he wrote competently as poet and essayist. The generic division is also partly chronological, for he was in his thirties and had written poetry for twenty years before turning to prose. My comments follow the main phases of his writing career.

In spite of wide disparity, in quality as much as in genre and outlook, Peacock's writings are all intimately related. To the benefit of his fiction, Peacock was an unabashed dilettante, and his novels may be said to dramatize his own many fads and pursuits. He loved the rural areas of Wales and England, while involved in the revival of Celtic studies and antiquarianism generally. He wrote with knowledge and foresight about American politics, steam navigation, and utilitarianism. He dabbled at play-writing and attended the theatre. He understood music and responded, if not to the great orchestral developments of his day, certainly to the opera and ballet. He wrote an essay on gastronomy and began a cookery book. He wrote about classical literature from Cratinus to Nonnus, about French literature from Rabelais to Paul de Kock, and he commented on many of the works of his English contemporaries. An outspoken enemy of industrial might, a feminist, a student of mythology, Peacock was an informed and opinionated writer, whose comments provide not only a clue to his own fiction, but also a fascinating insight into the intellectual life of the times. Since what will be said about the poems and essays bears directly on the discussion of the novels, I have introduced many of his works that are relatively unknown, incorporating them into a survey, though by no means an exhaustive one. While they may be read independently, the first two parts—on the poems and essays—serve as introduction to the third, which is a fairly full commentary on the novels.

Whatever its advantages, a survey creates problems of balance and bulk. If a number of poems and essays, as well as outlines of the novels themselves, seem to be described in excessive detail, the method itself may be at fault. My hope is that such descriptions are for the most part no longer than they need to be and that a reader familiar with the material will take them as simple reminders.

The question of biographical material and its relevance to a critical study raises a more difficult problem. But briefly, I have thought it useful to introduce at least a minimal biographical framework, partly because the arguments develop within a survey, partly because so much of Peacock's life seems pertinent for a study of his writings yet remains unfamiliar to most readers.

Peacock enjoyed a long life. In 1785, the year of his birth, the Bastille had not yet fallen; in 1866, the year of his death, the United States had lived through civil war and England was on the eve of the second Reform Bill. As a boy Peacock read the poems of Ossian, as a man the latest novel by Dickens. Dickens, who was born when Peacock was twenty-seven—and the author of several volumes of verse—accepted contributions from Peacock for *Bentley's Miscellany* (in 1837–8) some twenty years before Peacock wrote his final novel. And Thackeray, meeting Peacock in 1850, spoke of him as the 'charming Horatian' poet of *Maid Marian* (written thirty years before), not realizing that Peacock was still to write some of his best Horatian verse. In short, to speak about the works of a man whose life spans at least two literary generations, it is helpful to refer to biographical details. At the same time, this study adds little to what we know about the events of Peacock's life. It relies on Carl Van Doren's *Life* (1911), on the corrective biographical introduction to the Halliford Edition (1924–34), and on biographies—such as N. I.

White's *Shelley*—about certain of Peacock's contemporaries. There has been no satisfactory biography of Peacock—Van Doren's proved better as a critical study—possibly because, as Jean-Jacques Mayoux has written, Peacock *'n'a pas eu de vie extérieure'*, though more likely because he allowed few people into his confidence and left his biographers the sparsest of information. Reticent and reclusive, he lived a secret and private life, even among friends. As a young man he took solitary tours to Scotland and Wales and spent the greater part of his time in quiet country retirement. After joining the India House in 1818 (the year he published *Nightmare Abbey*) he travelled little, lost many of his earlier ties, and proved a responsible and influential but somewhat withdrawn public servant. Of his later relationships—for example, with his son-in-law, George Meredith, or James Mill, or Lord Broughton (John Cam Hobhouse)—and his meetings with people as diverse as Macaulay, Bentham, Thackeray, and Disraeli little is known, and more should be known. But such inquiry is beyond the scope of this project, which centres on the writings themselves.

Biography enters the discussion in another form. Peacock's friendship with Shelley (between 1812 and Shelley's death in 1822), while never entirely based on trust and understanding, never entirely intimate, seems as important to Peacock's writings as to his life, and I have speculated about the impact of Shelley and Shelley's friends on a number of Peacock's works.

II

Readers familiar with other studies of Peacock will recognize my indebtedness to earlier critics. My gratitude may be less in evidence. I have drawn especially on Jean-Jacques Mayoux's enormous and rather formidable assessment of what amounts to Peacock's intellectual and emotional response to his age. For bibliographical information I have relied on Bill Read's bibliographical study of Peacock and on the work of the Halliford editors, H. F. B. Brett-Smith and C. E. Jones. It is curious that, with the exception of several brief, introductory accounts, no full study of Peacock has appeared in English since completion of the Halliford Edition in 1934. During the time this study was in press, Howard Mills published *Peacock; His Circle and His Age* (Cambridge, 1969). There is no opportunity here to respond to Mr. Mills's book, except to say that it is another 'traditional' evaluation of Peacock as a writer of middling talents, and that, in the words of the preface, it is as much 'about Shelley, Coleridge and Byron' as about Peacock. Mr. Mills anticipates me on a number of points, but for the most part we have taken radically different approaches. Benvenuto Cellini's somewhat cursory book was published as early as 1937 and remains untranslated.

Not many of the specifically literary studies of Peacock retain their value. But there are exceptions. Discussions by A. Martin Freeman, J. B. Priestley, Olwen Ward Campbell, as well as the introductory notes to David Garnett's edition of the novels, all offer useful comments. Many of the best insights into Peacock's art occur in incidental remarks by Northrop Frye and Edmund Wilson, and some of the most provocative may be found in unsympathetic essays by Mario Praz and A. E. Dyson. Wherever possible, I have tried to make clear my borrowings from these and other writers. My disagreements with earlier critics are, of course, numerous; they range from specific quibbles to general objections. And, again, my assumptions about Peacock differ from those of most earlier writers, who, accepting the judgments of literary historians or the prejudices of Shelley's idolaters, have tended to apologize for him, to underrate his achievement—even when they pointed to his talents—or, like the Victorians and Edwardians, to treat him like a novel and naughty schoolboy who wrote delightful but trivial stories. Yet it goes without saying that for reasons both of point of view and the critical dialectic itself, disagreement is inevitable, and I have attempted neither to shout down the opposition nor to labour my own interpretations. This, then, is another voice in a continuing dialogue about a distinguished and intriguing literary career.

I have had the good fortune at various stages of writing to find patient and helpful readers. To Carl Woodring, who gave advice and kindness at the difficult times and who indeed made my work possible, I am deeply grateful. My thanks also to Thomas A. Carnicelli, W. H. Owen, James L. Clifford, Olga M. Ragusa, Gilbert Highet, Robert Langbaum, James Rieger, Seamus Dean, Esther Jackson, Lawrence D. Stewart, and Miss Eleanor L. Nicholes, who responded generously to the letter of inquiry from a stranger. Finally I would like to extend thanks to Barbara Schmidt of the Free University of Berlin, who cheerfully typed and edited the final draft.

I would like to thank Messrs. Constable & Co. Ltd., for permission to quote from the Halliford edition of the works of Thomas Love Peacock.

Berkeley, California.

BRIEF REFERENCE CHRONOLOGY OF
PEACOCK'S LIFE AND WRITINGS

1785   Born October 18 at Weymouth in Dorsetshire, his father a glass merchant, his mother the daughter of a Master in the Royal Navy.

1788?   After the death of his father (actual date unknown), removed with his mother to Chertsey, a village on the Thames some twenty miles from London. Spent most of his life in this area.

1791–9?   Attended school, his first and last, at Englefield Green. John Wicks, the Headmaster, said 'he would prove one of the most remarkable men of his day'.

1800   Employed briefly as a clerk in London. Won a prize for a poem, his reply to 'Is History or Biography the more Improving Study?' which appeared in *The Juvenile Library*.

1800–5?   Lived with his mother in London. Composed verse-letters and other boyhood poetry.

1804   Published as a pamphlet *The Monks of St. Mark*, a humorous poem anticipating the farce in his novels.

1805   *Palmyra and Other Poems* published (dated 1806). Evidently living in Chertsey again.

1806   Took a summer walking tour of Scotland.

1807   Began friendship with Edward and Thomas Hookham, who were to publish his writing from 1810 to 1837. Thomas had a reputation as a radical. Love affair with Fanny Falkner, later recorded in the poem 'Newark Abbey'.

1808–9   Secretary aboard the H.M.S. *Venerable* for several months, a warship anchored off the Downs, which he called a 'floating Inferno'.

1809   Excursion along the Thames to collect material for a new poem. Visited Oxford. Afterwards travelled to Wales and met his future wife, Jane Gryffydh.

1810   *The Genius of the Thames* published and for the most part favourably received.

1811–13   Worked on two farces that were never produced, *The Dilettanti* and *The Three Doctors*. Planned a volume of translations, 'Fragments of Greek Tragedy'.

1812   *The Philosophy of Melancholy* published. Introduced by the Hookhams to Shelley, who had praised his verses.

1813   Another visit to Wales. *Sir Hornbrook* published, a humorous 'grammatico-allegorical ballad' for children. Visited

Shelley and his friends at Bracknell, then travelled with Shelley and Harriet to the Lake District and Edinburgh.

1814 *Sir Proteus* published, a satiric attack on Southey (and another 'ballad'), anticipatory of Byron's *Vision of Judgment*. Contemplated founding a school in 'a beautiful retirement in the county of Westmorland', for which he began a prospectus. Strain in friendship with Shelley when Shelley eloped with Mary Godwin.

1815 Presumed engaged to Marianne de St. Croix, then arrested for debt after an affair with an unknown woman. Probably began about this time to receive a stipend from Shelley. Contemplated emigration, perhaps to Canada. Removed to the village of Marlow in Buckinghamshire, within walking distance of Shelley's house at Bishopsgate. Accompanied Mary and Shelley on a boating excursion up the Thames. Thomas Jefferson Hogg, mutual friend of Shelley and Peacock, called their winter of 1815–16 'a mere Atticism'. *Headlong Hall* published late in the year (dated 1816).

1816 Published *The Round Table*, a comic account of the kings of England for children. Began the story 'Calidore' (earlier version, 'Satyrane'), which he left incomplete. Worked on *Melincourt*. Death of Harriet Shelley. Shelley married Mary Godwin, who never liked Peacock.

1817 *Melincourt* published in March, 'by the author of *Headlong Hall*.' Shelley and Mary moved to Marlow, within a few minutes' walk from Peacock. Shelley's *Laon and Cythna* (*The Revolt of Islam*) and Peacock's *Rhododaphne; or the Thessalian Spell* written during the summer and autumn at a time of close co-operation.

1818 *Rhododaphne* published in February; said by one reviewer to put to shame 'our Scotts, Southeys, Byrons, Moores, Campbells, Wordsworths'. *Nightmare Abbey* published. Shelleys left once again for Italy. Wrote a diary for the summer and began his first essay, 'On Fashionable Literature', which he never finished. Worked on the first sections of *Maid Marian* in the summer and autumn.

1819 Began his thirty-seven-year employment with the East India Company in January, after probationary work in the autumn. James Mill employed at the same time. Corrected proofs for *The Cenci* and other of Shelley's poems.

1820 Married Jane Gryffydh after an eight-year interruption of their friendship. 'The Four Ages of Poetry' published in *Olliers' Literary Miscellany*.

1821 Took another trip to Wales. Resumed work on *Maid Marian*. Wrote several satiric poems, including 'Rich and Poor'.

1822 *Maid Marian* published, then adapted for the theatre. Birth of his first child. Purchased house in Lower Halliford, where he lived as much as his duties allowed. Shelley died in July. Peacock, with Byron—who was unavailable— executor of the estate. Busied himself on behalf of Mary Shelley and won her grudging respect.

1822–5 Met Jeremy Bentham, J. S. Mill, Edward Strachey, etc., at the India House. (There is no record of his having met Charles Lamb.)

1825–6 Worked on *Paper Money Lyrics*, a collection of satiric poems not published until 1837.

1826 Death of his daughter Margaret. Began a dramatic or narrative fragment, 'The Pilgrim of Provence'.

1827 Scathing review of Thomas Moore's novel *The Epicurean*, to be followed in 1830 by a similar attack on Moore's *Byron*. Wrote satiric verse at the expense of the new London University.

1829 *The Misfortunes of Elphin* published.

1829–36 Wrote music criticism, first for the *Globe*, later for the *Examiner*.

1830 Essays in the *Westminster Review* (the Utilitarian organ) on Moore, Thomas Jefferson, and London Bridge.

1831 *Crotchet Castle* published.

1833 Death of his mother, who had been friend and critic: 'after his mother's death, he wrote with no interest'.

1834 Key witness for the East India Company on steam navigation. The company later built ships, the 'iron chickens', to his specifications.

1835 A technical essay on steam navigation published in the *Edinburgh Review*. An essay on 'French Comic Romances' published in the *London Review*.

1836 Succeeded James Mill as Examiner, a high post in the India House. 'The Epicier' published in the *London Review*. Wrote the autobiographical piece, 'The Abbey House: Recollections of Childhood', which was to appear in *Bentley's Miscellany*.

1837 *Paper Money Lyrics* published.

1837–8 'The New Year' and several other pieces published in

Bentley's, under the editorship of Charles Dickens. (It is unclear whether Peacock met Dickens.)

1839 Met and established a friendship with Lord Broughton (John Cam Hobhouse), a former friend of Byron and at the time President of the Board of Control. Later met Thackeray and Disraeli at Broughton's house, Erle Stoke.

1839–50 Published nothing for twelve years.

1848 Writing again; began the fragment, 'A Story Opening at Chertsey'.

1849 Marriage of his daughter Mary to George Meredith—an unhappy match.

1851 Death of his wife, who had long been an invalid. 'Gastronomy and Civilization' published. Worked on a cookery book that he never completed, 'The Science of Cookery'. Met T. B. Macaulay.

1852 Began a series of essays on classical drama for *Fraser's Magazine* entitled *Horae Dramaticae*; finished three pieces.

1853 The Merediths living in Peacock's house at Lower Halliford.

1856 Retired from the India House. Succeeded as Examiner by John Stuart Mill.

1857 Death of his daughter Rosa Jane.

1858 Wrote the first part of the Shelley memoirs (parts two and three followed in 1859 and 1860, a supplementary notice in 1862), a corrective account 'to protest against this system of biographical gossip'. Published reviews of Demetrius Galanus and Müller and Donaldson's literary history of Greece.

1859 Began a formal 'Dialogue on Friendship After Marriage' that remained unfinished. Left several narratives unfinished in these years, including 'Boozabowt Abbey' and 'A Story of a Mansion'.

1861 *Gryll Grange* published, after appearing serially in *Fraser's* the year before. Wrote another autobiographical essay, 'The Last Day of Windsor Forest'. Planned 'A Collection of Miscellanies'. Death of Mary Meredith.

1862 *Gl' Ingannati, or The Deceived* published: a prose translation of the Italian play that was a source for Shakespeare's *Twelfth Night*.

1866 Died January 23 at Lower Halliford.

PART 1

Poetry:
The Courted Muse

But the best expression being that into which the idea
naturally falls, it requires the utmost labour and care
so to reconcile the inflexibility of civilized language and
the laboured polish of versification with the idea
intended to be expressed, that sense may not appear
to be sacrificed to sound. Hence numerous efforts and
rare success.

PEACOCK, 'The Four Ages of Poetry'.

1

Introduction

Sir, a man might write such stuff for ever,
if he would abandon his mind to it.

DR. JOHNSON to JOSHUA REYNOLDS
(on Ossian).

Like Cervantes and Fielding before him, Peacock turned to
the novel a seasoned writer for whom poetic fame had been a
pleasant dream of youth, but who had nevertheless a good deal
to say, and who found a more appropriate outlet in fiction.
He did not suddenly stop writing verse in order to write novels.
His last long poem, *Rhododaphne* (1818), followed the first of
his novels by two years, and the novels themselves are full of
songs, extravagant scraps on love and war and wine. There is
an easy cliché about Peacock's writings, that the prose is
classical, the verse romantic; but quite apart from the dubious
psychological assumptions underlying such a view, to pursue
the division is to misread the poetry as much as the prose. In
the first place, Peacock wrote more than one sort of verse. The
short lyrics have a different provenance from the poems
Peacock thought would make his reputation, and if, like many
works of the time, they take the form of ballads, glees and
catches, they belong to a verse tradition that reaches back to
Waller, Prior, Carey, and Cowper. Throughout his life
Peacock retained a gift for graceful and often light and playful
lyrics. Yet for about fifteen years he paid serious court to the
muses, composing earnest odes on Palmyra and rambling
panegyrics about the Thames. These are poems that not only
shun humour; at times they strongly condemn it. The author
of *The Philosophy of Melancholy* might have agreed with Shelley
that laughter must be 'put down'. The author of *Nightmare
Abbey* seems a different man indeed.

While Peacock's long poems are more easily classified than
the lyrics, they too—with the exception of *Rhododaphne*—are

3

hardly poems one would associate with the 'romantic generation'. They may be, like the characteristic works of Peacock's
great contemporaries, apparently outside any hard and fast
genre, but they are based on late eighteenth-century poetic
forms. They are essentially academic verse: odes and meditative topographical poems which have long and not altogether
distinguished traditions in the preceding century.

Like Pope, whom he so much admired—and whom, along
with Byron, he held up as an example for his contemporaries—
Peacock delights in the couplet. He also employs a given poetic
diction, accepts conventional personifications, and seeks to
express what had oft been thought. Unlike Pope, he avoids
strict adherence, except to some extent with the ode, to classical patterns. Always turning to Greek and Roman writers
for inipration, he rarely turns to them for models. This is true
of his short poems as well. The man who became a master of
epigrammatic prose wrote, for example, only two epigrams,
both as a young boy. In view of his love for classical literature,
his poetry is surprisingly empty of formal satires, such as
Gifford was imitating, pastoral dialogues, such as Wordsworth
was adapting, or classical dramas, so interesting to Shelley.
And though he sets *Rhododaphne* in ancient Thessaly, translates
passages from Euripides and Sophocles, and creates an 'Aristophanic Comedy' in *Gryll Grange*, he uses few of the ancient
genres.

His first long poem, *Palmyra* (1806), is an ode in the tradition
of Gray and Collins. *The Genius of the Thames* (1810), next in
the series, is a meditative, topographical poem, indebted to
Pope's *Windsor Forest*, Thomson's *Seasons*, and a host of their
imitators. *The Philosophy of Melancholy* (1812), more forbidding
in title than in fact, is a leisurely descriptive work with the
psuedo-epical overtones common to the generation of Beattie
and the Wartons. The three poems take slightly different forms,
but they belong to the same literary family and share certain
characteristics. All presuppose the relationship between picturesque nature and the solitary poet. All introduce the trappings
of blasted cities, emblematic figures, picturesque descriptions,
patriotism, and melancholy.

Essentially Peacock borrows both a poetic technique and a
philosophic stance; but it should also become clear that he

4

writes some of the best poems in whichever branch of the meditative-descriptive tradition he experiments. What Peacock took many years to recognize was that the tradition itself was worn out, or, put another way, that it had already lent itself to a new kind of poem. If we think of 'local poetry'—the term is Dr. Johnson's—as a long search by later eighteenth-century poets for form or genre, we will probably discover in some of Wordsworth's poems a culmination of the search.[1] For Wordsworth, after meandering in *An Evening Walk* and *Descriptive Sketches*, was to transform poetry of landscape in 'Tintern Abbey' and *The Prelude*. Wordsworth works away from sentimentalism by altering the terms of his response to natural objects—by escaping pastoral conventions—and so avoids the perils of the scene-painting eighteenth-century topographical poet who merely looked at his topic and pointed to its salient features, as if from a distance.[2] Wordsworth revolutionized meditative-descriptive verse, but in a way that Peacock found unacceptable. His reaction to Wordsworth is worth touching on.

When Wordsworth insists on 'natural' diction and 'spontaneous overflow', even in recollection, he is demanding direct and necessarily personal expression. Such a view of poetry Peacock vigorously opposed, just as he opposed generally the 'cult of personality'. Geoffrey Tillotson has written that it is the 'presence of a stage intermediary between the fresh response and the written poem that accounts for much of the difference between an eighteenth-century nature poem and a nineteenth-century one'.[3] If 'stage intermediary' implies an assumed pose and a conventional diction, if it involves, so to speak, the translation of a specific into a general personality, then Mr. Tillotson does account for the poetic attitude of many eighteenth-century nature poets and of poets, like Peacock, who carried the tradition into the nineteenth century. Peacock distrusted Wordsworth's preoccupation with himself, distrusted the matter-of-factness, the obsession with what, in his opinion, could only prove trivial.[4] A reserved man—and a defender of an author's privacy—Peacock fittingly retains the stage intermediary in his own writings.

His most successful caricatures and burlesques of early nineteenth-century writers were to be those that showed sympathy as well as understanding, and it is pertinent that, except briefly in 'The Four Ages of Poetry', he never managed a good parody of Wordsworth. Peacock misunderstood Wordsworth's insistence on subjectivity, confusing ends with means. He thought that Wordsworth wrote confessional literature, and he failed to realize that subjectivity was less the goal than the condition of Wordsworth's poetic intent.

The nineteenth-century critic Lord Houghton (Monckton Milnes) wrote that Peacock's long poems came of a time when verse could be considered as much a gentleman's art as a 'divine afflatus' and that they are rather depictions of current fashions in verse than important documents in themselves.[5] Peacock would perhaps have agreed with the first part of Houghton's statement; most readers of the poems would agree with the second part. In fact, neither of Houghton's points is quite accurate, since Peacock wrote his poems, not in the eighteenth century, but as a younger contemporary of Wordsworth, when poetic fashions and ideas about the nature of the poet had already undergone a great change. 'Another race hath been, and other palms are won.' What one can say, to accept part of Houghton's statement, is that Peacock as a young man considered poetry to be a gentleman's art and set out writing for other gentlemen.

His attitude towards readers of poetry changed drastically with the years. If, by 1820, he could write to Shelley that an intelligent reading public was a thing of the past, his earlier opinion had been quite different. To the young poet there could be no violent rift between the writer and his society, between creator and critic, because the poet was of society, his poetry for it. Fame would be the natural consequence of his genius and time. The response to his own poems proved anything but satisfying. A few generous reviews, a few scattered comments, were all that greeted his publications. No doubt one reason for his disillusionment with the readers of poetry was that they received his own efforts with insufficient enthusiasm.

But the problem went deeper. Peacock came to face what Wordsworth, Coleridge, Keats, Shelley, Byron, all struggled with: the question of whom to write for. Peacock was to recognize that the initial reaction to *Kubla Khan* and *Christabel* among the reviews and 'reading public' was childish and wrong. His first essay, an unfinished piece on 'Fashionable

Literature', denounces both readers and reviewers and laments the plight of the imaginative poet. Not always kind to Coleridge, Peacock was clearly aware of what he had to face. His response to his own readers is fascinating to watch. At about the time of his first novel (written in 1815) he sensed that there actually was no public to write for. He did not conceive, as Wordsworth had, of trying to create a responsive audience. He felt that such an audience as could listen to poetry was no more—had passed with the previous century when readers and reviews were more receptive. His decision was to stop writing for a particular audience, and the result was a series of iconoclastic novels and essays and, paradoxically, his best long poem—*Rhododaphne*. No longer bound by the idea of reviews, he was no longer tied to what he had thought the requisite sentiments and language for serious poetry.

Satire may not be, as Swift had suggested, written for the pleasure of the author alone, but much satire is both private and iconoclastic. It would be too simple to call Peacock's satiric writings revenge upon readers who had merely tolerated his poems. He himself apparently came to smile at his early efforts. And, of course, there may be dozens of reasons for his turning to satire. One thing, however, is clear. When, like Shelley, Peacock realized the limited nature of his audience, he stopped compromising. This did not enable him to be a great poet any more than it made inevitable his turning to the novel, but it did make a new kind of poetry possible for him.

The matter of the poet's audience helps to explain much about Peacock's writing, and it is a topic that will recur in later contexts. But Peacock was not created by his readers, nor could he wholly adapt to what he thought they wanted. Some characteristics of his poetry remain more or less constant throughout his seventy years of writing. All his verse, for example, is limited in depth or intensity of emotion. In the long poems this is especially obvious, for it is as though in these works he asks of himself more than he was capable of expressing, more perhaps—given the demands of such verse—than he was capable of feeling. In *The Misfortunes of Elphin* Peacock talks about the man who 'works himself up into a soliloquy of philosophical pathos, on the vicissitudes of empire and the mutability of all sublunary things, interrupted only by an occasional peep at his watch . . .'

(VI, 101). Although the specific target here is the 'picturesque tourist', the portrait applies just as well to himself as poet, when he wrote about matters which never wholly interested him, or at least to which he was never wholly committed. But the sense of engagement is not much more intense in the short lyrics than in the meditative poems, because Peacock nowhere abandons the 'stage intermediary'. Nor does he weep or moan or whisper sweet nothings to his mistress. Within his range he can write brilliant verse, but one is always aware of definite emotional limits. Peacock's granddaughter, Edith Nicolls, wrote shortly after his death that he had fine warm affections for people without any real passion.[6] Since she knew Peacock as an old man, her observation is of questionable accuracy; as a comment on his poetry it is perfectly apt.

2

Boyhood Verse and *Palmyra*

A Babylonish dialect
Which learned pedants much affect.

SAMUEL BUTLER, *Hudibras*.

There are no miraculous years in Peacock's literary career, no great periods of activity or corresponding declines. Like Walter Landor, he wrote into his 'ninth decade'; he also wrote with facility in his first. In the earliest of his poems that come down to us—written at the age of nine—there is a light and laughing quality befitting the future author of *Headlong Hall*. Making a distinction with a touch of prophecy, he has this to say:

> Dear Mother, I attempt to write you a letter
> In verse, tho' in prose, I could do it much better . . .

and adds, with ironic self-flattery,

> The Muse, this cold weather sleeps up at Parnassus,
> And leaves us, poor poets, as stupid as asses (VII, 153).

If he was not entirely a poet by this time, Peacock could at least put humorous lines together. 'Surely', says Clive Bell, 'the boy of nine years old who wrote this was destined to be something better than a minor poet.'[1]

Peacock was destined to be something better than a minor poet, but not all of the early verse offered such happy omens. His first published poem, written a few years later than the verse-letter, seemed to promise dullness and mediocrity. Responding to the question: 'Is History or Biography the more Improving Study' (in 1800), the earnest young poet lets History rout Biography in a list of abstractions:

> Hail then to thee, fair Hist'ry! 'tis for thee
> To wear the golden crown of Victory! (VII, 158).

9

Here too are foreshadowings, but not of *Headlong Hall*. *Palmyra* and *The Genius of the Thames* were also to reveal that their author nodded deferentially to Pope and to Pope's followers in the later eighteenth century and that it was not always the best of their qualities that he made his own.

The signs in both these poems may be clear enough. Each in its way depicts a characteristic of the poet and hints at the directions of his literary career. But, looked at as indications of Peacock's talents, many of the early verses will seem irrelevant. For Peacock wrote as a boy a greater variety of verse than he was later to find interesting. He tried his hand at miscellaneous types, some only once. He composed epigrams and acrostics and his only playful elegies; he wrote glees and rollicking narratives; he adapted passages from the Bible and from classical and Italian poets; and he wrote plays and poems in the Ossianic manner.

Most of his early verse is, naturally enough, slight and derivative, but there is already a qualitative difference between the 'serious' and the light poems that is to continue. Peacock is simply better with irony and humour than with the expression of emotion. One might think of Laforgue's ironic defences, his inability to maintain a serious pose or cope with emotions, for this was no less a characteristic of Peacock. Nor were there to be great changes in his sensibility or a measurable intensification with age. Arthur Symons' comment on Laforgue, that he was perennially an old man, also makes a certain amount of sense for Peacock's writings. (Symons, incidentally, had high praise for Peacock's verse in the study of English Romanticism.)

In the years between 1800 and publication of the *Palmyra* volume in 1805, Peacock was adapting lines from Ossian, translating Guarini's *Pastor Fido*, and, after the fashion of the eighteenth-century pindaric, paraphrasing sections from *Isaiah* and *Revelation*. 'The Storm' gives a clear idea of his more sober works of the time. It contains a stock hermit, so common in the countryside of late eighteenth-century poetry—and present even near Wordsworth's Wye—who says, 'thus 'tis with Man', as well as a regiment of abstractions, including Danger, who ' 'mid the lurid air/Sate darkly thron'd on high' (VII, 168). The moral of the poem, that pain and pleasure are transient as clouds, is appended as the final stanza. In 'The

Visions of Love' the young poet offers a sweeping survey of 'all-conquering Love', beginning with 'Eden's gate' and a Miltonic 'flaming sword', and closing mundanely with a comfy hearth. Addressing his sweetheart, he draws her attention to one 'vision' after another, in a way that foretells the technique of his longer poems. Peacock borrowed from eighteenth-century poets the 'as in painting, so in poetry' analogy. In 'The Visions', as in the later long poems, he depicts scenes, calls attention to things picturesque, and develops his material by visual progression. He also alludes specifically to James Thomson, long one of his poetic idols, by speaking of 'the whit'ning plains' and describing the earth according to its seasonal garb. 'Maria's Return', a poem of desolation and abandoned love, similarly includes the phrase 'whit'ning ground' and other touches from *The Seasons*. This poem remains an exercise in windy sentiment:

> With him to roam
> I fled my home;
> I burst the bonds of duty;
> I thought my days in joy would roll;
> But Henry hid a demon's soul
> Beneath an angel's beauty! (VI, 44).

Here as in a number of related poems Peacock allows himself more than a touch of bathos, though in fact he sometimes sinks before he rises. For example the 'Farewell to Matilda', intended to describe the speaker's emotions on parting with his mistress, opens in a way that invites laughter:

> Matilda, farewell! fate has doom'd us to part,
> But the prospect occasions no pang to my heart (VI, 71).

The abrupt, testy, and at the same time sing-song address excludes any sympathy a reader might be expected to feel for the presumably unfortunate lovers. Peacock writes this and other love poems hat in hand. Similarly the elegies, with one or two exceptions, prove flat and unmoving. These lines appear in a poem for Charles Pembroke:

> Upright and sincere,
> For public worth esteem'd, or private lov'd,
> Approving Virtue smil'd upon his life,
> And soft eyed sorrow consecrates his urn (vi, 67).

He is formal again and appropriately so, and he can turn his phrases—although he allows himself once more an unfortunate 'thus 'tis with man'. What tends to spoil the effect is the hiding of personal sentiment behind personifications and abstractions, for this remains a conventional eulogy, in which the subject's name might be inserted as on a dotted line.

Almost invariably the light verse is better. Reminiscent of 'Slender's Ghost', by William Shenstone, is 'Slender's Love Elegy', which contains the following admission:

> I cannot boast the art sublime,
> Like some great poets of the time,
> To sing, in lofty-sounding rhyme,
> Of amorous rage (vi, 9).

Slender is speaking to 'sweet Anne Page'. He might be speaking for his author. 'To a Young Lady Netting', an unpretentious lyric of three stanzas, develops the conceit that the young lady's hands weave a spiritual with the actual net 'no human pow'r can break'. If not inventive, this is gentle and pleasant, the kind of occasional verse Peacock probably read in Henry Carey, John Gay, or Matthew Prior. Two humorous elegies on a sweetheart's lap-dog also suggest Prior, especially his 'Epitaph on True, her Majesty's Dog'. 'The Comparison', at least in title, recalls Cowper's lighter verses. In this piece the young poet invokes Hermes and Jove to prove his 'Lucretia of Shacklewell [Engelfield] Green' more lovely than the Roman Lucretia of old.

Much of Peacock's early verse, like much of Keats's and Shelley's, takes the form of letters to friends and family. Typical is one written at fourteen to his grandmother, which he develops into a narrative poem about an upstart London merchant, Sir Peter Bohea. (Bohea: at the time a middle-grade tea.) Describing Bohea's meteoric rise from rags to riches, he alludes in passing to business ethics, London fashions, and cuckoldry. He may be writing according to models in, say, the *Anti-Jacobin*—then in its vigorous early days—but he is clearly watching his subjects and catching their follies:

By this time *Sir Peter* had realis'd clear
The *moderate* sum of three thousand a year!
His *lady* began her old friends to despise,
And look'd on the Cockneys with scorn in her eyes (vii, 165).

Elsewhere, in another verse-letter, he scoffs at 'The Man of Fashion',

A chap whose modish pucker'd shoulders
Create a laugh in all beholders—— (vii, 162).

and shows, for a young boy, an eye for absurdity and pretension, as well as an awareness of the humorous possibilities of feminine rhymes.

Peacock's later verse shows a technical control understandably lacking in poems of his youth, yet his early and late verse do share certain characteristics: in both there is a love of wordplay, of puns, of twisted rhyme—a desire to burlesque language. 'The Alarmists' affords a good early example of this quality. At a mock convention, spokesmen of various trades get up to air their patriotic grievances. Here, for example, is an irate cook:

John Bull once was fat, once he lived upon clover,
But he's now overdone and completely done over;
He's roasted, he's dish'd—Zounds! I broil with vexation!
Not one drop of gravy is left in the Nation (vii, 174).

The poem ends with 'let us all be unhappy together', a line Peacock will give to Christopher Glowry in *Nightmare Abbey* and make into a kind of refrain. Already in this poem he sets up absurd characters and lets them spout nonsense, while taking a Rabelaisian delight in their garrulity.

Two more poems should be mentioned before turning to *Palmyra*. The first is a glee, written when Peacock was eighteen:

Quickly pass the social glass
　　Hence with idle sorrow!
No delay—enjoy today,
　　Think not of tomorrow!
Life at best is but a span,
　　Let us taste it while we can!
Let us still with smiles confess,
All our aim is happiness! (VII, 185).

Here is the type of light, hedonistic verse that Peacock was to master and to scatter through his novels. Related to it is the longer, and independently published, *The Monks of St. Mark*, wherein the hedonists are cloister brothers, needing no exhortation to enjoy themselves. Peacock's second published work, it was issued privately in 1804, probably at the family's expense. Compounded of gambolling anapaests and chronic punning, *The Monks* is simply a poem of play. With the same buffoonery he introduces into his novels—but far more noisy—Peacock lets the monks kick and roll, poke and fall and gabble. They 'hold forth' 'by spirit inspired':

While Pedro protested, it vex'd him infernally,
To see such good beverage taken '*externally*'.

Their cloister offers a preview of Boozabowt Abbey, setting of a later, unfinished narrative, and of the drinking halls in *The Misfortunes of Elphin*. (Peacock's conception of cloisters and 'monkery' and of the Middle Ages was to develop little beyond that expressed in *The Monks*, as the later *Maid Marian* illustrates.) What develops into slap-stick chaos is, again 'by the spirit', soon resolved:

They reeled back to their bowls, laughed at care and foul
　　　　　　　　　　　　　　　　weather,
And were shortly all under the table together (VII, 192).

Peacock's early verse would not in itself warrant much attention unless it pointed to his later work. The little effort on behalf of history, for example, and the verse-letter to his mother hardly seem to have come from the same hand. The one is formal and academic, the other laughing and self-effacing. Peacock's later writings follow the early pattern, for they are almost invariably of unmixed types. The short poems prove either lightly satiric or, in a broad sense, elegiac, whereas the long poems express a distrust of laughter and include in their number a long apology for melancholy. The novels implicitly attack what the long poems defend.

When Frances Winwar wrote that 'Secretly Peacock knew that his talent did not lie in verse',[2] she was attempting to answer a question that is likely to occur to any of Peacock's readers: How could a poem such as 'The Visions of Love' or *The Genius of the Thames* have been written by the author of *Headlong Hall*? Miss Winwar's statement—which may be a shrewd guess, but which suggests an understanding of the poet's mind not easily come by—argues that the earnest poet and the laughing novelist are somehow irreconcilable, and she can only conclude that Peacock was no poet. Peacock's own statements make perfectly clear that, for about twenty years, he thought of himself as a poet. And since he wrote a number of fine poems, it is worth repeating that his talent was not for prose alone. The question, perhaps, is *why* he wrote in such dissimilar, if not contradictory, ways; and if no entirely adequate explanation can be given, one or two points are pertinent.

Nearly all of the great early nineteenth-century English poets developed their talents in close co-operation with a single friend, or defined themselves, if sometimes by antagonism, in relation to a literary circle or clique. The sense of the poet's isolation, since degenerated into a hackneyed catch-all to explain much more than it can explain, then seems to have turned poets, not merely in upon themselves, but towards other writers, as though poets began to consider themselves a group apart and to take confidence from the recognition of a common plight. Wordsworth may not have needed Coleridge as the midwife for *The Prelude*, but the knowledge that his friend could listen or was listening certainly lightened Wordsworth's enormous task. Keats and Shelley were nearly always associated with a literary circle, and both profited from sympathetic responses that were otherwise not forthcoming from a larger reading public.

Peacock was briefly to join Shelley's circle of friends, though not on very cordial terms, and with Shelley he formed a close relationship. The poem *Rhododaphne* (written in 1817) followed a period of close intimacy with Shelley, whom it was to influence, and from whom Peacock is likely to have had advice as well as encouragement and sympathy. But Peacock met Shelley after he had written all the long poems except *Rhododaphne*, the publication of which coincided with his friend's final departure from England. Apart from the brief friendship with Shelley, Peacock had few literary relationships; although he corresponded with Edward Hookham, his publisher, and met other poets—such as Keats and Leigh Hunt—he otherwise missed the type of working intimacy that sustained so many poets of the time.

Whether his poetry would have been much improved if he had known Shelley earlier, or if he had found a sympathetic fellow poet, is a matter for speculation. Peacock's aloofness, his reticence, his isolation from literary circles, nevertheless helps to define the kind of poet he was and, for that matter, the kind of poet he evidently wanted to be. His letters make clear that he identified poetry with the whole complex of responses and states of mind associated with an 'age of sensibility'. Perhaps because of his lack of contact with contemporary writers, Peacock's aesthetic positions largely remained those of a prior generation. As a young man he turned his eyes to this earlier poetic scene; he also lived in terms of the ideals of solitude, private meditation, and melancholy espoused by Gray, Collins, Thomson, Dyer, and other of his favourites.

From the beginning, Peacock seems to have been an estimably sane and stable person, but his stability was in part that of a man who submits himself to a given pose. Though we know relatively little about his life, and about the responses of his contemporaries to him, the few reports suggest a variety of postures, whether that of 'romantic' poet, wandering over hill and dale with his dog, or capable officer of the India House, a no-nonsense man, or flirt, or aloof, sceptical onlooker, smiling with a wry smile. There are postures in his writing: not only in his poems, but also in his novels and essays. Like Byron, who was himself much of a self-isolated man and a man of diverse personalities, Peacock prefers the ironical modes, because he maintains them with ease. He finds serious poems, love poems, for example, rather more difficult to handle. It is important to remember that no two men are at work in this literary career, but one man of complex sympathies and identifications.

As he worked on *The Genius of the Thames* Peacock took a trip to the river's source, and wrote to his friend Hookham:

> How is it possible that a river which is *perpetually flowing* can rise from a source which is *sometimes dry?*—The infant river in Kemble meadow is never totally dry, and to the source by which the stream there is constantly supplied can alone belong the honor of giving birth to the Thames. But this spring, Thames Head, would never be totally dry, were it not for a monstrous piece of machinery erected near it, for the purpose of throwing up its water into the neighbouring canal. The Thames is almost as good a subject for a satire as a panegyric.—A satirist might exclaim: The rapacity of Commerce, not content with the immense advantages derived from this river in a course of nearly 300 miles, erects a ponderous engine over the very place of its nativity, to suck up its unborn waters from the bosom of the earth, and pump them into a navigable canal! It were to be wished, after all, that the crime of *water-sucking* were the worst that could be laid to the charge of commercial navigation. . . .
>
> A panegyrist, on the contrary, after expatiating on the benefits of commercial navigation, and of that great effort of human ingenuity, the Thames and Severn Canal, which ascends the hills, sinks into the valleys, and penetrates the bosom of the earth, to unite the two noblest rivers of this most wealthy, prosperous, happy, generous, loyal, patriotic, &c, &c, &c, kingdom of England, might say: 'And yet this splendid undertaking would be incomplete, through the failure of water in the summer months, did not this noble river, this beautiful emblem, and powerful instrument of the commercial greatness of Britain, contribute to that greatness even at the instant of its birth by supplying this magnificent chain of connection with the means of perpetual utility—' (VIII, 172–3).[3]

He acknowledges two contradictory approaches to the subject, while assuming that a certain treatment must involve a certain type of thinking with a corresponding style. *The Genius of the Thames* does precisely what his hypothetical panegyrist outlines, and the first chapter of *Crotchet Castle* follows the suggestion of the satirist. To find fault with Peacock's formal verse involves, in a sense, criticizing the genres he adopts, for there is little of originality or novelty in these works. He is playing with borrowed counters, and the borrowing is wholesale. The young man with radical political leanings can therefore write poems that seem late apologies for the Whig establishment.

Palmyra, first of the long poems, may be understood in terms of an assumed point of view. Reverent toward the past and steeped in poetic conventions of the preceding century, Peacock naturally prefaced his work with a motto from Pindar, invoked the names of Ossian, Gibbon, and Longinus, and used the example of a ruined city to point a moral. But there is, additionally, a kind of biographical logic behind Peacock's turning to Palmyra and his particular handling of the subject. To clarify this, we need to turn briefly to a related topic.

In his memoirs of Shelley, Peacock describes Shelley's unfitness for Eton and Oxford and implies that Eton and Oxford were similarly unfit for Shelley. (In fact, it is hard to think of any institution where Shelley might have been content.) His assumption, and it runs through his entire writings, is that the public schools and the universities—'those dens of dunces', as Cobbett called them—consistently fail in their task of educating and have become places of stop-over for children of the wealthy. Hence his repeated charge in the novels that someone has 'finished his education', by which he means that time has been served but nothing learned. And as his various ironic strictures on educational theories—most notable those of Lord Brougham —make clear, the subject remained important to him. Once, after a brief trip to the Lake District, he envisioned a private school of his own, where he would offer 'classical education' to a small number of students, and he included under classical education study of the great English writers. Peacock's Plan came to nothing, but his prospectus remains as testimony to the belief in liberal—that is, literary—education, complemented by life in the country. He had read his Rousseau, and the plan is Rousseau methodized.

Peacock's own education took place largely in the country, under circumstances that Rousseau would have approved. There was, for example, very little formal schooling. His mother, a woman of intellectual interests, especially fond of eighteenth-century writers, served him first as teacher, later in that invaluable capacity of sympathetic listener.[4] For a few years, after his sixth birthday, he attended boarding school at Englefield Green, the Headmaster of which was a John Wicks, whom Peacock was later to describe as 'not much of a scholar' but capable of 'inspiring his pupils with a love of learning'. Wicks, who introduced Peacock to the study of French, Greek, and Latin, is reported to have had a high opinion of his student, expecting him to 'prove one of the most remarkable men of his day'.[5]

At the age of thirteen Peacock was doing nothing more remarkable than working as a clerk in London, the formal part of his education completed. That he never attended the university, never 'finished his education', Peacock rarely let his readers forget. His novels are full of attacks on the 'dens of dunces' and exude an unmistakable delight in extra-curricular, even anti-curricular, learning. Unlike the novels, the poems suffer, not because Peacock was an uneducated and unenlightened boor perpetrating nonsense, but because he let so much of his poetry turn into academic exercise. Never having been 'lashed into Latin by the tingling rod', he was unduly proud of his Latin— as of his learning generally. If he was not badly educated, he liked to think that others were, and, as often happens with a self-taught man, his learning tended to the out-of-the-way and the arbitrary. There is more than a touch of pedantry, though the practice was fashionable, in the way he buttresses his long poems with footnotes, as if he cannot entirely rely on his reader's knowledge. In the novels Peacock burlesques his own earlier practice, but even in the novels he delights in exhibiting his intellectual wares.

By the time he wrote *Palmyra*, Peacock had retired from his clerkship—which evidently lasted but a few months—and from London, and was living in the country at Chertsey. (For Matthew Arnold, as for Peacock, Chertsey was to be 'the poetic town of our childhood'.) *Palmyra*, a literary and academic poem on a topic that demanded research and that was foreign to Peacock's experience, seems the fitting product of a retiring, self-taught, and intellectual young man.[6]

Intent upon making his reputation, Peacock prefaced his work with a cento from the plays of Shakespeare, an honest sop 'To the Reviewers'. He assures them that his 'invention' can only thrive if they prove generous, and that he will speed 'under your good correction' (vi, 4). Perhaps he was aware of the poem's weaknesses; perhaps he simply wrote what he thought would please. In any case, he seems to have had no doubts about the wisdom of either his reviewers or the reading public.

The suitability of *Palmyra* as a poetic subject would have been obvious to readers of the eighteenth and early nineteenth centuries. The ancient city suggested travel, fascinating enough for lovers of excursionary verse; equally important, it conjured up ruins and the opportunity for reverie. In 1755 the poet James Grainger had noted, in his 'Ode to Solitude', that the lover of solitude could, in his homage to sublimity and contemplation, 'Tadmore's marble wastes survey'—Tadmore and its variations being other names for Palmyra—

> You, Recluse, again I woo
> And again your steps pursue.

Peacock, in 1805, followed Grainger's steps, which led him inevitably from observations on a ruined city to the Ruins of Time, of Art, of Nature herself. The ruins he depicts might be those of Pompeii, Rome, Fountains Abbey, or Stonehenge, other popular topics for poets similarly inclined.

A partly declamatory, partly elegiac ode of twenty-five stanzas—in form an open or 'false' Pindaric—*Palmyra* is a late symptom of what has been aptly termed 'the great *Pindarique* distemper'. Absorbed by the frailty of human things and the curse of time, Peacock says at length what Shelley says briefly and better in 'Ozymandias'. Too long and too windy, *Palmyra* does nevertheless sport its touchstones—and they resound:

> Where Desolation on the blasted plain,
> Has fix'd his adamantine throne,
> I mark, in silence and alone,
> His melancholy reign (vi, 8).

Desolation sitting on the throne involves only one of various positions assumed by army of abstractions. An excess of adjectives and, in the words of the *Critical Review*, 'sense that is not infrequently sacrificed to sound', are the poem's main faults.[7]

Looking back on the critical response to *Palmyra*, Peacock was to indicate that the poem had been unfairly received—a judgment not easy to understand. With one or two slight exceptions, the reviewers enjoyed his poem. Warmest praise came from that work-horse of the *Monthly Review*, Christopher Moody, who decided that the poet had clambered over the fence of a barricaded Helicon to sip of the fountain. 'Even those who are somewhat fastidious', he writes, 'will receive pleasure from the vigour of his conceptions, the elegance of his expressions, and the harmony of his numbers.'[8]

There is, predictably, no word in Coleridge or Wordsworth about Peacock's verse: Moody discovered just the sort of things they had grown to dislike. Shelley on the other hand was to read Peacock's work. As usual, generous in his response, he pronounced one section of *Palmyra* 'the finest piece of poetry I ever read'.[9] What won his applause, it should be added, was the revised version of the poem, which Peacock had recast and shortened.[10] The new poem expresses the same ideas with more force in briefer compass; it remains nevertheless basically the same poem, except that Hope in God has been supplanted by the Necessity of Virtue—hence perhaps some of Shelley's enthusiasm. The stanza that Shelley praised also reads a little like some of Shelley's own more abstract verse, in which subject and object dance off, to use Peacock's words, into the realm of 'ennui and magnanimity' (VIII, 39).

Of the poems issued with *Palmyra*, several were in the manner of the title poem, while others were experiments both in metre and form. Peacock's classical interest is apparent in a section entitled *Nugae*, a title he probably drew from Catullus and Tibullus. These little poems are satiric in part, as a motto from Juvenal would suggest, but their models would seem to have been eighteenth-century English adaptations rather than the Latin poets themselves. The *Palmyra* volume also included translations, notably from Peacock's early classical favourite, Pindar, and from a later model, Petronius.

Best of the poems in the collection are perhaps the Ossianic

ventures, 'Clonar and Tlamin' and 'Foldath', both brief imitations, and 'Fiolfar', a longer narrative in the Ossianic manner.
These were poems composed at a time when imitations of
Ossian were still in vogue—Byron and Coleridge, for example,
had both to outgrow their early infatuation with Macpherson's
writings. In spite of being modish, 'Fiolfar' is also a creditable
example of the genre as well as an indication of Peacock's
talent for certain poetic metres. Because they tend to gallop,
anapaests are not to every poet's taste, but Peacock, like Byron,
clearly enjoyed them, and 'Fiolfar' shows that he could use
them well. He varies the rising feet with iambics, sometimes
with spondees, and if the effect is not sublime, the pace is
lively—despite the grandiloquence of the words themselves:

> As the torrent, in eddies tumultuously tost,
> That lately has slumbered in fetters of frost,
> Descends from the mountain all turbid with snow,
> Shall Norway rush down on the fields of the foe (vi, 52).

The analogy used here, complete with its heroic clang, allitera-
tion, and fourth-line climax—the metre and couplet suggest a
kind of four-line stanza—appears elsewhere in the poem. Peacock finds the metaphors of waterfalls and spring floods, which
he may have picked up from Thomson, or from later topographical poets, suited to express a number of powerful emotions. He will use them again in *The Genius of the Thames* and
The Philosophy of Melancholy. He also introduces compound
metaphors, 'blood-dropping', 'time-honoured', and so on,
which mar some of his other verse, but which work in the context. Although conventional, such metaphors are appropriate
in a poem that is itself admittedly imitative. Its story of restored
love—the lady Nitalpha to the warrior Fiolfar, with the supernatural aid of Nerimnher—is carefully prefaced, as *Rhododaphne*
was to be prefaced, by an explanatory note on the myth. But we
do not have to remember Young Werther's poignant 'Ossian
has supplanted Homer in my heart', or Hazlitt's association
of Ossian with Homer, the Bible, and Dante, to appreciate
what powerful feelings Ossian had engendered in young poets.
A contemporary reviewer of the *Palmyra* volume found
Peacock's Ossianic poems worthy of Gray. If too generous, this

comment offers a reminder that Peacock had read Gray's work. Like Gray and perhaps with him as model, he cultivated the meditative, melancholic strain—and tended to use his poems as an excuse for footnotes. He was also to develop a genuine knowledge and appreciation of Celtic literature, far removed from modish Ossianism. Hazlitt wrote in his lecture on Gray and other eighteenth-century poets that the 'Pindaric Odes are, I believe, given up at present: they are stately and pedantic, a kind of methodical borrowed phrenzy'. His judgment is unfair to Gray but appropriate for Gray's imitators. *Palmyra* itself remains second-rate Gray.

Peacock's early verse invites comparison with the poems of Byron's apprenticeship, especially those in *Hours of Idleness*. Both men admire and imitate Ossian; both offer rather ponderous elegies—Byron on the statesman George Fox, Peacock on the naval hero Sir Ralph Abercrombie; and they write closely related poems in *Palmyra* and 'Newstead Abbey'. Byron's poem contains more than one line that could sit quietly in Peacock's: 'Here desolation holds her dreary court' is typical enough. Byron and Peacock both more than simply outgrew their early writings. It is as though their best work became a reaction to the more sentimental early efforts, to their years as literary carpenters, when they wrote easily and conventionally. Byron left *Hours of Idleness* far behind, for if the sentiments of 'Newstead Abbey' are still to be found in *Don Juan*, part of the laughter in the later poem is at the mawkishness of the young man. Similarly the sentiments and even the language of *Palmyra* recur in *Nightmare Abbey*—with its telling satire on Byron—and there too as objects of laughter. But in addition to self-parody, there is in both works, and indeed in all of Peacock's novels, satire upon 'fashionable' readers. If there is any consistent strain running through Byron's poem, it is the jeering at readers whose sentimental expectations are destroyed in the bathetic final couplet of so many of the stanzas. Peacock's laughter at his readers is not so pointed, but it is noticeable, and in the sense that all his novels deal with current fashions in ideas, they satirize the craving for such fashions among the reading public. Peacock's judgment of *Childe Harold* and Byron's youthful verse was severe. But he thought *Don Juan* the finest poem of his time.

3

Earnest Tidings:
The Genius of the Thames and
The Philosophy of Melancholy

And the sad truth which hovers o'er my desk
Turns what was once romantic to burlesque.

BYRON, *Don Juan*, iv.

I

Few of Peacock's ideas during the four years separating
Palmyra (1806) from *The Genius of the Thames* (1810) found
their way to burlesque; all too many, to invoke the other line
from Byron's couplet, partake of 'the sad truth which hovers
o'er my desk'. After a walking tour of Scotland in 1806, enjoying, as Brett-Smith comments, 'the scenery made fashionable
by Scott's narrative poems' (I, xxxv), Peacock put together,
though he never published, a poem called 'Time'. The title
perhaps identifies the type of poem as well as its subject, which
involves the same themes as *Palmyra*, Peacock invokes Ossian
again—in an epigraph—and introduces the somewhat glib
refrain 'Death comes to all'. 'The Vigils of Fancy' (1808), toying in anticpation of *The Philosophy of Melancholy* with
fashionable brooding, might be a weak sequel to Coleridge's
'Dejection': beginning with the poet alone at midnight, it
moves on to general reverie. Similarly 'Romance' (1808?),
a first-person narrative told by an abandoned woman, suggests
Wordsworth's 'Ruth', as if translated by an eighteenth-century
Pindar who omits details and strives for pathos:

> Hear a lost, forsaken maid,
> Mourn with wild emotion! (VII, 204).

In 1808 Peacock became a sea-going secretary—his family

had naval connections—aboard the H.M.S. *Venerable*. One result of his employment was the conventional 'Stanzas Written at Sea'—complete with 'white-rolling seas' and 'light-breaking zephyrs'—the title of which is not quite accurate. For the few months that Peacock served aboard, the *Venerable* remained at anchor; and though Peacock speaks of the ship, in a letter to Hookham, as a 'floating Inferno' where work is impossible (VIII, 162), his actual duties must have been negligible. He managed to write letters, with frequent requests for new books, and to do occasional prologues and epilogues for light dramatic productions aboard ship. He also wrote a laughing piece on 'The Art of Modern Drama', which includes a good-natured castigation of the stage and reveals that the author was already familiar, if not directly with the London theatre, at least with Pope and other earlier critics of its excesses:

> Confound in chaos all terrestrial things,
> Pugs, lovers, horses, charioteers and kings:
> The bellowing pit shall hail thy rash endeavour,
> And stage-box Jacky say: Gad's curse, that's clever!
>
> (VII, 211).

Peacock was to write more things at the expense of the 'bellowing pit', especially in his opera criticism. Ironically his own farces, composed soon afterwards, introduce some of the same theatrical techniques that he here mocks.

The floating Inferno evidently became tiresome, and Peacock abandoned the *Venerable* (in the spring of 1809) to continue his poetry. His goal was a new excursionary poem, his subject the Thames. He had completed a short draft aboard ship. By June he was tracing the course of the river in quest of material, at the same time supplementing his 'eye on the object' approach by reading earlier river poems. He finished the work a few months later, during a visit to Wales, and it appeared in the spring of 1810.

The 'proemium' to the first edition of *The Genius of the Thames*, a three-part ode, illustrates what is both the governing attitude of the poem itself and a sentiment common to all Peacock's writings: an intense nostalgia for the past. 'Ah!' he writes,

> whither are they flown,
> Those days of peace and love,
> So sweetly sung by bards of elder time? (VI, 10).

His implication is that modern poets write at a disadvantage, being years away from the times when Dryads frequented the Thames scene. 'We know too', as he was to say with wry irony in 'The Four Ages of Poetry', 'that there are no Dryads in Hyde-Park nor Naiads in the Regent's canal' (VIII, 19). But with luck, and with the muses' aid, the poet may yet sense 'a secret influence nigh' in the river's vicinity. Looking backward as he does and trying to re-create 'those days of yore', he echoes earlier apologists for the beauties of the Thames, and buttresses his own latter-day response with the fresher words of his forerunners.

> To thee I pour the votive lay,
> Oh Genius of the silver Thames! (VI, iii).

offers a distant echo of Robert Herrick's

> I send, I send here my supremest kiss
> To thee, my silver-footed Thamasis.

But one can hear echoes of Gray and Milton, of Thomson and the Warton brothers, and the patter of many smaller feet. Peacock obviously thought of the poem as taking its place in a great tradition of river poems, for he makes much of his indebtedness clear. He pays tribute to John Denham, father of English river poets, who in 'Cooper's Hill'

> The voice of truth to kings revealed
> and broke the chains of tyranny.[1]

Denham's famous quatrain, beginning 'O could I flow like thee', had lent itself to inspiration as well as to countless parodies. His blend of melancholy, patriotism, picturesque observations, and general reverie had guided many poets before Peacock.[2] Along with Denham, Peacock draws in Pope, whose *Windsor Forest* he has continually in mind.

26

Yet shall the ever-murmuring stream,
That lapt his soul in fancy's dream,
Its vales with verdure cease to crown,
Ere fade one ray of his renown (vi, 146–7).[3]

Peacock's encomiums are well-turned and appropriate, and he catches the sense of place and of accumulated tradition. Still, there are great weaknesses in *The Genius of the Thames*, possibly chronic weaknesses of its poetic family. Pope had chided in the *Essay on Criticism* rhymesters who repeat the same themes with the same phrases:

Where'er you find the *cooling Western Breeze*,
In the next Line, it *whispers thro' the Trees*;
If *Crystal Streams with pleasing Murmurs creep*,
The Reader's threaten'd (not in vain) with *Sleep*.

Familiar with Pope, Peacock read this and forgot:

Where now, by mouldering walls, he sees
The silent Thames unheeding flow,
And only hears the river-breeze,
Through reeds and willows whispering low (vi, 153).

His passage is not so much lacking in skill as derivative and dull. The phrases, the rhymes, indeed the whole emotional context, verge on pastiche of earlier writers. Peacock apparently came to discover what was at fault with *The Genius of the Thames*. He writes in 'The Four Ages', as part of his ironic survey of English poetry, what is a telling critique of his own earlier verse:

The changes had been rung on lovely maid
and sylvan shade, summer heat and green
retreat, waving trees and sighing breeze,
gentle swains and amorous pains, by
versifiers who took them on trust, as
meaning something very soft and tender,
without much caring what . . . (viii, 16–17).

In matters of language as well as emotional intensity, Wordsworth's 'Tintern Abbey' seems far away from *The Genius*

27

of the Thames, although both poems are based upon the same poetic tradition: that of musing near a river and letting description turn to larger statement. When reading 'Tintern Abbey' we forget the genre or find it so drastically altered as to be inappropriate. Peacock responded differently. He knew 'Tintern Abbey', as he knew most of Wordsworth, and he parodied the title as 'Lines written *en badinage*, after visiting a paper-mill near Tunbridge Wells, in consequence of the lovely Miss W., who excels in drawing, requesting the author to describe the process of making paper in verse' (VI, 294). His criticism, implicit in the mock title, that Wordsworth is too personal and too trivial in his verse, and that he ignores tradition, reflects on *The Genius*. With its studied impersonality, its epic paraphernalia—including invocations, prophetic visions, and phalanxes of marshalled rivers—Peacock's poems had been anticipated often in the preceding century, just as Wordsworth's in essential ways had not.

One of Peacock's not very distinguished predecessors, the poetess Anne Wilson, had blended misplaced eulogy with astonishing apostrophe to create the following lines: 'The model of the drains prepare to sing,/O sylvan muse!'[3] Peacock nowhere dampens the muse's feet in the drains, but he shares with Anne Wilson the desire to make his poem an almost encyclopedic survey of the river, as the 'Analysis' prefacing the first of the two parts demonstrates:

An autumnal night on the banks of the Thames. Eulogium of the Thames. Characters of several rivers of Great Britain [In *Windsor Forest* Pope had called them 'Sea-born Brothers']. Acknowledged superiority of the Thames. View of some of the principal rivers of Europe, Asia, and America [Pope listed some of these, too]. Pre-eminence of the Thames. General character of the river. The port of London. The naval dominion of Britain, and extent of her commerce and navigation [Compare Pope's 'Unbound Thames shall flow for all mankind']. Tradition that an immense forest formerly occupied the site of the metropolis. Episode of a Druid, supposed to have taken refuge in that forest, after the expulsion of the order from Mona (VI, 108).

Much of Peacock's extensive research for his poem spilled over into footnotes. Despite the helpful suggestion in one review of *Palmyra*, that the necessity of illustration should be 'sedulously' avoided, and despite the fact that the practice had often been satirized—there had been, for example, the *Anti-Jacobin*'s mauling of Erasmus Darwin—Peacock footnotes excessively. As he worked on one section of the poem, Peacock actually wrote to Hookham to request more books—for the purpose of 'manufacturing notes' (VIII, 176). In this matter Wordsworth also succumbed, adding the terse but essentially superfluous note to 'Tintern Abbey': 'The river is not affected by the tides a few miles above Tintern.' Even he could not resist.[4]

When introduced to a later edition of *The Genius of the Thames*, Shelley was to praise its 'genius and versification'. He also contested its assumptions, notably those about 'commerce' and 'prosperity'.[5] It is true that the poem occasionally reads like a pamphlet in favour of British trade:

> O'er states and empires, near and far,
> While rolls the fiery surge of war,
> Thy country's wealth and power increase,
> Thy vales and cities smile in peace:
> And still, before thy gentle gales
> The laden bark of commerce sails (VI, 119).[6]

The panegyric makes of Albion a sanctuary and of trade a panacea. Again, the metamorphosis was not uncommon. John Dyer, for example, had sung his unfortunate paean to the English wool trade in *The Fleece*, and Edward Young had conceived of the world as a 'great exchange', doubtless to the loss of poet and world alike.

In admiring the 'genius' of *The Genius*, Shelley seems to have intended his words without irony. One wonders exactly what he had in mind. That he was sensitive to Peacock's real strength is clear from his reference to versification. Technically—and here the *British Critic* and the (new) *Anti-Jacobin* agreed with him—the poem passed with high marks. Peacock's ear was nearly always good. If in the Thames poem, as in *Palmyra*, his vision gets blurry, if he takes 'on trust' rather too many of his scenes, he hears well. A happy anticipation of *Rhododaphne* are his passages having to do with music. When, in an otherwise conventional 'episode of a Druid', as he calls it, a Druid is dying and about to foretell the course of British history—in the manner of Gray's Druid in 'The Bard'—

> His harp, untouched by human hand,
> Sent forth a sound (vi, 126).

Elsewhere Peacock describes how 'deeper wonder' fills a Roman warrior's soul.

> When on the dead still air around,
> Like symphony from magic ground,
> Mysterious music stole (vi, 123).

But it is not in technical matters any more than in economic assumptions that the essential defect of the poem lies. For Peacock the river is merely a useful, if cumbersome, vehicle for a spate of observations, sketches, histories, and travel. Because he includes all these matters, he forgets the river, loses his focus, and wanders. (One thinks of Coleridge's term, the 'aggregating' power, by which he quietly dismissed poems of fancy.) In 'Tintern Abbey', Wordsworth creates his feelings in conjunction with the scene. The poem is, as Robert Langbaum puts it, 'located'.[7] No unifying feeling or series of impressions develops within *The Genius of the Thames*, nor could it develop. This is another way of saying that Peacock never found in these 'local poems' his real subject. And he did not learn, as Gray had learned in the essentially similar 'Eton Ode', to limit his focus. 'Observations on Man in reference to the Thames' can only lead to a series of unconnected passages, to a poetry of 'pseudo-statement', however good individual lines or sections may be. Perhaps Shelley missed this fault—obvious to later readers— because of his early tendency to wander. The young critic of Peacock's poem was in the midst of his struggles with *Queen Mab*.

II

Peacock remained in Wales some time after the completion of the Thames poem. It was there that he met his future wife,

Jane Gryffydh—'the most innocent, the most amiable, the most beautiful girl in existence' (VIII, 189)—although he was not to marry her for eight years, nor even correspond with her in the interim. A short poem, the 'Farewell to Meirion' (1811) illustrates Peacock's love for Welsh landscape and his disdain for most Welshmen:

> But can the son of science find,
> In thy fair realm, one kindred mind,
> One soul sublime . . . ? (VII, 211).

His answer is an emphatic, if rather querulous, no. He sounds much like Shelley, who was to bemoan the wretchedness of modern Italians while singing the praises of Italy. (Shelley responded wholeheartedly to the sentiment of 'Meirion'.) Evidently the Welsh, if they did not dislike, at least distrusted the strange outsider among them. According to a later report by Shelley, one pious lady reacted in this way: ' "Ah!" said she, "there Mr. Peacock lived in a cottage near Tan y Bwlch, associating with no one & hiding his head like a murderer"; "but", she added, altering her voice to a tone of appropriate gravity, "he was *worse than that*, he was an *Atheist*." ' [8]

What was the murderous-looking 'atheist' doing with himself during the months in Wales? If actually hiding his head, he must for the most part have been hiding it in books. The notes for *The Philosophy of Melancholy* (published in February 1812) tell of a heady range of studies, from Hoare's *Giraldus Cambrensis* to Dante and Virgil. Gibbon, William Drummond, Alfieri, Torquato Tasso—a favourite with Peacock as with Shelley and Byron—are all cited, in addition to several historians of Greece and Rome. Surprisingly, Burton and Milton, the two usual authorities for 'melancholy', do not appear, nor does Gray or Warton, but Mrs. Radcliffe does. Evidently Peacock considered Emily's 'Ode to Melancholy' in *The Mysteries of Udolpho* a worthy example of the melancholic tradition, or perhaps he appreciated the historical connection between Gothic romance and the elegiac tradition.

In any event, Peacock was quarrying from a variety of sources in preparation for his poem. He was also very likely 'communing' with Welsh grandeur. But he was writing little.

What he did write at this time took the form of translation, mainly from the Greek tragedians. (He planned a volume called 'Fragments of Greek Tragedy'.) As an older man he was to translate various passages from the classics into supple and idiomatic English, but in the years 1810 and 1811 he was forcing Euripides into ungainly verse. Why he chose Euripides, and to a lesser extent Sophocles, rather than his comic favourites can probably best be explained by his preoccupation with the subject of melancholy. Typical of his work at this time is 'Phaedra and the Nurse', from Euripides' *Hippolytus*, submitted to the *Morning Chronicle* in April 1814 (but probably written in 1811) with the following note:

> It may perhaps gratify some of your readers who are more conversant with the English than the Greek Drama, to bring them acquainted with a passage of Euripides, which bears a striking resemblance to a part of Hamlet's soliloquy. The original lines being anapaestic, I have given them in translation the form of that colloquial lyric, which seems to me to bear the most strict analogy our language will admit . . . (VIII, 481–2).

The verse itself begins,

> Oh ills of life! relentless train
> Of sickness, tears, and wasting pain!
> Where shall I turn . . . ? (VII, 216).

The letter to the editor is stiff and self-conscious: Mr. Mystic, of *Melincourt*, could have written it. The verse itself is markedly inferior, both to Peacock's own later translation and to work by Shelley, who was shortly afterwards to become acquainted with much Greek literature through Peacock's tutelage. It is, again, hard to avoid the conclusion that his translating, like the composing of excursionary verse, involved a pose, and an inappropriate pose, of which he himself was still unaware.

That Peacock was posing when he wrote *The Genius of the Thames* has been suggested with reference to his letter to Hookham, in which he differentiates between the 'satirist' and the 'panegyrist'. In that poem he assumed the role of panegyrist and played his part with scrupulous care. A few months after his letter to Hookham, Peacock proposed to his friend another theory. Discussing his tendency to both high and low spirits, he says:

> You saw this exemplified in me last summer when I was sometimes skipping about the room . . . at others doling out staves of sorrow, and meditating on daggers and laurel water. Such is the disposition of all votaries of the muses, and, in some measure, of all metaphysicians: for the sensitive and the studious are generally prone to melancholy, and the melancholy are usually subject to intervals of boisterous mirth (VIII, 183–4).

The observation—it reads like a character sketch for Scythrop of *Nightmare Abbey*—ascribes to temperament what Peacock had earlier explained by genre. The poetic result is the same. In *The Philosophy of Melancholy* as in *The Genius of the Thames*, the poet is 'prone to melancholy' and wary of mirth. Here the future author of *Nightmare Abbey* lets himself ask of personified Melancholy:

> Can a fantastic jest, the antic mirth,
> The laugh, that charms the grosser sons of earth,
> A joy so true, so softly sweet, bestow,
> As genius gathers from the springs of woe? (VI, 200).

The question is of course rhetorical, for the poet has consigned humour to 'the grosser sons of earth'.

Rambling through Wales and indulging in solitary musing serves as the foundation for *The Philosophy of Melancholy*. Part One deals with decay and change in nature—*The Seasons* is model once again—and suggests that contemplation of the natural sublime leads to virtuous living. Peacock is concerned here with much the same matter that had occupied him in the earlier poems, meditation on 'the universal mutability'. He finds contemplation best engendered by rugged scenery and mountain grandeur—by Wales, that is—so that wherever he travels in his 'philosophic' application, he has his eye on Cambrian mountains. In Part Two he discusses the happy effects of

D

melancholy on art, offering his principal examples from Gothic
romances and from the paintings of Claude Lorraine and
Salvatore Rosa, whom he refers to familiarly as 'Claude' and
'Salvatore'. Part Three insists upon the importance of decay to
social relationships, and love especially is said to benefit from
unhappiness, although in what way the poet fails to clarify.
Part Four, closing with a deistic hymn, argues, in the words of
the 'General Analysis', 'the mind perceives, that the existence
of a certain amount of evil is indispensible to the general system
of nature' (vi, 186). Wales provides Peacock with his sketch-
pad; Pangloss seems to be the tutelary spirit.

Three years after his poem on melancholy, Peacock sets
Headlong Hall in Wales, creating as a stage for comedy something more or less original. But when, in *The Philosophy of
Melancholy*, he waxes rapturous and earnest on Welsh scenery,
he is following a host of tourists, painters, and poets, who in
turn seem to have followed John Dyer in his trek up 'Grongar
Hill'. *Headlong Hall* and the later novels will caricature tourists,
those 'birds of summer', but *The Genius* and *Melancholy* are both
poems of local tourism, while *Palmyra* remains pseudo-tourism
beyond the English horizon.[9]

As an essentially descriptive poem, *The Genius* had traced the
imaginary wanderings of the poet from one scene to another.
The argument of *Melancholy* develops in the same way and
involved the same difficulties. A general observation either follows or precedes a pictorial emblem, and, as in the Thames
poem, Peacock offers a series of illustrative frames. Again he is
interested in the *ut pictura poesis* analogy and alludes to the
'sister arts'. In his study of *The Sister Arts*, Jean Hagstrum
isolates a technique in *The Rape of the Lock* that is relevant to
Peacock. 'The words "here", "there", and "now" ', he says,
'guide the eye to antithetically placed compositional masses . . .',
and he suggests that Pope, aware of the methods of painting,
uses analogous methods in his poem.[10] Peacock follows Pope's
device—it had developed into a mannerism in later eighteenth-
century verse—guiding with 'here', 'there', 'now', and with
'yonder', 'See!' and 'Hail!' Wordsworth had perhaps used this
technique to its best advantage in the opening lines of 'Tintern
Abbey' and 'Michael'. 'Melancholy' is closer to the Wordsworth of *An Evening Walk*.

34

A number of lines in *Melancholy* actually sound Words-
worthian, as, for example, 'More wildly sweet, nor less sublime,
the scene'; but the pervasive echo remains that of Pope, whose
pithy couplets Peacock seeks to emulate, and whose rhythm
and polish he sometimes catches:

Great nature's book unclosed beneath his hand,
And peace and science blessed a barbarous land (vi, 191).

The *Eclectic Review*, although pleased with the poem, and
particularly with its 'versification', thought that the author
dabbled too much in 'showy finery and sweet pretty nonsense'.[11]
About much of the poem their censure seems apt. It is when
Peacock pads his material that the poem falters; once more
he wanted enough material to eke out a complete volume. Then
he jogs along with superfluous Miltonic invocations or fills up
lines with 'pensive trains'. But generally this is better verse than
the earlier poems, as the following lines will show. 'O', he
writes, had some Genius

Traced, with prophetic gaze, the emblemed doom
Of earth's proud mistress, and his tyrant, Rome,
And watched the sea-breeze wave its rustling wings
Round the green tomb of unremembered kings (vi, 196).[12]

The weaknesses here are obvious. There is the struggle with
qualifiers, a problem that Peacock never overcame: a line with
two nouns, usually a whole clause, requires two supporting
adjectives, like 'emblemed' and 'proud', which tend to be vague
or hackneyed. But he has used the lines with care. His pauses in
the first couplet are calculated to emphasize the brevity of the
pause after 'watched' and 'breeze' and the almost imperceptible pause after 'tomb'. The carefully end-stopped lines of the
first couplet similarly emphasize the partial stop after 'wings' in
the last couplet. And 'round' shifts the accent and hence the
speed of the final line, which is also the final line of one section
of the poem.

Melancholy is the work of a competent poet, and it no doubt
accomplished what Peacock intended. At the end of a long
tradition of verse—of what Eleanor Sickels calls the 'Milton-

Gray-Collins-Warton composite'—and by no means a bad example of its class, it is reasoned and didactic and retains the cherished emotional detachment of an earlier generation. Keats's 'Ode to Melancholy', despite common origins and subject, is almost its antithesis. Keats's brief, sensuous ode makes *The Philosophy of Melancholy*—including its title—appear by contrast a kind of formal discourse, altogether not without intelligence and technical skill but wanting that 'fine excess'.

However competent, then, *Melancholy* represented for Peacock something of an aberration. He was not suddenly to leap from earnest young poet to playful novelist, and indeed the novels contains a good deal of submerged sentiment and affections. The novels are rather the reverse side of the early coin. The voice of *The Genius* and *Melancholy* becomes one of the numerous voices in the novels. This was not for Peacock a matter of finding his 'true' voice, for he stopped thinking of his works in an expressive capacity. It was a matter of recognizing his limitations and strengths and finding the better way.

4

From *The Dilettanti* to *Rhododaphne*

But still the heart doth need a language, still
Doth the old instinct bring back the old names.

<small>COLERIDGE, translation of *The Piccolomini*, 11, iv.</small>

I

Soon after the Hookhams issued *The Philosophy of Melancholy*,
Thomas Hookham forwarded a copy of *The Genius of the
Thames* and *Palmyra* to Shelley. Shelley's response, in August
1812, while friendly, expressed a distrust of Peacock's ideas that
was to culminate eight years later in the 'Defence of Poetry'.
'The poems', he wrote, 'abound with a genius, an information,
the power and extent of which I admire, in proportion as I
lament the object of their application.'[1] (After the publication
of 'The Four Ages', in 1820, Peacock received a letter from
Shelley expressing much the same point of view.) Encouraged
by the praise of the poems, the Hookhams managed an introduction between Shelley and Peacock shortly before Shelley
left London for Tannyrallt in Wales.

What on the Hookhams' part may have been intended
simply as a business gesture soon materialized into an important
friendship—important for both men, but especially so for
Peacock. Like Thomas Jefferson Hogg, and various other
members of Shelley's entourage, he seems to have been adopted
by Shelley, and it is fairly clear that Shelley's was the dominant
personality in the relationship. But Peacock had lived too long
by himself and too much enjoyed his privacy to become anyone's lap-dog. His independence suggests one of the reasons why
the friendship was not an entirely close or intimate one. There
has been a great deal of speculation about the nature of this
friendship, and several writers have expressed either surprise or
dismay—depending upon their allegiances—that any kind of
relationship should have developed at all. Some reasons are

easy to find. Seven years older than Shelley, Peacock knew much more, especially about the classics, and he was clearly of use to Shelley as a kind of unofficial tutor. At any rate, the two men shared an interest in Greek literature that always tied them together. They also shared certain political assumptions, as Thomas Hookham, a man of radical leanings, no doubt knew. On Shelley's part, then, there was the attraction for an older man who held similar ideas and who could prove useful in a number of ways. The elements in Peacock's attraction to Shelley are perhaps more inscrutable. He was probably interested in the first place by Shelley's title. (His radicalism never lifted him out of social snobbery.) But he was also a lonely man, with extremely few friends, and he was no doubt willing to be adopted by Shelley, who was anyway not the dullest company. He was also attracted by Shelley's enthusiasm, for if Peacock was reserved and sceptical, he had a corresponding desire for all that Shelley was and represented.

Shelley never became Peacock's constant companion, in part because he was seldom in England after 1815. But he did become Peacock's closest, in some ways his only close, friend. The two men met or corresponded until Shelley's death in 1822, after which Peacock served as executor of the estate. It comes as a shock to read the following comment by Shelley, expressed in a letter to Harriet: '[Peacock] is expensive, inconsiderate and cold: but surely not utterly perfidious. . . .'[2] Shelley may have been in a sour mood, or he may have been angry at a specific offence. But there are other signs, almost as pointed, scattered through his letters. Whether Shelley catered in his letters to what he knew to be the prejudices of his friends, or whether he was simply not honest with Peacock, is a matter for speculation. Apparently he never quite trusted Peacock's scepticism, just as Peacock never quite accepted Shelley's various enthusiasms. It was perhaps the antagonism as much as the attraction that made the two mutually useful.

In a sympathetic discussion of the friendship, Walter E. Peck speaks of its being

> of immeasurable profit to the genius of both in that their tastes in literature were broadened, deepened, and enriched by a mutual readiness to receive criticism and suggestion;

and without which it is impossible to understand the evolution of Peacock from 'The Genius of the Thames' to 'Rhododaphne' as that of Shelley from *The Posthumous Fragments of Margaret Nicholson* to *Alastor*.[3]

Shelley was not always to relish Peacock's criticism, and Peacock was to receive few specific criticisms from Shelley. Nor could one say with any certainty that the poetry of either would have proved much different if the two had never met. Peck's comments seem nevertheless both shrewd and accurate, and it is tempting to extend them. *Rhododaphne* took shape during months in which the two were together. It grew with Peacock's intimacy with Shelley, and may have benefited directly from Shelley's enthusiasm, if not from his suggestions. *Rhododaphne* was also Peacock's last long poem. Did he stop writing in this vein because Shelley was no longer around, either to criticize or to encourage? (Shelley did express curiosity about another poem begun after *Rhododaphne*.) A better guess is rather that Shelley, his own poetry maturing, unknowingly imposed upon Peacock the recognition of his limitations as a poet. But this is to leap ahead.

II

It was shortly before meeting Shelley that Peacock first tried his hand at comedy. His attempt was a versified farce, *The Dilettanti*, probably written in Wales at about the same time as *Melancholy* (1811 or 1812). He followed this with *The Three Doctors* (1813), which is slightly more sophisticated in matters of plot, line and verse, but otherwise similar.[4] Only a small part of the comedy that was to distinguish the novels can be found in the two farces. With Peacock, as with Dickens and many other novelists, there is the enigma that he could write brilliant dialogue in fiction but not in a play. Yet the seeds of the novels are there. The country house is the one obviously shared feature, lodging people with bees in their bonnets and bells on their toes. But here the characters are slapstick. They dance around, draw pistols, destroy paintings and landscape, let loose the hounds, remain overnight in closets—almost everything that buffoonery might devise. Peacock satirizes various professionals without creating any 'philosophers', and several figures emerge from the plays into the novels. But at this point they are little more than sketches. Theirs is the recognized language of the contemporary farce: quick, punning, and subservient to action. Peacock introduces none of the rolling sentences, periods, antitheses, none of the fun with pomposity that mark the novels.

One of the difficulties with *The Dilettanti* and *The Three Doctors* is the critical one of pacing; in performance a cast would race like a whirlwind through either, finishing breathless and puzzled. This is not to imply that there are no dull or dispensable passages: rather that all move with break-neck speed. Both plays blurt out a situation, aggravate it immediately, and resolve it, without shift in emphasis, a time to laugh, or a time to yawn. Songs and dialogue, jumbled together, are equally unheard. One or two of these songs are absurd enough to please, like nonsense of Lear or Gilbert, though they are not of the quality of most of Peacock's later verse:

> This trigger, if I pull it,
> Will emancipate a bullet
> That shall set our quarrels right (vii, 397)

sings the Irishman O'Fir in *The Three Doctors*. Gilbert might have written his lines, but Gilbert would also have constructed his play to frame them properly.

More financially successful than the two farces was a little work that appeared in Hailes' Juvenile Library in 1813. *Sir Hornbook* has been well-termed 'grammar without tears' (i, lii). It is a poem for children, a gentle story of knight-errantry, in which the participants are parts of speech. Seldom mentioned in histories of children's literature, it was nevertheless popular in its time—certainly more popular than the remainder of Peacock's poems; after running through five editions in five years, it was also revived half a century later. Only etymology comes off badly in this playful ballad, where prosody and syntax unite in brotherly love:

> There Etymology they found,
> Who scorn'd surrounding fruits;

> And ever dug in deepest ground,
> For old and mouldy Roots (vi, 276).

Although written in 1816 (and not published until 1817, the same year as *Melincourt*) *The Round Table; or, King Arthur's Feast*, a versified account of the kings of England, provides a companion piece for *Sir Hornbook*. Peacock toys in *The Round Table* with the 'Gods and Kings in Exile' theme, which was to have been the basis for his unfinished story, 'Calidore', begun about the same time. King Arthur, waiting disconsolate for a return to his kingdom, promised by the magician Merlin 'not in less than three hundred and seventy years', consents to give a feast to pass away the time; and the poem, again in jogging anapaests, and again for children, pulls forth the kings of England from the hat of the past, setting them down together to dine, with the foreseeable discord and drinking.

III

After another short trip to Wales in 1813, Peacock received Shelley's invitation to visit him at Bracknell, in Berkshire. With Shelley's friends at Bracknell, Peacock seems to have had little sympathy, and apparently laughed at their expense in company with Harriet Shelley. In a letter to Jefferson Hogg in November, Shelley was responding in this guarded way: 'A new acquaintance is on a visit with us this winter. He is a very mild, agreeable man, and a good scholar. His enthusiasm is not very ardent, nor are his views very comprehensive: but he is neither superstitious, ill-tempered, dogmatical, nor proud.'[5] Which is to say that, for Shelley, Peacock's virtues were largely negative. The month before, Mrs. Newton—like her husband a devoted vegetarian and reformer—probably drew a clearer picture of the group's reaction, also in a letter to Hogg. 'The Shelleys', she wrote, 'have made an addition to their party in the person of a cold scholar, who, I think, has neither taste nor feeling.' Peacock seems to have been thought of as a kind of mocking Urizen—Blake's spirit of cold reason—among the heralds of the new Jerusalem.

Neither side had to suffer the other for very long. With Shelley and Harriet, Peacock soon left Bracknell for what was intended to be a trip to the Lakes. They met, however, with the kind of bad luck that has since plagued so many would-be explorers of Wordsworth's homeland: they could find no adequate accommodation. So they dashed on first to Edinburgh, then back south to London. Peacock afterwards returned to the country and worked on his next poem, *Sir Proteus*.

For accepting the Poet Laureateship in October 1813, Robert Southey had incurred the hostility of the liberal Press, notably of Leigh Hunt's *Examiner*. His 'Carmen Triumphale for the commencement of the year 1814' prompted Peacock's satiric rejoinder, *Sir Proteus: A Satirical Ballad, 'by P. M. Donovan, Esq.'*, published in March 1814. Southey's protean qualities, his unaccountable praise of George III, that 'old, mad, blind, despised, and dying king', afford Peacock his main targets, but Scott, Coleridge, Wordsworth, and Byron come in for a drubbing too. Evidently as an afterthought, Peacock added a satiric dedication to Byron:

> This ballad is inscribed to the RIGHT HONOURABLE LORD
> BYRON, with that deep conviction of the high value of his
> praise and of the fatal import of his censure . . . with that
> admiration of his poetical talents . . . for versification
> undecorated with the meretricious fascinations of harmony,
> for sentiments unsophisticated by the delusive ardour of
> philanthropy, for narrative enveloped in all the cimmerian
> sublimity of the impenetrable obscure (VI, 280).

'Are we alive', quipped Byron, 'after all this censure?'[6]

Peacock attempts an attack on Southey and the other poetic 'turncoats' through a general parody of the ballad, but the intrusion of the dedication and of the footnotes involves the tacit admission that the ballad stanza is an inadequate vehicle. Actually most of the satire occurs in the very lengthy footnotes rather than in the poem itself. And it is satire that verges on simple invective. Peacock attacks among others William Gifford, in a way that anticipates both his attacks in *Melincourt* (1817) and William Hazlitt's attacks in the angry *Letter to William Gifford*. (Hazlitt called Gifford a 'literary toad-eater.) In this poem Peacock clearly aligns himself with the radical critics. Ironically, his treatment of the poets and reviewers is also comparable to, perhaps indebted to, earlier abuse of Southey in the *Anti-Jacobin*, though with the political bias adjusted to Southey's—as well as Wordsworth's and Coleridge's—changed positions.

Southey had to bear many attacks, the most potent and the most deserved of which was Byron's in *The Vision of Judgment*. Peacock's is a much clumsier weapon because less effective parody. Whereas in *The Vision* Southey is made the quintessence of poetic and political idiocy, in *Sir Proteus* he is buried under abuse. Peacock anticipates Byron by having the poet punish his listeners with vile music, for he

> grew completely hoarse,
> And croaked like any raven.

> They might have thought, who heard the strum
>   Of such unusual strain,
> That Discord's very self was come,
>   With all her minstrel train (vi, 308).[7]

But anything comparable to the magnificent scene that Byron was to create, in which the poet evokes chaos by his recital, making a hell at heaven's gate, is not to be found.

It would seem fitting for Peacock to have written satirical sketches, not only about Southey, but also about the individuals at Bracknell. Here certainly were likely targets. The immediate result of his encounters turned out to be a work of very different intent. Apparently after 1813, though before 1816, Peacock struggled with his most grandiose poetic scheme, an unfinished narrative that was to have treated in its twelve cantos the nature of the forces of evil and their 'historical' triumph over light. (Coleridge, among other writers of the time, also projected a poem on the origins of evil.) Intended as a more systematic analysis than *The Philosophy of Melancholy*, but fundamentally similar, it would have illustrated the 'deteriorationist' views of John Newton, who was, among his other vocations, a friend of Shelley and temporarily resident at Bracknell.

Ahrimanes never grew beyond a canto and a half, with a prose outline for the remainder, and its two fragments remained

unpublished until 1931. No one, however, could have missed
them, as the following, nerveless lines will indicate:

> Spake the dark genius truly, when she said,
> That Ahrimanes rules this mundane ball?
> That man, in toil and darkness doomed to tread,
> Ambition's slave and superstition's thrall,
> Doth only on the power of evil call,
> With hymn, and prayer, and votive altar's blaze?
> Alas! wherever guiltless victims fall,
> Wherever priest the sword of strife displays,
> Small trace remains, I ween, of ancient Oromaze (VII, 277).

Brett-Smith is far too generous when he contends that
'*Ahrimanes* is more promising than any of Peacock's previous
narrative poems; the handling of the Spenserian stanza is competent, and the story flows on with ease and dignity . . .' (I, lvii).
Peacock handles the stanza well enough, but not without
bathetic plunges or bows to the exigencies of rhyme. Stock
phrases and figures—such as 'I ween' and 'mundane ball'—and
clumsy constructions—such as 'Spake the dark genius truly'—
betray an unintended burlesque of Spenser's method or a
deference to imitators of Spenser in the eighteenth century.
What fragments remain of the story have little charm and less
topicality. Peacock himself could have had no high opinion of
his effort. He later used some of the rejected manuscript pages
for the draft of *Headlong Hall*.

During his labours on *Ahrimanes* Peacock met John Newton.
In the Shelley memoirs he describes both Newton's philosophy
and his person with whimsical indulgence, perhaps recalling his
own poetic effort in Newton's behalf. He writes that when
taking a stroll with Newton, the two men came to a public
house,

> which had the sign of the Horse-shoes. They were four on
> the sign, and he immediately determined that this number
> had been handed down from remote antiquity as
> representative of the compartments of the Zodiac. [Newton
> was to be caricatured, as the Zodiac specialist
> Mr. Ramsbottom in *Crotchet Castle*.] He stepped into the

public-house, and said to the landlord, 'Your sign is the Horse-shoes?'—'Yes, Sir.' 'This sign has always four Horse-shoes?'—'Why, mostly, Sir.'—'Not always?'—'I think I have seen three.'—'I cannot divide the Zodiac into three. But it is mostly four. Do you know why it is mostly four?'—'Why, sir, I suppose because a horse has four legs.' He bounced out in great indignation . . .' (VIII, 73).

The memoirs appeared many years later, long after Peacock had satirized Newton—along with the Zodiac and atrabilious melancholy and vegetarianism—in several novels. As an older man he could hardly have taken Newton, or what was by then his memory of Newton, without a pinch of salt.[8] Indeed he describes Shelley's entire acquaintance as deserving of laughter, each person riding an intellectual hobby-horse.

But it is typical of Peacock in these years that, while lampooning eccentrics and their various crotchets, he was at the same time intrigued by them. The level-headed young man who advised the ailing Shelley, victim of meatless regimen, to take 'Three mutton chops well-prepared' might have been composing a poem based on Newton's theories. Clearly attracted by Shelley's friends, especially by Newton, his difficulty lay in taking them seriously. He never finished *Ahrimanes*, but he also never really put Bracknell aside, for the eccentric society entertained by Squire Headlong found its ultimate genesis in Shelley's utopian circle of friends.

The 'spirit of darkness' found his way into another of Peacock's poems, 'Lines to a Favourite Laurel' (1814), which contains this gratuitous allusion to Ahriman:

> 'tis something yet,
> Even in this world where Ahriman reigns
> To think that thou, my favourite, hast been left . . .

Otherwise the poem is touching in its gentle sentiment and in the affection for natural objects. The description of a metamorphosed garden looks forward both to Shelley's 'The Sensitive Plant' and to Peacock's own *Rhododaphne*:

> the rank weed chokes
> The garden flowers; the thistle's towering growth

45

Waves o'er the untrodden paths: the rose that breathed
Diffusive fragrance from its christening bed,
Scarce by a single bud denotes the spot (VII, 231).

Peacock was not to write other short, elegiac lyrics for some
years, but 'Lines to a Favourite Laurel' anticipate several of
his later poems, most notably 'Newark Abbey'. Ahriman him-
elf, happily, vanished on the way.

IV

Between the publication of the poem on melancholy and
Peacock's next and last separately issued poem, appeared
Headlong Hall (in 1816) and *Melincourt* (in 1817). Six years had
elapsed, too, and Peacock was thirty-four when he finished
Rhododaphne. He was, in short, already a confident and diverse
writer when he turned to classic ground.

Rhododaphne grew out of Peacock's leisure in the autumn of
1817. Shelley, now married to Mary Godwin, was living
temporarily at Marlow, where he and Peacock read together in
the classics. Between April and September Shelley composed
Laon and Cythna, which Peacock helped to revise—he later said
it went 'beyond the bounds of discretion' (VIII, 107)[9]—and
which resembled *Ahrimanes* in general conception, as in its use
of the Spenserian stanza. Peacock probably began *Rhododaphne*
in the autum. By November Shelley could tell Hogg that
'Peacock has finished his poem, which is a story of classical
mystery and magic . . .'.[10] Delighted with the work, he persuaded Mary Shelley to transcribe it for him before the manuscript was sent off to Hookham. *Rhododaphne* was published in
February 1818, anonymously, as were the novels.

According to Shelley, the story of *Rhododaphne*—and this is
the first of the long poems with a story—involves 'the transfused
essence of Lucian, Petronius, and Apuleius'.[11] This distorts the
poem slightly. For Peacock takes seriously the accounts of
metamorphosis, in Ovid as well as in Lucian, Petronius, and
Apuleius, writers who themselves used magic as a springboard
into satire. *Rhododaphne* expresses the idealism of the Greek
romances, complete with innocence and pirates and true love
rewarded. The story is simple. Anthemion, a young man of

Arcadia, journeys to the Temple of Love at Thespia, hoping, by an offering to the deity, to find a cure for his dying sweetheart. When lo! Rhododaphne, a beautiful witch, enchants him. (Her name, Daphne of the rose, means oleander: something lovely but poisonous.) 'What ails thee, stranger?' she asks, and her lines anticipate those of Keats in *La Belle Dame*:

> Leaves are sear,
> And flowers are dead, and fields are drear,
> And streams are wild, and skies are bleak,
> And white with snow each mountain's peak,
> When winter rules the year (vii, 13).

She repeats, 'What ails thee, youth?', but her question is idle, for she knows well enough that Anthemion has come under her spell. To symbolize her love, she gives him a 'laurel-rose', which Anthemion, upon the advice of an old sage, casts into a stream. Then Rhododaphne reappears, kisses him, and, before he can break away, warns him that his kiss must bring death to another woman. Naturally, the sweetheart, Calliroë, does die when he returns to her. Anthemion wanders inconsolate until, as in all good romances, he is kidnapped by pirates. These rogues also kidnap a beautiful young woman, who not very surprisingly turns out to be Rhododaphne.

> The damsel by Anthemion's side
> Sate down upon the deck. The tide
> Blushed with the deepening light of morn.
> A pitying look the youth forlorn
> Turned on the maiden. Can it be . . . ?

It can. 'Too well he knows that radiant form' (vii, 54). Like Shakespeare's Prospero, Rhododaphne causes magic shipwrecks and magic rescues, and after a voyage rivalling that of the ancient mariner, Anthemion finds himself washed ashore with the sorceress on a deserted coast:

> The charmed waves in safety bear
> The youth and the enchantress fair,
> And leave them on the golden sands (vii, 61).

Anthemion flees his lady, but circles unwittingly back to her, and what had been, at the time of parting, merely a derelict cottage, emerges now a lavish palace.

> Mid gardens, fair
> With trees and flowers of fragrance rare,
> A rich and ample pile was there,
> Glittering with myriad lights . . . (VII, 72).

Anthemion, of course, submits to love in a palace. 'Now', cries the temptress, 'art thou mine!' Peacock's description of 'love in a palace' is suggestive rather than explicit, but it leaves little unsaid:—which Keats drew upon for 'Lamia'—

> The lamps grow dim,
> And tremble, and expire. No more.
> Darkness is there, and Mystery:
> And Silence keeps the golden key
> Of Beauty's bridal door (VII, 75).

Anthemion has submitted to Rhododaphne's beauty; his spirit nevertheless turns once again towards the dead Calliroë. Because the relationship in the palace of love is not of the soul, and because Rhododaphne has used devious methods to win her lover, the spirit of true love, Urania, kills the lovely witch. When Rhododaphne dies, Calliroë lives again—she had been spellbound, not dead, and she forgives Anthemion's infidelity, appreciating the irresistible lure of his seducer.

Rhododaphne did not take the literary world by storm. Indeed, there were only two reviews. But it did get attention enough to be pirated in Virginia and, because of its anonymity, to make readers wonder about its authorship. Among the candidates was Byron, who declined to acknowledge it, but who admitted he would gladly have 'fathered' 'the Grecian Enchantress'.[12]

The *Literary Gazette* apparently never considered Byron's authorship possible. With a peculiar blindness to so much poetry of the day, they wrote: 'Leaving our Scotts, Southeys, Moores, Campbells, Wordsworths, this reverts to classic ground.'[13] Peacock was hardly alone in his interests. The

reviewer might have included Walter Landor as another exception, another mind in exile, who wondered where the spirit of
Greece had flown and set about re-creating it. In fact Peacock
shared with many writers of the period a reverence for the
classics and a desire to use them in poetry in a way that most
eighteenth-century writers would have found objectionable.
Even Wordsworth, aside from his comments in the *Excursion* and
the poem 'Laodamia', wanted 'sight of Proteus rising from the
sea'. Keats, always preoccupied with Greek art and myth, spoke
in the Preface to *Endymion* of 'the beautiful mythology of
Greece'. And Coleridge, Byron, Shelley, all deferred to a new
preoccupation with classical themes.

It is true that Peacock is self-consciously turning to the myths,
and insisting that their meanings are irrevocably lost. 'Great
Pan is dead', he writes,

> The life, the intellectual soul
> Of vale, and grove, and stream, has fled
> For ever with the creed sublime
> That nursed the Muse of earlier time (VII, 30).

Perhaps the nearest equivalent for Peacock's dirge is Schiller's
lament for the passing of the Greek gods and the spirit they
embodied in *The Gods of Greece*. It was not only in *Rhododaphne*
that Peacock alluded to the shift in sensibility that obsessed
Schiller. When, in *The Four Ages of Poetry*, he offers an ironic
inversion of sentimental primitivism, he incidentally parodies
Schiller's famous essay *On Naïve and Sentimental Poetry* and the
general 'tyranny of Greece' over modern literatures.

Apart from the lament for ancient Greece, Peacock's 'rever-
sion' to classic ground needs further comment, because it
represented a specific focus in addition to the common sentiment. Peacock's interests link him with a type of literature that
is not exactly classic, nor, as Douglas Bush puts it, 'Hellenic',
except in a peripheral sense.[14] Although Shelley put a wrong
construction on Peacock's intent—at least as embodied in the
poem—he rightly pointed out the relation of *Rhododaphne* to
Apuleius, Lucian, and Petronius. These are of course important
writers, but they are not in what one would consider a mainstream: not Aeschylus or Sophocles, Homer or Virgil. Peacock

was a classicist of some distinction, but his response to classical authors was often wilfully, if not absurdly, idiosyncratic. J. B. Priestley aptly remarked that Peacock at times looked at 'classical culture as a kind of secret society'.[15] Often he did single out for praise writers who were considered then as they are now to be little more than literary footnotes. Nonnus, for example, author of the deservedly forgotten *Dionysiaca*, he ranked next to Virgil. J. B. Priestley, and for that matter most of Peacock's critics, interpret his classical tastes as an expression of personal whim, or a result of his informal education. They have another equally important origin.

In one of the notes to *Rhododaphne*, Peacock interrupts the narrative with the following aside:

'The dreaded name of Daemogorgon' is familiar to every reader, in Milton's enumeration of the Powers of Chaos [here Peacock footnotes his footnote to cite *Paradise Lost*, II, 964]. Mythological writers in general afford but little information concerning this terrible Divinity. He is incidentally mentioned in several places by Natalis Comes, who says, in treating of Pan, that Pronapides, in his *Protocosmus*, makes Pan and the three sister Fates the offspring of Daemogorgon (VII, 92).

Most readers of the time—Peacock thinks all—and some now would have followed his comments as far as *Paradise Lost*. Natalis Comes implies another world of learning altogether. To say that Shelley would have understood the train of allusion is to realize that Peacock was toying in *Rhododaphne* with the same sort of mythographical ideas and sources, and the consequent reinterpretation of literature, that underlie *Adonais* and *Prometheus Unbound*.

Edward Hungerford, in his pioneer study of such abstruse topics and their connection with poets like Blake, Shelley, Keats, and Goethe, cites Peacock in connection with the late eighteenth-century mythologists. Peacock's Mr. Ramsbottom of *Crotchet Castle*, according to Hungerford, represents the mythologist in his later stages, when new 'scientific' study of myth had reduced his theories to the laughable.[16] Ramsbottom is usually taken as a satiric portrait of John Newton:

he is also one of Peacock's many characters who represent the author's own treks into distant fields of learning. Peacock too searched through recondite literary and mythological treatises for poetic material. In his serious as much as in his parodic works he shows his familiarity with the syncretic mythologists and their own, often obscure, sources. Nonnus was one of many forgotten writers resuscitated at the time, and Peacock was not alone in finding him of interest.[17]

What I would like to suggest about *Rhododaphne* is that, no less than Peacock's earlier long poems, it is thematically and technically assimilative. It is a very literary poem. To a reader who wants to find Platonic elements, it includes enough to reward the search, to warrant a neo-Platonic interpretation. Peacock, for example, knew and evidently admired the antiquarian whom Coleridge referred to as 'the English Pagan'. Thomas Taylor, an acquaintance of Shelley, and a man involved with the revitalizing of myth as well as the interpreting of more standard Greek philosophy, may lurk behind *Rhododaphne* as John Newton lurks behind *Ahrimanes*. (Peacock does not refer to Taylor directly, but all of his acknowledged sources are older writers, excepting those subsumed as 'mythologists'.) The idea that Anthemion's 'supernatural'—though actually pandemic or vulgar or purely sexual—love must be of a lower order than that for the simple girl, whom Uranian love brings back to life, could certainly be understood in terms of Platonic grades and distinctions. But the point remains that Plato is one of many authors to whom Peacock turned for inspiration or information and whom he used to develop his story. A poem about the nature of love is a poem about the relevance of love to human relationships, and if Peacock naturally turned to Plato as an important authority, he also turned to Boccaccio, Plutarch, and all the 'mythological writers in general'. He speaks, appropriately, of Plato's 'mythological philosophy' (VII, 91). Had Peacock conceived of *Rhododaphne* as an *Epipsychidion*, a poem in which Plato or neo-Platonic thought is essential for understanding, he would have made his allusions more consistent and explicit. As it is, Apuleius's magic is almost as relevant as Plato's discriminations.[18]

Peacock's subordination of Plato to literary ends raises another question about *Rhododaphne*. While there is in this poem neither tame moralizing nor a clumsy surfeit of allusion, *Rhododaphne* is in some ways more learned, possibly more academic, than *The Philosophy of Melancholy*. The *Monthly Review* was not revealing an inclination to scatological interpretation when, after praising *Rhododaphne* as 'a very elegant little work', they credited Peacock with an extensive knowledge of ancient erotica.[19] He had such knowledge, and the poem builds upon it. Yet if it were not for a preface and a few almost gratuitous notes, a reader would be apt to overlook his knowledge *as* knowledge. To put this another way, Peacock's researches led him to find thematic support for fairly traditional narrative ends, and the narrative remains of first importance. He insists that love is the great civilizer, but he makes his point gently, shows what he means, and for the most part carries his learning with grace. Unlike Shelley, who introduces his learning as a conspicuous supporting system, Peacock merely uses what he thinks will enhance the story. An important corollary of this is that he is less interested in the didactic import or the contemporary application of ideas—as Shelley is—than in perfecting the self-sufficiency of the poem itself.

There is in this poem a clarity of image and of story line that indicates Peacock may have turned away from his earlier eighteenth-century poetic models. The naivety of the speaker— broken partly by generalized meditative passages at the opening of each canto—suggests certain sixteenth-century narrative poems by Drayton, Spenser, and Davies. And the full, tapestry-like descriptions as well as the speaker's non-committal stance are reminiscent of Ovid.

Some traces of eighteenth-century poetry remain in spite of the new echoes. The short, tetrameter lines, in couplets or alternating rhymes, look back as had those of *The Genius of the Thames* to writers like Thomson, who adapted Milton's octosyllabics. But here one is less aware of stock diction and abstract generalizing, endemic qualities in the earlier poems. Peacock admits a few of the old counters, the 'votive trains' and 'sylvan shades', but otherwise the words are simpler, fresher:

> Her sweet lips breathe a song so sweet,
> That the echoes of the cave repeat
> Its closes with as soft a sigh,

> As if they almost feared to break
> The magic of its harmony (VII, 33).

Another major difference between *Rhododaphne* and the earlier long poems lies in the new precision of imagery and association —which includes for the first time precision of colour. The lovely, homespun Calliroë appears by tall trees, whereas Rhododaphne is always found by short-lived, exotic flowers. The association, neither spelled-out nor belaboured, works persuasively: the lily of the day may be irresistible, but true love can outlive time itself. At the beginnings of some of the seven cantos—and the opening, meditative sections are comparatively flat—Peacock draws the enchantress among palm trees or among rank and insistent weeds. 'I need but love', she says. 'I seek but love' (VII, 68).

In the Preface to *Rhododaphne* Peacock speaks about the supernatural powers of music (VIII, v). Music is always important in his poems, as the references in *The Genius of the Thames* makes clear. And *Palmyra*, of course, is an ode, which, as Peacock knew, had a traditional association with music running back through Gray and Collins to Dryden's *Alexander's Feast*. Music is more important to *Rhododaphne* than to the earlier poems because it remains more central. The seductive witch uses the charms of music. Aboard the pirate ship,

> She rose, and loosed her radiant hair,
> And raised her golden lyre in air.
> The lyre, beneath the breeze's wings,
> As if a spirit swept the strings,
> Breathed airy music, sweet and strange (VII, 58).

Throughout the poem dialogue seems to be chanted or sung, and the vivid, slow-changing scenes evoke an operatic quality, appropriate from an admirer of Mozart, Bellini, and Donizetti. *Rhododaphne* is a narrative, but its better parts are dialogue and song as dialogue. Typical are these lines sung by the enchantress:

> And what if beauty slept, where peers
> That mossy grass? And lover's tears

Were mingled with that evening dew?
The morning sun would dry them too (VII, 16).

The music of *Rhododaphne* caught the ear of Edgar Allan
Poe, who knew nothing about the author and thought the
poem American.[20] He responded to its main strength. 'The
sense of musical delight with the power of producing it', as
Coleridge wrote, 'is a gift of the imagination.' *Rhododaphne* may
be Peacock's first and last imaginative poem in Coleridge's
sense of the word.

Shelley, enchanted by *Rhododaphne*, apparently began his
'Prince Athanase' soon after reading the poem, but the fragment, originally entitled 'Pandemos and Urania', has little of
the sensuous involvement of Peacock's poem, although Shelley's
story was to have paralleled that of his friend. *Rhododaphne* more
closely resembles Keats's 'Lamia'. The fatal lady—in both perhaps partly indebted to Coleridge's Geraldine—the account of
seduction, and the record of love between an ordinary man and
a supernatural woman, indicate an overlap of interests.
'Lamia' is Keats's most scholarly Greek poem, and *Rhododaphne*
is Peacock's most vividly sensual.

It was not a great coincidence that Keats and Peacock
should turn to similar themes and embody them in comparable
settings, because poetic romances were very much the order
of the day. But it is worth noting that Peacock, despite his
distrust of Keats, worked towards a related final statement in
his major poem, and that Keats, whose only recorded comment on Peacock is damning, drew from *Rhododaphne* for his
own poem about classical magic and love.

5

Later Verse

It is now evident that poetry must either cease to be cultivated,
or strike into a new path.

'The Four Ages of Poetry'.

I

In the months following the completion of *Rhododaphne*, Peacock
toyed with the idea of another narrative poem, this time on
'nympholepsy'—a state of frenzy or rapture inspired by
nymphs. He left only a prose outline of events, with no clear
formulation of what shape the poem might take or what the subject might have included. The prose outline describes a prince,

> a joyous and festive youth, a leader of Bacchic rites,
> beloved by many girls but indifferent to them all in the
> desire of the love of higher beings. He becomes suddenly
> dispirited and melancholy . . . [*sic*] The Nymph . . . has
> built an altar to Diana in a solitary grove and breathed on
> it a vow of chastity beneath the midnight moon. The
> prince has seen and loved her and been repulsed. The
> Prince is seized with the nympholeptic madness . . .
> (VIII, 463).

Enchantment and infatuation call up immediate thoughts of
Rhododaphne, though the evident similarities with Keats's
Endymion and 'Lamia' suggest that Peacock intended the term
'nympholepsy' in the sense of 'desire for the unattainable', and
therefore that he may have envisioned a poem not only about
divine and inspired states of mind, but about the writing of
poetry. This seems to have been Shelley's impression of Peacock's intent, or the construction he put upon their conversations about the poem. He writes to Peacock from Italy in
August 1818 in this somewhat enigmatic way:

Pray, are you yet cured of your Nympholepsy? 'Tis a sweet disease: but one as obstinate and dangerous as any—even when the Nymph is a Poliad [i.e. city nymph]. Whether such be the case or not, I hope your nympholeptic tale is not abandoned. The subject, if treated with a due spice of Bacchic fury, and interwoven with the manners and feelings of those divine people [the poets?], who, in their very errors, are the mirrors, as it were, in which all that is delicate and graceful contemplates itself, is perhaps equal to any. What a wonderful passage there is in Phraedrus— the beginning, I think, of one of the speeches of Socrates— in praise of poetic madness, and in definition of what poetry is, and how a man becomes a poet.[1]

In a later comment on Shelley's letter, Peacock identified the passage from Plato, a passage that offers a hint as to why he may have left the poem unfinished. Socrates, he says, speaks about a 'divine madness',

which proceeds from the Muses taking possession of a tender and unoccupied soul, awakening, and bacchically inspiring it towards songs and other poetry . . . but he who, without this madness from the Muses, approaches the poetical gates, having persuaded himself that by art alone he may become sufficiently a poet, will find in the end his own imperfections, and see the poetry of his cold prudence vanish into nothingness before the light of that which has sprung from divine insanity.[2]

Peacock may or may not have encountered the passage in Plato when working on the poem, unless he was still at work when Shelley's letter arrived. Yet it seems pertinent as a judgment about his poetry. His comments on Shelley in the memoirs, written many years after his poetic effort, imply a response that would associate Shelley with 'divine insanity', with the 'madness from the Muses'. If this was also his response to Shelley when the two were intimate, then the suggestion raised in an earlier section, that Shelley imposed upon Peacock the recognition of his limited powers as a poet, may be worth emphasizing. In 'The Four Ages of Poetry', written in 1819,

Peacock talks about 'poetry of civilized life', the polished, refined, but essentially insubstantial poetry of the Gray-Collins-Cowper variety. I have implied earlier that Peacock may have lacked the emotional power or sensibility necessary for the kind of poetry he attempted as a young man. This is a dubious kind of argument. But certainly he never had the poetic zeal of Shelley or the intensity of Keats, and one wonders if he did not associate himself with the poets of 'cold prudence', with the poets who are not inspired by Bacchus—and who are forced to recognize their limitations in the face of what they assume to be a true poet.[3] In Peacock's case, Shelley brought the shock of recognition.

Peacock was to say that he discontinued the new poem on seeing publication of Horace Smith's curiously titled *Amarynthus the Nympholept*. (Smith, who had neo-Platonic leanings, happened also to be an acquaintance of Shelley.) Actually, Smith's 'nympholeptic' story first appeared in 1821, three years after Peacock began his poem, and long, one suspects, after he had put it aside. Diverted for whatever reasons—and I shall offer another shortly—from continuing with the poem on nympholepsy, Peacock finished neither this nor any other long poem after *Rhododaphne*.

And he put aside more than the one poem in 1818, which was to be for him a year of false starts and new beginnings, as well as of real achievements. The great achievements were *Rhododaphne*, published in February, and *Nightmare Abbey*, published in October. Peacock's best poem and possibly his best novel appeared within a few months of each other. He began in addition several other projects. Not only did he conceive of the nympholepsy tale, he began another novel—*Maid Marian*—kept his one known journal, and attempted his first essay. All four of these projects were to be discontinued, and among them only *Maid Marian* was ever to see completion. One reason for the interruption of the writing was Peacock's acceptance of regular employment, which appears to have involved for him little less than the abandonment of his writing and the commitment to another, altogether different, career.

Through the auspices of a friend, Peacock was invited in the late summer of 1818 to apply for employment with the East India Company, his position in the India House itself, to approximate that of a well-paid civil servant. Some time in September his employers called him to London. A probationary period followed, and by the first week in November he had already submitted a report with the formal title, 'Ryotwar and Zemindary Settlements', which is said to deal systematically 'in precise official language, with the merits of the two specified systems of Indian Village taxations'. (His papers were returned with the comment: 'Nothing superfluous and nothing wanting.') (I, xcii–iii.) While awaiting confirmation of the appointment during the autumn, he evidently toyed once again with *Maid Marian*, without adding very much to it.[4] After January of the next year he was a public official, financially secure, and ensconced in new quarters in London.

What the new employment meant for Peacock, in a personal sense, he never really intimates—except in his incomparable summary of office routine:

> From ten to eleven, ate a breakfast for seven:
> From eleven to noon, to begin t'was too soon;
> From twelve to one, asked, 'What's to be done?'
> From one to two, found nothing to do;
> From two to three began to foresee
> That from three to four would be a damned bore (VII, 236).

However much of a 'damned bore', the job must have been a partial blessing. In a somewhat evasive and perhaps embarrassed letter to Shelley, Peacock speaks about it as 'employment of a very interesting and intellectual kind . . . in which it is possible to be of great service', but he seems most interested in the promise of 'a very sufficing provision' (VIII, 215). The India House position involved for Peacock the release from a situation that can only have been unpleasant. Leigh Hunt writes in his *Autobiography*: 'As an instance of Shelley's extraordinary generosity, a friend of his, a man of letters, enjoyed from him at that period a pension of a hundred a year . . . and he continued to enjoy it till fortune rendered it superfluous.'[5] The accusation is undoubtedly directed at Peacock. Some of Shelley's impatience with Peacock may have resulted from his thinking of the man, not only as a friend, but also as a hireling or hanger-on. He once tells Harriet that Peacock is 'expensive

. . . and cold'. Whatever his feelings on the matter, it seems that Shelley helped to support Peacock, and he could ill-afford the generosity. (When Peacock had moved into the new position, Shelley asked that Peacock procure him a job as secretary with an Indian Prince, a request that Peacock tactfully declined to sponsor.) If nothing else, then, the India House post assured him freedom from financial embarrassments. He was able to indulge himself in collecting an excellent library, to provide lodgings for his elderly mother—and also to marry.

The records of Peacock's relationships with women in the years prior to 1819 are obscure. Mary Shelley speaks in her diary about an affair with an heiress, who turns out to be no heiress. (Peacock afterwards found himself in gaol, evidently for debt.) There is more talk about Peacock and a woman called Marianne de St. Croix marrying and perhaps emigrating to Canada. But nothing is definite before November 1819, when Peacock—on official paper of the India House—writes to his old Welsh girl friend Jane Gryffydh and, with rather business-like despatch, asks her hand. Miss Gryffydh's response was wary acquiescence, and the two were shortly married. Little is known about their marriage, except that she became ill and remained an invalid for the last twenty-five years of her life. A few affectionate letters to her from Peacock are extant.[6]

In the 'Letter to Maria Gisborne'—where he speaks about Miss Gryffydh, without having seen her, as the 'Snowdonian antelope'—Shelley has this to say about 'English Peacock':

> have you not heard
> When a man marries, dies, or turns Hindoo,
> His best friends hear no more of him?

Shelley's verse letter also contains one of the warmest tributes to Peacock:

> his fine wit
> Makes such a wound, the knife is lost in it;
> A strain too learned for a shallow age,
> Too wise for selfish bigots. . . .

The praise is both fitting and generous, but several years were to elapse before that fine wit really showed itself once again.

Indeed, Peacock was to write almost nothing for the next three years. By all reports a very capable official, and faced with duties that must have been anything but onerous, he might have found time to continue his various unfinished literary projects.[7] As Shelley complains, he hardly even maintained his correspondence.

More than a real obstacle to writing, Peacock's position with the India House seems to have offered him an excuse, or, put another way, to have been the sign of his turning away from a literary career. The one significant piece of work that he completed during these years, 'The Four Ages of Poetry', is both a slap at contemporary poets and an expression of disgust with the readers of poetry. When Peacock began to write poems once again, it was with no accompanying aspirations to make a name for himself and with no deferential, if finally unflattering, prefaces to his readers. From this point his poems were to be short poems or, in the case of *Paper Money Lyrics*, collections of poems, written mostly in response to people and events.

II

Peacock not only put aside his poem about nympholepsy; he composed no more poems on those inevitably wearisome topics of necessity, time, fancy, or peace. One wonders if he knew Coleridge's censure of such poems—'the sundry odes and apostrophes to abstract terms' that reflected 'the madness prepense of pseudo-poetry'. In any case, like Coleridge himself, he stopped writing them. And he became a very capable writer of occasional poems. Most of the occasions he found were in the novels, and these poems will be touched on later. But Peacock wrote a number of other poems that deserve a reading. Of the earlier types of verse, he seems to retain just two, the elegiac and the lightly satiric, though within the categories the range is wide. Peacock's later poems are not really of a different kind so much as of different quality—better poems, but written in forms with which he had already experimented.

The elegiac poems, like the earlier ones on parting, disappointed love, or death, retain the same almost disinterested quality. Stylistic formality, if it is only that, carries over into the later elegies. I have suggested before, but it bears repeating, that Peacock refuses to fall upon the thorns of life and bleed. This is not to say that his apprehension of sorrow or suffering remains unexpressed, but rather that the manner of expression seems inadequate, will not carry the implied sentiment. Consider lines from his elegy to Lord Broughton's daughter:

> Accept, bright spirit, reft in life's best bloom,
> This votive wreath to thy untimely tomb.

Or,

> Yet, midst the many who thy loss deplore,
> Few loved thee better, and few mourn thee more (vii, 253).

The first of these couplets Wordsworth might have cited as an example of the diction he so much deplored. The words themselves seem to obtrude. The final couplet, while carefully turned, is again play with language, antithesis, and it is the phrasing that is conspicuous rather than the expressed sentiment. One exception to stilted elegy is a poem for 'Margaret Love Peacock', the poet's daughter, who died in 1826 while a young girl:

> Long night succeeds thy little day;
>   Oh blighted blossom! can it be,
> That this grey stone, and grassy clay,
>   Have clos'd our anxious care of thee?

It closes with a line of simple and touching beauty: 'The too fair promise of thy spring' (vii, 239).

Elegies are difficult verse; they must be formal without being stiff. And Peacock can hardly be condemned for having written few that succeed. Nonetheless, his elegies illustrate a characteristic of many of his poems. Even his love poems, rare as they are, have something of the stuffed shirt and cardboard of language. When Heine writes 'Du bist wie eine Blume' or 'Das Glück ist eine leichte Dirne'—a lyric either of love or of ironic comment—his words by-pass the decorum of prose and, with apparent simplicity, attain splendid emotional effect. Keats manages this too, with a narrower range of subjects. Burns certainly does it. But Peacock does not. He had much in common with Heine, and he can approximate the irony of the satiric poems, but of the love poem, the poem of regret and suffering, of despised love, of tears, of pain, he writes next to nothing.

Appropriately, his best-remembered and probably most successful lyric is a token of remembered love rather than a direct expression of emotion. 'Newark Abbey' is literally emotion recollected in tranquillity, a reminiscence of August 1807, written thirty-five years later. It records meetings with a girl called Fanny Falkner, with whom Peacock had been in love, and whose marriage and early death evidently troubled him throughout his life. Peacock's formality serves a purpose in this poem, because the passion is rightfully mellowed by time and associated with the original place of meeting, the Abbey, which reminds him of his age and of

> That gulf, unfathomably spread
> Between the living and the dead.

The poem opens in a way that foretells specific or vivid reminiscence:

> I gaze, where August's sunbeam falls
> Along these gray and lonely walls,
> Till in its light absorbed appears
> The lapse of five-and-thirty years.
> If change there be, I trace it not . . . (VII, 252).

But it is apt that the poem combines the memory of love with the dignity befitting an epitaph, and that the young lady should be the occasion for, rather than the whole object of, the meditation. Thus Peacock can introduce the somewhat hollow phrases 'Ruin's march' and 'imaged past' without detracting from the pathos engendered by the Abbey and by the association with the dead mistress.[8]

'Newark Abbey' offers a trace of Peacock's buried life that is more typically suppressed in his writing or turned into ironic commentary. Reticent by nature, and tending at crucial moments in his more serious poems to escape into stock or vague phrasings, he expressed himself with more ecse and with more skill in some of his lighter compositions. What works so well in the humorous verse is his setting aside both poetic manner and poetic diction to write wittily and playfully. Like

Landor's, Peacock's best verses are almost recreational: tuneful, laughing, unpretentious.

III

Peacock broke the silence following his employment at the India House with a little poem called 'Rich and Poor; or Saint and Sinner'. Suggested by one of William Wilberforce's questionable comments on the poor, its light irony contrasts with the bitter irony of Shelley's 'Masque of Anarchy', which is based on comparable assumptions:

> The rich man has a kitchen,
> And cooks to dress his dinner;
> The poor who would roast
> To the baker's must post,
> And thus becomes a sinner (VII, 147).[9]

Although Peacock proved both a capable and devoted public servant, he seems hardly to have been cowed by his employment. *Maid Marian*, completed around the time of 'Rich and Poor', also scoffs at the Establishment; and many of the poems after 1818 are sharply satiric. During the financial crisis of 1825 and 1826 Peacock wrote a series of poems called *Paper Money Lyrics*, a mischievous rendering of William Cobbett's *Paper Against Gold*.

Peacock agreed wholeheartedly with Cobbett's ill-considered tract—already by this time fifteen years old—and the *Lyrics* make a laughing attack on Scotch economists, free-traders, and paper money. (The point of view is that expressed in *Melincourt*, especially in the chapter entitled 'The Paper Mill'.)

> The Country banks are breaking:
> The London banks are shaking:
> Suspicion is awaking:
> E'en quakers now are quaking (VII, 101)[10]

he writes in 'Pan in Town', wherein Pan is not the pagan god, but an abbreviated 'Panic'. 'Great Pan', as he had written in *Rhododaphne*, 'is dead'.

Peacock assumed with Cobbett, as with Shelley and many others, that 'paper money' was a harmful innovation, designed rather to cheat the have-nots than to facilitate exchange, and that it brought about crises like that of 1825. He was mistaken about its ultimate utility but right about its immediate effects. He uses the *Lyrics*—perhaps because the topic lent itself to repetition—as much for a general parody of poets of the time as for economic comment. The poems are a rather more sophisticated version of *Sir Proteus*, published ten years before. One of the songs is supposedly written by 'S. T. C., Esq., Professor of Mysticism', whose topic 'The Wise Men of Gotham', lends itself to light travesty of *The Ancient Mariner*.

> The sea was calm, the air was balm,
>   Not a breath stirred low or high,
> And the moon, I trow, lay as bright below,
>   And as round as in the sky.
>
>   . . .
>
> I now divine each mystic sign,
>   Which robbed me oft of sleep,
> Three men in a bowl, who went to troll,
>   For the moon in the midnight deep (VII, 119, 121).

Another lyric comes from the pen of 'T. M., Esq.', entitled 'Love and the Flimsies' and offers an amusing take-off on Moore's anapaestic quatrains; another, from 'W. W., Esq., Distributor of Stamps', is called 'A Mood of My Own Mind, occurring during a gale of wind at midnight, while I was writing a paper on the currency, by the light of two mould candles'. Peacock never managed a successful verse parody of Wordsworth, often as he tried. Scott, identified merely as 'an enchanter unknown', and 'R. S.——, Esq., Poet Laureate', also come in for mockery—nearly all of which is lighter than that of *Sir Proteus*, if not entirely satisfactory as burlesque. Beneath Southey's imaginary Proæmium of an Epic', Peacock subscribes—from *Henry VIII*:

> His promises were, as he once was, mighty;
> And his performance, as he is now, nothing (VII, 101–46).

Enough of a rebel to compose the *Paper Money Lyrics*, Peacock was cautious enough to delay their publication for twelve years, presumably out of deference to James Mill, his senior in the India House, whose views they opposed. When they did appear (in a limited edition of 100 copies, in 1837), Peacock included additional related pieces. 'The Fate of a Broom', originally from an 1831 number of the *Examiner*, offers a good example of these largely political poems:

> Lo! In Corruption's lumber-room,
> The remnants of a wondrous broom,
> That walking, talking, oft was seen,
> Making stout promises to sweep clean,
> But evermore, at every push,
> Proved but a stump without a brush (vII, 149).[11]

Written on the eve of the passing of the Reform Bill, this remains an apt critique of 'lumbering' reform.

Throughout his years at the India House, Peacock composed such playfully satiric verse, part of which is related to his novels. 'Touchandgo', for instance, written a few months before *Crotchet Castle* (1831), characterizes the same rogue who, as father to Susannah, writes from America of his absconding and escape across the ocean. Peacock describes the repercussions of fleeing paper-money men in this way:

> Well done! Britannia rules the waves!
> A fleet to catch one brace of knaves!
> Thus paper-coinage sets in motion
> All England and the Atlantic Ocean (vII, 243).[12]

'The New Year', lines on a Cruikshank illustration, and written when Peacock was fifty-three, has a strength and a colloquial sureness missing in the early poems:

> A great philosopher art thou, George Cruikshank,
> In thy unmatched grotesqueness! Antic dance,
> Wine, mirth, and music, welcome thy New Year,
> Who makes her entry as a radiant child,
> With smiling face. . . .

The year will end, he says, in 'wasted means and broken promises',

and another Year
Will enter masked and smiling, and be welcomed
With minstrelsy and revelry, as this is (VII, 251).

Those readers of Peacock's novels who understand the comedy and happy endings as the expression of a chronically grinning writer would do well to read this exercise in hard and uninflated rhythm with its depiction of implicit tragedy. And Peacock's relation to Cruikshank might be elaborated, in that both are free-swinging commentators, agents of no party, deflators of all varieties of pomp. As a novelist, a writer of small, unpretentious works, Peacock is to Cruikshank what Fielding had been to Hogarth.

Unlike many of these later poems, the lines to Cruikshank were soon published. Along with the essay 'The Abbey House' and the poem 'The Legend of Manor Hall', they appeared in the newly-founded *Bentley's Miscellany* (for January 1838), as 'by the author of *Headlong Hall*'. The Cruikshank illustration referred to in the poem was not done for *Bentley's*, but Cruikshank did some of his best work for *Bentley's* and had already begun his famous illustrations for the magazine. (He had also illustrated *Sketches by Boz* and was soon to do *Oliver Twist*.) Whether or not Peacock met Cruikshank we do not know. Nor whether he met Charles Dickens, who had recently accepted the position of editor for *Bentley's*. Peacock's name occurs second, after Theodore Hooke, in a current list of contributors to the magazine, but there is no evidence that Dickens knew him, except as 'the author of *Headlong Hall*'.

Peacock's other poem for the *Miscellany*, published a year earlier, is a humorous ballad, a light account of a farmer who sells his grain and almost his soul to the Devil. He goes to Hell when his 'frugal dame' snatches money from the Devil's hand—money which allows her to win 'the vows of a younger spouse' (VII, 250). This is an uncomplicated narrative with scarcely a satiric thrust at anything contemporary. Since it was later included in *Bentley's Ballads* (1858), it may have been solicited by the editors of the *Miscellany*, whose format Peacock adopted. Another ballad, in full title 'A Goodlye Ballade of Little John,

Shewing how he raysed a Dyvell, and How he Coulde Notte
Laye Hymme', is more topical. Looking back to *Sir Proteus* and
several of the *Paper Money Lyrics*, its focus is political. 'Little
John' is Lord John Russell, who had recently baited the old
bear of Papal Aggression. Peacock includes in his satire comments on what one would now call 'isms' and on various
sects:

> And braw Scots Presbyters nimbly sped
>   In the train of the muckle black de'il;
> And, as the wild infection spread,
> The Protestant Hydra's every head
>   Sent forth a yell of zeal.

> And pell-mell went all forms of dissent,
>   Each beating its scriptural drum;
> Wesleyans and Whitfieldites followed as friends,
> And whatever in 'onian and 'arian ends,
>   *Et omne quod exit in hum* (vii, 255).

This is one of several topical poems that satirize either Parliamentary rhetoric or the using of religious intolerance for
political ends. Like the Cruikshank lines, they tend to be
colloquial and conversational. Among them are such sketches
as 'Oh nose of wax! True Symbol of the Mind', which tweaks in
passing 'Oxford's ancient nose of brass' (vii, 242),[13] and 'A Bill
for the Better Promotion of Oppression on the Sabbath', which
is similar to 'Rich and Poor'. The 'Bill', a thrust at legal im-
morality, with the kind of half-ironic outrage one finds in
Dickens, closes with a damning couplet in quasi-legal jargon:

> For no party whatever has aught to fear
> From said act who has more than £500 a year (vii, 238).

These are hard words, the kind that, according to Byron, 'stick
in the soft muses' gullets'. Peacock is not only shunning poetic
diction here; he is making an attempt—like Samuel Butler's,
whose phrase '200 pounds a year' he echoes, and like that in his
own verse-letters as a boy—to burlesque certain kinds of verse
decorum. This was a quality in Peacock's songs and poems that

struck Leigh Hunt, who, however, preferred Peacock's experiments with another kind of poem.

How rarely, wrote Hunt in 1854, do we find poems to make us happy, 'poems of a joyous impulse'; and how rarely in English do we find uninhibited poems on eating and drinking. Hunt finds an exception to this rule, not in Carey, Gay, Herrick, or Suckling, but in Peacock. As for songs of mirth, he says, 'There is a song, indeed, in the novel of *Headlong Hall*, fit to match any of them'. Ironically, Hunt says that the song of Headlong's ancestry in Peacock's novel is without a fellow, excepting a poem that has come to his attention in the Manchester *Examiner*, the author of which identifies himself as 'Horace'.[14] The poem, called 'A Can of Cream from Devon', appears to have been Peacock's. Hunt apparently had no idea that the exceptions he cites to an English lack of 'animal spirits' and poems on food were both by Peacock.

Hunt calls the 'Horace' of the Manchester *Examiner* 'more genial in some respects than his great namesake' and compliments him for taking liberties with language. Peacock, as the author of *Palmyra*, would never have received such a compliment. On the other hand, his liberties here leave something to be desired:

> It matters not, *then*, if I sink or swim;
> It matters not what may be my whim;
> Whether I float on the buoyant wave,
> Or in its deeps my limbs do lave:
> For oh! what a sensuous joy supreme
> Would *drowning* be in this Devonshire cream![15]

Peacock did of course write better verse than this on Devonshire cream, and Hunt, whose praise is excessive, might have cited any dozen poems from the novels to illustrate English drinking songs or songs of a 'joyous impulse'. Those of *Maid Marian* are especially pertinent.

The 'buoyant wave' in the 'Can of Cream from Devon' suggests another of Peacock's light poems that did not find its way into a novel. It was one of the last of his miscellaneous poems. Like several of his later works, it has a quality reminiscent of Landor, and might be compared with 'Finis' or 'To my

Ninth Decade'. Peacock speaks in this poem in what for him is rare—the first person:

Instead of sitting wrapped up in flannel
    With rheumatism in every joint,
I wish I was in the English Channel,
    Just going round the Lizard Point,
All southward bound, with the seas before me,
    I should not care whether smooth or rough,
For then no visitors would call to bore me,
    Of whose 'good mornings' I have had enough (VII, 272).

This is not quite the same sentiment as 'Alas! how soon the hours are over', but it involves the same admirable readiness to smile at oneself. In the following quatrain—an entire poem that expresses almost as much as *The Philosophy of Melancholy*—Peacock's lines might have been written by Landor himself:

The briefest part of life's uncertain day,
Youth's lovely blossom, hastes to swift decay:
While love, wine, song, enhance our gayest mood,
Old Age creeps on, nor thought, nor understood (VII, 261).

In 'Years' Landor begins:

    Years, many parti-colour'd years,
    Some have crept on and some have flown . . .

For the most part occasional—and again, Peacock's occasions were often his own novels—his later poems are invariably short and usually ironic. They may, as with 'The briefest part of life's uncertain day', be in couplets, or, like 'I wish I was in the English Channel', involve complicated metres. But except as ballads or parodies of ballads they are seldom examples either of classical or of English genres. In his shorter verse, as in his prose, Peacock preferred to ignore or to mix conventional forms. Clearly, his later verse has little in common with the earlier, the long, didactic efforts on behalf of mutability, melancholy, or the Thames. Only when he had abandoned poetry as a career, when he no longer purveyed those earnest tidings to the world, did he begin to write his best verse. Only then did the fickle muses acknowledge his long courtship. *Rhododaphne* marks a halfway point, for certainly it outshines as it builds upon the long poems before it. But *Rhododaphne* summarizes and fittingly closes a poetic career; and even this poem, however estimable, must be acknowledged as largely forgotten. The short poems, on the other hand, can still be found in anthologies—though Mario Praz and others resent their inclusion—and they have won the praise of critics as different as Leigh Hunt and Arthur Symons.

IV

This brief survey of Peacock's later verse has taken us far beyond the time when he began to write his essays and novels. Most of the miscellaneous verse mentioned here is that by an older man who wrote infrequently and at his leisure. 'Instead of Sitting', for example, Peacock wrote not long before his death, already to his 'ninth decade' having 'tottered on'. To pick up his beginnings as essayist we have to move back to that important summer of 1818, during which Peacock was following out the implications of his poetic career in the general indictment of 'Fashionable Literature', a fitting topic for a man whose poems had been politely but hardly ecstatically received, and who was abandoning the last of his big poetic projects—on nympholepsy—appropriately concerned with the nature of poetic inspiration and the role of the poet.

PART 2

Essays and Miscellaneous Prose: The Well-stored Past

Prior may say what he will in Verse . . .
in Prose I am sure he is of another Opinion.

MATTHEW PRIOR, 'Dialogue Between Charles the
Emperor and Clenard the Grammarian'.

1

Peacock and the Informal Essay: Introductory

> What is it in fact that we return to oftenest? What subjects do
> we think or talk of? Not the ignorant future, but the well-
> stored past.
>
> WILLIAM HAZLITT, 'On the Past and Future'.

A writer of essays for more than thirty-five years, Peacock offered book reviews, operatic notices, and disparate pieces on literature, politics, and gastronomy to various periodicals. Ironically, his first attempt at the essay—written shortly after the publication of *Rhododaphne*, when he was thirty-three— attacks periodical and other 'fashionable' literature. Perhaps a reluctance to cater to magazines dissuaded Peacock from regular contribution, for although he began his essays in 1818, and wrote them as late as the 1850's, he was by no means a prolific essayist. From about 1829 to 1834 he did regularly produce operatic reviews for the *Examiner*; otherwise his essays, like his poems and novels, appeared infrequently.

Peacock wrote relatively little, but he touched on a wide range of topics. His literary essays, for example, include appreciations of Cratinus, the Athenian writer of comedies, observations on popular French literature, and criticism of contemporary English writers. 'The Four Ages of Poetry' alone introduces people as diverse as Nonnus and Wordsworth; unquestionably Peacock's best-known essay, it is a kind of erudite 'Modest Proposal' with the suggestion that the 'egregious confraternity of rhymesters', mainly the Lake Poets, put an end to their abundant scribblings. In this, as in several other pieces, Peacock talks with a tongue-in-cheek whimsy reminiscent of Charles Lamb.

Yet little of his prose is so personal, so autobiographical, as Lamb's. Peacock insists in his memoirs of Shelley that a writer

73

deserves immunity from public gossip or sensationalism, and he himself seems to have been diffident by nature as well as on principle. In none of his writings do we sense the intimacy with the reader that is so basic to the essays of Lamb—or to those of Hazlitt and Leigh Hunt. Peacock is closer in this matter to Addison: he is usually good-natured and courteous with his reader, witty, but never unreserved. Whereas Hunt seems to poke his reader in the ribs or slap him on the back, Peacock chuckles with his in decorous informality. His few auto-biographical writings, such as letters, journals, and sketches of childhood, are pleasant and laughing—and Peacock shares with Lamb a delight in the circuitous—but they are never self-revealing as Lamb's 'The Superannuated Man' or Hazlitt's 'My First Acquaintance with Poets' is self-revealing.

Peacock may not indulge in the personal essay, but he writes a number of fine informal essays. Whatever the topic, he brings to bear acute judgments and wide learning; like Burton and Browne, he can be pedantic, though he is usually disarming and sensible. He also makes an almost automatic comparison between his own and earlier times. Apparently he prefers opera to concert music because opera corresponds more nearly to Athenian drama; he speaks warmly on behalf of London Bridge, about to be replaced by a new structure, because it is a symbol of the past; he lauds good food and hospitality, because these are old English as well as old Greek and old Roman virtues. Behind an almost boasted eccentricity, however, lies a considered point of view, for in his essays, as in his novels, Peacock insists upon traditional values of civilization. This is not to suggest that he is necessarily politically conservative or antiquarian. Actually he is neither. But he is a man avowedly at odds with industrial and intellectual trends of his time and laments the passing of a pre-industrial England. His loves are traditional loves: natural beauty, literature and music, conversation and conviviality. Few as his essays are, all insist upon the same ideals.

Sir Edward Strachey, who knew Peacock over many years, and who remembered him in a brief memoir, accounted for Peacock's literary reticence by suggesting that he was too scrupulous in composition, too conscious about style, to have written prolifically.[1] Had all of his writings been worked over and polished, such a theory might have been appropriate. The obvious fact is, however, that he often wrote rapidly and sometimes even carelessly, so that—apart from his distrust of periodical literature—the best explanation for his limited output must simply be that he was an amateur, neither dependent on his pen nor forever pushing it.

Part of Strachey's observation nevertheless makes sense, for Peacock seems to have been, if not always meticulous in his revision, still very conscious of his literary style. Dr. Folliott, of *Crotchet Castle*, scoffs at authors who write unquotable works— Scott is his main target—and Peacock himself is master of the epigrammatic phrase and the startling metaphor. He would have agreed with De Quincey, and have found nothing condescending in the opinion that 'the artifice and machinery of rhetoric furnishes in its degree as legitimate a basis for intellectual pleasure as any other'—that style itself, in other words, can be a desirable end, well worth cultivating. It may be appropriate to think of Peacock's writings, particularly the essays, as they relate to what Hazlitt called the 'truly English style'. In the essay 'On Familiar Style' Hazlitt offers an apology for one kind of writing to the exclusion of others: he lists the learned, the gaudy, and the vulgar. He might be referring to Hunt when he says that a writer is never 'at liberty to gabble on at a venture, without emphasis and discretion, nor to resort to vulgar dialect or clownish pronunciation'. But his target is Dr. Johnson when he exiles prose using 'tall, opaque words'. 'You must', he says, 'steer a middle course.'[2] Hazlitt's statements provide an apt description of his own taut, nervous prose; but if Hazlitt includes Lamb as a happy exception to his criteria, he shuts the door to dozens of other writers who write well, though not in a familiar style. (The term 'familiar' implies, of course, as much the relationship of the writer to his reader as it does a mode of expression.) Calling for a reformation in prose akin to that which Wordsworth had demanded in poetry, Hazlitt excludes and chastises to make a point. Essentially he calls for an English prose style that lacks 'style'—lacks, that is, the trappings of an old vocabulary and an old rhetorical syntax, without stooping to 'low' expressions. Southey, whose English is direct and unassuming, should have been his ideal. Peacock never could have been. We notice in Peacock—as we notice in Browne, Gibbon, Sterne, and De Quincey—style as style.

To some extent Peacock's prose does vary. There are times when his phrasing resembles that of quite different authors, whether of his own time or of the preceding century. Occasionally he echoes John Gay, Fielding, or Johnson, or quotes Steele within his own sentence, or paraphrases Cobbett and Coleridge. He can write terse and lucid prose, as the memoirs of Shelley will indicate, but he prefers to play with antithesis, parallelism, chiasmus, and other rhetorical devices. His most distinctive quality is a tendency to develop his paragraphs towards a final, often intentionally bathetic or surprising metaphor. And for this reason many of his sentences, while actually quite short, seem like clauses in the longer unit of the paragraph, which itself gives the illusion of being periodic. For those who respond to his ironic and sometimes cryptic manner, Peacock gives the lie to a number of clichés about style. He uses a great number of 'was's' and 'is's', and, rather than achieving his ends by 'strong' verbs, prefers to emphasize qualifiers. Sometimes he invents his own.

Although Peacock can write in the taut and direct manner of Hazlitt and although he consistently mocks the man infatuated with words, his characteristic style is less familiar than 'ornamental'. Hazlitt defended what Dr. Johnson, in the *Preface to Shakespeare*, had called writers of 'common intercourse of life'. Peacock's writing hovers somewhere between Johnson's other two categories, the learned and the polite.

Some of the divisions in this section may seem a little arbitrary: Peacock's political writings, for example, are never exclusively political. I have isolated two pieces and referred to others that seem to be largely political in emphasis. These essays reveal as much about what Peacock ignored as about what concerned him, for though he hammered at political issues in his novels, he was not a political essayist. Yet it makes sense to clarify what we can about certain of his assumptions, particularly as they bear on the novels. Like the political statements, those on gastronomy are brief; but again, they offer witty and erudite commentary as well as a clue to his novels. Peacock was indeed 'an English gastronome': he rarely shows himself in such good form as when he launches into the details of ancient symposia or quotes Martial on cookery.

Most of Peacock's collected essays are literary essays of one sort or another, generally factual and opinionated, digressive and tongue-in-cheek. Diverse, though also peculiarly limited, in subject-matter, they include both his first and last periodical works and serve as a good beginning here.

2

'The Four Ages of Poetry' and Peacock's Literary Criticism

We Poets are (upon a Poet's word)
Of all mankind, the creatures most absurd.

POPE: *Imitations of Horace*, II, i.

I am sometimes so very sceptical to think Poetry itself a mere
Jack a lanthern to amuse whoever may chance to be struck with
its brilliance—As Tradesmen say every thing is worth what it
will fetch, so probably every mental pursuit takes its reality
and worth from the ardour of the pursuer—being in itself a
nothing. . . .

KEATS, in a letter to Benjamin Bailey.

I

What chiefly distinguishes Peacock's critical positions from
those of many of his eminent contemporaries, including writers
as diverse as Wordsworth, Shelley, Coleridge, and Hazlitt, is
his reluctance to idealize the poet or to ascribe to poetry new
and, as he thought, alien powers. Sceptical about the claims
made for both poets and their work, Peacock tended to extreme
counter-statements, which he may elsewhere modify or outright
contradict; but he does remain consistent in his devaluation of
the poet. Appropriately, the term 'imagination', such a charged
and over-used word at the time, occurs seldom in his writings,
and whenever it does occur, the context is likely to be ironic.

Many of Peacock's contexts are likely to be ironic anyway,
and in this sense too he found himself at odds with what he
recognized as a major critical tendency. Peacock was not only
far more tolerant than most critics of the time to comic literature; he maintained a traditional approval of comic and satiric
forms—in part no doubt because his own talents manifested
themselves in comic fiction and because he was temperamentally sympathetic to comedy, but also because he recog-

nized the dangers, the new barbarism, in poets who judged all literature in terms of serious and meditative lyric norms.

Peacock's tastes and responses to poetry were limited, but he was neither an idle antiquarian nor, like Dr. Johnson's Dick Minim, a half-educated sophist. Apologists for the early nineteenth-century poets, especially for Shelley, often shrug Peacock off as a cold rationalist or as a naughty boy—or even, by a peculiar marriage, as both. This is to judge him by Shelley's own standards, which in many ways were more limited, and much more provincial, than Peacock's own. There is in most of Peacock's writing, whatever the lapses or the short-sightedness, a sustaining urbanity, an urbanity that enabled him to be on the one hand a tolerant reader of Shelley's poems, and on the other hand a lover of little and light works, of the bagatelles. Nor, among his contemporaries, was Peacock's appreciation limited to Shelley's work. If he never had, for example, Leigh Hunt's remarkable tolerance for welcoming new verse, he was rarely led, as Hunt often was, into indiscriminate acceptance. Peacock could praise Scott, Coleridge, Byron, and even at times Wordsworth, though he had a lasting prejudice against Keats. But he found these writers, however talented, to be children of a new kind of darkness, and, as though they were children, he publicly rapped their knuckles.

In many of his judgments Peacock anticipated Matthew Arnold's criticism of early nineteenth-century poets, since he demanded, as Arnold was to demand, a more balanced, a more critical, in short a more classical literature than he found being written. (However, he did not share Arnold's 'romantic' estimate of Pope and Pope's followers.) He wanted intelligence and clarity in art; instead of 'moods of my own mind', he wanted a more impersonal and a more dramatic poetry. At the same time, Peacock was even less sanguine than Arnold about the future course of poetry or about the audience for poetry. He had in him none of the underlying millenianism that sustained Arnold even in his gloomiest musings. He would also have distrusted Arnold's 'religion of literature', which in other guises he attacked in Shelley and Wordsworth. To inflate the task of literature was to make literature earnest and useful, to come to the philistines on their own terms.

To speak about Peacock as a literary critic, especially in

connection with Arnold, is not quite accurate. For a man whose novels offer what is probably the fullest and wittiest commentary on the intellectual life of his time, Peacock was at the most a part-time literary essayist. He offers no system, no series of extensive reviews, and only a smattering of the 'workshop criticism' by which he defends his own writing in commenting on that of others. His comments tend to be occasional, struck off in moments of impatience or anger, and the resulting essays are necessarily but a partial expression of his literary opinions. Reluctant to generalize, except in satiric contexts, he makes his best comments as it were in passing—feinting and darting, while avoiding direct assaults. This is a way of saying, not only that Peacock's novels took his main critical energies and offered the best medium for his commentary, but also that his essays are more or less asides, or discursive extensions of the novels, with a comparable tone and style. Especially true of 'The Four Ages of Poetry', the observation proves relevant for nearly all his miscellaneous criticism. For nearly all, but conspicuously not for his first venture into the essay, which was writing of another sort entirely.

Why, after writing two comic novels, each with telling satire at the expense of current writers and reviewers, Peacock should have begun the 'Essay on Fashionable Literature' can only be guessed at. Certainly the title offers hints. He started the essay, then laid it aside unfinished, in the summer of 1818, only a few months after the publication of *Rhododaphne*. Since the main thesis of the essay is that most literature gets produced for a mindless, consuming public, who treat poetry as they would treat a new article of clothing or a new piece of gossip, Peacock is probably expressing chagrin as well as disdain, aggravated by the tepid response to his poem. 'Fashionable Literature', like 'The Four Ages of Poetry', which followed a year or so later, is as much a salty goodbye to the profession of poetry as an exposure of the conditions inimical to the writing of poetry.

Peacock divides his comments into numbered and partly independent paragraphs, using them for the kind of urbane remarks—as opposed to what he calls the 'systematic cant' of professional despoilers like William Gifford—that one associates with the best periodicals of the eighteenth century. Had Peacock continued to write in the manner of the unfinished essay, we should have had a much fuller glossary on the judgments in the novels and in 'The Four Ages'. We should also have had intelligent and readable criticism in the *Spectator-Rambler* tradition.

Dr. Johnson himself might be speaking in parts of the essay. Not only do some of his opinions occur—that, for instance, 'originality will sometimes attract notice . . . by the mere force of excessive absurdity' (viii, 265)—but even patterns of phrasing. Peacock concerns himself with those 'easy books which command attention without the labour of application, and amuse the idleness of fancy without disturbing the sleep of understanding' (viii, 263). To 'disturb the sleep of understanding' may involve a strained figure, but it is clear that, with an eye on those of Johnson, Peacock has carefully and rather artfully turned his phrases. How intimate Peacock was with Johnson's writings would be difficult to say. Certainly the man who defines 'country gentlemen' as 'a generic term applied by courtesy to the profoundly ignorant of all classes' (viii, 268) knew the rhetoric of the *Dictionary*. In the Shelley memoirs Peacock speaks of Johnson as 'our literary Hercules', and although the phrase comes from a much later work, it is likely that he admired Johnson even while a young man. His tastes were not Johnson's, but his basic assumptions about literature seem not to have been too different.

The spirit of 'Fashionable Literature' is that of tolerant classicism, again not too far from Johnson's own. Throughout the satiric poems, essays, and novels, Peacock lampoons various writers of his time, most notably Coleridge, Byron, Wordsworth, Shelley, and Scott. In 'Fashionable Literature' he shows that he could respond positively to some of their work. Consider the following, almost Horatian announcement, which has an unexpected application. The role of poetry, he says, is 'to awaken the mind' by giving pleasure. Yet it is not Pope whom he singles out for praise, but rather Sir Walter Scott. (Like many people, he was aware of the 'Waverley' guise. 'Far from being a writer who teaches nothing' (viii, 275), Scott instructs as he entertains.

More unexpected and far more incisive than the apology for Scott is the final part of the essay, which contains an extended defence of Coleridge—object of a great deal of Peacock's laughter. Apparently Peacock began the essay as a vindication

G   81

of Coleridge, prompted by an anonymous attack in the *Edinburgh Review* (for September 1816), once ascribed to, but probably not written by, Hazlitt.[1] With devastating success, he uses the reviewer's own weapons against him. Bad reviewers, he says, have four or five routine charges to make against all works they cannot or will not understand. The reviewers of *Christabel* and *Kubla Khan* have relied on techniques that cast light only upon their own stupidity. By comparing the attacks with Coleridge's explanatory comments and lines from the poems, Peacock at once ridicules the critics and offers sensitive interpretation of the poems. He was one of the first to argue that, though published as a fragment, *Kubla Khan* makes internal sense and is both a beautiful and comprehensible poem (though admittedly easy to parody: Peacock himself parodied the 'damsel with a dulcimer' line a number of times). Of *Christabel*, which shocked and offended the reviewers, Peacock writes:

> But with all due deference to this Aristarchus [the adverse critic], let us examine the culprit on whom he thus summarily pronounces. *Christabel* is a ballad romance, a tale of wonder and mystery told with the simplicity of our elder minstrels, who depict every scene as it were passing under their eyes, and narrate their most marvellous legends with an unaffected *bonne foi*, that shows a mind fully impressed with the truth of its own tale. They never destroyed the appearance of self-persuasion by too much minuteness of detail. . . . Their style is at once simple and energetic, unincumbered [*sic*] with extraneous ornaments; the natural expression of distinctly conceived imagery, rising and falling with the elevation or homeliness of the subject. Such is the style and language of *Christabel* (VIII, 281).

Here of course is no echo of Dr. Johnson, but rather of Thomas Warton or Bishop Percy or the radical Joseph Ritson. Coleridge would have appreciated both Peacock's awareness of ballad tradition and his understanding of the poem's intent.

Coleridge would also have noted that Peacock uses some of Coleridge's own arguments in defence of the poems. He demands that the critic adequately understand the poem, or work of art generally, before venturing praise or censure, and in lashing out at the reviews he uses language reminiscent of Chapter III of the *Biographia Literaria* (which had appeared the year before).[2] He sympathized with Coleridge's concern about the impact of the reviews—those 'hardy veterans of corruption' (vIII, 268)—their making independent writing more and more difficult by setting up false standards, and their gradual subverting of unprejudiced readers. (Goethe, with Byron in mind, wondered how Englishmen could continue to write poetry in the face of the reviews and their poisoned subscribers.)

Peacock concerned himself in 'Fashionable Literature', therefore, with a central question of the time—that of the poet's audience. For whom, he was asking, could the poet write? Coleridge and Wordsworth evidently agreed, as Wordsworth writes in the 'Essay, Supplementary' of 1815, that the poet must secure his own audience, must create the taste by which he is to be enjoyed. Scott, deferring to his innumerable 'dear readers', could still argue that drama in his day was impossible because of uncouth and illiterate audiences. Byron at once pandered to and despised his readers. Peacock's response, once again, changed with the years. But by the time he wrote *Rhododaphne* he knew—as the Preface to the poem indicates— that there was no substantial readership for his own poems, and he assumed there was none for any but second-rate verse. What 'Fashionable Literature' attempts in a fairly straightforward manner, 'The Four Ages of Poetry' completes and expands by indirection and burlesque, the new vehicle providing tacit evidence that Peacock could no longer directly address himself to the 'reading public'.

II

To what extent Peacock was serious in his diatribe against poetry and what he actually intended are matters about which there has been little agreement, ever since Shelley responded to the essay with slightly disingenuous horror. George Saintsbury, who admired Peacock and who admitted the brilliance of the essay, could find no place for it in his *History of Criticism*. More recently, M. H. Abrams has acknowledged its relevance to early nineteenth-century criticism, at the same time maintaining 'it is idle to inquire about the exact boundaries of irony in this essay. . . . Peacock cannot be pinned down.'[3] The essay certainly is enigmatic, apparently with intention, and Peacock cannot perhaps be pinned down—if the phrase is appropriate. But much of his irony can and should be clarified, for it tells a great deal. Granted there is a risk of tilting at windmills.

Shelley, who sometimes agreed with Peacock more than he cared to admit, shared Peacock's estimate of the climate for poetry. Whereas Peacock's response was a kind of despair, masked by laughter, which made the further writing of poetry futile, Shelley's was both a voluble espousal of poetry and an admission that he must write, as he put it, 'simply for the esoteric few'. Actually both 'The Four Ages' and Shelley's 'antidote' or 'answer', as he called the 'Defence of Poetry', grew out of the same recognition that poetry had become a species of private communication. If only because Shelley's rebuttal bears upon Peacock's intent, it is worth recounting the circumstances behind this literary exchange.

Shelley's publishers, Charles and James Ollier, founded in 1820 a periodical called *Olliers' Literary Miscellany*. Whether Shelley suggested that they invite a contribution from Peacock or whether they approached him on the basis of former acquaintance—or as the author of *Nightmare Abbey*—is not known. Whatever the background, 'The Four Ages' appeared in the first and only number. By November Shelley was writing to Peacock that 'The box containing . . . your essay against the cultivation of poetry, has not arrived; my wonder, meanwhile, in what manner you support such a heresy in this matter-of-fact and money-loving age, holds me in suspense'.[4] When Shelley's books arrived, along with a letter from Peacock deriding the 'poetical reading public' (VIII, 219), Shelley responded: 'I received at the same time your printed denunciations against general, and your written ones against particular, poetry; and I agree with you as decidedly in the latter as I differ in the former. . . .'[5]

Shelley intended at first to write an immediate letter of rebuttal for the following number of the *Miscellany*, several drafts of which he left incomplete, full of omissions, corrections, false starts. Perhaps Shelley felt cramped by the necessarily limited scope of a letter to the editor; perhaps he was unsure about the extent of Peacock's irony and therefore puzzled about his reply. In any case, he left the letters unfinished. He then wrote the 'Defence', conceiving of it as the first part of a longer essay, and sent it off to Charles Ollier with a brief accompanying note. For what were probably economic reasons, the Olliers never issued a second number of the *Miscellany*. The 'Defence' was later to have appeared in Hunt's *Liberal* and was adapted by John Hunt so as to seem an independent and comprehensive treatise on poetry. Shelley's essay remained unpublished until 1840, when it was printed—as it is usually reprinted—in Hunt's revised form. It is, in Peacock's words, 'a defence without an attack' (VIII, 500). The first version, as he knew, responded on an almost point-by-point basis to 'The Four Ages'.

Among others, Milton Wilson has pointed out that Shelley's 'Defence' is something of a composite of Shelley's earlier critical remarks, refurbished for the occasion.[6] This is only partly true— it seems inapplicable to several of the important statements about imagination—but it suggests that Peacock's essay may have provided Shelley with the provocation he wanted, in order to re-enter a familiar arena.[7]

If Shelley used 'The Four Ages' as a convenient straw man, at least pretended that it was a straw man, he was baffled by its tone and incensed by some of its arguments. 'I had the greatest possible desire', he told Peacock, 'to break a lance with you within the lists of a magazine.' His urbanity, however, is inconsistent: 'your anathemas against poetry itself excited me to a sacred rage'.[8] One of Shelley's lasting sources of irritation was Peacock's readiness to argue what he did not believe, and Shelley immediately sensed a 'hobby-horsical' quality in 'The Four Ages'. In one of the draft letters he paid lip-service to his friend's wit—which elsewhere he encouraged and enjoyed—but the acknowledgement is a token gesture. 'So dark a paradox', he wrote, 'may absorb the brightest rays of mind. . . .' And, 'It is an impious daring attempt to extinguish Imagination which is the Sun of life'.[9] Peacock had probably not thought of himself in the capacity of anti-Promethean firefighter, although he may have thought Shelley something of an incendiary.

In another of the unfinished letters for Olliers, Shelley wrote that the author of 'The Four Ages' was engaged in a self-murdering attempt and that he resembled a pig swimming and inevitably cutting its own throat. The rhetoric of both the draft letters and the 'Defence', maintaining a position diametrically opposed to Peacock's, is no less overstated than the rhetoric of 'The Four Ages' itself. Shelley proposed to Peacock that they avoid the controversial manner of 'Mr. Price & Payne Knight, who like two ill-trained beagles began snarling at each other when they could not catch the hare'.[10] While the Payne-Knight-Price arguments—about the 'picturesque'—were common knowledge, Shelley may also have remembered that *Headlong Hall* (1816), Peacock's first novel, included two characters intended to parody the famous landscape experts. In other words, he may have been saying to Peacock: let us avoid a controversy of the sort that you yourself travesty in your fiction. He may also have sensed that Peacock was playing a rhetorical game. For the argument in 'The Four Ages' is almost entirely of the sort that is scattered through the novels. Like the characters in the novels, the voice in 'The Four Ages' is the voice of a travestied proposition, not unconnected with its author, but by no means his direct outlet. Peacock's method of dialogue is to force two or three spokesmen to ever more extreme positions, so that each casts doubt on the others. In 'The Four Ages', the author himself argues as though he had an antagonist—and perhaps he did have Shelley in mind. That his thesis is largely a spoof can be seen in the survey of the literature of the Renaissance.

From these ingredients [love, battle, and fanaticism] of the iron age of modern poetry, dispersed in the rhymes of minstrels and the songs of the troubadours, arose the golden age, in which the scattered materials were harmonized and blended about the time of the revival of learning; but with this peculiar difference [this is one of Peacock's favourite rhetorical devices], that Greek and Roman literature pervaded all the poetry of the golden age of modern poetry, and hence resulted a heterogeneous compound of all ages and nations in one picture; an infinite licence, which gave to the poet the free range of the whole field of imagination and memory. This was carried very far by Ariosto, but farthest of all by Shakespeare and his contemporaries, who used time and locality merely because they could not do without them, because every action must have its when and where: but they made no scruple of deposing a Roman Emperor by an Italian Count, and sending him off in the disguise of a French pilgrim to be shot with a blunderbuss by an English archer. This makes the old English drama very picturesque . . . (VIII, 15–16).

If some of the writing here—such as 'This was carried very far by Ariosto, but farthest of all by Shakespeare'—reads like an anticipatory parody of T. S. Eliot's essay style, most is clearly burlesque of neo-Aristotelian or Horatian dicta of the Rapin/Boileau/Rymer family. Obviously Peacock does not accuse Shakespeare of any real breach of propriety, nor does he confuse the paraphrased nuggets of earlier poetic credos with Shakespeare's actual achievement. His method is to compress judgments into the briefest compass, to state them in parallel with other distorted judgments, and to develop the resulting mixture into a final climactic piece of nonsense. The passage above ends by comparing the literature of Shakespeare's time to nothing more than a 'Venetian carnival'.

The argument of the essay is engagingly simple, comprising in its few pages an indictment of apparently wholesale proportions. Possibly its most remarkable quality is the nudity of its statement, the absence of what, in an attack upon poetry, one would expect to find prominent. Peacock's essay prompted Shelley to write the 'Defence', and since Shelley himself clearly turned to Sir Philip Sidney's classic apology for poetry, one naturally thinks of 'The Four Ages' in connection with Stephen Gosson's tract, *The School of Abuse*, an angry diatribe that served to provoke Sidney. Peacock uses as his motto a line from Petronius, to the effect that he who works in the kitchen must smell of food and hence lose all sense of discrimination. Gosson had written, 'For Hee that goes to Sea must smell of the Ship'. Like Gosson, Peacock directs his censure at the poets—though on intellectual rather than moral grounds—and his main thrust similarly concerns the undesirable effects of verse on the reader. But as it is in tone detached, supercilious, calmly assertive, his essay has little in common with Gosson's heated outburst. 'He that sitteth in the heavens', according to the psalm, 'shall laugh'; Peacock writes here as though his place aloft were assured:

A poet in our times is a semi-barbarian in a civilized community. He lives in the days that are past. His ideas, thoughts, feelings, associations, are all with barbarous manners, obsolete customs, and exploded superstitions. The march of his intellect is like that of a crab, backward. The brighter the light diffused around him by the progress of reason, the thicker is the darkness of antiquated barbarism, in which he buries himself like a mole, to throw up the barren hillocks of his Cimmerian labours (VIII, 20–1).

The allusiveness—he echoes *Hamlet* and refers to the *Odyssey*—the quiet overstatement, the careful building to the final metaphor, reveal a sophistication and wit far different from anything in Gosson.

Nor is the difference chiefly that of tone. Whereas Gosson's approach had been a sort of puritanical and derivative Platonism, Peacock's is surprisingly un-Platonic. Surprisingly so, because Plato offered the strongest traditional authority for an attack on poetry. To the extent that Peacock asserts the ill effects of verse, especially modern verse, and argues the need for another type of discourse, his argument might be Platonic. On these grounds, however, he had been anticipated by Bentham and Bentham's followers. Many of the standard Platonic arguments he leaves largely untouched. He does refer to various sorts of inspiration, among them that from 'vinous spirits', that *ascribed* to poets by the ignorant, as well as three more predictable 'ingredients': 'the rant of unregulated passion, the whine of exaggerated feeling, and the cant of factitious sentiment' (VIII, 21). Knowing quite well what Plato had done with comparable assertions, Peacock remains content with a few, undeveloped feints. On the matter of imitation he is also remarkably silent. Since he charges poets with letting loose undesirable emotions, and therefore imitating the worthless—their own morbid souls—one would have expected echoes of Plato's discussions of imitation in the *Ion* and *Republic*. It is curious that neither Peacock nor Shelley in his 'antidote' seems to recall that Plato had anything whatever to say at the expense of poetry. Shelley's reasons need no comment. One can only begin to understand Peacock's by asking about the intent of his essay. A man familiar with Plato, appreciative of his writings, who seriously wanted to denounce poetry, would surely have invoked both the name and the central arguments in an effort to buttress his case.

The usual estimate of Peacock is, to twist Shelley's words, that he would have preferred to 'be right with Horace' than to 'err with Plato'. But underlying 'The Four Ages', as it underlies most of his writing, is a respect for Plato and for Plato's ideas. The difference between Shelley and himself lies in allegiance to final answers, for Peacock refused to, or perhaps could not, commit himself to either speculative hypotheses or inclusive systems. Nevertheless, there is a great deal of Plato in his works, as *Rhododaphne* has made clear; and a great deal of admiration, as a number of his letters testify. Many details of his fiction are drawn from Plato. It was not by accident that Peacock entitled chapters 'Symposium', or that he fabricated his witty dialogues in mock-Platonic fashion, as though they were Socratic without an enlightening Socrates.

On receiving a copy of 'The Four Ages', Shelley suggested to Peacock that he should read the *Ion* again, implying that the counter to his argument could be found there. Ironically, Peacock had introduced Shelley, not only to less popular Greek writers, but even to parts of Plato. He probably knew the *Ion* as well as Shelley did. Was he then inviting a rebuttal to his argument based on Plato or on neo-Platonic grounds or, more precisely, did he expect his reader to see in 'The Four Ages' the other side to his arguments, so that the attack would be recognized as ironic? It seems more than likely.

While maintaining the charges against modern poetry, 'The Four Ages' becomes an implicit apology for the literature of older and largely, though not entirely, classical times. Because Peacock burlesques his own arguments as much as he mocks the poets, he excludes Plato from unflattering company. In any case, the ostensible argument of the essay is neither puritanical nor Platonic, but rather Utilitarian on the one hand and primitivistic or Viconian on the other. Both arguments overlap, and both contain Platonic elements, but they are also to an extent distinct. Peacock insists that poetry is inferior to various scientific and philosophical disciplines; he also introduces a historical and dialectical scheme, which at once points to the rise and fall of poetry and offers him a convenient organizational pattern.

Essentially the scheme underlying 'The Four Ages' is the old primitivistic view of history, common to dozens of earlier writers, and first known to us in Hesiod, significantly altered in order to make 'primitive' and modern poets—or primitive modern poets—appear ridiculous. 'Poetry', then, 'like the world, may be said to have four ages, but in a different order: the first age of poetry being the age of iron; the second, of gold; the third, of silver; and the fourth, of brass' (VIII, 3). It develops that poetry has not four but eight ages, four modern corresponding—as the shadow to the real thing—to four ancient. The effect is merely to emphasize the decline of poetry in modern times. Sentence pronounced, we can only wait, and perhaps with surreptitious glee, until the guillotine descends on Wordsworth and Byron. But again the scheme is too rigid, too pat, to be taken in earnest.

The idea of the cyclical scheme, though common to writers as different as Hesiod and Hegel, had found its fullest exponent in Giambàttista Vico, whose *The New Science* had appeared almost a century before 'The Four Ages'. Peacock describes, like Vico, the cycles of poetry and comes to the same intolerable conclusion that the expiration of the modern cycle—beginning for both men in the Middle Ages—has led to the virtual death of poetry. Since what remains to be written can no longer and should no longer be written in verse, and since science has eclipsed poetry, the poet has become a barbarian in a civilized community. The state of mind requisite for the creation of poetry having disappeared, it is idle to versify. When Peacock says, 'We know too that there are no Dryads in Hyde-park nor Naiads in the Regent's-canal', his argument parallels Vico's.[12] And the absurd associations and apparent glibness mask a nostalgia comparable to Vico's own.[13]

Just as the ancient cycle of poetry concluded with Nonnus, he writes, so the modern, in its early dotage, results in the Lake Poets and other 'confraternities of rhymesters'; but 'with a difference'—the phrase is Peacock's, and he uses it often. Nonnus, to his credit, could write occasionally beautiful passages, and he never expressed pernicious ideas. Modern poets are not so harmless. They are all

wallowing in the rubbish of departed ignorance, and raking

up the ashes of dead savages to find gewgaws and rattles for the grown babies of the age. Mr. Scott digs up the poachers and cattle-stealers of the ancient border. Lord Byron cruizes for thieves and pirates on the shores of the Morea and among the Greek islands. Mr. Southey wades through ponderous volumes of travels and old chronicles, from which he carefully selects all that is false, useless, and absurd, as being essentially poetical; and when he has a commonplace book full of monstrosities, strings them into an epic. Mr. Wordsworth picks up village legends from old women and sextons; and Mr. Coleridge, to the valuable information acquired from similar sources, superadds the dreams of crazy theologians and the mysticisms of German metaphysics, and favours the world with visions in verse, in which the quadruple elements of sexton, old woman, Jeremy Taylor, and Emanuel Kant, are harmonized into a delicious poetical compound (VIII, 19–20).[14]

What these poets have in common is a scornful disregard of lucid thought and clear language. Peacock's criticism is an orthodox one, reapplied to new conditions. His charge echoes that of Pope and Swift; it also anticipates those of Arnold, Irving Babbitt, and George Orwell. He sensed the political dangers as well as the dangers for literature in what he considered to be a misuse of the language. And he suggested that the misuse resulted from a new conception of the sources and purposes of poetry, recognizing in the poetry of his time the seeds of a cryptic and private communication. The new poets also compound their mischievous distortions of language and their misguided views of nature by theoretical defences. In parody of Wordsworth, Peacock writes: 'Poetical impressions can be received only among natural scenes: for all that is artificial is anti-poetical. Society is artificial, therefore we will live out of society. The mountains are natural, therefore we will live in the mountains' (VIII, 17).

A more central charge against Wordsworth's theories concerns Peacock's notions as to the public responsibilities of the poet, a matter already touched upon in relation to *The Genius of the Thames*. He accuses Wordsworth of a penchant for self-indulgence, of putting into his verse some inevitable 'phantastical parturition of the moods of his own mind' (VIII, 19). Again, he had nothing but contempt for expressive theories of art, for theories based upon 'the overflow of feelings', in part because he tended to confuse the object of imitation with the imitative work, in part because he found a Wordsworth's effusion less interesting than a Pope's craft.

Modern poets, in short, having lost the original function and the legitimate models of poetic writing, have also perverted what small role might have remained for them. If Peacock does attack poetry, it is largely these inheritors of the muse who receive his blows; Homer and Virgil, Milton and Pope, remain unmolested. (He calls Milton 'the greatest of English poets' [VIII, 16].) The argument, of course, includes an ironic complication, because if history follows a prescribed scheme, and poetry necessarily conforms to it, any condemnation of individual poets must be gratuitous. And if poetry becomes the victim of the times, the times themselves are to blame; in which case the real import of the essay becomes an unvoiced complaint about those factors making poetry impossible. To explore this question we need to glance at the utilitarian assertions within 'The Four Ages'.

Like his Platonism, Peacock's Utilitarianism tended to be a part-time commitment. There is no doubt about his acceptance of some of Bentham's principles, nor about his affiliation with Bentham and Mill, his professional connection with the new intellectual establishment. Peacock succeeded James Mill as Examiner in the India House.[15] (He was himself succeeded by John Stuart Mill, whom he also knew.) He is said to have been fairly intimate with Bentham, at any rate intimate enough to dine with him on a regular basis. Several of his major periodical essays were written for the *Westminster Review*, a Utilitarian journal. If guilt by association cannot demonstrate Peacock's toleration of the Utilitarians, his correspondence makes it clear. In letters to Shelley and to his friend and publisher Edward Hookham, Peacock expresses hope in a future conditioned by Bentham, who has laid 'a mighty axe to the root of superstition' (VIII, 206).

In his lectures *On Bentham and Coleridge*, John Stuart Mill was to make his well-known distinction between what he called negative and positive philosophers, those who attack and tear down, and those who found new systems. Bentham, he said, had both capacities. Peacock, as his statement about the 'axe to superstition' indicates, seems to have appreciated Bentham's attack on 'superstitions'. He could not respond to what he considered to be Bentham's own superstitions.

His objections to certain assumptions of the Utilitarians are best illustrated in Mr. MacQuedy of *Crotchet Castle*. MacQuedy is a Utilitarian, what Cobbett would call a 'scotch feelosopher', the new breed of social scientist from the 'New Athens', or Edinburgh. This 'son of a demonstration' proves a relatively amiable though essentially narrow thinker, far too certain of his own logic, and too sure of progress, especially technological progress. He is both contemptuous of history and smug about his systems, and for his errors Peacock trusses him up for sacrifice. MacQuedy's host, Squire Crotchet, whose intellect elsewhere is seldom keen, clearly speaks for Peacock when he defends an alternative point of view: '. . . where the Greeks had modesty, we have cant; where they had poetry, we have cant; where they had patriotism, we have cant; where they had anything that exalts, delights, or adorns humanity, we have nothing but cant, cant, cant' (IV, 96–7). To say that Crotchet speaks for Peacock in this instance is not to imply that Peacock subscribed to all of Crotchet's charges. The squire is involved in a dialectic, of which he is at once the perpetrator and the victim. Yet his general indictment holds. We are inferior to the Greeks; we have too much faith in social amelioration; and we subscribe to meaningless verbal systems.

If he distrusted the social and political assumptions of Bentham, then Peacock strenuously objected to his aesthetic conclusions. For, like Squire Crotchet, he could not and did not want to reject the past, and he did not find the 'cant' of political scientists any adequate substitute for the sweetness and light of earlier literature. Whatever Bentham's virtues as a thinker in other respects, his understanding of poetry was hopeless. His notorious comparison of poetry with 'push-pin' characterizes his almost quaint denigration of poetry to a minor, and far too aristocratic, source of pleasure. In this judgment Bentham was merely borrowing from certain empirical thinkers, notably John Locke, who on different grounds had argued similarly a century earlier. But Bentham extended the argument. He suggested that poetry may actually be harmful. 'The game of push-pin is always innocent; it were well the same could be asserted of poetry. Indeed, between poetry and truth there is a natural opposition.'[16] This combination of half-truths and unqualified overstatement is a quality of 'The Four Ages', and one object of Peacock's humour is evidently Bentham himself.

Peacock reduces to absurdity a number of stock Utilitarian ideas, at the same time poking fun at the 'superstitions' of modern poets. He argues that *all* poetry is Utilitarian in the crudest sense: poets are flattering and self-flattering Tommy Tuckers, singing for their suppers. The categorical absoluteness of the following passage might be a travesty of any page from Bentham—though the spectre of Adam Smith also creeps in:

> The natural desire of every man to engross to himself as much power and property as he can acquire by any of the means which might makes right, is accompanied by the no less natural desire of making known to as many people as possible the extent to which he has been a winner in this universal game. The successful warrior becomes a chief; the successful chief becomes a king: his next want is an organ to disseminate the fame of his achievements and the extent of his possessions; and this organ he finds in a bard, who is always ready to celebrate the strength of his arm, being first duly inspired by that of his liquor. This is the origin of poetry, which, like all other trades, takes its rise in the demand for the commodity, and flourishes in proportion to the extent of the market (VIII, 4).

His other objection is more centrally Utilitarian and more of a real charge against poetry. Concluding his argument, Peacock writes that in an age of 'mathematicians, astronomers, chemists, moralists, metaphysicians, historians, politicians, and political economists'—the Swiftian, polyglot list is itself damning—'who have built into the upper air of intelligence a pyramid, from the summit of which they see the modern Parnassus far beneath them . . .' (VIII, 24–5), poetry can find only an inferior place. Several types of irony, or at least directions of the irony, can be seen here. Peacock may, for example, have been responding specifically to a letter from Shelley, who had asserted—in a passage that reflects oddly on his 'Defence'—that he found poetry 'very subordinate to moral & political science' (VIII, 500). And he wrote after reading 'The Four Ages' that he would rather, 'for my private reading, receive political geological & moral treatises than this stuff in terza, ottave, & tremilesima rima, whose earthly baseness has attracted the lightening of your undiscriminating censure...'.[17] Peacock's censure included the very kind of 'stuff' for which Shelley confessed a preference; he failed to see the burlesque.

Thomas Carlyle was to speak about the 'cold voice of science' and the readiness of many writers of the previous generation to find poetry emasculated by science. The idea, if not commonplace, had been fairly widely invoked even before 'The Four Ages'. Peacock probably did not know that Keats speculated about the adverse effects of science—as well as of critics—on poetry, but he might have known the public statements by Francis Jeffrey and William Hazlitt.[18] One could read 'The Four Ages' as a travesty of Hazlitt's *Lectures on the English Poets*, with its remarks on the climate necessary for poetry and its historical survey of the major writers. Hazlitt says, for example, that poetry 'is not a mere frivolous accomplishment . . . the trifling amusement of a few idle readers or leisure hours'. Leave out the 'not', and one has Peacock's essential charge. But Peacock's arguments as to the present decline of poetry sound like echoes of Hazlitt, and they are in fact close in sentiment. Hazlitt writes: 'It cannot be concealed . . . that the progress of knowledge and refinement has a tendency to circumscribe the limits of the imagination, and to clip the wings of poetry. . . .' And: 'It is not only the progress of mechanical knowledge, but the necessary advances of civilization that are unfavourable to the spirit of poetry.'[19]

Implicit in Peacock's 'pyramid' of knowledge, with its suggestion of Babel and islands in the sky, is that haunting question of the time: Was there, indeed, any purpose left for poetry? Keats and Hazlitt, despite grave doubts, managed to arrive at an affirmation. Peacock skirts the issue by irony. But it is clear that his sympathies came closer to those of Keats and Hazlitt than to those of Bentham. If one remembers how Mr. Cranium of *Headlong Hall* and other specialists in Peacock's novels topple from their 'pyramids'—a tower in the case of Mr. Cranium—it becomes clear that Peacock chastises society itself, or these its representative intellectuals. Of the professions he lists as examples of an emergent common sense, nearly all are scourged in the course of the novels. That some prig should set himself up, whether as phrenologist or metaphysician, is to Peacock, as earlier it had been to Swift, at once the height of absurdity and the occasion for satire.

Just as he bemoans the passing of an intelligent audience for poetry and condemns those who insist on crying in the wilderness, so Peacock finds intolerable the fact that poetry succumbs to a false progress. Boileau is reported to have said about Descartes that he cut the throat of poetry: that rational inquiry and systematizing had made fancy obsolete. Peacock's ultimate irony is not so much that we have a Wordsworth where we ought to have a Milton, or a Byron where we might have had a Pope; it is that while we have a decline in poetry, we do not have any genuine corresponding 'march of mind'. In modern times it is learned barbarians in the guise of philosophers who cut the throat of poetry.

III

Excepting 'The Four Ages' and 'Fashionable Literature', Peacock's discussion of his English contemporaries is limited to a few reviews, to digressions in essays on other topics, and to brief and often cryptic asides in his altogether brief and cryptic correspondence. Again, the main critical energies were expended in novels. It is as though, while chaffing his contemporaries in 'The Four Ages' and in the novels, Peacock elsewhere snubs them. Perhaps only Hazlitt and Coleridge quote Wordsworth more than Peacock does, however much, in Peacock's opinion, Wordsworth would have been better lost in a Cumberland bog. Yet he has no essays on Wordsworth; only the incomplete passages on Coleridge in 'Fashionable Literature'; very little on Hunt; nothing on De Quincey or Lamb; no more than a few sentences on Scott, Campbell, or Proctor, whom, he said, wrote 'drivelling doggrel' (VIII, 219). What he thought about Landor, with whom he had so much in common —he relates that Landor, 'this frothy personage', has contributed a 'vapouring letter' to *The Times* (VIII, 218)—or of Hazlitt—unless the unpleasant Mr. Eavesdrop of *Crotchet Castle* caricatures Hazlitt—would be interesting to know, although presumably he had strong feelings about neither man. He wrote most extensively, as one might expect, about Shelley, but he also wrote two long essays about Thomas Moore, a writer he despised.

Peacock's criticism of Shelley takes the form of editor-to-author advice, which ranges from technical suggestions to general commentary about the state of poetry and the reading public. Shelley may have occasionally resented Peacock's objections and thought him a meddler, as his sharp criticism of Peacock to other friends would suggest. But he no doubt benefited from the advice and continued to seek it out. Of course Peacock was not Shelley's editor in any formal sense. What he did was to prepare Shelley's poems for the publisher, later correcting proofs and handling last-minute commissions. He served in the capacity of sympathetic and at the same time practical reader, who could advise as to what would or would not be accepted by the public, but who happened to share Shelley's contempt for the public. He can tell Shelley at one time that fame is something for the poet to avoid courting, while arguing elsewhere that 'The poetry of your Adonais is very beautiful; but when you write you never think of your audience. The number who understand you, and sympathise with you, is small' (VIII, 228). He is not so much inconsistent as disinterested, desirous of presenting alternatives to Shelley's extreme positions, and always with publication in mind. (Peacock's belated 'estimate' of Shelley in the memoirs is a work of public criticism, an eloquent apology, though one with serious reservations, the purpose of which is not specifically critical.)

The relationship with Shelley may help to clarify Peacock's rather abrupt dismissal of Keats's poems. Since he toyed with poetic themes interesting to Keats, and since he was often reminded by Shelley of Keats's powers, he may have come to think of himself as a rival to Keats, as it were, for Shelley's favours. This seems the best way of accounting for the strong feeling underlying his response to Keats's work.

Evidently Peacock met Keats in February of 1818—Hunt was a common acquaintance and they met at the Hunts'—for what was the only time. He neither took to Keats, nor did Keats take to him. In March 1818 Keats wrote: 'Hunt has damned Hampstead [and] Masks and Sonnets and Italian tales. [Poor Hunt! Elsewhere he robs Keats of his appreciation of Mozart, too.] Wordsworth has damned the lakes. . . . Peacock has damned sattire.'[20] By associating himself with satire, in other words, Peacock has spoiled it for Keats. But Keats had done something equally reprehensible to Peacock: he had profaned the Greeks. Among the few contemporary authorities for Peacock's opinion on this matter the most convincing is an article by Robert Buchanan, Peacock's first biographer. 'He had little or no appreciation for John Keats', Buchanan writes, 'for he could prove by a hundred quotations that the sleep of Endymion was eternal, whereas in the modern poem the Latmian shepherd is for ever capering up and down the earth and ocean like the German chaser of shadows.'[21] And replying in 1820 to Shelley, who recommended 'Hyperion' to him, Peacock insists that if he 'should live to the age of Methusalem, and have uninterrupted literary leisure', he would not find time to read the poem (VIII, 219).

It is no longer fashionable to see Keats as 'un-Greek' in his poems with Greek subjects, though some sympathetic, if not idolatrous, readers of Keats, Amy Lowell for one, have insisted that the Greek poems were about a Greece that never was on land or sea. This is Peacock's point when he accuses Keats of unhistorical frippery. He erred obviously on the side of pedantry. He failed to see the necessity of transforming the original sources, did not, apparently, understand that historical inaccuracy may be less a poetic sin than a necessary quality. He was therefore not ready to appreciate that Keats had made *his* imaginary Greece relevant for his own times, whereas *Rhododaphne* remains a beautiful but static and ornamental piece of historical tapestry.

Yet one can find in Peacock's reaction to Keats more critical acumen than all this would indicate. For he was responding, not to 'Hyperion', 'Lamia', or the odes, but to *Endymion;* and has anybody honestly worked through *Endymion* without a comparable effect of bewilderment and a sense of the poet's baffling cross-purposes? Even if Peacock had appreciated the poem's brilliant passages, this would not have affected his estimate of the poem as a whole work. He was wrong-headed not to follow Shelley's advice to read more of Keats, but his reluctance to caper 'up and down the earth' in another search after German —or pseudo-Greek—shadows is at least understandable. The author of *Endymion* was a long way in achievement if not in years from the poet who wrote the 'Ode on a Grecian Urn'.

If Peacock thought that Keats sinned, he found Thomas Moore a heretic. Outside of Lockhart, Croker, and Hazlitt there are few more devastating articles than Peacock's attacks on Moore. The first, a review of Moore's novel, *The Epicurean*, appeared in the *Westminster Review* for October 1827. *The Epicurean*, according to Peacock, had popularized, misrepresented, distorted, spoiled. About Moore's love and adventure story he speaks with absolute contempt, scoffing at everything from faulty imagery to basic unintelligence; but at the centre of his argument is disgust with Moore's portrayal of the ancient philosophy. Endeavouring to please fashionable readers—Peacock says he will please them—Moore is 'traducing the noblest philosophy of antiquity, and setting forth the impotence of philosophical education in the formation of moral character' (ix, 67). Having made 'a vain parade of scraps and fragments, which will be found, on due examination, to be not the relics of a rich table, but the contents of a beggar's wallet', Moore should be treated like a 'mischievous boy in a flower garden, and turned back into the fields . . .' (ix, 66–7).[22] He is, in short, neither scholar nor philosopher enough to do more than toy with the subject, which he has simply made an excuse for a vaguely Oriental adventure story.

Peacock's review of Moore's *Letters and Journals of Lord Byron* followed the *Epicurean* review after three years, but the interval can hardly be said to have warmed Peacock towards the 'mischievous boy'. On the contrary. After citing passages from Moore, correcting them, or merely scoffing; after chastising him for misrepresentation at worst and gullibility at best, he says:

We have given very fair specimens of the matter and manner of the volume before us, and an outline of its contents, with such remarks as were imperiously demanded from us by our sense of the moral duty of exhibiting to our readers the real scope and purpose of a series of shallow sophisms and false assumptions, wrapped up in bundles of metaphors, put forth with a specious semblance of reason and liberality, and directed towards the single end of upholding all abuses and delusions by which the aristocracy profit (IX, 138–9).[23]

By modern standards, Moore's work remains a valuable compilation—it is *mostly* compilation—to which later biographers of Byron have had to turn. Moore probably conceived himself as a sort of hurried Boswell. To Peacock, Moore's book represented an unforgivable breach of decency (I shall discuss his views on biography later), in that Moore was making money by gossiping about friends—and writing badly at that.

Understandably chagrined by the review and anxious lest the attack continue, Moore succeeded in persuading the *Westminster* (where Peacock's article had appeared) to refrain from comment on the second part of his work. He cannot be blamed. A final sentence from Peacock's dogged though partly warranted attacks will illustrate what Moore wished to avoid. Peacock quotes a passage from Moore: 'There is a healthfulness in the moral feeling so unaffectedly expressed in this letter, which seems to answer for a heart sound at the core, however passion might have scorched it.' And he comments: 'What is the relation between scorching and a sound core? Half the metaphor is from a rotten apple, and half from a roasted one' (IX, 136). So much for Moore's *Byron*.

Peacock does not introduce many of his own opinions about Lord Byron in this essay, being too intent upon worrying Moore. With the exception of the brilliant parodies in *Nightmare Abbey*, he actually has few comments to make about Byron. For a number of reasons, one would have expected more. Byron's disenchantment, if not with Thomas Moore, with so many other writers of his age often approximates Peacock's, and it may even take the same kind of response. Just as Peacock speaks about progressive 'ages of poetry' and labels his own age that of 'brass', Byron entitles a poem 'The Age of Bronze', both perhaps glancing back to a comparable satiric scheme in Juvenal. Byron's wish that Coleridge would 'explain his explanation' is close to Peacock's criticism in *Melincourt* and *Nightmare Abbey* of the intentionally obscure and 'Cimmerian' philosopher-poet. Similarly, Byron's censure of the matter-of-fact and self-centred Wordsworth essentially parallels Peacock's. And both men, with an almost stubborn blindness, mixed dislike for Keats's poetry with a patronizing contempt. About Robert Southey, as *Sir Proteus* and *The Vision of Judgment* make clear, they were in full harmony, finding him at once a pretentious and bad poet and a political turncoat.

The two men not only shared objects of attack; to some extent they shared the ideals and standards that gave direction to the attack. Politically, for example, they were never far apart. But what I have in mind here is their common admiration for Pope and the eighteenth century, for certain standards of the Enlightenment, which they used to flail the poetic innovators of their day. Peacock's acceptance of these standards, including the ideal of a common idiom and established taste, went farther than Byron's; and though he could appreciate some of Byron's work, Peacock often included him among the apostles of darkness. His most direct comments on Byron reflect apparently extreme positions. At one time he tells Shelley that *Childe Harold* is 'really too bad' (VIII, 193)—a judgment with which Shelley agreed—at another time he says: '*Cain* is very fine; *Sardanapalus* I think finer; *Don Juan* is best of all. I have read nothing else in recent literature [this to Shelley!] that I think good for anything' (VIII, 228). Characteristically, he does not elaborate, though from the novels and from other references, one can piece together his reaction. He despised *Childe Harold* for whatever it represented in the way of pubescent morbidities and fashionable *Weltschmerz*. And he probably liked *Sardanapalus* because he preferred the impersonality of drama to undisguised personal expression. In the masked and ironic *Don Juan*—begun shortly after his own *Nightmare Abbey*—Byron had both escaped from mere personalism and re-created some of the spirit and wit of Augustan satire. Byron was also to write in a way sure to win Peacock's approval:

> The days of Comedy are gone, alas!
> When Congreve's fool could vie with Molière's *bête*
> (canto xiii).

Byron not only applauded satire and comedy; like Peacock, he mocked what he thought overly sober poetry of his own day.

Yet even *Don Juan* remains essentially at odds with what Peacock affirms, both in the critical statements and in the novels. Implicit in his writings is a desire for social and hence for aesthetic order and a corresponding assumption as to the limits of the poet's role. With no more faith than Byron in the advent of an ideal society, he nevertheless refuses the alternative trumpeted in *Don Juan*, that aristocrat's *Beggar's Opera*, with its paradoxical apology for social anarchy and poetic retrenchment.

Peacock occasionally associates poetry with passion, but he would never have agreed with Byron's claims that poetry *is* passion, or 'exalted' passion, including the correlative assumption that the poet is always more than the poem he creates. Implicit in the censure of Moore's work on Byron is the accusation that Byron has asked for just the kind of indiscriminate hero-worship with which Moore has remembered him.

The Moore reviews were Peacock's last specific treatments of English writers, excepting the memoirs of Shelley. He turned next to some French writers, and these essays are perhaps best introduced by a short digression on a very different sort of author.

Carlyle disparaged the eighteenth century, with its restraint, politeness, rationalism, scepticism, lasciviousness, and what he considered a lack of sincerity and inspiration. James Sutherland characterizes his method particularly well, suggesting that 'For addressing his public . . . Carlyle had evolved an artificial . . . falsetto, [and] exclamatory style that we should normally associate with a literary mountebank'. Mr. Sutherland contrasts this moral haranguing with the restraint of the 'earlier romantics', who 'had their roots in the eighteenth century and retained some of its intellectual discipline'.[24] Although Peacock does not refer to Carlyle, Carlyle stood for everything, including a mode of address, that he found abhorrent, and, with his own roots firmly in the eighteenth century, he would no doubt have been appalled by Carlyle, as he was by other contemporary 'mountebanks'. 'Mountebanks' is one of his own words of censure.

Carlyle turned away from eighteenth-century or Enlightenment ideals; he also turned away from France in his admiration for Germany. Peacock on the contrary was partial to France and to the French language, which, like Greek, Latin, and Italian, he read with ease. He never learned German, and in some ways he was quite unsympathetic with things German; he lets one of his characters win an argument by quoting Porson to the effect that life is altogether too short to learn German.

He was not entirely anti-German. What he disliked was the German fashion of the time, the fad for 'horrid mysteries', grotesque theatre, and the insufferable descendants of Young Werther. He sensed that what was worst of a vast intellectual movement had been welcomed in England. (But he included the importation of Kant and German philosophy among the worst.) On the other hand, German scholarship represented to him an admirable achievement. He writes in a letter to Thomas L'Estrange: 'I took to reading the best books, illustrated by the best critics; and amongst the latter I feel especially indebted to Heyne and Hermann [German classical scholars, for both of whom, incidentally, Carlyle had high praise]. Such was my education' (VIII, 259). He also allows Dr. Folliott, of *Crotchet Castle*, the following comment: 'I run over to myself the names of the scholars of Germany, a glorious catalogue! but ask for those of Oxford—Where are they?' (IV, 114).

Still, his preference in imaginative literature was for the French, and among the French it was not only for the great writers of satire or comedy. Indeed, some of the authors he read and wrote about were, by anyone's standards, the odd fellows of literature. The posthumous catalogue of Peacock's books, for example, shows that he owned over one hundred and fifty volumes of Paul de Kock, a writer who today is virtually forgotten—except for non-literary reasons, as the nominal delight of James Joyce's earthy Molly Bloom.[25] Peacock does not have especially high praise for Kock, but he writes about him at some length, and in a context that includes 'Cervantes—Rabelais—Swift—Voltaire—Fielding'—just the writers about whom one would like to have Peacock's comments, and about whom he merely says that they 'have led fancy against opinion' (VIII, 275). Part of the reason for Peacock's defence of Kock and other French romancers may simply have been the slowly diminishing estimation of French literature in the England of his time. Hazlitt, typically, considered the French lacking in 'gusto': 'Neither Van Dyck nor the French have it', he wrote, lumping together a painter and a nation, in spite of his appreciation of individual French authors. He does say at the close of his essay and with a characteristic about-face that, among prose writers, Rabelais is distinguished for gusto.

Peacock not only admired French literature; he was especially attracted to the comic romance, of which Rabelais was at once the great model and the single giant. In his first two essays on French literature—both announced as prologues to a piece on Kock that never appeared—Peacock clarifies a number of his literary opinions. 'French Comic Romances' (issued in the *London Review* for October 1835) turns into an implicit defence of comic literature. 'An intense love of truth', he writes, 'and a clear apprehension of truth, are both essential to comic writing of the first class' (IX, 262). He argues that the comic writer is not—as Aristotle had so long condemned him to being—essentially frivolous or a writer of secondary talents. Hence Rabelais is 'one of the wisest and most learned, as well as wittiest of men' (IX, 258). This emphasis on the man rather than the work involves a back-door apology for comic literature akin to the *ad hominem* attack on poetry in 'The Four Ages', yet it was the sort of apology that still had to be made.

Many of Peacock's observations are apt, but they tend to hang, as though gathered together from a series of notes. (Conspicuous is the overuse of Latin tags, very few of which are more than decorative.) Most interesting, if undeveloped, are the opinions that bear on his own fiction. He calls comic romances unassuming—though whether he has tone or intent in mind is unclear—while saying that they make an important 'tilt at popular opinions' and thereby help to improve the general intellectual climate.

Like several of his essays, this on comic romances flags into plot summary, which in fact takes up half the space: Peacock uses the opportunity to translate long passages from two little known, and deservedly forgotten, eighteenth-century romances. But the matter of tilting 'at popular opinions' involves a recurring and to some extent a unifying idea. The age demands, he says, and artists supply. A Shakespeare living today would write libretti for light opera—as Jean Paul also insisted. This is a concept Peacock had toyed with in 'Fashionable Literature' and 'The Four Ages'; it underlies all his comments in 'The *Epicier*'. Just how the comic writer can reflect or be determined by the intellectual and social conditions of his time and still tilt at opinion, is a question Peacock leaves unanswered. He seems to argue that the great comic writers are more independent than writers working in other genres and therefore represent a more consistent source of fresh and honest criticism. And so, though he calls Wordsworth's appeal for another Milton silly—because the age would not listen—he implies that a Swift, a Rabelais, an Aristophanes might have a voice.

However, his basic point is that the age gets what it deserves. 'So with philosophy', he writes in 'The *Epicier*'. 'So with literature.' A Hobbes emerges only when the age tolerates free inquiry, a Pigault-Lebrun—the popular eighteenth-century romancer—only in times of political activity.

> So with literature. Among a people disposed to think, their every-day literature will bear the impress of thought; among a people not so disposed, the absence or negation of thought will be equally conspicuous in their literature. Every variety of mind takes its station . . . in the literary market (IX, 294).

This argument of 'French Comic Romances' and 'The *Epicier*' is not so much a simple-minded conception of literary causality as Peacock's way of confronting what for many writers had become a distinct source of worry. Coleridge writes in one of his lectures:

> After the Revolution, the spirit of the nation became much more commercial than it had been before; a learned body, or clerisy, as such, gradually disappeared, and literature in general began to be addressed to the common miscellaneous public. That public had become accustomed to, and required, a strong stimulus; and to meet the requisitions of the public taste, a style was produced which by combining triteness of thought was calculated at once to soothe ignorance and to flatter vanity.[26]

The argument of 'The *Epicier*' (it followed 'French Comic Romances' in the next number of the *London Review*) might be a gloss on Coleridge's comments, except that its ostensible focus is France rather than England. Peacock compares the politically-minded Pigault-Lebrun of the last century with the non-political Paul de Kock; but he is less interested in literary qualities than in defining the climates in which they wrote. As to the title, intended to suggest 'philistine' rather than the literal 'grocer', Peacock uses it to slap at modern arbiters of taste. The *épicier*, in his fear and conservatism, is not only the silent sponsor of a government of *status quo*, he is also the patron of the arts—or rather no patron at all. There is in fact no worthwhile audience for literature, and writers in self-survival are having to cater to the *épicier*'s folly.

Just as 'Fashionable Literature' might be understood as a defence for Peacock's unread *Rhododaphne*, so 'The *Epicier*' seems relevant as a comment on the limited audience he had found for his novels. In 'Fashionable Literature' he had praised Scott's talents, though he had hedged on the matter of Scott's 'opinions', on the question as to whether Scott actually had anything to say. He writes in 'The *Epicier*': 'When works of fancy run out to the extent of those of Paul de Kock, or Walter Scott, we may be sure that the authors have chimed in with the predominant tastes, as well as the predominant opinions, or negations of opinions, of a great body of readers' (ix, 296). According to Henry Crabb Robinson, Wordsworth judged Scott similarly. 'He assented', Robinson writes, 'to the observation "that the secret of Scott's popularity is the vulgarity of his conceptions, which the millions can at once comprehend".'[27] It would be hard to say how much of Peacock's or Wordsworth's response is, like Coleridge's, disinterested commentary on the reading public, and how much is literary pique. Both men seem to indicate, and with a trace of regret, that their work is too iconoclastic to win great popularity.

Much later than the essays on comic romances, Peacock wrote an appreciative essay for *Fraser's Magazine* (it appeared in April 1858) on 'Chapelle and Bachaumont'. Re-telling Chapelle and Bachaumont's *Voyage* with easy good spirits, he shows how popular the two writers have been, how justifiable their popularity is. That Voltaire read them with pleasure, he suggests, is recommendation enough, and he adds his name to Voltaire's. The essay is typical of Peacock's later work for periodicals. It offers little in the way of new insight, little analysis or theory. Peacock's interest in contrast to that in 'Fashionable Literature' or 'The Four Ages' is in 'impression-istic' commentary, his strength, to use Madame de Staël's term, 'the animated description of masterpieces'—or the not-so-masterpieces. The tone approximates that of *Gryll Grange* in its relaxed, conversational manner. As it were incidentally, Peacock throws off an occasional and often dubious observa-tion, such as: 'Our French contemporaries have the advantage over us in more than one branch of literature. In the drama, the balance of trade is decidedly against us. We have imported much, and exported nothing' (x, 91). His point, in essence, is merely that he enjoys French drama as he enjoys French narratives. And he is thinking about both, but as intellectually engaging or emotionally moving literature, but as splendid entertainment. As an old man, Peacock has withdrawn from the battlefield, and books are his recreation.

These characteristics of 'Chapelle and Bachaumont' recur in Peacock's other essays of the time—in the years, that is, preceding *Gryll Grange*—wherein he talks about the drama. But not about French drama. In 1852 he began a series of three essays called *Horae Dramaticae* for *Fraser's* (two appeared in 1852, the third in 1857). The subject of these essays might well have been classical French drama, or Elizabethan drama, or drama of the Restoration; but it is typical of Peacock in his later years that he turned increasingly to classical literature and appropriate that he should write about it.[28]

Macaulay, who met Peacock briefly and found him 'a clever fellow and a good scholar', noted that Peacock intended to edit the *Supplices* of Aeschylus. Macaulay found this a little absurd. He and Peacock, Macaulay writes, were 'strong enough in these matters for gentlemen',[29] but scholarship ought to be for scholars. And Peacock he supposed to be no scholar. Peacock never did edit Aeschylus, evidently never began the work—perhaps the whole plan was born and died in conversa-tion with Macaulay. But he was a more capable classicist than Macaulay guessed.

His allegiance to classical literature has been relevant in

earlier contexts, but it is worth a further comment. The charge sometimes brought against him of dilettantism is not always appropriate and, when appropriate, not always damning. Yet there is a sense of minor proprietorship in his response to Greek and Latin literature, which we have seen already in reference to *Palmyra* and in the slightly disingenuous Preface to *Rhododaphne*. Peacock shared with Shelley, Landor, Byron, Proctor, and Keats an intense commitment to the classics. Unlike Keats's, sometimes like Proctor's, his response was not all imaginative. One recalls Byron's definition of poetry as a vision of the past and future. For Peacock it was much more a vision of the past alone. And what is characteristic of his poems may be seen in his essays. His contemporary, the neo-Platonist Thomas Taylor—who was important as a translator of Aristotle as well as of Plato—nicknamed Peacock 'Greeky-Peaky'. However affectionately he may have intended the name, it portrays a slightly ludicrous figure riding the classical hobby-horse; and there is indeed and something of an imbalance, something of a militancy, in Peacock's espousal of Greek literature. He would have amended Shelley's pronouncement 'We are all Greeks' to 'We rather ought to be'.

As a young man, Peacock tended to wax shrill in his defence of classical writers, whether Plato or Nonnus, Homer or Athenaeus, and he never quite lived down his pedantry. But as an old man he wrote mildly, as though—sure of his own tastes—he no longer cared about those of others. 'It is our purpose', he wrote by way of introducing the essays for *Fraser's*, 'to present our views of some of these subjects, in the forms of analyses or criticisms; not following any order of chronology or classification, but only that in which our readings or reminiscences may suggest them' (x, 4). He writes, in short, as a gentleman amateur, as a man with loves to share rather than axes to grind.

The essays themselves are of recognizable types. About the first of his topics, *Querolus*—one of the few extant Latin comedies —he offers a work in popularization. As he puts it, '*Querolus* is not only . . . a great literary curiosity, but it is in itself a very amusing and original drama'. (He would have allowed himself neither the tone nor the standards in 'Fashionable Literature', with its attack on the rage for the curious and novel.) 'It is little known in this country' (x, 4). He merely sets out to make it better known, introducing textual, historical, or critical comments as he moves leisurely along.

The next piece, of a different but common enough type, attempts a reconstruction of Euripides' *Phaethon*. It reveals Peacock's familiarity with both original and scholarly material and recalls a description of him, as a much younger man, by an appreciative admirer: 'He was at the time studying Greek, was reading some Greek dramatist and a commentator, and excited the wonder of the farmers who came into the house by reading, as they said, two books at once.'[30] In this, as in the first essay, he cites Goethe often—presumably from translation—and for the most part agrees with his opinions, yet he shows no hesitation in disagreeing with other scholars— notably the distinguished Hartung and Hermann, who had reconstructed dozens of plays. If, as in most cases of reconstruction, Peacock's Euripides essay provides a more valuable comment on the scholar than on the original, it makes clear that Peacock knew Euripides' work and that, to use his own phrase, he 'never finished his education'.[31]

Five years elapsed between the Euripides and the final article of the series, which begins with a discussion of *The Flask* by the Greek comedian Cratinus, but works into a pleasant *tour de force* on 'the bacchic birth of poetry'.[32] Quite naturally, Peacock warms to Cratinus, who, according to some sources, died repentent for his sins at a very old age. 'No', he says, 'Cratinus remained what he was to the last: or Aristophanes could never have said that he died of a broken heart on seeing the running to waste of a barrel of wine which had been fractured in a Lacedaemonian incursion' (x, 75). With what delight Peacock works towards the end of his sentences! Who would not have written 'Spartan attack' for 'Lacedaemonian incursion', and placed it unnoticed somewhere at mid-sentence? This is the manner of the piece: full of quotation and anecdote and quite verbal play. His theories about the development of Greek comedy as a matter of the waxing and waning of the role of Bacchus, or good drinking, prompt some astute comments, and the essay quite informally anticipates Nietzsche's thesis in *The Birth of Tragedy*:

The Old Comedy, though not all poetry, abounded with poetry of the highest order. The New Comedy never soared into the sky to build a Cuckoo-city-in-the-clouds; nor ferried over the Styx, beating time with its oars to the accompaniment of a chorus of frogs. It stood quietly on earth, and held the mirror up to human life. The Muses of the Old Comedy were never found without Bacchus (x, 86–7).

His love of names and pleasure in re-telling, his purposely slow pace and contrived emphasis, his balance, and his wit—they are all there. One of his best sleights results from an application of his theories to some modern poets, especially Wordsworth. The odd thing is that Wordsworth, ranking low as a tippler, scrambles through as a poet. Peacock's depiction is witty and apt:

Wordsworth, though himself a water-drinker, could sympathize with Fancy and Feeling in their Bacchic expression . . . Wordsworth's own genius is in no respect Bacchic: it is neither epic, nor dramatic, nor dithyrambic. He has deep thought and deep feeling, graceful imaginings, great pathos, and little passion. Withal, his Muse is as decorous as Pamela, much of a Vestal, and nothing of a Bacchant (x, 77–8).[33]

About forty years earlier Peacock had written to Edward Hookham, wondering if 'Wordsworth [is] sleeping in peace on his bed of mud in the profundity of Bathos, or will he never again wake to dole out a lyrical ballad?' (viii, 164). He had spoken in 'Fashionable Literature' of the *late* Mr. Wordsworth. By the 1850's, with Wordsworth dead, bathos had mellowed to pathos, and the poet, representative already of the old order, had become at least unobjectionable.

Politics of Scepticism and Faith

I look with well-grounded confidence to a period when there
will be neither slaves among the northern, nor monks among
the southern Americans. The sun of freedom has risen over that
great continent, with the certain promise of a glorious day.

> Mr. Fax, in *Melincourt.*

Without magnetism we should never have discovered America;
to which we are indebted for nothing but evil. . . .

> Doctor Opimian, in *Gryll Grange.*

I

Although a man of strong political feelings, Peacock had few
and incomplete political ideas. The reasons for this is partly his
having chosen ironic or satiric forms for the expression of his
opinions, yet the choice itself may reflect the anti-theoretical
bent of his mind. A satirist's ideas are often enough not ideas
at all, but attitudes or beliefs. The pages that follow take the
form of conclusions, drawn from a variety of contexts, about the
quality of Peacock's political beliefs.

What becomes clear from reading Peacock is that, in spite of
the diversity of argument and the profusion of targets, there is a
coherence to his criticism. He shares with Arnold, though
writing before him, the violent discontent with Press, Ministry,
Party, and Technology; and like Arnold's his discontent goes
beyond specific grievances to a general state of mind. He too
judges in terms of a hypothetical culture, of tradition, which he
holds up as desirable alternatives to a society increasingly given
over to external values, increasingly dominated by its ostensible
servant, machinery.

Lord Houghton, who spoke about the difficulty in ascertain-
ing Peacock's political views from his books, found 'a singular
continuity of impressions lasting through the whole course of his
writings, which indicate that at no time in his life would he have

been what is commonly called a consistent member of a political party'.[1] Houghton's periphrasis elaborates what must be evident to most of Peacock's readers. Already in the 'Essay on Fashionable Literature' he makes clear his aversion, not only to Whigs and Tories, but to the entire system of political parties, and on this matter, as almost any of his works will testify, he remained consistent. He was from the beginning an independent. To assert his dissociation from party is not of course to imply that he was unaffected by political dogmas and theories. The contrary is true. He knew the classical theorists of Greece and Rome, diverse eighteenth-century theorists of the Enlightenment, as well as contemporaries like Cobbett and Bentham. His views are very much an amalgam.

II

Outside of his novels, Peacock wrote little that is exclusively political. 'French Comic Romances' and the 'Essay on Fashionable Literature' reveal a political concern, and 'The *Epicier*', ostensibly literary, includes political judgments. These are, however, peripheral comments. A report on steam navigation to India, while reinforcing the fact of Peacock's nationalism, with its plea for immediate action to forestall Russian initiative, is specifically concerned with political issues. Written at the directive of the India House—which still, in that crucial period of its history, retained some semblance of 'a state in the disguise of a merchant'—it retains little interest for modern readers, being technical, dry, official, if extremely informed. (It appeared, ironically, in the *Edinburgh Review* for January 1835— that object of so much of Peacock's earlier satire.)[2]

Peacock wrote two further essays that speculate more broadly on political matters. 'London Bridge' blends the technological skill evident in the India pamphlet with the irony and whimsy common to the novels. Less factual, though more comprehensive, is his review of Thomas Jefferson's *Memoirs*. (Both articles appeared in the October number of the *Westminster Review* for 1830.)

In the essay on London Bridge, purportedly a straightforward presentation of facts with a desire to establish sane building policies—this when the old bridge was being replaced

by the present structure—Peacock betrays a sentimental regard
for the demolished bridge and an aversion, more than fiscal, for
the new one. (One wonders how he would have responded to
the shipping of the present bridge, the one he opposed, to the
American desert.) Admitting finally that he opposes any un-
necessary change in the face of London, he belies the earnest
and practical arguments he has so carefully marshalled. 'We
have not touched on the question as a matter of sentiment.
But, even on this ground, we do not like these sweeping changes
. . . which obliterate every visible sign that connects the present
generation with the ages that are gone' (ix, 219). He becomes
reminiscent, not only of his own Prince Seithenyn in *The Misfortunes of Elphin*, that spokesman for the tottering and enemy
of change, but also of Edmund Burke. Burke's phrase 'wise and
salutary neglect' would have sat comfortably in his argument.
Peacock 'looks back', as Burke has it, 'to his ancestors'. He cites
Christopher Wren's views on building, and had Homer been
apposite, no doubt he would have invoked him too. Yet basic
to his argument are significant questions of political principle.

Peacock shared the dilemma of many utilitarians, who
desired the efficiency of a strong, central administration and
feared the consequences of State interference. It was left for
John Stuart Mill and Matthew Arnold to point out that liberal
ideas might be reconcilable with powerful government. Peacock's desire for such a government is qualified by the recognition of its likely misuse. Upset by the fact that the public is
deceived by the sponsors of the new bridge, and therefore, too,
by the government, he hints that increasingly complicated
building projects may involve unscrupulous officials and a
bullied public. 'Rapid movement', as Kingsley Martin writes,
'was exhilarating and men forgot, in the midst of scientific
discovery and industrial change to ask in what direction they
were hurrying.'[3] For Peacock, London Bridge becomes a
poignant symbol of fruitless, mechanical change, ordered in the
name of progress. Although Peacock wrote 'London Bridge' for
the *Westminster*—organ of John Bowring and the Utilitarians—
he recognized that Utilitarianism could be confused with
expediency, a concept that he, like Coleridge, detested.

If we consider the essay on London Bridge and with it, for a
moment, the comments on America in *Gryll Grange*, Peacock's

admiration for Thomas Jefferson will have no obvious motive. Jefferson was an American, whose principles bespoke independence, and who, additionally, pledged international allegiances to France rather than England. Peacock had written in a rather ill-advised letter once that

> The Saxons—the Saxons are the staple commodity of human nature, and the great hope of their species. . . . [Whereas] Violence when violence is possible, cringing fraud when it is not; consummate dishonesty and inveterate selfishness always,—such are the invariable traces of Frenchmen. . . . Let no such men be trusted (VIII, 206–7).[4]

Apart from the reminder that Peacock came of a naval family and that the wars with France were scarcely over when he wrote this, one can only call it nonsense akin to that of Gobineau's, or say with Heine, '*Wie eng, wie englisch!*' The letter makes even more puzzling his attitude towards Jefferson, who not only admired France but affixed a conspicuous signature to an anti-English document.

At first glance, Jefferson ought not to be Peacock's hero. It is, however, not difficult to account for his praise, which arises from at least two related causes. For the first I must mention again *Gryll Grange* and its date, 1860. In that novel and at that time, Peacock finds little good to describe either in America or in things American, and depicts through the words of Dr. Opimian, and from admittedly secondary reports, a country given over to gross materialism. Opimian's account might have been summarized by Granville Hicks: 'In a society that regarded chaos as natural, that made greed a virtue, that placed financial achievement before personal integrity, culture was not likely to flourish. When things are in the saddle, the artist . . . is almost certain to be trampled underfoot.'[5] Except for a few nineteenth-century apologists for America, like Lord Acton, most Englishmen concerned about the fate of 'culture', and a good many who were not, would have agreed with this estimate, though they might have smiled at the metaphors. Matthew Arnold, writing at the time of *Gryll Grange*, speaks about the pressing danger of becoming 'Americanized', assuming that his public will share his fear, which he does not bother to explain. To Peacock, American society afforded much to be condemned: from slavery and rapacious industrialism as major evils, to badly-cooked food as an annoying drawback. In 1830, when his review of Jefferson's *Memoirs* appeared, he admired a younger America, the unspoiled child of England's and France's Enlightenment—whether the picture was true or not—and a statesman independent of mind, honest, capable, learned.

> And the interests of America being peace and liberty, were and still are the interests of mankind. He [Thomas Jefferson] was a great instrument in the foundation of her liberties in 1776; the main instrument in their restitution in 1800. He lived to see the community of which he was a member, proceed from infancy to maturity: he lived to see it . . . grow strongly and rapidly into one of the most noble and important communities of the world; and he left it in a fair train for becoming the very greatest of nations (IX, 186).

America first held for Peacock, as for many nostalgic writers before him, the possibility of a better, an intellectual, and a moral, life. Peacock saw in Jefferson the representative of an earlier ideal, the humanist politician, the good man in a state not totally bad. No less important, he shared with Jefferson the thorough admiration for ancient Athens, for its political theorists as well as its political model.

In addition to the appreciation of Jefferson as a man and the pleasure in discovering a literate statesman, Peacock delighted in the recognition that Jefferson shared fundamental political assumptions. Both men assumed that the writings of Locke, as well as those of Rousseau and other liberal French writers of the eighteenth century, must underlie any healthy political outlook. Just as Peacock's tastes in popular literature ran to eighteenth-century France, so many of his political attitudes seem to have come from the *philosophes*. We find him, *à la* Condorcet, defending the rights of women; like Montesquieu, championing toleration and speaking out against clericalism and slavery; like Holbach, warning against the credulity and tyranny of custom. Of course the influence of French political thought was widespread in England, and since many of

Peacock's opinions were mere commonplaces, it would be hard to establish influence. With Voltaire and Rousseau, who were public knowledge as much as public villains, this is especially true. One can only point out that Peacock alludes to these writers and clearly approved them.

It would also be difficult to say whether Peacock drew his assumptions from the French thinkers and their English followers or whether he shared with them the common source in John Locke. Probably one supported the other. In any event, there can be no doubt about his respect for both, and he found a similar respect in Jefferson's writings. Peacock calls the *Essay on Human Understanding* 'the very best foundation of an enlightened system of study' (VIII, 176) ;[6] Jefferson rarely writes two pages without a similar comment. As students of Locke and his French disciples, the two shared a faith in intellectual and, consequently, in political enlightenment—as well as in popular sovereignty—though both could appreciate the difficulties in realizing their ideals. When, for example, in *Crochet Castle* Peacock attacks Henry Brougham's plan for educating the working classes, he is attacking the plan itself rather than the principle that men should be educated ;[7] when in 'The *Epicier*' he quips that the French Revolution has implemented the rule of Ho Fum in place of Fum Ho, he is simply making a sceptical historical observation. In neither case does he announce his political assumptions. Yet Peacock assumes, as Jefferson does, certain things to be self-evident. That, for instance, natural rights are anterior to the State and must be respected and maintained by the State. 'The *Epicier*' reveals a muted envy of Pigault-Lebrun, who, Peacock says, 'lived in the days of the Rights of Man, Political Justice, and Moral and Intellectual Perfectibility'—the capital letters are his. His own times, when he finds parties and politics unsaved by idealism, only win his contempt. The essay on Jefferson is Peacock's expression of pantisocratic sentiments. He can speak here about the 'good sense of the people', and if he means specifically the American people, his statement remains an endorsement of popular rights.

There remain, clearly, certain paradoxes in Peacock's views, and they are paradoxes common enough to his age. 'London Bridge' must be explained in terms of nostalgia, rather for the sentimental associations of history than for the actual generations that kicked up dust on the old bridge. (Today there are those who even resent the demolition of ugly and dirty railway stations on the grounds of sentiment.) Peacock's nostalgia, then, includes an older England, of which London Bridge is one of few remaining signs. But again his primitivism includes Greece —even includes, according to some of his poems, the nameless realms where solitude and melancholy rule in picturesque serenity. However earnestly he might advocate the introduction of steam shipping along the Euphrates, or argue on the basis of utility for the preservation of London Bridge, he remains capable of damning 'the march of the mechanics',[8] with its dark, satanic tread.

In his book on the political ideas of the English romanticists, Crane Brinton has pointed out that one of the commonest ideals of those tending towards primitivism, towards a glorified view of historical times, was the parallel desire of finding a modern, though distant, setting where men lived as they ought to live. For many men America offered that setting.[9] To read Jefferson, a man devoted to moral and political ideals and capable of expressing them, is to be convinced that America offered great promise. Here was a free land, a 'pandemic' hope, the possibility of dignity in public office. In short, a modern Athens. To read Dickens on America—in the *American Notes* —is both to appreciate the limits of that promise and to realize that fuller understanding of political and social conditions necessarily mitigates an ideal. Peacock's later views on America lack the open-mindedness of the *American Notes* and approximate the Dickens of *Chuzzlewit*, with its angry and rather crude diatribe against New York society and Mississippi swamps. Perhaps Dickens too shared the disappointment of a man tempted by the original innocence of the New World, who had seen it develop into what he recognized as a frightening parody of the Old.

III

A nineteenth-century Englishman's response to America may well characterize his political attitudes. Certainly Peacock reveals himself in his esteem for Jefferson as a man of liberal sentiment, to whom the Rights of Man are more real than, say, the quantitative politics of a Bentham, and who, over the course of years and in a way perhaps unnoticed by himself, becomes more conservative.[10]

In the Jefferson essay Peacock allowed himself spirited praise of broad-based suffrage. Yet it was not long after the Jefferson essay that he told an India House Committee he feared nothing more than the mob.[11] Is one to assume that he considered Englishmen of the lower classes less responsible than their American counterparts? Or that he was simply swept up by his admiration for Jefferson? Questioned about his statement in the essay, he would possibly have clarified his opinion in this way: 'When I say representative government, I intend government elected by "free" property-holders; a man without land is a man without responsibility, consequently without the requisite state of mind suitable for the democratic process.'

In his distrust of mobs, which included both the rural dupes of the rotten borough and the unenfranchised urban workers, Peacock is probably reminiscent, not only of the *philosophes*, but also at times of Burke. He would not, however, have responded happily to any statement linking him with 'the whole honourable band of gentlemen-pensioners', of whom he considered Burke the prime offender. In a superfluous and unfortunate footnote in *Nightmare Abbey*, he says about Burke that he was, according to other 'gentlemen-pensioners', a very sublime person, particularly after he had prostituted his own soul, and betrayed his country and mankind for 1200*l.* a year' (III, 90). In *Melincourt* and *Maid Marian*, despite his own apprehension about mobs—which was probably less pronounced at this time than when he addressed the India House Commission—he joins the common radical mockery of Burke's phrase 'swinish multitude' and links Burke with all that he considers reprehensible and self-seeking in contemporary politics. Elsewhere his comments are less committal; it is not until August 1818, apparently, that he actually seems to have looked into Burke: 'Read Burke's *Letter to a noble lord* and some parts of his other works' (VIII, 440). But we are dealing with essays written after 1818, and the question remains whether, his animus against Burke notwithstanding, Peacock might not have shared some of Burke's political attitudes.

The problem is complicated by his reticence as much as by

his misunderstanding of Burke, whom he associated with Eldon and other reactionary politicians of his own day. But it can be said, I think, that his conservatism is of a different sort from Burke's, that in a sense it is conservatism which finds in political change the protective instrument for what is important to conserve—and that would not include rotten boroughs or French queens. He thinks radical change a necessity and is impatient with gradual reforms. He shares with Hunt and Shelley dismay with a corrupt and unenlightened nation. But is he, like Hunt, or, in a different way, like Shelley, a consistent radical? Apparently not. Peacock's seems to be a radicalism much more akin to that of Cobbett, a radicalism predicated on an essentially conservative belief, but temporarily or from time to time allied with radical opinion, perhaps out of impatience. He responded as Cobbett did to the terrifying social consequences of a dispossessed rural England, and he would have agreed with Cobbett, to use Arnold's words, that 'faith in machinery is our besetting danger'. (Though he favoured steam navigation—away from home and in the name of national emergency.) No Little Englander, he nevertheless looked back to times when England was a self-sufficient and small state, peopled by stout yeomen. If he knew of political unrest and social injustice in earlier England, he looked back with reverence at its intact social fabric, its cohesive and meaningful rural life. The dream was a common one, shared by writers as disparate as Joseph Ritson, Wordsworth, and Scott. Even radicals like Hazlitt and Hunt subscribed to it in part. Essentially it represented a gilding of history and repugnance with its barren inheritance.

But however much Peacock agreed with Cobbett's radical agrarianism, his humour saved him from seeing the past as all charming idyll. As *Maid Marian* and *The Misfortunes of Elphin* show, he could at once acknowledge a nostalgia for things past and laugh at the nostalgia. His ideal past is an amalgam, almost never drawn from a particular epoch. Voltaire, whose words are perhaps echoed in 'The Four Ages', said in his typically deflating way that the so-called 'golden age' wasn't golden at all; it was iron. Peacock would probably have agreed. He would also have added that there was enough that was worth preserving: one can re-create a golden age out of the best that has been thought and said.

A final comment on Peacock's response to Utilitarianism may be appropriate here. While he could respond to Bentham's attack on 'superstitions', and while he could credit Bentham with a healthy programme for reform, he divorced himself from Bentham's kind of Utilitarianism in the two ways I have mentioned. In the first place he disagreed with Bentham's rejection of Natural Law and Natural Rights (and shared Coleridge's opinion that people should be weighed instead of counted). More central was his distrust of unhistorical attitudes. Burke was probably mistaken when he maintained that 'people will never look forward to posterity who never look backward to their ancestors'. After all, Bentham consciously shunned history precisely in order to look forward. Burke's comment is, however, appropriate for Cobbett and Peacock, both of whom looked forward on the basis of a love of the past. That past of course was an ideal rural past. Neither put much faith in the dark, noisy future of a Leeds, Manchester, or even a London.

In short, Peacock neither allied himself with a political party nor ever committed himself to any coherent political system. If he could share a faith in Enlightenment, he could not accept technology and technological progress as a means to that end. If he recognized in Bentham the necessary instrument for social change, he feared Bentham's assumptions and Bentham's methods. He would have agreed with F. H. Bradley's estimate of Utilitarianism as the great temple of Philistia, even while preferring Bentham's temple to Burke's.

4

Music Reviewer for the *Examiner*

erotick and irrational entertainment.

DR. JOHNSON, *Life of Hughes.*

I

Peacock might have agreed with Dr. Johnson's description, if not the implied estimate, of operatic music. Erotic and irrational? So much the better, for music has its own powers and creates its own laws; if it has a 'civilizing effect', it also makes its appeal through the emotions and moves the listener by inscrutable means. For Peacock, operatic music is at once the most civilizing and the most appealing of musical forms.

A lover of music and a theatre-goer, Peacock began in the late 1820's a series of musical reviews for periodicals. Exactly when he began and for which periodical we do not know. In a July 1829 issue of the *Atlas*, William Hazlitt wrote an attack, largely on the *Westminster Review* and the Utilitarians, but including a few lunges at Peacock. His criticism of the Utilitarians is similar to Peacock's own: they are, he says, 'seized with the same *hydrophobia* of music, painting, and poetry, as their pious predecessor', the Puritans.[1] A Bentham can tolerate neither poetry nor theatre. Hazlitt's attack on Peacock is rather more cryptic. He associates him with the *Westminster* and hence with the Utilitarians, but his point seems to be something other than guilt by association. Peacock's sin, he implies, is not aesthetic hydrophobia but indiscriminate flattery of certain actresses and singers. Whatever the import or the justice of Hazlitt's comments, evidently Peacock had been reviewing prior to this time, or at least Hazlitt assumed he had. However, the only known reviews by Peacock are dated 1830 and after, and they occurred not in the *Westminster*, but in the *Globe and Traveller* and later in the *Examiner*.

Most of Peacock's notices remain uncollected—though the

Halliford editors offer a representative sampling[2]—and critics seem to be agreed as to their unimportance. A number of these writings are trivial, and nearly all are brief. At the same time, Peacock's comments on musical productions—which incidentally make up the largest part of his miscellaneous writings—illustrate his strengths as much as his weaknesses as a writer.[3] Occasional reviews seldom have the virtues of considered essays: some of Peacock's do. He ranks, with a man like George Hogarth, among the finest reviewers of the time. And this was a time of capable reviewers. In addition to Hogarth and Leigh Hunt and Keats's friend, Edward Holmes, there were the writers for the *Harmonicon,* one of the first and most influential musical journals. The *Harmonicon* regularly included commentaries on theatre productions and concerts throughout most of the 1820's and 1830's. Peacock could accuse its reviewers, as occasionally they might have accused him, of dispensing 'with the small preliminary of being present at the performances they criticize',[4] but standards were generally high. From them, and especially from a correspondent who called himself 'The Dilettante', Peacock apparently adopted a manner of reviewing. He shares their preoccupation with specifically theatrical matters, with staging, costume, ticket prices, condition of the house, and manners of the audience.

Stylistically formal but witty, detached if not entirely disinterested, Peacock's critiques are informative and sensible without being violently involved. In their allusiveness and turns of phrase, they introduce a wide range of literary reference and maintain a tone of non-professional competence. Like the *Harmonicon* reviewer, Peacock was also a musical dilettante. He could, and usually did, include technical matters, but his point of view was that of an amateur who knew music and appreciated it, whose main concern, however, lay in entertainment. He seems to have thought of himself as something like the epitomized good sense of the audience.

When Hogarth wrote his brief, informative, and remarkably unprejudiced *Musical History* (in 1836), he took pains to describe what he recognized as the significant musical events in England during the early part of the century: the founding of the Royal Academy of Music (1823), of the Vocal Society (1832), and, even more important, of the Philharmonic Society

(1813). He commented on the work of Victor Novello, who was a composer and organist, but who is best and rightly remembered for his inexpensive editions of music and for the Soho publishing firm that bears his name. If English composers of the time were no more gifted than, say, Henry Bishop and Samuel Webbe, English scholars and audiences were concerned with music as perhaps never before. Members of the Philharmonic Society sent money to Beethoven; English audiences welcomed Rossini—as previously they had welcomed Handel and Haydn —with open arms and purses, and they at least tried to listen to Berlioz. Peacock shared the reverence for Beethoven and Rossini, and of course for Mozart, whose powers were universally acknowledged. But when he thought of their music it was opera that he had in mind. *Fidelio*, for instance, he considered 'the absolute perfection of dramatic music' (IX, 432–3), but he wrote little about Beethoven's other music. He said: 'There is nothing perfect in this world except Mozart's music' (IX, 430), while thinking specifically of *Don Giovanni*. Of Rossini he wrote that if 'there be any Italian opera (we speak not of those of Mozart) pre-eminently entitled to the appellation of divine, it is decidedly . . . Rossini's *Semiramide*' (IX, 434). Peacock shared with another great ironist, Stendhal, an exclusive preference for opera. He did not share with Hogarth and so many contemporaries the new excitement about orchestral music. Nowhere, for example, does he mention the Philharmonic Society, and though he seems to have been acquainted with Novello, he was presumably as deaf to his achievement as Charles Lamb pretended to be deaf to his music in the 'Chapter on Ears'.[5]

To a large extent Peacock's tastes in music are conventional eighteenth-century tastes. Like Rousseau and, in England, like Charles Burney and John Hawkins, whose histories of music he read and owned, he felt that perfect music must be vocal music. He did not welcome, as Burney had, every new Italian opera, but he did prefer the Italian opera and he demanded a certain amount of 'novelty'. If in some ways a musical conservative, his assumptions about the power and the importance of music are bolder. Peacock associates music with passion, with the irrational. He also speaks of responding to the soul of the composer; almost like Carlyle, he affirms music's power of transport. But, again, Carlyle offers a far better contrast than comparison. Whereas Carlyle could exclaim about the beauties of Rossini, Mozart, and Bellini, he had nothing but disdain for opera-going. Peacock equivocates about the audience, but he never forgets the need for the illusion of the stage. He may admit that Bellini's songs sound better in a private apartment; he nevertheless attends and comments on the theatre.

His ideals in opera, which will emerge in the following pages, may be inferred from his predilection for Greek drama. Thus he preferred the music of the Italian opera while admiring the productions and the ensembles from Germany. Appropriately he praises Carl Maria von Weber, because he recognized in Weber coherent and dramatic constructions in which arias bear some relation to the whole ensemble and to the story line. In this sense Peacock responded to the new operatic movement, the great shift away from operas that catered to individual performers, to truly dramatic and unified works. Like Wagner, of whom his comments are sometimes anticipatory, he equated modern opera, or an ideal modern opera, with Greek drama. Often he criticizes productions for lacking the virtues, the coherence, the power, as well as the wit, of the Athenian stage. Wagner might not have tolerated the application, but he would have appreciated the sentiment behind Peacock's admiration for Bellini's *Somnambula*. 'It came upon us', he writes, 'as a shadow of the Athenian stage' (IX, 437)—a somewhat insubstantial shadow, one would guess—and this is his highest praise. I do not want to suggest by invoking Wagner that Peacock thought in definite terms about *Gesamtkunstwerk* or even that Wagner would have satisfied his hopes for opera. In fact, he would have thought the works too long and the orchestra too important in Wagner. But the point is that he theorized relatively little about the nature of opera, just as he did about the nature of poetry. His talent was descriptive and also reflective of general demands for better opera and better productions. Part of the interest of his comments is that he was describing a time, the late 1820's and early 1830's, which, without too much hyperbole, has been called 'precisely the great period of grand opera'.[6]

II

Perhaps the best way to characterize Peacock's reviews is to compare them with those of Leigh Hunt, who, about ten years earlier, also wrote music criticism for the *Examiner*. If Hunt tended—using Hazlitt's words—'to gabble on at a venture', still he wrote at his best with spontaneity, with a dash, and above all with an intimacy, which most of Peacock's writing lacks. When Hunt reviews an operatic production, he joins in the performance, urging his readers to share his pleasure. Colloquial, rapid, in good spirits, he lets the production live again in his notice. One of his descriptions of a singer reads: 'He wears bells on his toes and rings on his fingers. He will run divisions upon the most insignificant words, and trill, quaver, and roll about you without remorse. He lights up, as it were, fifty candles to exhibit a nutshell. . . .'[7] Hunt tells of another, who 'while standing still, as an Irishman would say, keeps writhing and bending himself about like an elephant trunk'.[8]

Now here are two comparable descriptions by Peacock—without, among other things, Hunt's favourite 'as it were':

Signor Arnaud . . . while a tempest of paternal rage was a bursting on the head of his mistress, stood, with a face empty of all meaning, twiddling his thumbs, on the out-skirts of the party, presenting no earthly image but that of a hovering tailor, watching for an opportunity to take measure of one of the old gentlemen (April 8, 1832, 229).

Again in this, as in the following, Peacock saves his metaphor for the end:

His element is in bustle and volability; he cannot force himself into the personation of a moody villain, which he principally endeavours to achieve by standing with his arms folded, with one side to the lamps, and with his head look-ing over his shoulder, like Canova's 'Venus', or rather like a gentleman about to receive satisfaction in the shape of a bullet (April 17, 1831, 242).

Peacock's sentences are not, strictly speaking, periodic, but their whole effect comes from balanced elements in phrasing, and from a final impact unfolding from a slowly-paced syntax. Hunt has raced along, and the speed as well as the effect of his sentences result from a kind of one-way pattern: final elements in the sentences have little or no structural connection with the opening statements, as though his progression were narrative. He tells the story of his visit to the opera, with personal and colloquial touches—'as an Irishman would say'—that give a warmth and a sense of participating. Peacock has neither of these qualities. He stands ironically apart and offers formal, sometimes mock-formal, comments, whereas Hunt gives himself up like a delighted child.

Unlike Hunt, Peacock also spends little time on specifically technical aspects of the opera. When he does mention the orchestra it is to chasten it for containing incompetents or to accuse the conductor of a lack of taste, such as 'incessant tapage' of the baton. Or he will say sharply that the orchestra's performance 'was not without lapses, which we wish the worthy conductor would correct by some less cacophanous and misleading signal than hissing' (July 15, 1832, 453). As a music critic, Peacock concerns himself with few criteria, and on these he is adamant: varied programmes, and 'novelty', companies working well together, intelligent stage management, and fresh and pretty ladies, who are not overworked in concerts, or too egotistical to sing in a team. 'Good operas', he says, 'either new to this stage, or not grown stale by repetition, unmutilated, and effectively performed' (February 24, 1833, 117). These are his ideals, and they seem reasonable enough. But despite the improved quality of operas themselves, London managers at the time mutilated by habit. Peacock reports that in one production the first act of a Rossini opera—*Semiramide*—was followed, as though naturally, by the second act of a Bellini opera—*Il Pirata*. His comment, with an aptly-changed couplet from *Kubla Khan* is:

> A damsel with a fish's tale
> In a vision once I saw.

—It was the muse of this theater. Under no other auspices could such a dramatic monster have been dreamed of (April 21, 1933, 117).

Peacock records with disdain the various tactics of 'tomahawk managements' to placate audiences, and insists that tampering with musical works not only involves bad artistic policy but bad economic policy as well. He is also concerned, as Scott or Carlyle were concerned, with quality for audience. He shows an intense dislike for ill-mannered, ill-dressed, or simply boorish people. The following comment was made during the year of the Reform Bill; it hints that Peacock's radicalism may not have extended beyond the strictly political:

> When we said, about three weeks since, that we left it to the critics of the *Court Journal* to determine the question of the proper dress for this theatre, we did not mean to imply that there is any necessary connexion between liberal opinions, and a rough great coat redolent of cigars, or a pair of dirty boots, ostentatiously displayed, as we have sometimes seen them, on the seat cushion, the wearer sitting on the rail with a hat on his head (February 5, 1832, 85).

Propriety, then, and decent manners, are almost as important to him as a good performance.

On dirty boots, dismembered works, tired voices—on whatever he discusses—Peacock makes a judgment. Sometimes his haste to judge involves a stiffness of expression, as in the following, where he begins with Francis Jeffrey's notorious phrase: 'This will never do, Mr. Mason'—Mason was the theatre manager.

> We are told that Madam Puzzi is a very pretty concert singer. We will take it upon trust. She has no qualifications for a *prima donna*. She sings tolerably in tune, and that is all. The tone of her voice is positively disagreeable: it is at once thin and harsh. Her action is freezingly passionless. She certainly moves our feelings, but it is in the wrong sense. The part suffers instead of the heroine . . . (March 18, 1832, 181).

Disregarding the question of the singer's talents, which were no doubt as unhappy as Peacock depicts, we still have a crabbed and caustic passage, heavy-handed in its wit. In the 'Essay on Fashionable Literature', Peacock had condemned reviewers for hasty and damaging judgments; but, like all periodical reviewers, he too blunders occasionally when he takes up the weekly pen.

Quiller-Couch, in an essay on W. S. Gilbert, says that it puzzles him to see Gilbert enjoyed as a happy-go-lucky comedian, whose works are the bubbling over of an irrepressible good nature. Especially in his attitude towards ageing women, Quiller-Couch insists, Gilbert can be not only harsh but even cruel, and much of his humour results from exploiting this vein.[9] Quiller-Couch's point has some relevancy for Peacock. Consider for a moment the ladies in Peacock's novels. They are young, beautiful, intelligent creatures. With few exceptions, Peacock excludes unlovely ladies from his books. Indeed, almost none of the heroines still have their mothers. His novels chastise vanity, especially intellectual vanity, but by and large they are removed from the ugliness and sorrow of the world. The reviews, directly concerned with the London theatres, can be less amiable. 'Memory', he writes in one witty but cutting review of a faded soprano, 'will keep up to a later period the attractiveness of a performer whom we have known in her bloom; but St. Cecilia herself, if she were to descend in an English theatre as a matron of forty, would exhibit to empty benches' (April 17, 1831, 242). And when he finds vanity coupled with rudeness, Peacock writes harshly. Bemoaning the overcrowded conditions of the King's Theatre, home of the Italian Opera, he scorns

> those walls of gauze, lace, silk, velvet, or plumage, which some women, with a selfish disregard of the comfort of others, are in the habit of building on their heads; to say nothing of an occasional square foot of tortoise shell, professing to be the top of a comb. . . . It is curious and true . . . that the volume of the head-dress increases in mathematical proportion to the ugliness of the wearer (May 22, 1831, 325).

Possibly displeased by his lapse into invective, Peacock caught himself and softened the final sentence in a later edition. But it remains as testimony to a recurrent quality in his reviews. Of course it also shows that Peacock's harshness is not, finally, like that which Quiller-Couch finds in Gilbert. Peacock is not impatient with the ugliness and the incapacities of age but with its vanities, for his scorn, with very few exceptions, is directed at pretence rather than at incapacity. And he is often at his best when he laughs at female vanity, off or on stage:

> . . . we must have *pirouettes*, and the ladies must make some exhibition of under drapery. This is most commonly a sort of elastic fawn-coloured pantaloons, of tolerable substance, which at the most, gives a flying glimpse of something like a Venus, sculptured out of the same sort of stone as Tam O'Shanter. . . . The only alternative is in volumes of muslin drawers, which set forth the shadowy semblance of something like a Dutch farmer's wife skating to market in a high wind (IX, 429).

Intermingled with his opera notices Peacock introduces an occasional dramatic review and, extremely rarely, a comment on non-operatic music. Both he and Leigh Hunt wrote about performances by the gifted and curious Paganini, who was then ruling the music centres of Europe as his own demesne. A comparison of reactions to Paganini might also include Heinrich Heine's impressionistic account in the *Florentiner Nächte*. Hunt describes the violinist's playing in a lively but fairly straightforward manner, as though relating to friends. 'Our wizard', Hunt calls him.

> A lucky interval between a gentleman's head and a lady's bonnet favoured our endeavour, and there we beheld the long, pale face of the musical marvel, hung, as it were, in the light, and looking as strange as need be. . . . He is like a great old boy, who has done nothing but play the violin all his life. . . . His playing is indeed marvellous. What others can do well, he does a hundred times better. . . . How perfectly his bow talks. It remonstrates, supplicates, answers, holds a dialogue.[10]

Like Hunt, Heine speaks of Paganini as a magician, makes of

his performances something prelusive of Thomas Mann's *Zauberspiel* in *Mario and the Magician*, and so lets his imagination play that he sees Paganini first in shoddy black, then in festive dress, then different again, as he measures his fantasy against the dolts in the audience, who exclaim after one piece that the entrance price is already well repaid. His complex illusion, built and broken, certainly soars beyond Hunt's little account, but it is based upon assumptions similar to Hunt's. Superb music emancipates the mind by creating splendid fantasy. It is perhaps a comment on Peacock's inventive powers that although he affirms 'the supernatural powers of music' and recognizes Paganini's achievement, he does so without any imaginative flights. He acknowledges the artist's magic, but unlike Heine or Hunt he comments on, rather than soars with, the music:

> Paganini draws forth from his instrument notes and combinations which (in the modern world) none before him have produced or dreamed of: wild and wonderfully alike in the strongest bursts of power, and in the softest and sweetest touches, air-drawn and evanescent as the voices of distant birds. . . . The real magic is not the novelty of the feat, but the surpassing beauty of the effect. . . . It is this transcendent beauty and effect, that hushes his crowded audiences into an attention more profound than we ever witnessed in this usually gossiping theatre (IX, 444–5).

While similarly couching his critique in terms of audience effect, Peacock's tribute is of the three the most considered. It reveals far less about the writer than Heine's, and far less about the circumstances than Hunt's, but it does ample justice to Paganini's skill.

III

Apart from the opera notices, Peacock wrote two musical essays: a review of Lord Mount-Edgcumbe's *Musical Reminiscences*, and a commemorative piece on Bellini. In 1834 the fourth edition of Mount-Edgcumbe's *Reminiscences* was published in London, 'containing an account of the opera in England from 1773'. There is little remarkable about this volume, but it was considered significant at the time.[11] Peacock, among others, admired the work and reviewed it in the *London Review* (April 1835).

Apparently written without haste, his review has none of the barking that even the best reviewer falls into, none of the hackneyed sentence rhythms that can be applied and re-applied to suit the topic. But it expounds familiar opinions. Peacock uses Mount-Edgcumbe as a stepping-stone to his own pronouncements, intimating that he has had the good sense to anticipate him. Mount-Edgcumbe praises companies that sing together harmoniously, likes a pretty singer, and disapproves of the star system. Orchestra interests him, as it does Peacock, very little; he insists on the audience dressing for a performance; and he condemns tampering with an opera—although, unlike Peacock, he rarely seems to be sure when the deed has been done.

George Hogarth, who began reviewing for the *Morning Chronicle* in the same year that Peacock began with the *Examiner*, but who was, in sharp contrast to both Peacock and Mount-Edgcumbe, a professional musician, wrote in 1838: 'it is no small recommendation of Lord Mount-Edgcumbe's elegant book, that though he is (and with good reason) a *laudator temporis acti*, his admiration of the great works and great performances of a former day has not rendered him unjust to the merits of the moderns'.[12] Quite often Peacock refers to himself as the *laudator temporis acti*, and a common theme in his incidental criticism, including his music criticism, is precisely the implied comparison that Mount-Edgcumbe makes and Hogarth emphasizes between art of the past and present. Yet, like Mount-Edgcumbe, he can appreciate the moderns, as his response to Vincenzo Bellini makes clear.

To the music of Bellini, already popular in France and Italy, Peacock at first was cool: the young composer had used too many 'tricks', had failed in creating real 'style' or dramatic effect (IX, 435). Within a few weeks his opinion had begun to change. He came to see qualities that had first escaped him; and through the next months and seasons he expressed a gradually developing appreciation. He sensed that Bellini was better suited to melodrama than tragedy and that 'the predominant characteristic of the music is a graceful playfulness.

Bellini's is a dancing spirit' (IX, 436). Not all of Bellini pleased him, however, and *Romeo e Giulietta* he found 'a dull affair at best'—one of his common phrases of censure. 'A dull affair Bellini found it, and a dull affair he has left it. . . . We may, therefore, consider it condemned' (IX, 437). But he had soon taken in the composer as a favourite and could insist that the management, with its usual incompetence, had 'ill-killed' a Bellini work. 'The mangling of old favourite operas', he writes of one production, 'has been carried to a pitch of more than common audacity' (June 23, 1833, 389). He never says of Bellini what he says regularly of Beethoven and Mozart—that their music approximates perfection—but his praise is high.

In 1835, still in his early thirties, Bellini died. One of the finest tributes to his life and music was Peacock's essay in the *London Review*, printed in the following spring. The beginning is restrained: 'The composer Bellini, who died in the vicinity of Paris on the 23rd of last September, is as great a loss as the musical stage, in its present circumstances, could well have sustained' (IX, 315). But soon he seems to go beyond the mere theatre-goer's disappointment entailed by the loss of a good musician:

> Musical critics, who hear by rule, have laboured to discredit Bellini. Fortunately reputations grow in despite of these systematical doctors. The feelings of the ordinary unsophisticated and unprejudiced hearer [presumably, nevertheless, a well-groomed one] are always in advance of their rules. . . . Listening one evening with great pleasure to some beautiful modulations in one of the operas of Rossini, we were edified by a learned Theban near us, who could hear nothing but a profuse use of the diminished seventh. . . .
> It is fitting that there should be rules in science, because they are the collected and concentrated experience of ages; but they are not to be converted into pedantic fetters to bind genius through all future time (IX, 335–6).

These comments, which, in a time when theatre conditions were rapidly changing, provided a sensible defence of Bellini—he wrote for small companies with limited resources—precede comments that are both prophetic and bold: 'As there is no possible sequence of sounds to which human passion does not give utterance, so there is no possible consonance or dissonance which will not find its fit place in dramatic music' (IX, 336). Here Peacock might be defending a Berg as much as a Bellini, and he continues with equal good sense and justice:

> Akin to the pedantry of inflexible rules is that of entrenching the want of tact and feeling behind the authorship of great names—saying 'This is nought, because it is not like Mozart, or Haydn, or Beethoven, or Handel;' and thus sweeping away all modern music as with the fire of an impregnable battery (IX, 336).

Even Beethoven, he reminds his readers, had been considered 'a madman who wrote crazy music which nobody could perform'. He adds: 'Handel and Bononcini; Gluck and Puccini; Mozart and Rossini; the world of music has, in all these cases, been wide enough for both' (IX, 337). Than Mozart there may be nothing more perfect, yet he recognizes—as did Chopin— the virtue of Bellini's music, particularly the melodies, 'which cannot die' (IX, 338). In short, he offers a defence of Bellini that is tolerant, convincing, and apt.

In one sleight of phrase, Peacock sums up his attitude toward bad criticism and aesthetic dogmas generally, which he found as dangerous to musical as to literary writing. 'The oracle shakes his head, and the profane take it for granted that there is something in it' (IX, 337). He has, needless to say, contradicted his earlier opinion that the public chooses in spite of the critics— an opinion that had been, perhaps, less fact than hope—but the sentence outweighs a dozen contradictions.

IV

Carl Van Doren insisted that Peacock's musical criticism was unlike his other work and hardly worth perusing.[13] But this was to judge the quality of a large number of essays on the basis of a few. If his reviews occasionally suffer from hasty composition or from a kind of axe-grinding, this is to be expected from the weekly routine. It does not mean that a great many of his reviews, in addition to the two longer essays, are without his usual grace and wit or wanting acute and discriminating comments. Quite apart from their intrinsic value, these are also intriguing accounts of the London operatic world at the time. For a man who loved singing, this was a happy time in opera. Peacock records with appreciation his response to such singers as Malibran, Pasta, and Grisi—names that still suggest excellence in singing—and to such a dancer as Taglioni, apparently one of the truly great artists of ballet. 'When he discovered an artist . . . of whose skill he approved', as the Halliford editors write, 'no man could praise more warmly . . .' (IX, 413). (Although Peacock scorns 'the overweening vanity and absurd pretensions' of various performers, Hazlitt rightly pointed out that he erred on the side of flattery.) Furthermore, in Peacock's reviews we find a full account of operatic life, from ticket prices and the number of doors in a particular theatre to the reception of Mozart, Rossini, Donizetti, Bellini, Weber, Meyerbeer, and Beethoven on the English stage.

It is difficult and not always appropriate to compare critics who wrote in different times and from different presuppositions, but it is nevertheless tempting. Peacock is closer in his comments, not to Hunt or Mount-Edgcumbe or Hogarth, but to George Bernard Shaw, who, about sixty years later, was to be writing about many of the same topics. Of course by Shaw's time Weber, for example, was not being discovered but rediscovered after years of neglect. Shaw was to share with Peacock the devotion to Mozart, whom he also considered 'the greatest master of them all'.[14] But, unlike Peacock, Shaw thought it necessary to bring operas up to date, and therefore defended what Peacock would have insisted was 'garbling' or 'mangling' them. Shaw, moreover, writes as 'I' and speaks more personally, perhaps more vividly. And he touches on a far greater number of topics. Yet, allowing for changes in the musical climate—the advent of Wagner, say, or Verdi, or Gilbert and Sullivan—allowing for differences in personality and intent, some points of accord still seem relevant. Both critics insist on the importance of the musical amateur, while distrusting the learned or half-learned pundit. Both write musical criticism that is allusive and that can touch on remote works of literature as well as topical London. Like Peacock,

Shaw enjoys saving his metaphor for the end—and often directs his barbs at vanity in ageing women. 'I need say no more of Miss de Lussan', Shaw writes in a review of a *Don Giovanni* production,

> who does not grow more interesting as her voice loses freshness and sustaining power and her manner becomes perter and trickier, than that she is one of those Zerlinas who end *Batti, batti,* on the upper octave of the note written, as a sort of apology for having been unable to do anything else with the song. The effect of this suburban grace can be realized by anyone who will take the trouble to whistle Pop Goes the Weasel with the last note displaced an octave.[15]

Peacock himself might have written this. And if Shaw's writing is more consistently excellent, Peacock's best reviews do not suffer by comparison.

The relevance of Peacock's interest in and comments on music should become clear when we turn to the novels, for music is as essential to the novels as it is to the poem *Rhododaphne.* James Robinson Planché, with little effort, adapted *Maid Marian* for the stage, and, with music by Henry Bishop, its songs won a certain popularity. Peacock's novels are really much more than light opera, but they include elements of light opera. Music affects the characters, provides them with conversation, reveals their strengths and weaknesses, and alters the course of the story. Edmund Wilson is quite right to speak about the importance of Mozart in Peacock's novels.[16] Peacock is not a novelistic Mozart, but he is a writer steeped in Mozart's works, a man who thought *Don Giovanni* the highest imaginative achievement and who perhaps did seek an equivalent for comic opera in novels of songs and talk.

5

Personal Writings and a Theory of Biography

> And so, perhaps, biography might have pursued its way, draping the robes decorously over the recumbent figures of the dead, had there not arisen towards the end of the eighteenth century one of those curious men of genius who seem able to break up the stiffness into which the company has fallen by speaking in his natural voice. So Boswell spoke. . . . Once we have heard those words we are aware that there is an incalculable presence among us. . . . All the draperies and decencies of biography fall to the ground. We can no longer maintain that life consists in actions only or in works. It consists in personality.
>
> VIRGINIA WOOLF, 'The New Biography'.

I

In none of his personal writings does Peacock reveal anything at all intimate or surprising. He would have sympathized with Jane Austen's sister, who, out of propriety, destroyed the novelist's most intimate and revealing letters and let a world wonder.

The memoirs of Shelley (published in three parts between June 1858 and March 1862) illustrate Peacock's views on biography in general and specifically on the vogue for intimate biography and confessional literature, either by the author himself or by his camp-following admirers and detractors. Deploring the 'appetite for gossip' in the 'reading public', he says that most biography 'is the old village scandal on a larger scale': 'and as in these days of universal locomotion people know nothing of their neighbours, they prefer tittle-tattle about notorieties to the retailing of whispers about the Jenkinses and Tomkinses of the vicinity' (VIII, 39). Peacock objected to what Walter Scott had called, in his own little autobiography, the rage for literary anecdote and private history. If Peacock agreed with the desirability of biographical censoring, he did so for reasons that are defensible, if currently unpopular, feeling that some part of an author's life—maybe the larger part—ought to be his own domain, and ought not to be offered to an excitable public for its titillation. Such a view of biography, no doubt quaint to modern readers, is related to a view of criticism that seems more modern.

Whether Peacock would have agreed with George Santayana, who held that a lack of knowledge about a poet is actually advantageous, is questionable; but he does suggest that in some cases 'it is better to let the whole story slumber in silence'. 'I could have wished', he writes of Shelley, that 'he had been allowed to remain a voice and a mystery . . . and that he had been only heard in the splendour of his song' (VIII, 42). A poet must be known by his poetry. Within limits, other facts and considerations may be introduced, but they remain incidental to the main task, which is to look at the work itself.

That—given such opinions—he should still see fit to write a memoir, Peacock explains in this way to Claire Clairmont: 'My purpose in undertaking the article for *Fraser's*, is: first, to protest against the system of biographical gossip: second: to present an outline, clear of all offence to the living: third: to correct errors . . .' (VIII, 249). Peacock thinks in this, as in so many other matters, at a polar extremity from Carlyle, for it was just such a negative view of biography that Carlyle mocked. 'How delicate, decent,' he wrote, 'is English biography, bless its mealy mouth!'[1] Carlyle wrote this while praising Lockhart's *Life of Scott*. He had written earlier in praise of Boswell—and Peacock might have been responding to him directly in the thrust against gossip—'. . . may the earnest lover of Biography expand himself on all sides and indefinitely enrich himself. Looking with the eyes of every new neighbour, he lives with every neighbour's life, even as with his own.'[2] Behind Carlyle's ranting stands the achievement of Boswell, the advent of biography without its 'draperies and decencies'. Appropriately, although he alludes to events in Dr. Johnson's life, Peacock has nothing to say about Boswell. He knew his work, and his own retailing of anecdotes about Shelley sometimes approximates Boswell's telling. But he is, given Carlyle's assumptions, mealy-mouthed and uncourageous in his account of Shelley. If he is not advocating the ceremonial 'life and letters', he is advocating propriety. But one wonders whether his account of Shelley—with a wit and brevity that is almost like that of Strachey, but with a much gentler irony—is not more useful than Carlyle's *Life of Sterling*. It is certainly as readable. And, also, whether his apology for restrained biography might not offer an appropriate model in our own time of massive 'lives', those interminable grandchildren of Boswell. In any case, Peacock's point of view need not be thought of as 'typically Victorian'. He echoes Addison's plea that biographies be withheld until interested parties are dead; and Wordsworth, who said that our business was with a poet's books; and he echoes Coleridge, too, who wrote, 'The spirit of genuine biography is in nothing more conspicuous than in the firmness with which it withstands the cravings of worthless curiosity, as distinguished from a thirst after useless knowledge'.[3]

The Shelley memoirs aim at providing useful knowledge and at avoiding what Peacock considers gossip. A balanced and honest statement, they served as a necessary corrective for works on Shelley—some foolish, some mistaken, some idolatrous —which already by the mid-century were appearing voluminously. Peacock tells us a great deal about Shelley, most of which has become common knowledge and needs no restatement. Perhaps the most important correction Peacock made— and his represented one of the first appraisals of Shelley that remained both appreciative and honest—was his account of Harriet Westbrook, whose role in the *ménage à trois* he made clear, without attempting a posthumous thrashing of Shelley. Richard Garnett attacked Peacock's work, especially this part, accusing him of a lack of disinterestedness; but with admirable candour Garnett himself later characterized his opinion as 'unjust and uncharitable'.[4] Throughout the memoirs Peacock makes clear that he appreciates Shelley's talents, but he admits his shortcomings too, both in the poetry and in the man, among them his tendency to hallucinate and his peculiar treatment of his first wife. Because Peacock retells some of the events of Shelley's life, not only with appreciation but also with humour, and because revelatory details support the general narrative, Shelley lives in Peacock's short biography.

In a quiet, unobtrusive way, the author also lives. Without being unfair to Shelley, or distorting his account, Peacock introduces his own tastes, interests, and opinions. For example, he tells how he introduced Shelley to the opera. (Comedy, with its 'withering and perverting spirit' [VIII, 81], was going too far, but Shelley did respond to opera, and delighted to 'see human beings so civilized' [VIII, 115].) And he inserts his own comment about the decline of opera: 'I hope I am not unduly given to be the *laudator temporis acti*, yet I cannot but think that the whole arrangement of the opera in England has changed for the worse' (VIII, 115). But he admits to more than a mere affection for the past. He intimates that he is given to being alone, that he loves the country and country walks; he shows himself capable of friendship, but also careful in friendship, for his description of Shelley reflects his own ambiguous response of scepticism and admiration. Underlying the whole account is the native reticence and the implication that he is writing as it were against his will.

But the result, instead of being stiff and unreadable, is a skilful portrait. Peacock's impartiality, his discernment, his quiet humour at the expense of the Bracknell people, his fairness to Shelley and Mary, even when he considers them at fault, might well remain as models for Shelley's biographers. 'There have been', as Ian Jack says, 'few saner summings-up.'[5]

II

The unfortunate concomitant to Peacock's reserve, theoretical and otherwise, is that he wrote extremely little about himself. What he did write, in addition to being meagre, has the formality, and seems to have the disinterestedness, of his work on Shelley. Carl Van Doren, in his *Life* of Peacock, appreciates the difficulty of his subject, and his recording of the 'external' facts, a few guarded indulgences, and some anecdotes—often apocryphal—leaves him with the works themselves as autobiography. The 'personality' of the man for the most part eludes him. A typical illustration of the biographer's difficulty is offered by Peacock's diary for the summer months of 1818. Another man might have recorded impressions, or mused about whatever preoccupied him; or perhaps described the faces or manners of people he met. Peacock notes that he planted flowers, or sailed on the river, or wrote to Shelley, or suffered from hot weather. Typical is his entry for August 27: 'Rowed from Windsor to Cookham alone. Constant rain: wind adverse:

stream strong.—Walked from Cookham to Marlow and laid desperate siege to a cold beef-steak pie and tea' (VIII, 442). The heart of his journal is an extensive reading schedule in classics. Presumably the diary was intended for his own later perusal, but as an intimate record it remains about as engaging as a grocery list.

Peacock's correspondence is similarly restrained and not at all extensive. If, as Dr. Johnson wrote to Mrs. Thrale, a man's 'soul lies naked' in his letters, which are 'the mirrour of his breast', then Peacock never bared his soul. It may be that a large part of his letters have not survived, but those that do crop up add little to those already collected, either by way of fact or revelation of opinion.[6] When having had to rely on scanty evidence for the writing of Peacock's biography, Van Doren was justly criticized for spinning out his material, the fault was as much Peacock's as his own.

Peacock's letters to Shelley—in Italy—give a clear indication of the kind of personal correspondence he wrote; and Shelley's letters to Peacock, some of them his best letters, offer a revealing contrast. Shelley did not, as a matter of fact, write to Peacock in all confidence, or spill over with affection. Indeed, he exhibits a certain reserve towards his friend, disclosing in personal matters little more than the fact that he misses England. But he describes his work carefully and in detail, relates his tourist's observations, and says what in the realm of ideas has preoccupied him:[7]

> The curse of this life is, that whatever is once known, can never be unknown. You inhabit a spot which before you inhabit it is as indifferent to you as any other spot upon the earth, & when, persuaded by some necessity you think to leave it, you leave it not,—it clings to you [and] . . . revenges your desertion. Time flows on, places are changed; the friends who were with us, are no longer with us; yet what has been seems yet to be, but barren and stripped of life. See, I have sent you a study for *Night Mare Abbey*.[8]

Peacock wanders from one topic to another, inevitably mentioning what he elsewhere calls 'the alpha and omega' of English conversation—the weather:

A letter from you is always a joyful advent to my solitude.
That of the 16th of August came a day or two after I had
sent off my last. I have not heard from Ollier [Shelley's
publisher], nor seen any of the proofs you mention. Much
as I regret your absence, I think you will do well at least
to winter in Italy. A cold and stormy autumn has succeeded, with very sudden change, to our brilliant summer,
and gives no favourable promise of the coming winter. I
thought I had fully explained to you the object of *Nightmare
Abbey* . . . (VIII, 204).

Even if the topics respond to Shelley's questions, or comment on
Shelley's own topics, the tone remains desultory. Besides, a
good letter-writer takes the initiative himself.

Not all of Peacock's letters are dull and mechanical. Discussing Plato in August 1818, he indulges in his usual sally against
modern tendencies and the great falling-off of learning. Plato,
he says, 'certainly wants patronage in these days, when philosophy sleeps and classical literature seems destined to participate
in its repose' (VIII, 202-3). But there is rarely a sense of
intimacy, even intellectual intimacy. He might be addressing
anyone. A hint as to the trouble with his letters occurs in the
following note to Shelley, where he apologizes for his writing:
'I wish I could write you more interesting letters; but there is a
great dearth of political news, and my own mode of life admits
of no varieties worth detailing . . .' (VIII, 193). Matter-of-fact
and impersonal, this is reminiscent of his letter to Jane
Gryffydh, in which he asks her hand in marriage, dispatched
with the formalities of the India House. Time and again Shelley
asks him, with the disguised chagrin and loneliness of the
traveller, what he is about, what he is writing—although he
refrains from personal inquiries, perhaps because of his lasting
distrust of Peacock, perhaps because he knew that nothing very
intimate was forthcoming. '*Nightmare Abbey* is finished. Well,
what is in it? You are as secret as if the priest of Ceres had
dictated its sacred pages.'[9]

The diffidence in Peacock's letters is matched in two autobiographical accounts he wrote late in life—his own modest
counterpart to the autobiographies put out by so many of his
contemporaries, from Coleridge to De Quincey. 'The Last Day

of Windsor Forest' appeared in 1887, long after Peacock's death, with a note by Richard Garnett: 'It was in all probability intended for *Fraser's Magazine*, but never appeared there, nor, so far as can be discovered, elsewhere.'[10] He gives the likely date of composition as 1862, which would make it roughly contemporary with the Shelley memoirs. 'Recollections of Childhood: The Abbey House' is much the same sort of essay. It appeared in Peacock's lifetime (in *Bentley's Miscellany* for February 1837), though certainly not with any accompanying sacrifice of the author's privacy.

A short, whimsical recounting of a boyhood incident, 'Recollections of Childhood', is too slight in subject and too suave in manner to be thought confessional. The Abbey House is an idealized portrait of a country residence in the old style—and similar in its attractions to the houses in the novels—where Peacock as a boy had been a welcome and happy guest.

> The mother and daughter had all the solid qualities which were considered female virtues in the dark ages. Our enlightened age has, wisely no doubt, discarded many of them, and substituted show for solidity. The dark ages preferred the natural blossom . . . the enlightenened age prefers the artificial double blossom, which falls and leaves nothing. . . . These ladies had the faculty of staying home (VIII, 32).

Peacock not only echoes the sentiments, he actually uses the language here of his own 'medievalist', Mr. Chainmail of *Crotchet Castle* (1831); and, as often happens in his essays, his whimsy invites him to take irony too far, to become a faintly absurd spokesman for a half-truth. Peacock remained a confirmed feminist, arguing throughout his writings for improved education for women and for an end to social, especially conversational, segregation. But in pursuing his censure of 'enlightened' times, he plays a different tune. He once wrote, incidentally, that the only bright spot in the 'dark ages' was the kitchen fire.

An England of simpler, more honest virtues, with pleasures to match, is the ideal of the Abbey House as it is of Chainmail

Hall; and Peacock fashions his ideal with the same contrast of past and present and back-handed praises of modern times that run through his entire work. As a young man he might have seen himself, the apostle of science and progress in poetry, as the *buccinator novi temporis*—and 'philosophy sleeps', he wrote, in the country of Bacon. But again, as in the Shelley memoirs, the essay on London Bridge, the music criticism, as well as in the novels, he is confirmed *laudator temporis acti*. His praise of past times is related to a preference for the rural and unsophisticated —common enough to most writers of the time, except honest Charles Lamb. And Peacock's Abbey House is akin to Mary Mitford's 'The Old House at Aberleigh' in *Our Village*: both writers blend an admiration for old traditions with a faith in the countryside as the last, though vanishing, uncorrupted haven. Goldsmith had sung the same dirge in *The Deserted Village*. And Wordsworth, with less sentimentality, had treated the subject in 'Michael'.

The family of the Abbey House, which Peacock idealizes for his purposes, have definite qualities unknown to Wordsworth's shepherds, for they are all very social. They 'dined early and maintained the old fashion of supper. A child would not easily forget the bountiful and beautiful array of fruits, natural and preserved, and the ample variety of preparations of milk, cream, and custard, by which they were accompanied' (VIII, 33). The suppers sound rather like a child's version of the banquets in the *Thousand and One Nights*. They also serve as another indication of Peacock's lifelong delight in good food and conviviality. Without anticipating the writings on gastronomy, it can be noted here that Peacock insists on his tastes and preferences as though they too represented moral virtues. Eating early becomes an old English virtue, as does playing musical instruments, of which the house—again like Peacock's novelistic houses—has a good store. The ladies, he suggests, play beautifully.

Towards the close of the essay Peacock shifts from the ostensibly personal recounting to a satiric aside. Describing how his friend Charles, condemned to his room, plays with 'an accumulation of lead, which he was casting into dumps', he moves off on a witty and irrelevant tangent:

Dumps, the inexperienced reader must know, are flat circles of lead,—a sort of petty quoits,—with which school-boys amused themselves half a century ago, and perhaps do so still, unless the march of mind has marched off with such vanities. No doubt, in the 'astounding progress of intellect', the time will arrive when boys will play at philosophers instead of playing at soldiers,—will fight with wooden arguments instead of wooden swords,—and pitch leaden syllogisms instead of leaden dumps (VIII, 35).

Anticipating Dickens on Gradgrind pedagogy, he is also indulging in a love of digression similar to that of Lamb's. Peacock's digression is neither so elaborate nor so supple as Lamb's, but it reflects a related turn of mind. He mixes every detail with a large opinion, and comes back slowly, atop a pun or two, to the narrative. If he did not share with Lamb the devotion to country pleasures, he did share the love of things past, and especially older literature. And like Lamb he was dismayed by the easy optimism suggested in 'the march of mind', a phrase and a concept that both men satirized.

More than twenty years after 'Recollections of Childhood', and slightly later than *Gryll Grange*, Peacock wrote his other autobiographical essay, 'The Last Day of Windsor Forest'. *The Genius of the Thames* had illustrated Peacock's familiarity with local scenery along the river, and from childhood he had known the country intimately. 'Windsor Forest' offers the reflections of an old man on the favourite haunts of his youth; it is his prose 'Newark Abbey'.

Peacock looks backward in this short reminiscence, describes the places and impressions of his daily walks—many of the scenes are almost identical with those depicted in *Crotchet Castle* and *Gryll Grange*—comparing what was with what is. Windsor Forest has been enclosed since he first wandered there, so that a lovely area and, just as important, a personal enjoyment have been denied by law. With an anecdote from the reign of William IV, and a discussion of a modern-day Robin Hood—a poacher who capitalized on a flaw in the enclosure ordinance by chaffing the Keeper and hunting the deer, and whom he makes to resemble his own Robin Hood of *Maid Marian*—he writes a pleasant little account of something essentially trivial.

Once more he links a personal taste with national policy, and speaks about the decay of a better way of life—but not without ironic asides:

> I do not express, or imply, any opinion on the general utility of enclosure. For the most part, they illustrate the scriptural maxim: 'To him that hath much, much shall be given; and from him that hath little shall be taken away, even the little he hath.' They are, like most events in this world, 'Good to some, bad to others, and indifferent to the majority.' They are good to the landowner, who gets an addition to his land: they are bad to the poor parishioner, who loses his rights of common: they are bad to the lovers of rural walks, for whom footpaths are annihilated: they are bad to those, for whom the scenes of their youth are blotted from the face of the world. These last are of no account in ledger balances, which profess to demonstrate that the loss of the poor is more than counterbalanced by the gain of the rich; that the aggregate gain is the gain of the community; and that all matters of taste and feelings are fitly represented by the cypher. So be it (VIII, 148–9).

How would Cobbett have expressed this, with his invective, his slang, with what Hazlitt rightly called his unquotable but powerful style. Peacock could admire Cobbett's writing without trying to emulate it. 'It is impossible', he had written forty-five years before to Shelley, 'that [Cobbett's] clear exposure of all forms of political fraud should fail of producing a most powerful effect' (VIII, 193). His own writing by contrast is light, urbane, and far less committed. The abrupt 'So be it' in the passage just quoted reflects a quality that was increasingly characteristic of the man and always characteristic of the novels. There is a prefatory note to *Gryll Grange* about the New Forest that closely anticipates the passage in 'Windsor Forest'. If the young man, in words satirized in two of the novels, 'had a passion for reforming the world', the older man merely looks on with subdued and ironic dismay.

Peacock's final description of the deer, as they were herded into Windsor Park, 'the most beautiful sight I have ever witnessed', includes a distinctive touch: 'For, with the expulsion of the deer, the life of the old scenes was gone, and I have always looked back on that day, as the last day of Windsor Forest' (VIII, 154). When he wants to express an opinion, Peacock sometimes abandons his great words and his involved and apparently periodic sentences, to speak with limpid simplicity; but in this he can be deceptive. The final clause above, working perfectly, is broken by a comma, there the necessary rhetorical pause.

III

Apart from the two essays of reminiscence and the correspondence, those who would know about the man Peacock are limited to few materials, which for the most part are anecdotes about him as an older man. Most interesting, if probably the most unreliable of these is by Robert Buchanan, the Scottish poet, remembered if at all for his pious attack on 'The Fleshly School of Poetry'. Buchanan was impressed by the white-haired gentleman, who forbade his smoking in the house. 'And this old man', he writes,

> had spoken with Shelley, not once, but a thousand times; and he had known well both Harriet Westbrook and Mary Godwin; and had cracked jokes with [John Cam] Hobhouse [Shelley's friend and later an important public official], and chaffed [Brian] Proctor's Latinity; . . . and had dined with Jeremy Bentham; and had smiled at Disraeli, when . . . he stood chatting . . . with the countess of Blessington; and had been face to face with that blond Rhodamathus, Chief-Justice Eldon; and was, in short . . . a living chronicle of things past, and men dead. . . .[11]

Peacock also knew the Mills. (John Stuart Mill, though occupying an office near Peacock's in the India House, fails to mention him in the *Autobiography*—a conspicuous omission.) He met Victor Novello, Leigh Hunt, and T. B. Macaulay. About these relationships we know little, and it would be interesting to know more. Peacock may not have had, as Jean-Jacques Mayoux writes, 'an exterior life' in the sense of wide travel, involved affairs, or great social intimacies.[12] But if only as a 'chronicle',

146

his life would be worth more attention. As poet, novelist, public official, he was involved with many of the important events and rends of the nineteenth century .

Buchanan raised another point about Peacock that wants scrutiny. He suggests that while 'Nothing could be more gentle, more guarded, than Peacock's printed reminiscence of Shelley', the private account was something altogether different.[13] And the two accounts reflect two quite distinct lives, the public—whether as author or India House official—and the private. Perhaps revealing more about his own dismay with things 'fleshly' than about Peacock, Buchanan writes: 'It must be admitted . . . that his mind was in itself a terrible "*thesaurus eroticus*".' Just what he intended by this, except the Philistine disapproval, remains a matter for speculation. He may simply have echoed the reviewer of *Rhododaphne* who credited the poet with a vast knowledge of ancient erotica. But it is also possible that Peacock indulged a wide range of interests, including the collection of 'forbidden books'. (He is said to have admitted absolutely no one to his library.) Did he then insist on an author's privacy partly because he himself maintained his secret life? Or was the display of erotic lore merely a joke at the expense of the young puritanical Scot?

All this is merely speculative, perhaps idly so. But it would seem that when a new biography of Peacock is written, it must scrutinize more closely statements like Buchanan's, and also admit a wider range of questions. Peacock himself was surely wrong in his defence of an author's privacy, if we conceive privacy as anything that might be shocking—assuming that people still may be shocked—nor is the matter of 'offence to the living' any longer an issue. And Virginia Woolf was surely right in seeing the advent of Boswell's *Life* as the advent of personality in biographical writing. No account of Peacock really tells us about the personality. The kind of cosmic gossip that Carlyle advocated is not what I have in mind here, but rather a fuller and richer study of so elusive and intriguing a writer.

6

An English Gastronome

Not all on books their Criticism waste;
The Genius of a dish some justly taste,
And eat their way to Fame.

EDWARD YOUNG, 'The Universal Passion'.

I

Peacock's first novel, *Headlong Hall*, is tolerant but not overly friendly towards the hedonistic attributes of the Anglican divine, Dr. Gaster, whose name betrays both his real vocation and his model in Rabelais. *Gryll Grange*, the final novel, strikes a more benevolent note, for although Dr. Opimian owes his name to the most famous of Roman wines, the gentleman himself escapes censure. Dr. Folliott of *Crotchet Castle* had already provided a basis for the gastronomic clergyman who is at once scholar and wordling, as well as a witty addition to the dinner table. Opimian, nevertheless, is the apotheosis—precisely the kind of churchman that Richard Graves had admired, as opposed to the troublesome and puritanical Methodists—and Peacock, with a distaste for the ascetic, is unquestionably fond of his creation. Not only does he give Opimian an appropriate Latin or Greek phrase whenever relevant, he lets the Doctor participate in the Aristophanic comedy, comment on and facilitate desirable love-matches, and above all expatiate on good eating. One of the Doctor's achievements is his 'domestic' wife, with whom he supplies a stock of cookery books and many a private recipe too. Like Folliott, who can cite Athenaeus in an apparently casual talk of fish, Opimian has familiarized himself with the entire science of cookery. He pontificates on everything from Madeira to meat-carving.

He is the ultimate in Peacock's characters who love their food —there are very few who do not—and he embodies a quality that Peacock seriously admired. Peacock himself wrote a large part of a cookery book. Never printed, and presumably never completed, the volume was to have been called 'The Science of Cookery'. Its purpose becomes clear from the introductory remarks to one recipe. Peacock writes: 'The boiling of Bacon is a very simple subject to comment on—but our main object is to teach *Common Cooks* the art of dressing common food in the best manner' (IX, 447). There was a tradition of this sort of book in the earlier handbooks on cookery, most famous of which had been Mary Kettilby's, Dr. Kitchener's, Mrs. Rundell's, Mrs. Raffald's, and Mrs. Glasse's—ascribed by Johnson's friend Dilly to Dr. Hill, but which Johnson said had to be by a woman, because the book had too many mistakes.[1]

Peacock's qualifications for writing a cookery book were particularly high. He seems, like Dr. Opimian, regularly to have prepared recipes for his cook, indeed to have taken a lifelong interest in food. Whether

> It snewed in his hous of mete and drinke,
> Of alle dayntes that men coude thinke,

as Chaucer says, at least from his culinary knowledge and his praise of hospitality it would seem so. His problem would have been limiting his appeal to common cooks, for as the Halliford editors comment, 'The volume is popularly intended, but the author could not quite renounce the classics, and the receipt for "Hare" is headed by Martial's "*Inter quadrupedes gloria prima lepus*" ' (IX, 448). The tone as well as the allusiveness seem not always designed for the audience of common cooks:

Lamb

Is a delicate, and commonly considered Tender meat,—but those who talk of tender Lamb—while they are thinking of the Age of the Animal, forget that even a Chicken must be kept for a proper time after it has been killed, or it will be tough picking.

Woeful experience has warned us to beware of accepting an invitation to Dinner on Easter Sunday, unless commanded by a thorough-bred Gourmand, our Incisors, Molares, and principle viscera having protested against the Imprudence of encountering young tough stringy Mutton under the Misnomer of Grass Lamb. The proper name for 'Easter Grass Lamb' is 'Hay Mutton' (IX, 453).

Yet if this is strutting prose, it works in the context. More appropriate for the intended audience are the less ornate sections, as, for example, the following, which would grace any cookery book:

> It is said there are *Seven* chances against even the most simple dish being presented to the mouth in absolute perfection; for instance a Leg of Mutton.
> 1st. The Mutton must be *good*.
> 2nd. Must have been kept a *good* time,
> 3rd. Must be roasted at a *good* fire,
> 4th. By a *good Cook*,
> 5th. Who must be in a *good* temper,
> 6th. With all this felicitous combination you must have *good* luck, and
> 7th. *Good* appetite,—the meat & the mouths which are to eat it must be ready for each other (IX, 448).

This is not the place to detail Peacock's varied recipes, although it should be noted that most of them are English, and look back to a time when, according to Peacock, the English ate with 'republican' moderation and 'wholesome' gusto.

According to Boswell, Dr. Johnson 'boasted of the niceness of his palate' and actually theorized about writing a cookery book that sounds in intent like Peacock's. 'You shall see,' he is supposed to have said, 'what a Book of Cookery I shall make.' When Mrs. Seward replied, 'That would be Hercules with a distaff indeed,' Johnson said, 'No, Madam. Women can spin very well; but they cannot make a good book of cookery.' Neither Johnson nor Peacock realized his ambition, but both insisted on works based on 'philosophical principles' and on a kind of Attic simplicity. Johnson says that 'Pharmacy is now made much more simple. Cookery may be made so too.'[2] Peacock, as though with a view towards the 'Two Cultures', seems to reply: 'We have brought chemistry into our kitchens, not as a handmaid but as a poisoner' (IX, 394).

That last sentence comes from an essay which, unlike the

cookery book, did see publication; *Fraser's Magazine* (for December 1851) printed it, however, as by M(ary) M(eredith), Peacock's daughter. Very probably the article was Peacock's— the Halliford editors say 'obviously'—or at least a collaboration, he doing the actual writing. One or two sentences, such as 'We have been present at some balls in France . . .' indicate that his daughter may have added something to the piece, but the format, the allusions, the style are characteristic of Peacock.[3]

It may be true, as J. W. Duff has written—whether it has always been so is another matter—that a Roman and a 'Gallic interest in food is not understood in England, where people do not talk about their meals as they did at Rome and do in France'.[4] Certainly food has been from time to time a suspicious topic of conversation, whether because the English have not cared about food, or whether food has been considered something vaguely infantile, a necessary embarrassment. Still, many Englishmen have been interested in their meals, beyond the point of merely eating them. In Peacock's time there were several writers seriously involved with gastronomy. Charles Lamb was an entertaining dilettante in the field, as was Leigh Hunt. Keats's letters tell of a forthright love of food and drink. Christopher North devoted volumes to his dining in *Noctes Ambrosianae*. More informed was Isaac Disraeli—the novelist and father of Benjamin Disraeli—who wrote eruditely and wittily about 'Introducers of Exotic Flowers and Fruits', 'The Introduction of Tea, Coffee, and Chocolate', and 'Drinking Customs in England'. Many of these essays in the *Curiosities of Literature* anticipate Peacock in their method, and the essay on drinking customs in particular reads like a companion-piece for 'Gastronomy and Civilization', although Disraeli's essay preceded Peacock's by thirty years. Disraeli handles his learning with somewhat less grace than Peacock, but he can smile at himself and his topics. Like Peacock's, Disraeli's talk about food and drink is usually involved with literature.

About fifteen years after Disraeli's *Curiosities* appeared, Abraham Hayward, then a young man of thirty-two, reviewed for the *Quarterly* that great fountain-head of culinary lore, the *Physiologie du Goût*, by Brillat-Savarin. Hayward's essay, which he subsequently published with a review of Thomas Walker's *Original*—another work based on anecdote, food, and theories of the good life—as *The Art of Dining*, may also have been Peacock's model for 'Gastronomy'. Less literary in his allusions than either Disraeli or Peacock, Hayward nonetheless unfolds a wide store of learning. Like Peacock, though more briefly, he treats of the history of gastronomy, working towards the culinary state of modern England. His essay, prompted by other works on the subject, clearly depends on a developed interest in kitchen doings. And these years were in England, as they were in France, a time of concern with gastronomy and its relation to civilization.[5] Aware of Francatelli—one-time chef to Queen Victoria—Ude, as well as Walker and the great Brillat-Savarin, Hayward might be glossing their works. 'Gastronomy and Civilization' is not a review but a complete and independent essay. Yet it too came in response to a developed interest in cuisine.

'Gastronomy' is Peacock's most self-sufficient essay apart from 'The Four Ages', the format of which he loosely applies to the development of eating habits. Running titles of the essay, as it appeared in *Fraser's*, convey the range of its topics: 'Social Habits of the Greeks; The Feast of Trimalchio; Festal Amusements among the Romans; Eastern Banquets; The Feasts of our Ancestors; A Feast in the Time of James the First [given, by the way, for the East India Company: it was an immense repast, according to the recipes, and it had its modest counterpart in the early days of Peacock's employment, when the company provided a breakfast for all officers arriving before ten o'clock]; Gastronomy in France; and Modern English Cookery' (IX, 457). To illustrate his material, Peacock draws on authorities as unlike as India House archives and Athenaeus. Only Rabelais, whom he normally cites, might be considered a significant omission, his great gluttons and catalogues not appearing in this work at all.

If the general pattern of 'Gastronomy' resembles that of 'The Four Ages', its tone is quite different. Lighter and less ironic, dependent rather on quip than on mock grandiloquence, it is full of anecdote and culinary lore. 'The philosopher', Peacock writes, 'though he may be very positive about what he does know, is equally ready to admit what he is deficient in. "I am told you are a great epicure, Mr. Hume," said a lady to the distinguished historian. "No, madam," he replied. "I am only a glutton" ' (IX, 400). (Hume himself had planned to write on the 'science of cookery'.) Even a teetotalling Puritan would have to smile at some of Peacock's theories, as for instance: 'We have recorded, as historical evidence, that the most incorruptible republicans were austere and abstemious; but it is still a question whether they would not have exerted a more beneficial influence, and have been better men, if they had moistened their throats with Madeira and enlarged their sympathies with grouse' (IX, 400–1). Sometimes he plays leap-frog with his own ideas, laughing his way from one illustration to another: 'Whatever the habits of others may be, the true republican is invariably simple in his manners. Mirabeau's stomach was stronger than his conscience, but then his convictions were unsettled: Danton and Demouslins talked of Spartan broth and quaffed champagne . . .' (IX, 389). The conversation in *Headlong Hall*, where Mr. Escot, enjoying his beef, holds forth on the evils of meat, is one earlier suggestion for this passage. But Peacock's lasting delight lay in mocking those who speak one way and live another. He finds the ideal man given to self-restraint, at the same time honest enough to have pleasures, though as the title of the essay itself indicates, he does not disapprove of the epicure. Witness his applause for Voltaire's letter to the Comte d'Autrey: ' "*Je trouve fort étranges . . . les gens qui mangent sans boire, et qui ne savent pas même ce qu'ils mangent*" ' (IX, 388). He might have quoted Johnson, too, who made much the same comment: 'Some people (said he) have a foolish habit of not minding, or pretending not to mind, what they eat.'[6]

More than with simply eating well, Peacock concerns himself with what good food involves. 'Hearts expand', he says, 'simultaneously with mouths'; and 'we agree with Addison, that "he keeps the best table who has the best company at it"; but the table must have its own recommendations to attract the best company' (IX, 396).[7] He speaks for much the same virtues that Fielding had in the 'Essay on Conversation': social grace, good talk, good dining, and a warm welcome. 'It is wonderful', he writes, 'what a humanizing effect this habit of decorous conviviality has on men' (IX, 397). His 'decorous conviviality' is little different from Fielding's 'good breeding'; both writers assume a wordly and common-sense character in their readers, agreeing that a hospitable table and good conversation rank among life's highest pleasures. Here is Fielding on the topic of the unskilled host: 'The order in helping your guests is to be regulated by that of placing them equitably. . . . I have sometimes seen a large dish of fish extend no farther than the fifth person, and a haunch of venison lose all its fat before half the table tasted it.'[8] And Peacock on a similar topic: 'There are not many who can make their friends feel at home when they have them there. Hospitality is not to be measured by the square inch, and calculated by cubic feet of beef and mutton: it is dependent more on quality than capacity, and requires generosity, delicacy, liberty, and a taste for its true administration' (IX, 396).

In spite of its relationship with a mid-nineteenth-century interest in cuisine, 'Gastronomy', like 'The Four Ages', has its basis in eighteenth-century values. The parallels with Fielding and Johnson, the quotations from the *Tatler*, from Hume, from Pope, and from Shenstone, are not accidental. In this essay, as in so many of his others, Peacock is saying that the good times have gone and that the best of English habits, conviviality and hospitality especially, are disappearing. But his argument here is more explicit. Even more than in 'The Four Ages', 'London Bridge', and 'Recollections of Childhood', he insists upon the traditions and the old virtues of civilization, and civilization means above all leisure and talk. If only because of the rhetorical position or the nature of the topic, 'Gastronomy' is, significantly, the one essay that suggests conviviality may be a greater good than solitude. For this reason it becomes important to the setting of Peacock's novels, all of which revolve about convivial banquets.

II

Of the feasts and symposia mentioned in 'Gastronomy', nearly all make a showing in the novels. Before turning to the novels themselves, it might be appropriate to mention some of Peacock's favourites. Undoubtedly the oddest literary banquet to win his affection was that incredibly protracted one of Athenaeus. Peacock often confesses, perhaps rather boasts, that he is reading the *Deipnosophistae* (the 'sophists at dinner'), which —throughout its fifteen books—records the wide-ranging dinner-table talk of diverse 'philosophers' and writers at the home of one Laurentius. Peacock also knew Plutarch's *Symposiaca*, Lucian's *Symposium*, and the ancient tradition generally that related cookery and civilization. Greek conviviality, as C. B. Gulick writes, 'was not incompatible with more or less sober discussions, and to make a banquet the scene and setting of philosophical discourse seemed natural'.[9] Of course a large part of the classical banquets were sober in neither sense of the word. Peacock was familiar with the mock banquets in Horace —as well as in later writers like Rabelais.[10] Most pertinent for his novels, and one he alludes to time and again, is Trimalchio's banquet in Petronius's *The Satyricon*. The immense and noisy feast of the Roman *parvenu*, despite its obscenity and profound difference in tone, may well have provided the germ for *Headlong Hall* and *Crotchet Castle*, wherein wealthy dilettantes entertain such varied house-guests as they think requisite to a feast of minds.

Peacock's attachment to Plato, his feeling that Plato 'wants patronage in these days', needs no further elaboration. Of Plato's works he seems to have preferred the *Symposium*, in which, as in his own writings, ideas and humour play dramatically together. Peacock occasionally entitles chapters 'The Symposium', and when, in *Melincourt's* Symposium, he concludes the conversation he might be doing a good-humoured burlesque of Plato's work. Just as Plato's drinking party, as an organized session, breaks up: 'suddenly a band of revellers entered, and soiled the order of the banquet', so Peacock's ends with an English equivalent: 'The summons to tea and coffee put a stop to the conversation' (II, 189).

PART 3

The Novels:
In Pursuit of Comedy

There are plain reasons why the comic poet is not a frequent apparition, and why the great comic poet remains without a fellow. A society of cultivated men and women is required, wherein ideas are current, and the perceptions quick, that he may be supplied with matter and an audience. The semi-barbarism of merely giddy communities, and feverish emotional periods, repel him; and also a state of marked social inequality of the sexes; nor can he whose business is to address the mind be understood where there is not a moderate degree of intellectual activity.

GEORGE MEREDITH, 'An Essay on Comedy'.

I shall not look on myself as accountable to any court of critical jurisdiction whatever; for as I am, in reality, the founder of a new province of writing, so I am at liberty to make what laws I please therein.

FIELDING, *Tom Jones*.

1

Backgrounds for Peacock's Comedy

It would be difficult to say what his books are; for they are neither romances, novels, tales, nor treatises, but a mixture of all these combined.

Review of *Nightmare Abbey* in the *Literary Gazette*.

I

When, in 1815, Peacock turned over the sheets of the unfinished poem *Ahrimanes* and launched into his first novel, he created an original and at the same time brilliantly eclectic fictional form. Why he began a novel instead of continuing with poetry—he was still to write *Rhododaphne*—is a question that has arisen in earlier sections and will be pertinent again in connection with *Headlong Hall*. There may have been financial problems, or dissatisfaction with the public response to his poems, or recognition of his limitations as a poet, imposed upon him by the relationship with Shelley. Whatever the reasons, his novels are another kind of art, predicated on a new attitude towards his readers. Peacock turned over more than the pages of *Ahrimanes* when he began *Headlong Hall*. At the same time, and if only by a process of inversion, the novels remain intimately connected with the earlier poems.

Ahrimanes developed out of the relationships between Peacock and Shelley's friends, who gathered around him in 1813 at Bracknell. Peacock's later comment on the group in his memoirs of Shelley indicates why he failed to get the poem done or why, temperamentally, it must have caused him a great deal of trouble. Shelley's friends, especially John Newton, were, he decided, individuals of peculiar mental equipment. Although they 'wore their rue with a difference', each one of them had 'nevertheless some predominant crotchet of his or of her own, which left a number of open questions for earnest and not always temperate discussion' (VIII, 70). If Peacock found himself less than welcome among these people, the explanation seems obvious: he simply thought their crotchets too hilarious to be taken seriously. This certainly is what he implies in the memoirs and what may be inferred from Mrs. Newton's letter—quoted in Part I—about the nasty sceptic among them. Yet Peacock's response was not so unambiguous.

Carlos Baker argues that Shelley gathered people about him as though to create a private world, a tailor-made microcosm, which he substituted for the reformed world that was obviously not forthcoming.[1] Whether Shelley's mind actually worked in this way remains questionable. One could argue that his urge for exile, if not ultimately for suicide, made him impatient with any group, and that his hangers-on were the accidental effects of his generosity and personal or social attraction. Whatever Shelley's relationship with the group may have been, Peacock's, ironically, grew to approximate what Mr. Baker describes. In spite of his finding them absurd, he was attracted by individual members of the group and by their ideas—as 'Ahrimanes' testifies. More important, he was attracted by the group itself. It may be that, as a lonely man, Peacock created the little worlds of his novels as Shelley—if we accept Mr. Baker's suggestion—had created his with diverse acquaintances. His motives must remain inscrutable. The point here is that he recognized in the encounters with Shelley's acquaintances a potential comedy. Just as he found these people noisily ensconced in their country houses, so he places his characters in isolated settings where they gather to attack 'a number of earnest questions' in 'not always temperate' and never entirely serious discussion. His fiction suggests barber-shop reflections of the Bracknell assembly, mirrored and re-mirrored into new shapes and extended to include other representative faddists of the age.

But this is not to say that Peacock's seven novels, or the five 'novels of talk' are mere *romans à clefs*, as it were exhausted when the various portraits are deciphered. After one has identified Mr. Mystic of *Melincourt* with Coleridge, Scythrop of *Nightmare Abbey* with the young Shelley, relatively little has been accomplished. For Peacock's characters are at once more and less than the individuals they suggest or on whom they may be based. They and the books wherein they live become increas-

ingly independent of the world they seem so unmistakeably
to burlesque.

Peacock may have conceived of his satiric portraits as a way
to quit himself for his exclusion at Bracknell; if so, his method
tends to work against him, or at least to reveal his more complex response. A remarkable change occurs in his novels, for
though they begin by satirizing intellectual fads, they move
away from satire into the realm of comedy. The process here is
generic as much as biographical. By an almost imperceptible
process, light, intellectual irony usurps the initial militancy.
Works that begin as mock utopias, as showcases for a collection
of harmless lunatics, gradually turn into play utopias, of which
the narrator approves and about which his laughter is gentle.

Ahrimanes suggests another, rather more elusive, quality of
the narrator himself. Peacock wrote the poem, which is learned
and dull, as an intellectual, and presumably *for* an intellectual
audience. Shortly afterwards—if not at the same time in his
two farces—he was satirizing intellectuals, both by dramatizing
into absurdity his own earlier pursuits and by lambasting what
he thought foolish and misguided readers. 'The Four Ages of
Poetry' and 'Fashionable Literature' have indicated a major
change in Peacock's attitudes towards fashionable readers,
whom in the early poems he addressed with unqualified respect.
The novels raise intriguing questions about the manipulation of
the audience within the narrative; most of these topics will
recur later, one or two are relevant here.

Among Peacock's favourite writers of narrative were Boccaccio, Chaucer, and Rabelais, all of whom maintain some sort
of informality and intimacy with their readers, and Fielding,
who indulges in chit-chat with his readers, often laughing with
them at the expense of the characters.[2] Whatever his admiration
for these writers, Peacock's own narrative rarely effects, or
tries to effect, intimacy between the speaker and the reader.
One corollary of this is that Peacock is independent of tiresome
bows to 'my dear reader'. Indeed, through his narrator he plays
a variety of puppeteering games that are often directed at the
reader himself. Whereas in *Ahrimanes* and the other long poems
Peacock footnotes allusions and documents interpretations,
with the unfortunate result of undercutting the speaker's
credibility, in the novels he footnotes both the narrator and the

M

characters, using the device to emphasize the separation of what Wayne Booth calls the 'implied author'.[3] In short, Peacock calls into question the narrator's judgment, and he implies throughout the novels a standard of values almost as much beyond the narrator's as it is beyond the characters' understanding. The reader, having no intimate—or as it is in so many novels, avuncular—guide to interpret for him, must work through a series of points of view.

When Shelley wrote in the 'Letter to Maria Gisborne' that Peacock would find his recompense for present lack of popularity 'in the serener clime of years to come', he was incidentally defining the range of audience likely for such fiction. But it is not only because no serener climes have been forthcoming that Peacock's audience has remained, and will remain, relatively small. After first lusting for poetic fame, Peacock created in his fiction a private and exclusive imaginative world, and there runs throughout his novels an undercurrent of contempt for fashionable readers, for his own readers, whether the few admirers of *The Genius of the Thames* or those that pick up 'the newest new nothings', the little novels that at first glance resemble his own. With his scorn Peacock of course differs from a writer like Walter Scott—at once the most popular and most patronizing novelist of the time—for he had neither Scott's literary tact nor that which underpinned it, a desire to accommodate. He implies that the show is his alone, produced for his own entertainment rather than directed at a particular audience. To those who pick up his books he seems to say: follow me if you will and if you can, but you must do so on my terms.

Traditionally, Peacock is understood to have written two distinct types of fiction: the 'novels of talk' and the 'satiric romances'. For purposes of convenience I have accepted the classification. It can, however, be misleading. Peacock's novels are, as Frances Russell called them, 'probably the most monomorphic little group to be found in literature'.[4] If *Headlong Hall* and *The Misfortunes of Elphin* at first appear to have as many differences as points of accord, they differ essentially in what is a balance of common features. *Nightmare Abbey* hovers somewhere between the two; satire and romance, narrative and talk, are in that story at a kind of equipoise. The following comments centre mainly on the novels of talk, but they are based on the assumption that all seven books, if not strictly speaking of the same genre, are still closely related, and that many of the generalizations about the novels of talk will also be applicable to the satiric romances.

II

Comedy need not, despite George Meredith's insistence in 'An Essay on Comedy', find its setting in the wealthy houses of 'polite society', where people may prattle in isolated leisure, the world notwithstanding. Aristophanes and Shakespeare alone prove otherwise, as Meredith himself, while singing their praises, seems tacitly to acknowledge. But Meredith's observation offers a relevant insight into the world of Peacock's comedy. Whether Peacock creates his characters in twelfth-century Sherwood Forest or in nineteenth-century Wales, he places them in a remote and idyllic setting and in self-imposed exile. The various castles and abbeys where they gather to talk are set in 'green' worlds, away not only from the city, but from all substantial cares.

Peacock shared with William Cobbett, as with many Augustan writers, a faith in rural manners and customs, but unlike Cobbett he is interested less in the farm-hand than in the gentleman farmer. In *Crotchet Castle*, Captain Fitzchrome, who may be Peacock's variant on the traditional *miles gloriosus*, woos his lady by describing the virtues of love in a cottage. 'I dare say', she replies archly, 'love in a cottage is very pleasant; but then it positively must be a cottage ornée: but would not the same love be a great deal safer in a castle . . . ?' (IV, 37). About love it would be difficult to speculate, yet Peacock's novels are safer in a castle, because he can better handle and often cares more about polite and intellectual talk than social problems or human suffering. In the castle, or hall, or abbey, he finds the ideal stage for his carefully limited comedy.

Not the first novelist to set his books in Wales or Sherwood or the Lake District, Peacock was the first to combine the rural setting with particular types of character and dialogue. There were, however, a number of writers who might have offered him suggestion. The country house itself is an important feature

in many eighteenth-century novels. One thinks of Sterne,
Smollet, Clara Reeve, Horace Walpole, Mrs. Radcliffe, Maria
Edgeworth, and William Beckford, who are all, to be sure for
diverse reasons, interested in remote houses. In *Nightmare
Abbey* Peacock might be parodying Mrs. Radcliffe and other
Gothic romancers, but the Glowrys' residence is more than a
burlesqued Gothic abbey. It approximates in one respect
Allworthy's house in *Tom Jones*. Like Fielding, whom he very
much admired and to whom he was indebted for a variety of
narrative techniques, Peacock turns his country houses into
emblems of a state of mind. Fielding makes of Allworthy's
estate a parodic but credible garden, from which Tom Jones
is expelled and to which he returns triumphant after wandering
in a fallen but comic world. (In a sense, despite the general
remarks about the middle-class epic, it is specifically Milton's
story that Fielding re-writes for the new audience.) Without the
formal allusiveness surrounding Fielding's, Peacock's estates
convey the same sort of values in miniature. A major difference
is that Peacock brings his characters to the garden, and presents,
instead of Fielding's elaborate and formalized picaresque, something of a conversational picaresque, a parlour *Lazarillo*.

Fielding stood high among Peacock's list of great writers, but
there are several lesser novelists who used country-house settings
in ways more pertinent for Peacock's own method. In the works
of Thomas Amory, Richard Graves, and Robert Bage he could
have found novelists who isolated their characters for the main
reason of letting them talk.

Amory, who wrote the rambling *Life and Adventures of John
Buncle* (1755), built his novelistic edifices in wild regions,
making Westmorland and Yorkshire somewhat resemble the
northern tundra. His novel is digressive, at times tedious, and
far too long, but Peacock, who owned a copy, was probably
amused by the book—which Lamb and Hazlitt also read with
pleasure. Buncle is an innocently immoral man who wanders,
encounters colonies of 'philosophers' in the wilds, muses, and
talks. He discovers numerous castles and mansions, in which
enlightened and improbably beautiful young ladies exist in
intellectual retreat. Here may have been hints for an Anthelia
Melincourt or a Susannah Touchandgo, comparably beautiful
and isolated heroines in Peacock's novels. Amory's band of

philosophers, gathered together in a rural setting, also anticipates the ideological phalanxes marching on Headlong Hall
and Crotchet Castle.

Richard Graves, who was an epicurean eighteenth-century
clergyman with the tastes and erudition of Peacock's Dr.
Folliott and Dr. Opimian, foreshadowed Peacock in several
respects. He shared the delight in Samuel Butler's *Hudibras*,
which led him to conceive of characters like 'the spiritual
Quixote' with bees in their bonnets, and which directed his
attack on assorted forms of hypocrisy. Graves's links with
Butler are tighter than Peacock's, but Peacock did, significantly,
introduce three of his novels and many of his chapters with
mottoes from *Hudibras*. In *Columella* (1776) Graves anticipates
Peacock in another way. While introducing no spokesman like
Peacock's, he creates a situation distinctly like that in *Headlong
Hall*, though in one way or another common to all Peacock's
stories. Columella and two friends, a garrulous trio, gather
together and discuss sundry matters at Columella's country
farm. The balance of the three, each representing a general
point of view, and some of their topics, such as landscape
gardening, look forward to *Headlong Hall* and indicate that
Peacock may have known Graves's novels when he began to
write.

But the closest of Peacock's novelistic predecessors, in time
and method, was undoubtedly Robert Bage. *Mount Henneth*
(1781), Bage's first novel, takes place in Wales. Like several of
Peacock's novels, it depends upon the device of a host inviting
various acquaintances to his country retreat for the related ends
of friendship and conversation. This novel includes topics and
activities uninteresting to Peacock; it is also epistolary. But
Bage's later works, especially *Hermsprong* (1796), involve a
narrative method that prefigures Peacock's own (a matter I
shall return to).

Not only does Peacock erect halls, abbeys, and castles in
remote regions, he peoples them with remarkable hosts—
Squire Headlong, Squire Crotchet, Squire Gryll. Different as
they are, each of these gentlemen is intent on pumping his
guests and himself full of food and drink, always in the hope of
livelier conversation. The guests who descend on the various
residences are quite obviously not ordinary people, if indeed

any of them are intended as people at all. Peacock suggests in his essay on 'French Comic Romances' that there are

> two very distinct classes of comic fictions: one in which the characters are abstractions or embodied classifications . . . another in which the characters are individuals. To the first of these classes belong the fictions of Aristophanes, Petronius Arbiter, Rabelais, Swift, and Voltaire; to the latter those of Henry Fielding, his Jonathan Wild perhaps excepted (IX, 258).

Aside from ignoring questions of genre here, Peacock casually overlooks an obvious fact. After all, any creation of fictional characters—and even of actual characters in biography—involves some degree of stylization. Tom Jones and Joseph Andrews, not to mention 'Allworthy' or 'Square', can be considered individuals only by contrast with a Candide or Trimalchio. Yet taken as a comment on Peacock's own fiction, the classification can be helpful. With the exception of those in *Gryll Grange*, his characters belong to the first of his two categories, but with this difference: they are abstractions or caricatures of intellectual rather than social or psychological types, embodiments of what Swift called the 'Fanatick Branches' of learning, though also of current fads and tastes. Even 'embodiment' invites the assumption that they are more than Peacock in fact makes of them. His characters are rather voices—witty, garrulous, and monomaniacal. Peacock's is a variety of 'humour' comedy, devoted to intellectual aberrations.

Because so many of his characters are rather abstractions or personifications of ideas than attempts at full characterization, Peacock's narrative is as circumscribed as the characters themselves. Except briefly in *Melincourt* and *Gryll Grange*, he rarely indulges in sub-plots or relates biographies of his characters. In the realistic details of a Smollett, the psychological intricacies of a Sterne, or the atmospheric complexities of a Mrs. Radcliffe, he shows little interest. His are short novels, as restricted in action and complexity of character portrayal as they are in setting. Characters perform constantly in the foreground or, to shift the metaphor, on stage. They seldom have either private lives or private thoughts. Peacock scarcely bothers to tell his reader about the outward appearance of the characters: the ladies are conventionally beautiful, the men sketched quickly or not at all. Most of their actions are stage actions. They may take excursions, but usually they dine, they dance, they topple from chairs and towers. These remain movements independent of character—they are perhaps specifically the movements of farce—and Peacock employs them merely to create a laugh or to shift a scene. The characteristic action is the dialectical fencing of the conversation.

Again, Peacock may have been led to write conversational works with the ancients as examples. Plato's *Symposium*, the *Dialogues* of Lucian, the talkative banquets in Petronius and Athenaeus, all seem relevant to his novels. In Peacock's time Athenaeus was undergoing a minor literary vogue. Isaac Disraeli, whose novels will be pertinent later, and Horne Tooke, author of the *Diversions of Purley*, one of Peacock's favourites, are among several writers who speak of Athenaeus with praise. Tooke may have modelled the *Diversions* on the literary frame of the *Sophists at Dinner*, on the idea of letting representative spokesmen of current points of view visit together in a quiet residence and talk over food and drink. Lord Houghton mentioned that Peacock himself found Athenaeus 'a perpetual banquet'.[5] Certainly his characters allude to the *Sophists at Dinner* during their own banquets and drinking sessions. Like Horne Tooke, Peacock writes with the classical banquets in mind. However, the literary form of the dialogue, no doubt without the help of Athenaeus, had already found apologists and practitioners in the earlier eighteenth century, with some of whom Peacock was familiar.

Peacock knew Richard Hurd's *Letters on Chivalry*. Hurd's tastes, like Peacock's, included classical as well as local antiquities, and another of Hurd's works, often printed with the *Letters*, offers English dialogues based on classical models. In the introduction to *Moral and Political Dialogues* (1788), Hurd writes:

> When every other species of composition has been tried, and men grown so fastidious as to receive with indifference the best modern productions, on account of the too common form into which they are cast, it may seem an attempt

of some merit to revive the only [genre] almost of the
ancient models, which hath not yet been made cheap by
by vulgar imitation.[6]

Hurd did indeed light on a fine classical form, but he was
not remarkably inventive after all. When Landor began the
Imaginary Conversations in the next century, he had, or may have
had, as models, not only Lucian, Plutarch, Cicero, Plato, but
also Shaftesbury, Addison, Berkeley, Payne-Knight, and—to
suggest writers closer to his own work—Lyttelton and Prior.
Dialogue was as basic to eighteenth-century literature as to
eighteenth-century life, and Hurd was not the first to interest
himself in classical precedent. Dialogue, moreover, almost
independent of narrative—at least independent of furthering
the story proper—became important to a number of eighteenth-
century novelists, both in England and France. Peacock knew
Voltaire, Diderot, and Marmontel as well as he knew the
writers of formal dialogues. Marmontel announced in his Preface to the *Moral Tales* that he would 'banish the "said he" and
"said she" ' from his reported dialogue. 'When I make my
characters speak', he wrote, 'all the art I employ is to fancy
myself present at their conversation, to write down what I
imagine I hear.'[7] Marmontel had his followers in England,
Maria Edgeworth among them; and George Saintsbury, having
discovered that Peacock borrowed a character's name from the
French writer, indicated that his stories were fashioned after
Marmontel's.[8] In part they may have been. Except, however,
for Peacock's nostalgic love of the country and an insistence, to
use Ian Watt's phrase, on 'elegant concentration',[9] his stories
have little in common with those of Marmontel. There had
developed in the latter decades of the eighteenth century a
whole tradition of conversational novels—almost as a substitute
for the stage itself—of which Marmontel is but one example.
When (in 1788) the *Critical Review* called Dr. John Moore's
Zeluco 'a series of conversational pieces',[10] the description would
have been equally applicable to many novels of the late
eighteenth and early nineteenth century. Thomas Holcroft,
Mrs. Inchbald, Isaac Disraeli, Thomas Day, and Robert
Bage all let their characters speak without an identifying 'said
he'.

Just as Peacock may have found his idea for a novelistic setting in Bage's *Mount Henneth*, so in *Hermsprong*, Bage's final novel, he may have found a useful precedent for a novel of talk. Bage delights in conversation. When he tires of introducing a topic, or closing it, or has a character witty enough to speak for him, he steps aside and places the name before the speech, as though, like Marmontel, a mere recorder of the words. His Mr. Hermsprong, an 'ideal' young man and an *ingénu* from untainted America, is ready, as any of Peacock's characters is ready, to voice his opinions with forthright alacrity. Hermsprong looks forward to Peacock's Mr. Forester, of *Melincourt*, or to Mr. Falconer, of *Gryll Grange*, but he blends with Forester's ingenuous gusto Sir Oran Haut-ton's native chivalry—native, that is, to the trees of Angola. Bage's characters are generally affluent enough to find leisure to talk, and like those in Peacock they do little else. Both Bage and Peacock were feminists and both, partly and self-consciously for that reason, create women characters who are more sensible than the men. Bage's Miss Fluart anticipates the blue-stocking heroine of *Melincourt* and Lady Clarinda of *Crotchet Castle*.

The lady novelist Mrs. Barbauld, while commenting on the novels of her colleague, Mrs. Inchbald, pleaded that dialogue could never prove a very effective means of persuasion; and she would probably have found Bage and Peacock, as she found Mrs. Inchbald, given to the epigrammatic instead of the 'solid'. While Mrs. Barbauld's assumptions about forms of persuasion are no doubt questionable—what does one do with Socrates?— she makes a legitimate historical association. Regardless of whether novelistic dialogue can influence a reader as effectively as first person narrative or 'essays' or emblematic 'characters' within the narrative frame, a whole generation of English novelists thought that it could. Many writers relied on dialogue for militant social and political ends. One of Peacock's appreciative critics exclaimed it a great pleasure to encounter his doctrinaire novels after reading such of his literary forbears as Elizabeth Hamilton, George Walker, Charlotte Smith, Thomas Holcroft, Mrs. Inchbald, and Mrs. Barbauld.[10] In fact, Peacock was not a writer of polemical fiction, despite the polemical beginnings of his stories. Whatever his intent and whatever he might have picked up from these all too prolific novelists, essentially he has different interest and creates another type of fiction.

Even from Bage, who may be thought of as a polemical writer, a 'sort of inferior Fielding who has read Rousseau', in the words of one unflattering critique,[11] Peacock remains sharply distinct. Bage looks forward like any self-respecting reformer to better times, but Peacock's glance is backward. He is as sceptical politically as he is radical and he anticipates little progress. Bage also needs a villain so that good may triumph over evil, whereas Peacock's 'villains' are mostly harmless intellectual fools. Capable of infinite folly, they are seldom guilty of vice. Peacock's targets are sometimes political and social grievances; more typically they are 'perversions of intellect' (viii, 18) or what he sees as dangerous cultural trends.

What is true of Peacock's connection with Bage is, therefore, so much more true of his indebtedness to other novelists with whom he has less in common. A man who read fairly widely, Peacock borrowed widely too, and if his books are related to those of many earlier writers, they are at the same time unmistakably his own.

III

In speaking about matters of setting, characterization, and dialogue with reference to Peacock's manipulation of borrowed techniques, I have skirted a central problem, a problem that has disturbed many readers of Peacock and caused some to misjudge him. What in a formal or generic sense are these books, wherein a variety of spokesmen drink and dine and spout ideas, creating their own societies in remote parts of the kingdom? To call them novels as I have been doing—and will continue to do—is to invite misunderstanding, for these are not novels according to usual expectations. To speak of Peacock's *novels* is to associate him with Fielding or Richardson, Dickens or George Eliot, and his writings are of another family, disappointing or seemingly inadequate if we expect of them what they were clearly not designed to offer. Yet if *novel* is a vague term or an imprecise catch-all, it can be useful as such. As G. K. Chesteron wrote, evasively but aptly: 'In the sense in which there is such a thing as an epic, in that sense there is no such thing as a novel.'[13] To describe certain types of prose fiction there are simply no better terms available.

Northrop Frye, who has struggled with the question of fictional genres as urgently as anyone, says of Peacock that 'he is as perfect in his medium as Jane Austen is in hers'. For Mr. Frye, 'in his medium' is the operative phrase. We fail to understand, let alone find the means of talking about, a writer of fiction, unless we pay more than lip-service to his particular form and method. There are creditable books that are not fiction like George Eliot's or suitable addenda to the great tradition. Mr. Frye proposes that the introduction of more specialized and more accurate categories offers the best approach to apparently unconventional fiction; and in setting aside the moral categories of Mr. Leavis and his followers or the lumpish categories of those readers bred to enjoy only realistic modes, he introduces the more useful category of genre.[14] He suggests that all seven of Peacock's comedies belong in the literary tradition of Menippean satire, of *anatomies*, along with Rabelais's *Gargantua*, Burton's *Anatomy of Melancholy*, and Melville's *Moby Dick*.[14]

Unfortunately, the very listing of Peacock with Rabelais, Burton, and Melville involves the recognition of enormous differences between them. In contrast to the encyclopedic and sometimes grotesque works of these writers, Peacock's novels are small and polished, what Swift might have praised as *bagatelles*. He called one section of his first book of poems *Nugae*, and the term in its original sense is just as apt for his fiction. Peacock is to Rabelais what Ovid is to Virgil. He is a writer of restrictive and essentially modest works.

The recognition that Peacock's novels differ in form or conception from most novels—less from Fielding's, incidentally, than Melville's—need not lead to the conclusion that Peacock, any more than Rabelais, Burton, or Melville, writes largely within the conventions of Lucian and Petronius, or that he creates something analogous. He knew and borrowed from Petronius, as I shall indicate, but probably no more than he borrowed from Plato or Walter Scott. In short, if it is necessary to justify an author by accounting for him in terms of a given genre, then Peacock's justification may best lie in Menippean satire. But if we are aware of his magpie approach to fiction, we realize that, important as it is, even this category will finally not do.

To raise the matter of plot, that bugbear of many critical inquiries, is to see why associating Peacock with the anatomy can be as misleading as to talk about him as a lesser Fielding. It is true that like writers of Menippean satire he mixes prose and verse and incorporates otherwise unconnected elements in a kind of intellectual whirlpool. Apparently, too, his novels are disjointed and bulky, resembling narrative bags haphazardly filled with assorted ingredients. Whether such narrative disorder is limited to Menippean satire is another question. Henry James described the English novel, not traditional narrative satire, as 'a paradise of loose ends'—in an ironic aside that cannot be wholly derogatory. In any case, the chaos in Peacock's stories is only apparent.[15] The songs work towards a specific end; the various incidents or episodes, while loosely connected, fit together in a number of essential ways. If, as Alvin Kernan has argued, the characteristic plot of narrative satire involves a conspicuous lack of resolution—in that matters are no better for the characters at the end than they were at the beginning, and may be worse—then Peacock's plots are not those of satire.[16] They are rather episodic comic plots. Peacock resolves individual scenes, occasionally with a physical upset, more often with a song or a call to dinner, which impose a temporary harmony—so that all may begin once more. However, the process is not merely repetitious or arbitrary. The resolution of specific scenes prefigures the ultimate resolution of the whole story, the unmistakable signs of which are feasts and weddings.

There is a great deal of traditional comedy in Peacock, both 'Old' and 'New'. His energetic debates reveal an admiration for Aristophanes, as, more specifically, does his 'Aristophanic Comedy' in *Gryll Grange*. There are scapegoats, the implied virtues of 'common sense' and social standards, as well as the constant reminders of rituals larger than the individual participants. But the tone, the conception of character interrelationship, and the plots more nearly approximate the descendants of New Comedy. Despite the frequent references to Aristophanes and the essay on Cratinus, one is more likely to associate his works with those of Molière, who has a related interest in forms of anti-social monomania, and who finds his common-sense antidote as much in beautiful women as in *honnêtes hommes*. Or one would associate him with Restoration and early eighteenth-century comedy. His references to Congreve and his quotations from other Restoration writers suggest that their sharp, crackling talk helped him to develop his own.

Peacock offers variations on the themes of recognizable new comedy plots. He gradually lets his characters, especially the 'select party of philosophers and dilettanti' (I, 150), the developing social group, enact the traditional roles of comedy. They continue to spout their ideas, while what they say becomes increasingly severed from what they do. Beneath the largely unresolved dialogue there is always the progress of a love story, and the time span of the novels—with one partial exception—approximates a short courtship. Music ravels story and characters together, and the novels close on a note of imposed social harmony, with young men winning their ladies, old age conciliated, folly thrashed, and scapegoats punished.

Peacock's is, then, a type of narrative comedy with models or analogues in a variety of earlier literature. Except in specific instances, when he quotes another writer or obviously echoes a passage, not much can be gained by insisting on *sources*. Nor does Peacock's posthumous library catalogue offer any certain guide to his reading or his borrowing, since he often alludes to writers whose books he evidently did not own.[17] To refer to earlier writers is merely to piece together in sketchy manner Peacock's eclectic form. Urbane yet learned and widely allusive, tending towards gentle mockery, though at times sharply indignant, his novels are amalgams of diverse attitudes and literary forms yoked together for new purposes. The frame is always 'novelistic', or narrative, but within the frame conversation is of first importance.

2

Headlong Hall: 'the Wand of Enchantment'

But they wore their rue with a difference. Every one of them
adopting some of the articles of the faith of their general
church, had each nevertheless some predominant crotchet of his
or her own, which left a number of open questions for earnest
and not always temperate discussion (VIII, 70).

'Memoirs of Percy Bysshe Shelley.'

I

Headlong Hall grew out of Peacock's discarded farces, *The
Dilettanti* and *The Three Doctors*, which provided a few names, a
song, and the country setting, but it is in every way a better
piece of work.[1] 'We suspect', wrote the *Critical Review*, that the
author is 'no novice'.[2] And though this was Peacock's first
novel, they were nevertheless right. *Headlong Hall* does not have
the sparkling wit of *Nightmare Abbey*, the rolling periods of
Crotchet Castle, or the easy-going confidence of *Gryll Grange*, but
with virtues of its own it is of their class. Peacock served his
apprenticeship with verse; when he turned to fiction he was
already a capable and self-assured writer.

We know little or nothing about the genesis of the novel,
since there are no references available in either Peacock's letters
or personal papers. By the end of 1815, however, it was in the
hands of the publisher, Hookham, and, with the 1816 dating
and an anonymous title-page, appeared shortly before the new
year. (Anonymous publication of novels was still the rule rather
than the exception, but it is worth noting that some of the earlier
long poems carried Peacock's name on the title-page, while
Rhododaphne followed the practice of the novels. All of Peacock's
novels appeared anonymously. Even *Gryll Grange*, published
almost half a century later, was issued as 'by the author of
Headlong Hall'.) Peacock probably began his novel during the

174

winter of 1814–15, completing it in the following autumn. During the summer months he indulged in his usual pastimes of walking and boating, and seems to have worked little, if at all. Shelley's friend Charles Clairmont described him in this way: 'He seems an idly-inclined man; indeed, he is professedly so in the summer; he owns he cannot apply himself to study, and thinks it more beneficial to him . . . entirely to devote himself to the beauties of the season, while they last; he was only happy while out from morning till night.'[3] Clairmont unknowingly touched on two aspects of the author relevant to *Headlong Hall*. This is a book about, or at least predicated upon, the leisure of its characters, and it is no less a book about 'study', diverse topics and ideas being represented in its spokesmen and in the laughing allusiveness of its narrator.

After August 1815 Shelley was living at Bishopsgate, within long but possible walking distance of Peacock's home at Marlow, and the two men saw a great deal of each other. Perhaps Shelley, who seems to have taken more interest in Peacock's novels than in his verse, at first persuaded him to attempt a novel. Peacock's silence on the matter invites speculation both as to why he began a novel and why he chose for his genre the novel of talk. Shelley, apart from his teenage romances, had conceived of and perhaps begun (in 1812) the novel 'Hubert Cauvin', a work of political commentary; and he seems to have added something to Thomas Jefferson Hogg's *Leonora*.[4] No longer occupied with a novel himself, he may have thought it the ideal form for 'cold' Peacock, just as he had earlier found it ideal for the less-talented Hogg. Shelley would have envisioned a polemical work, a fictionalized pamphlet related to the doctrinaire works of Holcroft, Day, and Mrs. Inchbald, and, like those earlier works, based upon a conversational format. If *Headlong Hall* actually was Shelley's suggestion, his attempt to find a substitute writer for a medium he himself had put aside, he must have found the novel a disappointment. *Melincourt* was to please Shelley, because it proved more clearly polemical, but *Headlong Hall* involves a kind of comedy that Shelley could hardly have welcomed.

Aside from such speculation, what can be said about the writing of the novel remains meagre. We have, according to descriptions like Clairmont's, the picture of a man devoted to physical and intellectual leisure and a man capable of play, who somehow managed to dash off an entertaining novel of talk. The phrase 'dash off' is appropriate, at least for the opening sections, for Peacock seems to have spent little time revising or polishing. Within the first three pages he casually repeats the words 'various knotty points' and gets himself into a minor problem of time sequences. The later parts, evidently more carefully worked, may reflect Peacock's changing response or commitment to his work. Yet one flaw continues—a flaw endemic to his prose as to his poetry. He allows himself, as the following passage indicates, an overuse of stock and superlative language:

> The vale [of Llanberis, in North Wales] contracted as they advanced, and, when they had passed the termination of the lake, their road wound along a narrow and romantic pass, through the middle of which an impetuous torrent dashed over vast fragments of stone. The pass was bordered on both sides by perpendicular rocks, broken into the wildest forms of fantastic magnificence (1, 72).

Peacock sounds here rather like Mrs. Radcliffe effusing about the Alps without having seen them. He need not have been in Wales to have produced his 'picturesque' description. As his letters and notes to poems show, he was familiar with Mrs. Radcliffe's stories. But he also knew Walter Scott's work, and his description of the vale may offer another slight clue about the genesis of the novel. Consider the following passage from *Waverley*, published two years before *Headlong Hall*. Waverley and his guide are hiking into the Highlands:

> The path, which was extremely steep and rugged, winded up a chasm between two tremendous rocks, following the passage which a foaming stream, that brawled far below, appeared to have worn for itself in the course of ages. A few slanting beams of the sun . . . reached the water in its darksome bed, and showed it partially, changed by a hundred rocks and broken by a hundred falls.[5]

It seems possible that Peacock, who was soon to defend Scott in the 'Essay on Fashionable Literature', wrote *Headlong Hall* with an eye on 'the enchanter of the north'. (Apparently his eye, like Scott's, was not upon the object.) This is not to argue that he actually tried to do for Wales what Scott had done for Scotland; his outlook was altogether different. Yet Scott would have provided authority for two things: fiction that centred in rural localities and fiction that sold. Peacock had not yet landed his position with the India House. He was in 1815 still short of money. With Scott as an example, a novel set in a far-away place might have seemed to him a good gamble.

However, if Scott offered a kind of authority, he proved no model for Peacock's story. Instead of characters like the 'romantic' Waverley and the Scottish chieftains, Peacock introduces 'philosophers' into the countryside and creates Headlong Hall, a bastion of good food and conversation and home of the epicurean Squire Headlong. Whereas in his meditative poems Peacock had used natural scenery as an excuse for solitary musings, his focus in the novel is upon a convivial group. But in the novels no less than in the poems Peacock's love of rugged landscape is evident, and it is tied with a presupposition as to the uses of the country. Natural surroundings represent an ideal alternative to city and society, a dissociation from ordinary places and ordinary cares, and thus the novels work out the pastoral desires that underlie the verse. At the same time, although Peacock introduces set-pieces—like the description of the Vale of Llanberis—in most of his novels, description becomes incidental to the characters. Peacock no longer concerns himself with the emotional impact of landscape, which, despite its importance for so many aspects of his fiction, he has relegated to the capacity of painted backdrop.

II

As with all of Peacock's novels, the story of *Headlong Hall* is simple in the extreme. The novel opens with 'the ambiguous light of a December morning' revealing four travellers within the Holyhead Mail:

A lively remark, that *the day was none of the finest*, having elicited a repartee of *quite the contrary*, the various knotty

points of meteorology, which usually form the exordium of
an English conversation, were successively discussed and
exhausted; and, the ice being thus broken, the colloquy
rambled to other topics, in the course of which it appeared,
to the surprise of every one, that all four, though perfect
strangers to each other, were actually bound to the same
point, namely, Headlong Hall . . . (i, 5–6).

Such mock-formal language—mixing 'exordium' and 'meteorology', which are merely upholstered clichés, with actual clichés
like 'the ice being . . . broken'—reinforce the intention to
burlesque, already anticipated by the book's motto:

> All philosophers, who find
> Some favourite system to their mind,
> In every point to make it fit,
> Will force all nature to submit.

To meet the four 'philosophers' in the Holyhead coach is to
recognize immediately that they are philosophers according to
Swift's description: men, that is, of 'favourite systems', and that
Peacock is interested, as Swift himself had been, not only in the
proper use of language, but in certain implicit standards of
common sense. After letting in a little daylight on the 'four
insides', Peacock allows the travellers to spout their ideas, which
they manage to do despite their initial conversational fumblings.
He follows them to breakfast, then shifts the scene to Headlong
Hall so as to await these and other guests.

He has bounced into the story in a way that reflects on his
whole writing method. There is a studied impersonality as
noticeable in the first page of his novel as in his poetry and
essays. Peacock refrains from introducing his narrator and from
making entirely clear just who the narrator is or what he knows,
in short, how much we may rely on him. In the opening
passage the narrator's mockery implies greater knowledge than
that of the characters, whom he evidently knows to be fools, but
he does not actually offer additional information. Later he will
venture asides, like the following, which have the effect of
undercutting the narrative itself, but also of laughing at the
expectations of the reader: 'Various other songs succeeded', he
says, 'which, as we are not composing a song book, we shall lay
aside for the present' (i, 134). At times the narrator will also

indulge—after the manner of Fielding, Richard Graves, and Hannah More[6]—in brief but essentially irrelevant essays, which may draw him closer to the reader, with whom he shares the observations. His more usual role is to put ideas into the mouths of characters, or, as in the opening scene, to paraphrase their talk while posing as the anonymous, inconscient recorder, at once urbane and aloof.

The anonymity of the narrator approximates a quality in Jane Austen's novels, for her speakers are often as circumspect. Jane Austen makes her values and her judgments on characters quite clear, and she creates a much more intricate world of social interrelationships, but like Peacock she maintains a separation between herself and the characters on the one hand and herself and the readers on the other. The illusion in both writers is that of the stage, as though, operating like a stage manager, the narrator were presenting a series of intact and immediate scenes. Whereas Jane Austen's narrative offers the novelistic counterpart of comedy of manners, Peacock's—as the reference to Swift's 'philosophers' makes clear—comes closer to a comedy of ideas.

Again, the stage for Peacock's first comedy is Headlong Hall. Harry Headlong, of prodigious ancestry—his name stemming ultimately from a waterfall—has invited assorted intellectuals and dilettantes to his Welsh estate. Although, 'like all other Welsh squires', fond of 'shooting, hunting, racing, drinking, and other such innocent amusements', Squire Headlong

> had actually suffered certain phenomena, called books, to find their way into his house; and, by dint of lounging over them after dinner, on those occasions when he was compelled to take his bottle alone, he became seized with a violent passion to be thought a philosopher and a man of taste; and accordingly set off on an expedition to Oxford, to inquire for other varieties of the same genera, namely, men of taste and philosophers; but, being assured by a learned professor that there were no such things in the University, he proceeded to London, where . . . he formed as extensive an acquaintance with philosophers and dilettanti as his utmost ambition could desire . . . (1, 7–8).

In short, Headlong is a self-styled '*Maître d'Hotel* of Philosophy', something of a Welsh Baron Holbach who creates his own rural and parodic salon. Among his newly-formed acquaintances are Mr. Nightshade and Mr. Mac Laurel—probably caricatures of Robert Southey and John Wilson; Sir Patrick O'Prism and Mr. Marmaduke Milestone—based on Sir Uvedale Price and Humphrey Repton, though informed by Payne-Knight, 'Capability' Brown, and a whole generation of theorists about landscape gardening; and Geoffrey Gall and Timothy Treacle, 'who followed the trade of reviewers'—Gall bearing some resemblance to Francis Jeffrey. Peacock carries to an extreme the old comic and satiric convention of giving significance to names, often explaining them with multilingual etymologies or whimsical onomastic accounts. The more obvious cases among Headlong's guests include Dr. Gaster, who must be a gourmand; Mr. Cranium, who must be a phrenologist; Mr. Chromatic, who similarly must be an addict to music; and Mr. Panscope, who, owing something to Coleridge, conceivably might be a 'chemical, botanical, geological, astronomical, mathematical, metaphysical, meteorological, anatomical, physiological, gal-vanistical, musical, pictorial, bibliographical, critical philo-sopher' (I, 28).

Apart from Squire Headlong, the four gentlemen discovered in the coach prove the most talkative and the most central characters. They are Mr. Escot, a 'deteriorationist', Mr. Foster, a 'perfectibilian', Mr. Jenkison, a 'statu-quo-ite', and Dr. Gaster, who, as gourmand, begins as a satiric portrait of wordly clergymen. The three philosophers may at first have been intended as ironic portraits of Peacock himself, Shelley, and Thomas Jefferson Hogg, their mutual friend. But they become, as David Garnett puts it, 'the mouthpieces of ideas' rather than actual portraits of men.[7] And they dominate the talk at Headlong Hall. Escot, as the spokesman for 'decadence', and Foster, upholding 'progress', re-enact the traditional Battle of the Books—though the terms of the debate have changed slightly since the days of Swift—and Mr. Jenkison weighs the respective merits of the ancients and moderns, com-mitting himself to neither. Even Squire Headlong, quite a sane gentleman in contrast with most of his guests, embodies what W. H. Smith calls 'the wealthy amateur with eccentric architectural tastes'.[8]

Once together at Headlong Hall, the philosophical guests and the family of the squire launch into conversation. They converse at table, at exercise, at all costs. Action in the novel remains at a minimum, and Peacock seems already to have realized in this first novel that he could better depict verbal than physical movement. Indeed, such actions as there are seem contrived either to offer the characters an opportunity to speak or to provide the narrator with a means of cutting them off. The narrator describes a tour of the grounds by the squire, accompanied by his landscape gardeners;[9] he lets Escot, Foster, and Jenkison promenade in constant debate to nearby Tremadoc —in order to see the embankment that had intrigued Shelley, and where, incidentally, Shelley had been arraigned for debt; and he describes an explosion, which jolts the two parties back together again. As his name makes clear, Squire Headlong is impetuous. Inspired by Marmaduke Milestone's plan to 'wave the wand of enchantment' over his estate, Headlong wants to see immediate results.[10] Dynamite being produced to shatter a protruding rock, the squire lights the fuse. Too late does he realize that Mr. Panscope and Mr. Cranium are perched in a nearby tower. No one is injured, but the explosion proves detrimental to the poise of Mr. Cranium, who

> bounded, under the elastic influence of terror, several feet into the air. His ascent being unluckily a little out of the perpendicular, he descended with a proportionate curve from the apex of his projection, and alighted, not on the wall of the tower, but in an ivy-bush by its side, which, giving way beneath him, transferred him to a tuft of hazel at its base, which, after upholding him an instant, consigned him to the boughs of an ash that had rooted itself in a fissure about half-way down the rock, which finally transmitted him to the waters below (i, 88–9).

Cranium's bathetic plunge emphasizes Peacock's delight in burlesque. The pseudo-exhaustive account, wholly out of proportion to the fall, might be a parody of Milton's Satan, when he enters the Garden and 'o'er leaps all bounds'; it reduces Cranium, one of the most pompous of Headlong's guests, into a mere bouncing object, cascading in slow motion down a series of absurd clauses. Peacock introduces similar falls with similar language in several of the later novels.

Mr. Escot arrives at the scene of the explosion as if on cue. Not being himself 'destitute of naratorial skill', he rescues the hapless phrenologist, who is then plied with Madeira and given 'ten thousand lame apologies' by the squire. A little later, Escot takes a solitary walk, and finding in a local graveyard a gigantic skull, which he claims is that of the local hero Cadwallader, he secures the means of bribing Mr. Cranium to part with his daughter. Cranium has been undaunted by the rescue, which he ascribes in behaviouristic terms to Escot's automatic response. But, as the traditional reluctant father, he is finally won over, so that Escot—joined by Headlong, Foster, and O'Prism—can marry. Dr. Gaster officiates at 'the spiritual metamorphosis of eight into four' (1, 150), and the novel comes to a happy, an easy, an incredibly tidy end. The guests part on the assumption that Headlong's hospitality will unite them in the not too distant future.

III

Looking back on *Headlong Hall* in his Preface of 1837, Peacock was to write:

> Perfectibilians, deteriorationists, statu-quo-ites, phreno-logists, transcendentalists, political economists, theorists in all sciences, projectors in all arts, morbid visionaries, romantic enthusiasts, lovers of music, lovers of the pictur-esque, and lovers of good dinners, march, and will march forever, *pari passu* with the march of mechanics, which some facetiously call the march of intellect (1, 2).

He might be speaking here like a many-eyed Samuel Butler, scorning the pride of self-deceiving fools; but the list, like those in 'The Four Ages', needs a second look. Ostensibly a black-list of undesirable types, all the objects of Peacock's satire, and more besides, it happens to include 'lovers of the picturesque', 'lovers of music', and 'lovers of good dinners'—pertinent cate-gories for Peacock himself. The list also admits the assumption, in the word 'forever', that neither his own nor anyone else's books are going to change matters. Both are relevant points for an understanding of Peacock's satire. Already in *Headlong Hall* he is peculiarly tolerant towards most of his characters, or tolerant of the opinions for which they are spokesmen. Dr. Gaster, for example, a 'lover of good dinners', might have remained the gluttonous clergyman who sprains his ankle in his haste to get to breakfast; instead, Peacock transforms him into a desirable companion.

Perhaps with Gaster in mind, one of Peacock's reviewers was to complain about 'the bad taste that has led its author to give his *dramatis personae* names strongly indicative of their characters', and to insist that 'if they require such, it argues that the characters are neither strongly marked nor consistent'.[11] It does not, of course, argue anything of the sort, as Rabelais, Ben Jonson, Fielding, and any number of writers would illustrate. The danger lies in the characters being too 'strongly marked', too purely caricature.

Yet in one sense Peacock's characters are inconsistent. Gaster obviously mellows in the course of the story, despite his unflattering name. With Escot and Foster the process is somewhat more complicated, since neither begins with Gaster's handicap. Both are honest, forthright, and sociable, ready, so to speak, to be married-off. At the same time, both are quite consistent in their ideas, from the moment the story opens to the point where Escot, like Bernard Shaw's Tanner, submits to marriage while railing against it. As the story progresses, Peacock dissociates these two, with Gaster, Headlong, and Jenkison, from the more brittle exponents of ideas and tastes, so that by the time of the weddings only the chosen group remains on stage, the others having been packed off as undesirables.[12] Escot and Foster are, then, consistent, but Peacock alters their relationships with the rest of the cast and consequently with the reader too.

The progress of the comedy may be seen in the tenor of the dialogue, which is not all of a kind in *Headlong Hall*. The more unsympathetic the character, the more acrid becomes the conversation and the more clearly the undesirables become scapegoats to 'the select group of philosophers'. And so we find Peacock introducing a series of traditional comic victims.

When Mr. Panscope defends 'authority' and shuns understandable discourse, he might be aping any number of pedantic ancestors, not only in Erasmus and Rabelais, but also in eighteenth-century essays and novels. In the introduction to William Beckford's *Azemia* (1797), the narrator, offering a 'defence' for the book, ponders: 'Who at this æra of felicitous luminosity shall adventure on the perilous undertaking of superadding, with due ratiocination, to the accumulation of vernacular entertainment? This is familiar enough as a stock treatment of pedantic nonsense; and Mr. Panscope sounds just as familiar in his self-defence:

> The *authority*, sir, of all these great men [he has cited for half a page writers as disparate as Pindar, Zoroaster, and Smollett] whose works, as well as the whole of the *Encyclopaedia Britannica*, the entire series of the *Monthly Review* . . . I have read through from beginning to end, deposes, with irrefragable refutation, against your ratiocinative speculations, wherein you seem desirous, by the futile process of analytical dialectics, to subvert the pyramidal structure of synthetically deduced opinions . . . (I, 54).

When an awed Squire Headlong pronounces this to be 'the very best speech that ever was made', Mr. Escot adds: 'It has only the slight disadvantage of being unintelligible.' If unintelligible, it remains stock humour. Panscope puffs himself up and Escot explodes him. Similarly, Miss Philomena Poppyseed —based on the ideas of the novelist Mrs. Opie, and master of the art of sinking in novels—finds herself at first ignored, then forgotten. The first sign of Dr. Gaster's 'taste' being more than gastronomic is his falling asleep at Miss Poppyseed's recitation of her latest plot.

Whenever Escot, Foster, or Jenkison speaks, Peacock's irony underlies their clashing dialectics. Consider the following interchange between Escot and Foster, with Jenkison a silent third. They have stopped during one of their peripatetic sessions 'to contemplate a little boat which was gliding over the tranquil surface of the lake below':

'The blessings of civilization,' said Mr. Foster, 'extend themselves to the meanest individuals of the community. That boatman, singing as he sails along, is, as I have no doubt, a very happy, and, comparatively to the men of his class some centuries back, a very enlightened and intelligent man.'

'As a partisan of the system of the moral perfectibility of the human race,' said Mr. Escot,—who was always for considering things on a large scale, and whose thoughts immediately wandered from the lake to the ocean, from the little boat to a ship of the line,—'you will probably be able to point out to me the degree of improvement that you suppose to have taken place in the character of a sailor, from the days when Jason sailed through the Cyanean Symplegades, or Noah moored his ark on the summit of Ararat.'

'If you talk to me,' said Mr. Foster, 'of mythological personages, of course I cannot meet you on fair grounds.'

'We will begin, if you please, then,' said Mr. Escot, 'no further back than the battle of Salamis; and I will ask you if you think the mariners of England are, in any one respect, morally or intellectually, superior to those who then preserved the liberties of Greece, under the direction of Themistocles?'

'I will venture to assert,' said Mr. Foster, 'that, considered merely as sailors, which is the only fair mode of judging them, they are as far superior to the Athenians, as the structure of our ships is superior to that of theirs . . .'
(1, 32–3).

The absurdity of the logic, the applications, and the force of commitment on the speakers' part makes judgment impossible. Whatever and whoever enters such conversation must enter in kind—and become laughable. Peacock does not punish these speakers nor upset the delicate balance of their absurdities. After Escot and Foster have fenced for a few pages, the narrator calls a draw in a simple manner: 'Mr. Foster was preparing to reply' —'preparing' seems just the right word for their elaborate arguments—

when the first dinner-bell rang, and he immediately com-
menced a precipitate return towards the house; followed
by his two companions, who both admitted that he was
now leading the way to at least a temporary period of
physical amelioration: 'but, alas!' added Mr. Escot, after
a moment's reflection, 'Epulae NOCUERE repostae!'
[Peacock's translation, in a footnote, reads: 'Protracted
banquets have been copious sources of evil'] (I, 36–7).

Peacock has closed his scene—as well as his chapter: the two
are usually synonymous—with an exclamation, but what
satiric point can he have made?

Of course there is satire in *Headlong Hall*. Panscope is a satiric
butt; so is Miss Poppyseed; so are Milestone and Cranium; so
are Gall and Treacle. Peacock censures these characters by
making the talks in which they take part more vitriolic and by
letting the inner group get the better of them in debate. Despite
a general intellectual waywardness, Escot, Foster, Jenkison,
and the squire himself become satirists in their own right, not at
any time speaking wholly for the author, because always pushing their arguments too far, but from time to time identified
with his viewpoint. Several of Escot's comments, for example,
anticipate almost phrase for phrase what Peacock himself
expresses directly in the 'Essay on Fashionable Literature' and
other later writings.

The turn-about of values in *Headlong Hall* parallels a related
turn-about in Cervantes' *Don Quixote*, which sees the translation
of a self-deluding fool into a man of perverse wisdom. Like
Cervantes' knight, Peacock's characters do not remain merely
the ludicrous victims of their reading. An original standard
of common sense, with which the characters are at odds,
is slowly supplanted by a new standard, of which the characters,
the quixotic philosophers, are representative. And as Quixote
remains a gentle and generous soul, whatever unwitting
follies he may perpetrate in *this* world, so Peacock's central
characters—a kind of collective hero—remain free from
the more dismal aspects of their arguments and manage to act
disinterestedly. Whereas Mr. Gall acts according to his name,
Escot, a spokesman against the eating of meat and against the
institution of marriage, downs his roast beef and weds his lady.

His marriage suggests a related question, already touched upon. George Meredith called attention to the importance of women in comedy, as in 'civilized' life: the necessity for quick-witted, and lovable, and marriageable beauties, around whom everything seems to move. Again Meredith's observations are relevant to Peacock, who creates gracious and intelligent ladies in their prime. The central characters in Peacock's novels are in a sense neither the hosts nor their eccentric guests—with *Nightmare Abbey* and *Elphin* excepted—but the young ladies: Caprioletta, Cephalis, Anthelia, Marian, Lady Clarinda, Morgana. They recall similar and related heroines in other comedies: Lysistrata, Rosalind and Miranda, Dekker's Rose, Congreve's Millamant, Molière's Célimène, Jane Austen's Elizabeth. Never are they fatal ladies or repositories of excessive sentiment. They smooth discord, they sing, they speak with sense and sensibility. Sometimes they are blue-stockings or *femmes savantes* but they are not 'philosophers'. Caprioletta Headlong beams 'like light on chaos, to arrange disorder and harmonise discord', and contrives to prepare Headlong Hall for her brother's guests. Tenorina Chromatic—all have such unlikely names—quietly contradicts Marmaduke Milestone's bad taste in landscape by preferring the natural and untouched countryside. 'The beautiful Cephalis'—Peacock took her name, as George Saintsbury pointed out, from Marmontel—sings 'with feeling and simplicity' a song of 'Love and Opportunity':

> Oh! who art thou, so swiftly flying?
> My name is Love, the child replied:
> Swifter I pass than south-winds sighing,
> Or streams, through summer vales that glide (1, 69).

Most of Peacock's heroines sing, and their singing is an emblem of 'civilized' qualities, especially the ability 'to harmonize discord'. When, in one of the earliest and one of the best studies of Peacock, A. Martin Freeman wrote, 'The desideratum of a Peacockian character is that he be able to talk',[14] he might have added the corollary that the desideratum of a Peacockian lady is that she be able to sing.

A generation before Peacock, William Blake had partially anticipated his genial comedy with the satiric *Island on the*

Moon, in which caricatures of current spokesmen converse and sing. To encounter early versions of 'Innocence' songs arbitrarily punctuating satiric dialogue is to wonder about Blake's purpose, or to understand why he left the work unfinished. Peacock's songs are more central to his story, because they are related both to the context and to the kind of the comedy he creates. But they are not at all gentle lyrics like 'Love and Opportunity'. The bantering, nonsensical gusto of the Headlong 'Chorus' suggests another muse entirely:

> Hail to the Headlong! the Headlong Ap-Headlong!
> All hail to the Headlong, the Headlong Ap-Headlong!
> The Headlong Ap-Headlong
> Ap-Breakneck Ap-Headlong
> Ap-Cataract Ap-Pistyll Ap-Rhaiader Ap-Headlong!
>   (I, 135).[15]

Related to the 'Chorus' is a 'Glee', typical of much of Peacock's later verse and, characteristically, a drinking song:

> A heeltap! a heeltap! I never could bear it!
> So fill me a bumper, a bumper of claret!
> Let the bottle pass freely, don't shirk it nor spare it,
> For a heeltap! a heeltap! I never could bear it! (I, 58).

Drinking songs, glees, ballads, as well as the love songs, all emphasize the significance of an underlying comic ritual and its intimacy with traditional festivities. *Headlong Hall* opens in December in order to close at Christmas, for it mixes the seasonal celebrations with the celebrations of the recently-formed group. Squire Headlong has invited his guests to argue 'over his Old Port and Burgundy', which may remind us that Peacock himself associated the emergence of comedy with drunken revels—witness his praise of Cratinus.

In the same year Peacock wrote his Preface for *Headlong Hall* (1837), Charles Dickens was publishing *Pickwick Papers*. Possibly unfamiliar with Peacock's story, Dickens nevertheless approximated some of its qualities; for he too relieves the satire by introducing alternatives closer to his wishes. Dickens modifies the original laughter at Pickwick by making both the

Chairman and his club into more than wandering vehicles for the author's witty observations.[16] An indication of the changed attitude is Dingley Dell, which is no less a retreat than Headlong's estate. Dickens keeps Pickwick's activities near to farce, as the spill through the ice makes clear, but he provides him and his friends the opportunity for convivial celebrations, which like Peacock's take place at Christmas. One essential difference between *Pickwick* and *Headlong Hall*, in form as well as viewpoint, is that Peacock keeps his characters in their retreat. They wander only about Headlong's secluded estate and in their preposterously allusive conversation.

IV

Despite its varieties of satire, then, *Headlong Hall* cannot be thought of as a novel of engagement. Rather like Christopher North's *Noctes Ambrosianae* (begun a few years later), Peacock's first novel presents an ideal and of course 'unreal' world. It is in a sense an other-worldly novel. This is not to argue that Peacock knew cosmic intellectual or spiritual realms or that he presents characters with aspiring souls. All are very worldly in the matter of requiring physical enjoyments. The point is they are fortunate enough to have such enjoyments. Like Jane Austen, Peacock creates an adult world—both authors refer to characters by their last names—but if his characters are more aware of 'ideas', they are much less aware of social responsibilities and cares. The conversation in Headlong Hall takes place assuming their leisure, away from children, wives, and duties. Moreover, if one of Peacock's characters is not himself wealthy, he can always rely on the larger income of his host. Wealthy or not, most of his people are in a position to agree with the parasite in Athenaeus, who says: 'That is the life the gods lead, when you can dine at another's expense with no thought of the reckoning.' Squire Headlong's guests are as remote from daily toils as Headlong Hall itself is remote from 'the march of mechanics'.

3

'Calidore' and *Melincourt*: Hints from Spenser and Voltaire

Laugh and be well. Monkeys have been
Extreme good doctors for the Spleen.

MATTHEW GREEN, 'The Spleen'.

I

Of the two new novels that he began in the months following completion of *Headlong Hall*, Peacock finished only one. The fragment 'Calidore', entitled 'Satyrane' in its early version, apparently occupied him first, and he worked on it in the spring months of 1816.[1] The material of this regrettably incomplete story suggests a kinship with 'The Round Table', since in both the poem and the story Peacock is toying with Arthurian legends. 'Calidore' is also related to *Melincourt*, for both are *ingénu* literature, heirs of Montesquieu and Voltaire.

At about the same time that Peacock was writing 'Calidore', Keats also began a work by the same name—of course in verse. His poem has little in common with Peacock's story, saving its incompleteness and its title, which both men drew from Spenser; yet Peacock had only recently put aside 'Ahrimanes'— written in Spenserian stanzas—when he undertook the satiric tale.[2] Like Keats, Peacock opens his story with a boat on the water, but he shows immediately that the intent is ironic rather than lushly exotic or evocative of *The Fairie Queene*. He describes 'a very handsome young gentleman, dressed not exactly in the newest fashion', broaching the Welsh shore in something resembling a skiff (VIII, 303). Enter Calidore. No sooner has the hero landed—presumably none the worse for having crossed the ocean in a tiny boat—than he meets two local maidens, with one of whom he promptly falls in love. (Peacock not only

married a Welsh woman; he considered Welsh women generally to be exceptionally handsome.) Calidore, who proves as
courteous as his forbear in Spenser, questions the young ladies
and surprises them too. He does not know the meaning of the
word 'bishop', and is even unsure what he wants when he
requests the way to an inn. He turns out to be a sort of Anglican
primitive, inhabitant of an island where Jupiter and King
Arthur, together with the retinues of Olympus and the Round
Table, survive in syncretic and timeless exile.[3] Jaded or mal-
content, Arthur dreams nostalgically of a heroic return to
Britain, to which he sends periodically an unmated young man
for the ostensible purpose of finding a wife and a court 'philosopher' and for the real purpose of spying. He has learned from
reports of fanatical uprisings, beheading of kings—not very
auspicious—as well as the grumblings of the 'swinish multitudes', and being at heart a deteriorationist, he despairs of
success. The wizard Merlin, Arthur's counterpart as perfectibilian, maintains the king's hopes.

Latest of the secret agents, Calidore is admirably conceived—
the son of a lovely nymph and a heretofore puritanical clergyman shipwrecked on the island—but he is a better *ingénu* than
spy. Peacock uses him as the traditionally uninitiated outsider
who makes implicit criticism of customs and institutions. Arriving in London, he argues naïvely with the clerks of Thread-
needle Street, because they insist on returning paper slips—
paper tokens of 'paper prosperity'—for his 'Arthurus Rex' gold
pieces. Having found a wife on the opening page, he goes in
search of a 'philosopher', much as Squire Headlong does in the
first novel. Various crotcheteers and burlesqued poets emerge,
among them representatives of Wordsworth and Coleridge.
Then, abruptly, the episodes end. For his final sequence Peacock probably borrowed an idea from Lucian's *Sales of Lives*
(or 'Philosophers for Sale'). Like Lucian, he reduces ideas to
absurdity by putting them and their spokesmen in the capacity
of marketable products. He was to exploit this satiric device a
few years later in 'The Four Ages of Poetry' and, more immediately in *Melincourt*, where poets measure their success in
terms of pensions.

Because 'Calidore' remains incomplete and survives in five
somewhat inconsistent sections, it can hardly be discussed as a

finished work. Nevertheless, it indicates some of Peacock's opportunities for humour, as well as his difficulties with sustained narrative. His problem—and it was to be the problem with *Melincourt*—seems basically to be one of balance. In the device of confronting an outsider with matters not bearing examination, Peacock depicts, like Voltaire in *L'Ingénu* and Goldsmith in the *Citizen of the World*, another innocent abroad. (He was familiar with a wide range of related books, including Lucian's *True History*, Rabelais' *Gargantua* and *Pantagruel*, Cervantes' *Don Quixote*, and Swift's *Gulliver*.) But the final pages shift to another kind of story: conversation again, with a battery of spokesmen like those in the earlier novel. Peacock's stories are usually quite flimsy, incidental in fact to the dialogue. At home with dialogue, he may have found 'Calidore' too demanding, or, more likely, unsuitable as a format for a conversational work. In any case, after sketching his background and opening his scenes, he went on to write a related but more congenial work. Calidore became Sir Oran Haut-ton, Bart., of *Melincourt*.

II

Melincourt appeared about a year later than *Headlong Hall* and was advertised in the second edition of that novel in the summer of 1816. Enlarged during the autumn of 1816 and added to at least as late as January of the next year, *Melincourt* is a much longer and more committed novel than *Headlong Hall*. It is also much more topical. Peacock aims directly at current political and literary targets, is rather less concerned with intellectual fads, offers caricatures of sundry public figures, and directly attacks political targets, including rotten boroughs, slavery, post-Waterloo reactionism—and a recent number of the *Quarterly Review*.

Peacock's motto for *Melincourt*, from Horace's *Art of Poetry*, is *Vocem comœdia tollit*, 'Comedy raises its voice'. Out of context, it implies either a process from satire to comedy—a promise that *Melincourt* partly fulfils—or the imposition of a comic order on material suggestive of another treatment. Whatever Peacock intended by his epigraph, it is certainly true that the comedy in *Melincourt* is less dominant or less genial and consistent than in the novels that preceded and followed.

Most recent critics of *Melincourt* have been dissatisfied with the book because it is more pointedly satiric and hence more private than Peacock's other novels, and also because its satire is at once more obvious and more complex. While no less sensible in this novel, no less observant, Peacock offers a great deal of social commentary that has lost its impact with the passing of time. Yet this is an accusation that can be made about much satire, in that satire tends more than any other literary mode to be bound to its time. 'I want,' wrote Sherwood Anderson in a statement applicable to many satirists, 'to take a bite out of the now.' Successful satire often manages, none the less, to speak beyond its own generation; and for modern readers the important question about *Melincourt* is not so much whether it provides a telling satiric portrait of the time, but whether as a literary work it holds together. And in this sense the book falters.

It is misleading to judge earlier fiction—especially works that make no pretence to realism—in a post-Jamesian way, thinking, that is, in terms of tight constructions and consistent points of view. However, an author's inconsistencies will often make clear his problems. In *Melincourt* Peacock leaves a number of loose ends, repeats himself, drops characters, and arbitrarily suspends topics. A symptom of all this is the narrator's bewildering shifts in point of view. In one sequence he speaks directly as 'I', and though otherwise he speaks as the more formal or elusive 'we', his function and his powers change conspicuously. E. M. Forster's usefully evasive remark that a novelist may change point of view, but only if he can get away with it, applies here. Despite his introducing characters who express opinions for him, the narrator in *Melincourt* tends to obtrude in a way that the narrator of the earlier novel does not. At one point he introduces a topic by speaking of the 'virtuous', 'amiable', and 'sublime' Condorcet—clearly without irony—and regardless of the French philosopher's virtues, the adjectives necessarily determine the direction and the tone of the ensuing dialogue. At their best, Peacock's novels have what Oliver Elton called 'the true air of impromptu', and if, as Elton implies, the dialogue is actually far from being impromptu, the strenuous dialectics do give the impression of it, as though the narrator were recording a type of intellectual *commedia dell' arte*.[4] Wit involves concision, and Peacock's interest in *Melincourt* lies in more formal and far more extensive debate.

Whatever its faults, *Melincourt* is also an intriguing novel, to a few readers Peacock's most intriguing, for it has its own riches— they are closely related to its flaws—and it offers a complexity of detail and reference missing in the other stories. It is a kind of satiric intellectual odyssey, full of incident and wonderfully improbable happenings, which presents 'a whole treasury of . . . exuberant and overflowing folly'. Some of its scenes and characters are among Peacock's most inventive, and the boldest of the creations is, doubtless, Sir Oran Haut-ton, Bart.[5]

Melincourt is in essence a sophisticated beast fable, reaching back in its pedigree to the fables of Aesop—and, like Aesop, not without a social message—but also parodying a century of *ingénu* literature and theories about the nature of man that were still current in Peacock's time. Sir Oran reveals Peacock at his whimsical best, exploding settled opinion and mocking ideas, at the same time creating in his *ingénu* the principal agent for the establishment of a happy and harmonious ending. The title of the 1856 edition of the novel was, fittingly, *Melincourt, or, Sir Oran Haut-ton.*

Sir Oran is no ordinary English gentleman. When Sir Telegraph Paxarett learns that he has been 'found' in Angola, and when Mr. Hippy muses, 'I wonder who he is . . . manifestly dumb, poor fellow! a man of consequence, no doubt: no great beauty, by the by . . . (II, 109), Peacock is laughing at the startled reactions of his characters to a civilized orang-outang. (By orang-outang he apparently understood any large ape.) For information about the theory that held certain apes to belong to the species of man, Peacock turned naturally to Buffon and Rousseau; but most of his extensive footnotes— Peacock footnotes his novels, especially *Melincourt*, almost as much as his long poems—are quotations from that eccentric, Rousseauistic, Scottish gentleman, James Burnet, Lord Monboddo. In several of his works, though especially in the *Origins and Progress of Language* (1773–92), Monboddo concerns himself, purportedly, with a systematic analysis of speech. However, he becomes so enamoured of both irrelevancies and apes that he essentially presents apologies for the orang-outang. His writings offered an ideal springboard for Peacock's hairy innocent. Yet

Peacock is not harsh with Monboddo; he simply uses Monboddo's theories as an ironic vehicle for satire that is largely political. Sir Oran becomes a capable musician, a convivial gentleman, ultimately even a Member of Parliament. He rescues ladies in distress, shows 'civilized' traces of a tendency to romantic love, while retaining a natural capacity for uprooting trees. Of *Melincourt's* two interrelated story lines, the more important is that of Sir Oran's career, a career remarkable in its achievement because Sir Oran lacks the quality most requisite for wordly success and for success in Peacock's other novels: he shares with ordinary apes the inability to speak. But in name and in fact he has *ton*, a favourite Regency term of social approbation.

Peacock's concern with Sir Oran's 'dumb discourse' and his generally humorous treatment of the orang-outang indicate that part of *Melincourt* may have grown out of hints from the novels of Isaac Disraeli. Disraeli laughs in *Flim-Flams* (1806) at craniology, much as Peacock laughs in *Headlong Hall*, and he draws a variety of scenes as well as satiric portraits that find parallels in Peacock's novels. *Flim-Flams* also has fun with Monboddo, and with extensive footnotes, and reduces Monboddo's ideas by ironic paraphrase. Toying with the question of language among animals, Disraeli touches on a line of humour and a prejudice close to Peacock's own. 'Leibniz', he writes, 'to illustrate his origin of language on mechanical principles, contrived to force a dog to bark several words! And as these were German, he probably did not find his philosophical experiment very difficult.'[6]

But, again, Sir Oran cannot learn to speak, nor even to bark. If he is the strong, he is also the silent hero, not always upstage in a novel of talk. Having perhaps learned from the difficulties in 'Calidore', Peacock does not treat exclusively the adventures of one individual but creates, as in *Headlong Hall*, a core of garrulous spokesmen. One of the disappointments of the novel is that Sir Oran, at first so central to the story, performs less and less in the later parts—until his triumphant rescue of the heroine. The heroine is Anthelia Melincourt, who, along with Sylvan Forester, provides the focus for the conversation.

Melincourt has no unifying group comparable to that of *Headlong Hall*. Whereas in the earlier novel the most unlikely of companions, without ever really agreeing, continue to talk in each other's company, in *Melincourt* characters very often agree but they do not for the most part remain together. Some of the best characters—Mr. Sarcastic, for example—appear but briefly; some of the least interesting characters—such as the Reverend Mr. Grovelgrub—recur throughout, though not as part of the coterie surrounding Forester and Anthelia. At times there is a sense of a stage unit, 'the very few congenial friends' but there is no sustaining dialectic, which is the main virtue of *Headlong Hall*.

III

The events of *Melincourt* take place largely in the vicinity of Melincourt Castle, ancestral home of Anthelia's family. A medieval edifice perched on a crag in a wild region of Westmorland, the castle is comparable in its remoteness and its hospitality to Headlong Hall.

Peacock first introduces Anthelia enjoying the solitude and privacy of her northern retreat. She is, like Thomas Amory's Ayora in *John Buncle*, an intellectual and idealistic young lady. She is also both rich and orphaned. Such a woman in such circumstances naturally precipitates an invasion of would-be bridegrooms or their informal agents, like the match-making Mrs. Pinmoney; and, in an effort to protect herself, Anthelia invites a hypochondriac but gregarious uncle, in the person of Mr. Hippy, to act as her major-domo. He is to meet the guests, while his niece spends her time with the Italian poets—in the library. (Anthelia's name and her tastes recall Shelley's 'friend' at Bracknell, Cornelia Turner.) The narrator describes the unbalanced situation at the opening of the story in this way:

> Among the numerous lovers who had hitherto sighed at her shrine, not one had succeeded in making the slightest impression on her heart. . . . Her knowledge of love was altogether theoretical; and her theory, being formed by the study of Italian poetry in the bosom of mountain solitude, naturally and necessarily pointed to a visionary model of excellence which it was very little likely the modern world could realize (11, 12).

Anthelia's visionary model of excellence fortuitously materializes in the person of Sylvan Forester—whose moralistic iconoclasm suggests Shelley—a wealthy, idealistic, and reclusive gentleman, who lives with Sir Oran in nearby Redrose, formerly Rednose, Abbey, and who also reads Italian poets.

Peacock introduces Forester and gives his first detailed account of Sir Oran by describing the reactions of Sir Telegraph Paxarett. Travelling as a suitor to Melincourt, Sir Telegraph finds himself after a day's journey distressingly far from an inn. He finally chances on Redrose and recognizes in Forester an old acquaintance. The ensuing conversations fill in a certain amount of background material and give Sir Oran an opportunity to run through his acts, among them downing bumpers of wine and vanishing through windows. Forester turns out to be the chief member of the Anti-Saccharine League, composed of those who abstain from sugar because it is the product of slave labour. (Peacock himself so abstained.) He has always been, according to his guest, 'fond of railing at civilized life, and holding forth in praise of savages' (11, 34). Hence his attachment to Sir Oran, whom he serves as a Rousseauistic Pygmalion. Because of his sympathies, Forester proves the perfect match for Anthelia. Unfortunately, he also proves a little tedious, because, unlike Escot and Foster, he has 'the strange habit' of practising what he preaches. Like Escot, Forester is partly ridiculous, but since he is even more of an intellectual and more of a prig, he should have been, at least at the beginning of the story, a more obvious butt of comedy. 'The ridiculous increases', as Peacock's contemporary, Jean Paul, pointed out, 'with the rationality of the ridiculous character'. Peacock of course knew this, yet he lets Forester get the upper hand in debate so consistently and lets him talk at such length that he strains the reader's sympathy.

Soon after Sir Telegraph leaves Redrose for Melincourt, Forester also discovers a reason for going. Lord Anophel Achthar, one of Anthelia's disappointed suitors, has taken legal action against Sir Oran, who, by rescuing Anthelia from a flooded stream, has roused Achthar's envy and ire. Peacock admits little love for lords in this his most politically radical book, and he makes Achthar into a coxcomb.

Already intrigued by the report of Anthelia's generosity to a local family, Forester is at their meeting even more impressed by her charms. Peacock lets the two talk, appropriately, in the library. After a brief period of mutual scrutiny, Sylvan and Anthelia—one hopes they find other names of endearment—realize that they have found their ideals, and admit their love.

Peacock's characters usually reveal their affections with alacrity—and Peacock no doubt remembered Miranda's candour, or that of Robert Bage's heroines. In Anthony Hamilton's *The Four Facardins*, with which he was probably also familiar, the narrator longs for the good old days when women were candid in their love.[7] Peacock felt much the same way, and he creates forthright heroines. While admirable as a matter of sentiment, however, such honesty invites certain difficulties in matters of plot. Apart from Sir Oran's adventures, *Melincourt* depends for its plan on thwarted love, and as the main characters fall in love almost immediately and have nothing to keep them apart except the meddling of Lord Achtar, who tries once and once succeeds in abducting the heroine, Peacock even deprives himself of this most rudimentary of plot devices. Had Sir Oran maintained a chief role in the book, the inadequate love story would not have mattered. The plot would then have depended on a consistent focus or on the continuing dialectic of Sir Oran's 'friends'. But Peacock gradually reduces his importance, so that *Melincourt*, like the other novels, relies on the controlling principle of the love story, and the difficulty is that the illusion breaks down. In *Gryll Grange*, a similarly long novel, Peacock will add complexity to his love story; he will also confine his satire to the immediate setting, allowing his speakers to range in conversation rather than in fact.

With Forester's arrival at Melincourt, the company is for the time being complete. Peacock records a series of conversations, wherein Feathernest, a caricature based on Robert Southey—and one that is little less scathing than that in the poem *Sir Proteus*—Derrydown, a curious mixture of Scott and Burns, Fax, based on Thomas Malthus, and others, come in for drubbings. Peacock is still anti-clerical in *Melincourt*, and treats the two clergymen, especially Grovelgrub, with unmitigated contempt. Portpipe, who reads Rabelais and Swift, shows signs of mollifying, like his predecessor, Gaster, but he remains incomplete.

In a chapter called 'The Symposium' Peacock lets his diverse assembly raise their voices in none too esoteric debate. 'A dry discussion,' says Mr. Hippy, when Feathernest launches into a spirited defence of his own 'prudent' conservatism. 'Pass the bottle and moisten it.' Portpipe and Sir Telegraph Paxarett then join Harum O'Scarum, 'the sole proprietor of a vast tract of undrained bog in the county of Kerry', in singing 'A Glee— The Ghosts':

In life three ghostly friars were we,
And now three friarly ghosts we be.
Around our shadowy table placed,
The spectral bowl before us floats:
With wine that none but ghosts can taste,
We wash our unsubstantial throats.
Three merry ghosts—three merry ghosts—three merry
                                    ghosts are we:
Let the ocean be Port, and we'll think it good sport
To be laid in that Red Sea (II, 183).

If he does not up-end someone, or close a scene with a call to dinner, Peacock usually smooths the conversational waters with music. In the chapter following 'The Symposium', appropriately entitled 'Music and Discord', debates that are at the point of becoming acrimonious are again relieved by songs. Once more Peacock's agent is Mr. Hippy, who deems it 'expedient to interpose for the restoration of order', and entreats Anthelia 'to throw in a little musical harmony as a sedative to the ebullitions of poetical discord' (II, 197).

When, in 1854, Leigh Hunt commented on Peacock's songs, he evidently took Peacock at his word, suggesting that 'his satire often runs off into purely jovial song'. Yet Hunt was probably the first critic to appreciate the relationship between Peacock's satire and songs. 'Momus', he writes, 'returned to his satire in our own days in the classical guise of Mr. Peacock'— Hunt is thinking specifically of 'The Symposium' and its 'Glee'. He adds that 'Peacock's wit could never rid his imagination of the gods and goddesses who possessed his first affections, especially those of the lyrical order....'[8]

The harmony produced by the songs is short-lived. Achthar, aided by his sycophant Grovelgrub, soon attempts to abduct

Anthelia. Sir Oran, fortunately nearby, foils their plot—without being able to reveal their identities. Thereafter, Forester, Anthelia, and several companions journey to the borough of 'Onevote' in order to elect Sir Oran to Parliament. This is the most humorous sequence of the novel, in addition to being the climax of Sir Oran's improbable career. When Sir Oran and his friends arrive in 'the large and populous city of Novote, which was situated at a short distance from the ancient and honourable borough of Onevote'—Onevote is a rotten borough in the control of Mr. Christopher Corporate—

> Sir Oran signalized his own entrance by playing on his French horn, *See the conquering hero comes!* Bells were ring-ing, ale was flowing, mobs were huzzaing, and it seemed as if the inhabitants of the large and populous city were satisfied of the truth of the admirable doctrine, that the positive representation of one individual is a virtual representation of fifty thousand (II, 225–6).

Prior to the election, Forester and his group encounter Sir Oran's 'brother candidate', Mr. Sarcastic, who is really more frank or cynical than sarcastic. He has the disarming charac-teristic of telling people the truth. Peacock seems to use Sarcastic to indicate the nature of his satiric intent in *Melincourt*, where, more than in the other novels, the narrator himself poses as the traditionally plain-talking satirist. Even if Sarcastic is not his author's mouthpiece, his method resembles that of the narrator. 'Custom,' he says, is the pillar round which opinion twines, and interest is the tie that binds it. It is not by reason that practical change can be effected, but by making a puncture to the quick in the feelings of personal hope and personal fear' (II, 233). Sarcastic not only sounds like Juvenal, he also quotes him, and in *Melincourt* Peacock unmistakably approaches Juvenal's tone, his rhetorical pose that of the incensed honest man compelled to speak out.

The plans to install Mr. Sarcastic and Sir Oran run smoothly at first: Mr. Christopher Corporate, 'free, fat, and dependent burgess', has been duly paid for the Parliamentary seat: Sarcastic has performed the necessary address—Sir Oran pre-serving his wonted reticence—and the residents of Novote have been plied with a sufficient quantity of ale to render them uncaring. Then Peacock indulges in one of his favourite rumpuses. Sir Oran tacitly refuses to be chaired by the ecstatic mob, and an effort to apply gentle force results in the unleashing of his 'natural instincts':

> . . . he seized a stick from a sturdy farmer at his elbow, and began to lay about him with great vigour and effect. Those who escaped being knocked down by the first sweep of his weapon, ran away with all their might, but were soon checked by the pressure of the crowd, who hearing the noise of the conflict, and impatient to ascertain the cause, bore down from all points upon a common centre, and formed a circumferential pressure that effectually prohibited the egress of those within . . . (II, 249).

One of Peacock's contemporary reviewers complained that he equated polysyllabic verbosity with wit; and he can be accused of using the long word and the periphrastic construction when the short one would do. So of course can any number of comic writers. The passage above gains its humour from a change in diction. Beginning with a subdued, earthy account, Peacock moves to an inflated rhetoric. He does not elaborate individual faces, or smells, or panic, but the increasingly formal style—as though he were turning the whole thing into a geometric problem or recording the advance of Spartan phalanxes on Athens—makes for successful humour. A disparity between content and manner is Peacock's most constant source of verbal humour, and it is clear that Rabelais and Butler were among his lessons well read.

When the inhabitants of Novote have been mollified by the intercession of Forester and Sarcastic, who speed an antidote to revolt in the form of another supply of ale, Forester and his friends can return without further disturbance to Melincourt, secure in Sir Oran's election and in their ideals. With celebrations, with a 'Chess Dance'—an idea taken from Rabelais—and with the anticipated marriage of Forester and Anthelia, the novel might have ended at this point. Possibly in one version it did.

Brett-Smith conjectures that the printer found 'the tale . . .

too short for three volumes . . . and too long for one', and that
Peacock may have taken the opportunity to extend his novel
(I, lxx). Whether or not the case, this offers a useful hypothesis
for approaching the rest of the novel. Peacock then postponed
the wedding celebrations by having Lord Anophel Achthar
finally succeed in abducting Anthelia—in a sequence reminiscent of Robert Bage's *Barham Downs*. The search for Anthelia
becomes a peculiarly rambling one, in that Forester appears less
concerned about his lady than about towns ruined by 'paper
money' and benevolent squires squeezed by urban economics.
Accompanied by Mr. Fax and Sir Oran, whose role is minimal,
Forester wanders like another Quixote, alien in a world that
he think he understands.

Forester does admit to being baffled in one sequence, entitled
'Cimmerian Lodge'. In this chapter Peacock depicts Moley
Mystic—another portrait reminiscent of Coleridge—the 'poeti-
copolitical, rhapsodicoprosaical, deisidaemoniacoparadoxi-
graphical, pseudolatreiological, transcendental meteorosophist'
at home on his island of 'pure intelligence' (II, 328).[9] The
journey taken by Forester, Fax, and Sir Oran across Mystic's
'Stygian pool', light-hearted burlesque of the traditional cross-
ings of the Styx—and with specific echoes of Aristophanes and
a scene in Disraeli's *Flim-Flams*—is followed by a parody of
lines from the *Ancient Mariner*:

> The fog was here, the fog was there,
> The fog was all around (II, 333).

Peacock insisted in his 1865 Preface to *Melincourt*, for Bentley's
Standard Novels, that he had never 'trespassed on private life'
(II, 2). No doubt he was sensitive to the fact that among his
novels *Melincourt* comes the closest to personal invective. But his
statement remains true, if only just true, even of *Melincourt*
itself. Even though Mystic is a puffed-up fool, whose foggy
rhetoric hides a profound ignorance, it is futile to call his
portrait an unfair slur on Coleridge. For Peacock is merely
prodding what amounts in modern parlance to the public
image of the man—and probably not only the one man—who,
as with the portrait of Panscope in *Headlong Hall*, is distinct
from the actual person.[10] Nor is it relevant to say, as A. E.

Dyson does, that Peacock is incapable of appreciating eccentric genius. We know the contrary to be the case. Mr. Dyson notes specifically Peacock's limited response to Coleridge and Shelley.[11] The 'Essay on Fashionable Literature' defends Coleridge on the basis that hasty critics cannot appreciate his individual talents; and the Shelley memoirs remain for many readers, an almost unimpeachable defence of 'genius'. The point here is that the novels depend upon an ironic mask. The outlandish caricatures in the novels are themselves an indication that, whatever their basis in fact or opinion, they have been transformed by the medium.

Not all the later chapters prove as inventive as 'Cimmerian Lodge'. Indeed, most involve another type of satire. In an episode called 'The Paper Mill', Peacock records in some detail the distresses of a rural community where ' "Messieurs Smoke-shadow, Airbubble, Hopthetwig, and Company, had found themselves under the disagreeable necessity of suspending their payments"; in plain English, had found it expedient to fly by night . . .' (II, 319). He introduces several random characters who are strangers to Forester, and lets them elaborate their woes at undue length. Forester himself gives charitably to a few of the victims, but the episode otherwise bears little relationship to the rest of the book. This is equally true of other chapters, such as 'The Deserted Mansion'—again suggestive of Goldsmith and Mary Mitford—'The Vicarage', and even of 'Mainchance Villa', in which some familiar characters turn up for a final round. 'Mainchance Villa' contains rather heavy-handed caricatures of Wordsworth in the person of Mr. Paperstamp, Canning as Mr. Anyside Antijack, John Wilson Croker as Mr. Killthedead, and others, who—with their refrain 'The church is in danger!'—become tiresome enemies of liberal thought.

That Peacock can denounce representatives of Canning and Southey, not only in the same chapter, but on the basis of a shared guilt, emphasizes a quality peculiar to the satire of this novel. Peacock usually comments on political assumptions and events, but for the most part incidentally, his main target being, for want of a better phrase, a 'state of mind'. In *Melincourt* his focus is largely upon the condition of politics, in relation to which his poets are representative turncoats or hired apologists for the *status quo*. Again, Southey is not Southey the man, but the Poet Laureate, stabled by the Establishment and symbolized by the butt of sack.

IV

It is clearly not true, as Albert Cook would have it, that because comedy affirms 'social order' it automatically precludes social criticism; and that when a writer like George Bernard Shaw introduces social commentary into his plays he no longer writes comedy.[12] In the first place, the social order within comedy often represents an alternative order to the outside world. Then, too, comedy tends to be an inclusive rather than exclusive mode. Much of Shaw's writing may be unsuccessful, but when he lets his characters discuss social questions he is not lapsing from comedy so much as exploring its capacities. The same can be argued about Peacock. Theoretically, he might have introduced almost any kind of comment into *Melincourt* without necessarily ruining the comedy. Yet there is in fact a problem with the chapters he added, not because they attempt what comedy is incapable of achieving, but because they raise the nagging question of relevancy. Ian Jack, in his admirable commentary on Peacock, insists that *Melincourt* has no problem except undue length. Compared with a novel by Dickens or Scott, however, it is not long at all. The reason that it *seems* long is that Peacock added only one type of chapter—the rambling, episodic sort, directed at a specific evil—without, as in the early part of the novel, balancing them with a 'percussion of ideas'.[13]

But what is often overlooked about the novel, and what Mr. Jack rightly suggests, is that the later scenes resemble several of the earlier episodes. Throughout *Melincourt* Peacock punctuates his story with discussions that are at best tangential to the people and the events at Melincourt Castle. A pair of chapters, 'Desmond'—presumably after Charlotte Smith's novel by that name—and 'The Cottage', are illustrative. In both Peacock lectures on that respectable topic of cultivating one's garden.

Early in the story Forester, Fax, and Sir Oran stroll to Melincourt. Fax, on a somewhat pat cue, relates the story of an unfortunate man called Desmond, after which the three gentlemen arrive at Desmond's cottage and learn the happy outcome of his previously unhappy life. Desmond, after finding himself unable to subsist in the corrupt city, has retired with his bene- factor to the country. Left at his friend's death with no means of supporting his family, and victim of outside economic forces, he is nearly destitute until saved by Anthelia's generosity. She places him on a comfortable little farm, where he can finally lead the good moral life. This story within a story serves tech- nically like Fielding's chapter about the 'Man on the Hill' in *Tom Jones*, while the sentiments echo Rousseau and Words- worth. Wordsworth's stories of Michael and Margaret contain related assumptions, but Wordsworth follows his own logic and brings his characters to their inevitably pathetic ends. Peacock's account of Desmond ought to have ended similarly, for Anthelia's kindness is an arbitrary gesture on a stage otherwise without hope.[14] Hers is a true and a rare act of charity, yet one that must remain an inadequate antidote to the evil Peacock has drawn.

Peacock does imply at various points in *Melincourt* that it is the dispossessed who suffer most—indeed, whose lives are tragic. What mitigates his observations is the contrast between his chief characters and the examples of suffering that they encounter. They do not themselves have any real cares, even if in this novel—hardly at all elsewhere—they are called upon to witness and to alleviate the cares of others. In this sense Peacock diverges from Voltaire, whom he admired and with whom he shared certain predilections. He creates an old man, for example, who has witnessed suffering but suffered little him- self, and who seems to speak for his author in the summing-up of his life: 'I eats my beef-steak and drinks my ale, and lets the world slide' (II, 350). Despite the righteous tone, the talk of 'puncturing' feelings, the political tirades, this essentially is the resolution in *Melincourt*. Voltaire, whose Candide's final turn with a hoe is a stoical move from worldly palaver to the realization that things are bad and must be accepted as such, writes satire that broaches on tragedy. Peacock, leading his characters to a similar philosophic vantage-point, presents his satire as subordinate to comedy.[15]

How much Peacock's narrative method is indebted to Vol- taire's would be difficult to say, although he clearly knew and enjoyed Voltaire's stories, as 'French Comic Romances' will illustrate. In *Melincourt* he is at his closest to Voltaire, not simply because his characters learn to cultivate their gardens, but also because he introduces to this story the wider range of incident. One wonders also whether Peacock knew the works of George Walker, a grudging disciple of Voltaire. A man of mixed political sympathies and strong political hatreds, Walker employed Voltaire's techniques to attack Voltaire's ideas. (His *Vagabond* appeared a few years before *Melincourt*.) Essentially both Walker and Voltaire offer an ideological picaresque, wherein action derives meaning from a fixed body of opinion. Voltaire—and Walker to a lesser extent—holds his readers' concentration by inventive story-telling, one event following hard upon the heels of another, almost without respite. Even in *Melincourt* this is not Peacock's way of presenting material. The actions of his characters always remain at a certain remove from their conversation, as if in fact independent of it, and whatever external actions or events impinge on the characters serve at most as points of departure for the dialogue. Peacock never holds the mirror up to the dusty road or tumbles his people in filthy inns, never, that is, submits them to physical realities, and therefore never creates the illusion of picaresque.

Melincourt closes on an affirmative note similar to that of *Headlong Hall*, without offering such a dazzling spate of headlong weddings. Sir Oran having finally rescued the beleagured heroine, Forester wins his lady. Lovers of the country, of humanitarian principles, of food and drink, and of the good life talk their way to a happy conclusion. Forester himself speaks about pernicious vinous beverages and admonishes Sir Telegraph to 'Read ancient books, the only source of permanent happiness in this degenerate world' (ii, 272). At the same time he acts the part of a traditional comic hero.

If in *Melincourt* Peacock writes comedy almost in spite of himself, or at least in spite of the dictates of his satire, comedy does nevertheless raise its voice. It is the final as well as the first voice we hear.

4

Nightmare Abbey:
a Little Daylight on
the Atrabilarious

C'est une compagnie étrange
MOLIÈRE, *Le Misanthrope.*

I

In February of 1819, some three months after the publication
of *Nightmare Abbey*, Mary Mitford spoke of Peacock's novel in a
letter to a friend: 'I have been laughing at *Nightmare Abbey*, the
pleasantest of all Mr. Peacock's works, whether in verse or
prose, *Rhodo-daphne* and *Melincourt* included. I have not met
with a more cheerful or amiable piece of *raillerie*.'[1] Miss Mitford, herself devoted to the 'cheerful' and 'amiable', knew what
she was praising. Peacock could hardly have found a more
proper or sympathetic response to his work. He had written to
Shelley in September 1818 that the purpose of the novel was
'merely to bring to a sort of philosophic focus a few of the morbidities of modern literature, and to let in a little daylight on its
atrabilarious complexion' (VIII, 204). His most carefully
ordered and carefully written story, *Nightmare Abbey* does more
than merely let in a little daylight—but it does that too.[2] It
offers a trenchant critique of certain tendencies of thought and
literary types of the period, before the *idea* of an English
romanticism actually became current. Written shortly before
the 'Essay on Fashionable Literature', *Nightmare Abbey* makes
some of the same judgments as the essay, but it makes them, as
Miss Mitford realized, with good-humoured raillery.

Peacock seems to have begun the novel in the spring of 1818,
and Shelley, who left for Italy in March, must have had some
prior information. He concludes a letter from Milan, in April,
with this laughing admission: 'See, I have sent you a study for

Night Mare Abbey.'[3] Shelley's letters of these months are filled
with requests for information, either about Peacock's activities
or about the new work. As usual, Peacock tells little about himself, but he suggests in May that he thinks 'it necessary to
"make a stand" against the "encroachments" of black bile'
(VIII, 193). Although a stronger rationale for his novel than that
of 'merely' letting in daylight, he wrote this before the novel
itself had been completed, and he modifies his statement with
the irony of the quotation marks. Shelley, taking a hint from the
phrase 'black bile', forwarded to Peacock a passage from Ben
Jonson. 'We have found an excellent quotation', he writes, 'in
Ben Jonson's *Every Man in His Humour*. . . . The last expression
would not make a bad motto.'[4] He refers to Stephen's lines,
'Have you a stool there, to be melancholy upon?' Peacock
found the whole passage an apt motto, and added it to the
novel, which he had completed by mid-June.

Nightmare Abbey appeared about eight months after the
publication of *Rhododaphne*. It was Peacock's first novel after the
close of his poetic career; it was also the last novel he completed before entering the service of the India House. Had it
perhaps sold more (there was no second edition before 1837),
the 'author of *Headlong Hall*' might have proved a more prolific
novelist. But it is hardly likely that he would have proved a
much different one, for there is nothing of public service or of
the India House in the later works: *Gryll Grange*, despite some
changed ideas, is no less iconoclastic than *Nightmare Abbey*.

Once again a novel of the proportions of *Headlong Hall*,
Nightmare Abbey is, as Miss Mitford remarked, a literary rather
than political satire. Whereas *Melincourt* drubs Coleridge,
Southey, Scott, Croker, and Wordsworth in passing, it con-
centrates largely on social ills, and treats the poets as political
spokesmen and examples. *Nightmare Abbey* has little mention of
politics and also, significantly, no character resembling Wordsworth, whom Peacock attacked in *Melincourt*, not as poet, but as
political turncoat. Mr. Flosky—Peacock's best caricature of
Coleridge—may speak parenthetically about the Revolution:
'Tea has shattered our nerves,' he says, 'late dinners make us
slaves of indigestion; the French Revolution has made us
shrink from the name of philosophy, and has destroyed, in the
more refined part of the community (of which number I am

one), all enthusiasm for political liberty . . .' (III, 50),[5] but excepting this and one or two other sallies—including the footnote at Burke's expense, mentioned earlier—the focus of the satire rests elsewhere. There is some slight indication that Shelley, himself a minor pamphleteer, played a part in the conception of *Melincourt*. In *Nightmare Abbey* Shelley provides hints for what Mario Praz might call the eclipsed hero of the work, Scythrop Glowry. ('Scythrop': 'of a sullen countenance.') Few would deny that Shelley, especially as young, unacknowledged legislator, serves better as the object than as the perpetrator of comedy.

II

As in *Headlong Hall* and *Melincourt*, Peacock creates in *Nightmare Abbey* a 'venerable family mansion' for the setting of his story. But he limits himself even more in this novel, since nearly all of the action and talk occurs in either the main chambers of the Abbey or in Scythrop's secret quarters. Scythrop and his father, Christopher Glowry, live in their isolated residence, 'pleasantly situated on a strip of dry land between the sea and the fens' (III, 1). Like nearly all of Peacock's young heroes and heroines, Scythrop has no mother. Presumably he is better off without her. Christopher Glowry, having 'offered his hand, from pique, to a lady, who accepted it from interest', has led a married life no better than 'the life of a dog'. Fate, happily, makes recompense, for 'one morning, like Sir Leonine in Christabel, "he woke [*sic*] and found his lady dead", and remained a very consolate widower, with one small child' (III, 1–3). The one small child is Scythrop, who has grown up to share his father's practical love of Madeira and his theoretical love of melancholy.

After 'finishing his education', Scythrop has returned to the Abbey. He occupies his own tower, where, in delicious moroseness, he dabbles in metaphysics and dreams about the reformation of mankind. Although at an early age and in the family tradition crossed in love, he is, unlike the elder Glowry, an idealist about women, whom he wants to see 'emancipated', and also something of an intellectual. Already he is a budding author, his first publication having sold to the promising tune of seven copies.

Scythrop proceeded to meditate on the practicability of
reviving a confederation of regenerators. To get a clear
view of his own ideas, and to feel the pulse of the wisdom
and genius of the age, he wrote and published a treatise,
in which his meanings were carefully wrapt up in the
monk's hood of transcendental technology, but filled with
hints of matter deep and dangerous, which he thought
would set a whole nation in a ferment; and he awaited the
result in awful expectation . . . and some months afterwards he received a letter from his bookseller, informing
him that only seven copies had been sold, and concluding
with a polite request for the balance.

Scythrop did not despair. 'Seven copies,' he thought,
'have been sold. Seven is a mystical number, and the omen
is good' (III, 16).[6]

A kind of male counterpart to Jane Austen's Catherine Mor-
land (*Northanger Abbey*, though written earlier, appeared in the
same year as *Nightmare Abbey*), Scythrop similarly fashions his
ideals and his expectations on diverse strands of 'Gothic'
literature, although he reads more widely than Catherine. Like
Jane Austen, Peacock thrusts his ingenuous character into a
situation not anticipated in his literature, and the result is a
comparable series of awkward recognitions and a gradual
weaning away from the poison fruit.

Nightmare Abbey itself has not merely an untenanted wing
like that in Northanger; it boasts the full-scale ruined wing that
Gothic romancers owed to Clara Reeve. It also has a fitting
complement of morose servants, such as Raven and Crow. A
sometime footman was Diggory Deathshead, who, unfortunately for Mr. Glowry's temperament, 'was always grinning,
—not a ghastly smile, but the grin of a comic mask'. Diggory's
'comic mask' and his ringing laughter bring about his dismissal, but not before he has made 'conquests of all the old
gentleman's maids, and left him a flourishing colony of young
Deathsheads to join chorus with the owls, that had before been
the exclusive choristers of Nightmare Abbey' (III, 8).

Devoted as he and Scythrop are to melancholy, the elder
Glowry nevertheless creates a distinctively hospitable residence;
and if solitude and pensive musing are his ideal, at the time of

the story the Abbey is paradoxically full of diverse guests. In addition to Mr. Flosky, there are Mr. Toobad, 'the Manichaean Millenarian', based on John Newton; Mr. Listless, the lethargic fop, perhaps owing something to Lumley Skeffington, a friend of Shelley;[7] the protean Reverend Mr. Larynx, 'who was always most obligingly ready to take a dinner'—in short, the traditional parasite; Mr. Asterias, 'the ichthyologist', forever searching after mermaids; and Mr. Cypress, a fine portrait of the Byronic hero, who is about to leave for distant climes. Only Mr. Hilary, a good-natured and epicurean gentleman, and an *adversarius* for the other characters, verges on anything resembling balanced intelligence. Though a relative, he is to the Glowrys the least welcome of the guests who converge on the Abbey to air their respective distempers.

Peacock does not create a caricature related to William Godwin, but he introduces the spirit of Godwin when Mr. Flosky comments with unexpected lucidity on Godwin's *Mandeville*: ' "*Devilman*, a novel." Hm. Hatred—revenge—misanthropy—and quotations from the Bible. Hm. This is indeed the morbid anatomy of black bile' (III, 39). The novel was a morbid anatomy, and a depressingly long one. If Shelley, who had shortly before reviewed Godwin's novel, admired Godwin with an energy second only to Hazlitt's, Peacock's reaction was adequately distilled into Flosky's apt synopsis. A small point that has been overlooked about *Nightmare Abbey* and seems worth remarking is that part of Peacock's intent is to burlesque Godwin's book. *Mandeville* had appeared in the preceding year; it was one of those 'fashionable' books, which Mr. Listless describes as being rushed by mail-coach from Edinburgh to London, then forwarded express to the reading public. The setting of a large part of Godwin's story is the fens, 'a striking scene of desolation' with 'portions of bog and marshy ground'. Godwin's narrator, with Godwin's usual circumlocution, says, 'The whole situation was eminently insalubrious'. And in the insalubrious situation Godwin creates a castle with 'one wing only that was now tenanted', and draws a character who, crossed in love, lives there because the gloom and fog 'suited the frame of his mind'. 'He loved his sadness, for it had become a part of himself' is an absurd line, like many others in *Mandeville*, that Peacock echoes in *Nightmare Abbey*.[8] There can be little doubt that one of the offending perpetrators of black bile against whom he directed his irony was the author of *Mandeville*.

Much of the story of *Nightmare Abbey* also seems to lampoon *Mandeville*, especially its sentimental love complications, but one could argue that Godwin himself was the unwitting lampoonist of a whole rash of earlier Gothic and sentimental romances, from Mrs. Radcliffe's to the Marquis of Grosse's— whose *Horrid Mysteries* raises its head in *Nightmare* as in *Northanger Abbey*—and therefore that the resemblances are accidental.

Another fact that argues against Peacock's twisting *Mandeville*'s plot in the burlesquing mirror of his mind is the more obvious similarities his story has with two of Goethe's works that were famous at the time. To the silliest aspect of *Mandeville*, its self-parodic setting, Peacock appends situations from Goethe's *Stella*, with its classic Goethean love triangle, and from the *Sorrows of Young Werther*, with its sentimental catastrophe. (In 'The Four Ages' he speaks of Werther as a 'drivelling puler'.)[9] And he alludes specifically to both *Stella* and *Werther*. The story of *Nightmare Abbey* does not need the reference to Goethe in order to make sense, but our awareness of the relationship makes its humour that much richer. The plot in this novel is rather more complex—with its recognition scene and reversal— than is usual in Peacock's fiction, and Peacock takes pains to develop it.

For about the first quarter of the story there is noticeably less of the crotchet-brandishing that fills *Headlong Hall*; instead Peacock develops situations with a view towards the ultimate catastrophe. Scythrop's attentions are at first directed to Miss Marionetta Celestina O'Carroll, the niece of Mr. Hilary. Marionetta exhibits 'in her own character all the diversities of an April sky':

> Whether she was touched with a *penchant* for her cousin
> Scythrop, or was merely curious to see what effect the
> tender passion would have on so *outré* a person, she had
> not been three days in the Abbey before she threw out all
> the lures of her beauty and accomplishments to make a
> prize of his heart . . . he soon became distractedly in love;
> which, when the young lady clearly perceived, she altered

her tactics, and assumed as much coldness and reserve as
she had before shown ardent and ingenuous attachment
(III, 21–2).

Meanwhile, Mr. Toobad—whose main conversational gambit
is that 'the devil is come among you, having great wrath'—
together with Mr. Glowry, has been trying to arrange a marriage between Scythrop and Toobad's daughter, Celinda.
Unfortunately, Celinda is an 'emancipated' young lady,
strongly opposed to any such parental authority. Rather than
submit to her father's will, she runs away and, being one of the
seven mystical readers of Scythrop's treatise, understandably
seeks refuge with just the man she is trying to avoid. Scythrop
conceals her in secret chambers.

The two ladies, in some ways reminiscent of Shelley's Harriet
and Mary—Shelley himself at times lived a parody of sentimental romances—place poor Scythrop in an awkward predicament. He finds himself in love with them both. Peacock
naturally exploits the humorous possibilities of having a beautiful young lady parading ghost-like about the Abbey. Mr.
Asterias is convinced that he has seen his long-awaited mermaid
—for him, mermaids are 'the orang-outangs of the sea'—and
Mr. Flosky can expatiate on the philosophical and personal
implications of ghosts. 'I can safely say'—this in parody of
Coleridge's notorious comment—

> I have seen too many ghosts myself to believe in their
> external existence. I have seen all kinds of ghosts: black
> spirits and white, red spirits and grey. Some in the shape
> of venerable old men, who have met me in my rambles at
> noon; some of beautiful young women, who have peeped
> through my curtains at midnight (III, 120).

To which Mr. Listless adds, 'And have proved, I doubt not,
"palpable to feeling as to sight".' Peacock leaves the sexual
innuendo, like several others in *Nightmare Abbey*, as innuendo.
Byron was to go a step farther. The ghostly friar in Canto xvi
of *Don Juan* who materializes as her frolic Grace, Fitz-Fulke,
conceivably owes her existence to Peacock's mysterious lady.[10]
If Don Juan knows what to do after his confrontation,

Scythrop does not. Unable to choose between the 'enlightened'
Celinda—who calls herself 'Stella' after Goethe's character—
and the fickle Marionetta, and finally discovered in conversation with the secret lady, Scythrop contrives to lose both his
loves at once. And to divide, here, is to take away, for both
ladies promptly disappear and just as promptly marry Flosky
and Listless. Werther-like, Scythrop plans, or rather threatens,
suicide if the elder Glowry fails to return with either Celinda or
Marionetta—he doesn't care which. But he neither gets his
wish nor pulls the trigger. His father, sounding like Enobarbus
on the death of Fulvia, consoles him; and Scythrop abandons
himself once more to self-imposed and disingenuous despair.
The novel ends with his call to 'Bring some Madeira'.[11]

III

Madeira—or port, or claret—a regular ingredient in all of
Peacock's novels, affords the fitting antidote, not just to
Scythrop's fashionable brooding, but equally to the sombre
pronouncements of most of the characters. Typically, but with
his own lucid directness, Mr. Glowry says, 'Let us all be unhappy together.' Clearly most of the characters have assembled
in the Abbey to enjoy 'the dark lantern of the spirit', the gloom
that Peacock himself had peddled in *The Philosophy of Melancholy*. Their ideas, however, remain one thing, their actions
another, for all of Glowry's guests pass the bottle with despatch
and talk and drink with glee. Because they share a gloomy
conviviality, they can propose the following remarkable toast:

MR. GLOWRY: You are leaving England, Mr. Cypress.
There is a delightful melancholy in saying farewell to an
old acquaintance, when the chances are twenty to one
against ever meeting again. A smiling bumper to a sad
parting, and let us all be unhappy together.
MR. CYPRESS (*filling a bumper*). This is the only social
habit that the disappointed spirit never unlearns.
THE REVEREND MR. LARYNX (*filling*). It is the only piece
of academical learning that the finished educatee retains.
MR. FLOSKY (*filling*). It is the only objective fact which the
sceptic can realize.

SCYTHROP (*filling*). It is the only styptic for a bleeding heart.

THE HONOURABLE MR. LISTLESS (*filling*). It is the only trouble that is very well worth taking.

MR. ASTERIAS (*filling*). It is the only key of conversational truth.

MR. TOOBAD (*filling*). It is the only antidote to the great wrath of the devil.

MR. HILARY (*filling*). It is the only symbol of perfect life. The inscription 'NON HIC BIBITUR' will suit nothing but a tombstone (III, 100–1).

As the bumper to a sad parting helps to illustrate, the dialogue in *Nightmare Abbey* takes a somewhat different turn from that in *Melincourt* and more nearly approximates the conversations in *Headlong Hall*. One problem with *Melincourt* is the length of the speeches, the tendency of the characters to talk beyond the point where their comments remain witty and to become long-winded. What is true of the characters in *Melincourt* is also true of the narrator himself, who is seldom willing enough to let his characters carry the burden of implication. *Nightmare Abbey* looks back to *Headlong Hall* in its rapidity and economy of movement, but its dialogue and narrative are, for want of a better word, more sophisticated than those of the first novel. Although the voices and the combinations of dialogue are to some extent varied in *Headlong Hall*, almost every character speaks with the same rhetorical patterns; in *Nightmare Abbey* Peacock alters his dialogue, adjusting it to meet the needs of the story and the traits and moods of the characters.[12] For this reason his using the motto from Ben Jonson was apt, not only because he satirizes melancholy, in its various postures, but because he effects here a relationship between the voices and the humours they represent. Mr. Cypress, the morbid and self-pitying young poet, speaks a continual pastiche both of ordinary sentimental jargon and of Byron's actual lines:

I have no hope for myself or for others. Our life is a false nature; it is not in the harmony of things; it is an all-blasting upas, whose root is earth, and whose leaves are the skies which rain their poison-dews upon mankind. We

wither from our youth; we gasp with unslaked thirst for
unattainable good; lured from the first to the last by
phantoms—love, fame, ambition, avarice—all idle, and all
ill—one meteor of many names, that vanishes in the smoke
of death.

Mr. Flosky speaks with a comparable egotism but with the
syntax of a pedant:

A most delightful speech, Mr. Cypress. A most amiable
and instructive philosophy. You have only to impress its
truth on the minds of all living men, and life will then,
indeed, be the desert and the solitude, and I must do you,
myself, and our mutual friends, the justice to observe, that
let society only give fair play . . . to your system of morals,
and my system of metaphysics, and Scythrop's system of
politics . . ., and the result will be as fine a mental chaos
as even the immortal Kant himself could ever have hoped
to see; in the prospect of which I rejoice (III, 104–5).

And Mr. Toobad—a sort of one-stringed Alceste—speaks in a
garbled admixture of *Revelation* and *Isaiah* together with the
shrill tones of a John Newton or Joseph Ritson:

It is our calamity. The devil has come among us, and
has begun by taking possession of all the cleverest fellows.
Yet, forsooth, this is the enlightened age. Marry, how?
Did our ancestors go peeping about with dark lanterns,
and do we walk at our ease in broad sunshine?

We see a hundred men hanged, where they saw one. We
see five hundred transported, where they saw one. We see
five thousand in the workhouse, where they saw one. We
see scores of Bible Societies, where they saw none. We see
paper, where they saw gold.

In short they saw true men, where we see false knaves.
They saw Milton, and we see Mr. Sackbut [Robert
Southey] (III, 105–6).

Whereas in *Melincourt* Peacock takes sides too often, letting his narrator sound little different from, say, Mr. Fax or Mr. Forester, in *Nightmare Abbey* he creates a relationship between the narrator and the characters that is much more satisfactory. In the first place, he paraphrases brilliantly, allowing the dialogue to emerge from the recounting of events, so that the talk may be brief and to the point. At times he dispenses with ordinary and space-consuming narrative by the abbreviation of stage directions, often mock stage directions. He interrupts a monologue at one point by saying : '(*Mr. Flosky suddenly stopped : he found himself unintentionally trespassing within the limits of common sense.*)' Elsewhere he inserts the italicized comments into a speech, so as to present with absurd abruptness, the reactions of the other character. For this device he may be indebted to Sterne, who uses it with similar effect throughout *Tristram Shandy*. Marionetta says:

> I see, Mr. Flosky, you think my intrusion unseasonable, and are inclined to punish it, by talking nonsense to me. (*Mr. Flosky gave a start at the word nonsense, which almost overturned the table.*) I assure you, I would not have intruded if I had not been very much interested. . . .—(*Mr. Flosky listened in sullen dignity.*)—My cousin Scythrop seems to have some secret preying on his mind.—(*Mr. Flosky was silent.*)—He seems very unhappy—Mr. Flosky (iii, 76).

In addition to the stage directions or asides, Peacock uses another technique to achieve humour and concision. In the brief dénouement he moves out of dialogue and narrative altogether and, in parody of *Werther* and of so many other epistolary novels of sensibility, relates information by letters from Scythrop's departed lovers. This is not typical, but it is illustrative of his general tendency in this novel to experiment with a greater range of narrative devices and also to give the illusion of a story that tells or shows itself, as though the narrator merely introduced characters or prepared the stage to let things happen. One is aware of a story-teller, of a manipulating and ironic personality. But Peacock makes sure that he never quite loses his anonymity, never quite comes on stage.[13]

Reflective of the economy and brevity of *Nightmare Abbey* is the unusually small number of songs. Despite references to Mozart and other composers, the characters perform only three songs—though what they do perform rank among Peacock's best. One, 'a catch', has often found its way into anthologies. It offers another example of the light, uninhibited song about food or drink that Leigh Hunt found too little represented in English verse:

> Seamen three! What men be ye?
> Gotham's three wise men we be.
> Whither in your bowl so free?
> To rake the moon from out the sea.
> The bowl grows trim. The moon doth shine.
> And our ballast is old wine;
> And your ballast is old wine (III, 112).

The other song, fittingly performed by Mr. Cypress, offers an incomparable parady of *Childe Harold*; George Saintsbury, among others, called it one of the best parodies in the language:

> There is a fever of the spirit,
>   The brand of Cain's unresting doom,
> Which in the lone dark souls that bear it
>   Glows like the lamp in Tullia's tomb:
> Unlike that lamp, its subtle fire
>   Burns, blasts, consumes its cell, the heart,
> Till, one by one, hope, joy, desire,
>   Like dreams of shadowy smoke depart.
>
> When hope, love, life itself, are only
>   Dust—spectral memories—dead and cold—
> The unfed fire burns bright and lonely,
>   Like that undying lamp of old:
> And by that drear illumination,
>   Till time its clay-built home has rent,
> Thought broods on feeling's desolation—
>   The soul is its own monument (III, 111).

Evidently highly amused by Mr. Cypress, Byron requested that Shelley forward a rose-bud to Peacock in token of his appreciation, and perhaps to compliment him at the same time on *Rhododaphne*. Byron, like Mary Mitford, realized the amiable quality of the novel. Shelley himself could write: 'I am delighted with *Nightmare Abbey*. I think Scythrop a character admirably conceived & executed; & I know not how to praise sufficiently the lightness, chastity & strength of the language of the whole. It perhaps exceeds all your works in this.'[14] Shelley even compared the tower of the Villa Valsavano, where he composed *The Cenci*, to Scythrop's tower, and, as Peacock wrote in the memoirs, 'took to himself the character of Scythrop'.

IV

Peacock's portrait of Scythrop and Mr. Cypress and Byron's and Shelley's response to the portraits reintroduce a matter touched on in earlier sections that is pertinent to *Nightmare Abbey*. The novel has been enjoyed by generations of readers after Shelley and Byron—it remains, very likely, Peacock's best-known novel—and has been objected to only by 'some of Shelley's admirers [who] have resented *Nightmare Abbey* on his behalf'.[15] There is no need here to labour the argument that Shelley the man has little to do with Shelley as Scythrop, except to emphasize that for the most part this portrait too depicts the public personality and incorporates more than the young Shelley's foibles. There are, however, related questions about the nature of Peacock's criticism, and the nature of a book that poses as mere burlesque, which need to be raised.

In a pair of essays about what he calls the 'social satires' of Peacock, John Draper maintains that because Peacock is a critic, or because he consistently finds fault—Draper equates the two—for Peacock 'human nature is gone wrong'. Draper merely summarizes what has been a fairly common response to Peacock's writing, but it is a response that simply will not do. After all, what reader of *Nightmare Abbey* could seriously argue that Peacock 'affirms the intellectual pessimism and social bankruptcy' of his times?[16] Listen to Mr. Hilary, who seems so often to speak for his author, and at least speaks against the advocates of intellectual pessimism and social bankruptcy within Nightmare Abbey:

To expect too much is a disease in the expectant, for which human nature is not responsible; and, in the common name of humanity, I protest against these false and mischievous ravings. To rail against humanity for not being abstract perfection, and against human love for not realizing all the splendid visions of the poets of chivalry, is to rail at the summer for not being all sunshine, and at the rose for not being always in bloom (III, 107–8).

Mr. Hilary's words are typical of the kind of statement Peacock scatters throughout his writings, typical of his satire upon just the sort of easy negativism of which Draper summarily accuses him.

Hilary's comments and the narrator's collaborating irony make clear that Peacock judged many of the intellectual trends of the age in terms of their ill-effects on the way men lived as well as the way they wrote. (This was of course to be a central concern in 'The Four Ages', written a little over a year later.) It is true that 'If he provides a moral, it concerns outlook, not conduct',[17] though it is no less true that he offers a fairly consistent antidote to what he thought to be unfortunate intellectual as well as mechanical tendencies of the early nineteenth century.[18] One does not have to agree with the terms of his criticism, but one must recognize that he has a legitimate criticism to make, and that anger itself has not only a privilege but a disguise. Peacock speaks in *Nightmare Abbey* about the road connecting, or separating, the Abbey from 'civilization'. Like *Headlong Hall* and the other novels to follow, *Nightmare Abbey* offers an alternative civilization of its own, which Peacock makes clear is not much more representative of mankind's 'crazy fabric' than the world out there. He uses the term 'civilization' as he was to use it in 'The Four Ages' with more than a touch of irony. Nevertheless, he thinks in terms of civilization—of common sense, of a humane epicureanism, of tolerance, of a theoretical social order—all of which underlie his laughter at types of mental bondage.

Related to the point of view that sees Peacock simply as a misguided, embittered or shallow pessimist is that which admits his critical acumen but denies him talents of any other kind. More important because more acute and sympathetic than Draper's statements is a little essay by Humphry House, who argues that Peacock 'is not primarily an artist or novelist, but

a critic, a critic abnormally sensitive to the important movements of the mind and spirit of his age'. There are several
questionable assumptions underlying Mr. House's comment.
The phrase 'abnormally sensitive', for example, implies an
unhealthy critical response or a mental quirk. It recalls the
kind of charge that used to be brought against Swift and Pope,
the kind of biographical explanation that may have been fact
but that can be misleading in assessing the works. But this
is not the chief problem with the argument. 'Peacock is not
primarily an artist', says Mr. House—because he is a critic. He
is 'doing in his own medium the same sort of thing that Hazlitt
was doing in . . . the *Spirit of the Age*; and Hazlitt is the best
introduction to Peacock'.[19]

Certainly *Nightmare Abbey* is analogous to the *Spirit of the Age*,
offering a series of portraits, if not of individuals, of representative writers and thinkers, and implying that the best
literary times are past. But to compare Peacock with Hazlitt is
to recognize an essential difference between the two, a difference
made evident by the phrase 'in his medium'. Hazlitt's characteristic mode of criticism is the essay, a genre that he uses for
direct and personal commentary. Even Hazlitt's lectures have
the virtues and take the form of the personal essay. Peacock, too,
writes critical essays. He has the reviews of Moore, 'Fashionable
Literature', the memoirs of Shelley, and 'The Four Ages'. But
his characteristic mode is fiction. When Hazlitt tried his hand
at fiction the result was the painful, the terribly honest but ill-
considered *Liber Amoris*. Peacock neither could nor wanted to
write confessional literature. He was no more capable of writing
a *Liber Amoris* than a series of essays like the *Spirit of the Age*, any
more than Hazlitt was capable of writing a *Nightmare Abbey*.
For Peacock, Robert Owen becomes Mr. Toogood of *Crotchet
Castle*; Malthus becomes Mr. Fax of *Melincourt*; Monboddo, or
his theories, are transformed into Sir Oran; Coleridge turns
into Mr. Mystic or Mr. Flosky. Such men are treated ironically
within fiction, within a medium in which everything and everyone is substantially changed—changed sometimes beyond the
point where recognition is important.

And this surely is an 'artistic' medium. *Nightmare Abbey* is a
precise, a complete, a beautifully manipulated fictional world.
The Abbey, moreover, would live if the poets or ideas it depicts

were forgotten—as in part they already are—because it has gained an independence from mere portrait-painting and because its humour rests on more than burlesque. It may be, as Leigh Hunt wrote, that Peacock, as a necessary spirit of satire, was Momus alive again in the nineteenth century. But Momus in fictional guise is another spirit entirely.

Maid Marian:
the 'Masked Ball'

Honour to bold Robin Hood,
Sleeping in the underwood!
Honour to Maid Marian,
And to all the Sherwood-clan!
Though their days have hurried by
Let us two a burden try.

JOHN KEATS, 'Robin Hood' (1818).

I

Maid Marian was one of the three or four literary projects that
Peacock put aside when, in January 1819, he accepted employment with the East India Company and left the village of
Marlow for London. Unlike the poem about nympholepsy and
the essay 'Fashionable Literature', *Maid Marian* did see completion, although not for several years to come. Apparently
most of the book had taken form in 1818, and one wonders
about Peacock's reluctance to finish it. Was his time really so
limited during the next three years? Or was he perhaps inclined
not to finish a work about which he had doubts, knowing that
there were faults in it related to those in the fragment 'Calidore',
which he had left incomplete two years before?

Questions arise about *Maid Marian* because it represented for
Peacock another direction in fiction from either *Melincourt* or
Nightmare Abbey, another experiment in narrative and in the
possibilities for satire. Although in certain respects a culmination of what had been pointed to in the earlier stories, it was also
a new venture and a venture that was only partly successful.

To suggest that *Maid Marian* is Peacock at his closest both to
the *Waverley* novels and to John Gay's *Beggar's Opera*, and that
two literary modes are at work within the story may offer a
way of pointing to Peacock's difficulties. *Maid Marian* is an

in-between book: half comic opera, half novelistic idyll; or half social satire, half genuine, if humorous, romance. Of course an attempt to mix characteristics of both genres was not inevitably to fall between the two stools. Behind Scott's stories there is often the sustaining chuckle of the uncommitted narrator; behind Gay's burlesque there is the rural or pastoral ideal, an insistent if implicit alternative to the corrupt and false values in the England of the time. Peacock's story of Robin Hood and Marian is largely narrative, or presents dialogue in a narrative frame, and it is set like some of Scott's stories in a distant past. It is also a work that, more than Peacock's other novels, approximates comic opera; and in its 'airs' as in much of its satire it is reminiscent of Gay's burlesque opera. What Peacock fails to do in this work is to establish his, and thus the reader's, response to the material—to the love story, to the satiric inversions of the time and place—and the result is a book discontinuous in structure and inconsistent in tone.

If Gay was at the back of Peacock's mind when he conceived of *Maid Marian*, Scott was clearly in the foreground, possibly too much in the foreground, when he wrote. The relationship between *Headlong Hall* and *Waverley* has been touched on earlier; the relationship between *Maid Marian* and *Ivanhoe* is much more direct.

It need not be, as Henry Newbolt wrote, 'a remarkable coincidence' that two men should begin works about Robin Hood at roughly the same time (the summer of 1818), but it may seem remarkable that Peacock was one of them.[1] Who would have expected of the author of *Nightmare Abbey* a work about the folk hero of Sherwood?

When he published *Maid Marian* in 1822, Peacock added a prefatory note: 'This little work, with the exception of the last three chapters, was written in the autumn of 1818.' *Ivanhoe* had appeared in 1819, and Peacock evidently felt the need to indicate that he had not borrowed from Scott's work or that he was not intentionally burlesquing it. (He had, as a matter of fact, borrowed from one of Scott's own sources, Joseph Ritson's *Robin Hood*, though he had not used Ritson on a hint from Scott.) At first glance, the prefatory note draws attention to a link with *Ivanhoe* that few readers would otherwise have considered, for Peacock's treatment of the Robin Hood legends seems markedly different from Scott's. Whereas Peacock casually ignores everything but the adventures of Robin and Marian in and about Sherwood, 'the enchanter of the north' draws a historical panorama in which the outlaw band plays only a decorative role. There is nothing in *Maid Marian* of the dark, silent hero—nothing of the shadowy Ivanhoe. Nor is there anything of Rowena or Rebecca; Peacock's Marian has, according to one account, not the silent modesty of Scott's heroines, but 'beauty, grace, wit, sense, discretion, dexterity, learning, and valour' (III, 10). She can shoot a bow and arrow, wrestle with King Richard and she adopts the green attire of the foresters. Yet she maintains a certain modesty and is said to keep her forest vow of chastity. Unlike Rowena's, but quite like Rosalind's, her songs are light, her words satiric. She is a livelier version of Anthelia Melincourt and a recognizable figure of romantic comedy. Appropriately, she, not the talkative but essentially simple and hedonistic Robin Hood, accounts for the title.

There are a few parallels between the two novels. And perhaps before publishing *Maid Marian* Peacock lifted one or two phrases or even scenes from *Ivanhoe*. His 'siege' of Arlingford Castle could easily be a literary spoof on the related scene in Scott, perhaps added when the story was essentially complete. But Peacock's note need not be discounted; nor, on the other hand, does it make any less immediate his relationship with Scott's works. He had been reading Scott's lays and romances for some time, had recently congratulated Scott in 'Fashionable Literature'. That he did have Scott in mind as he worked on the novel is indicated by his having quoted from *Marmion* at the head of Chapter I. Pleased with Scott's works, he may have wanted to submit the material of romance to a comic mode— as Cervantes, Fielding, and so many other of his favourite writers had done before—and in a way which, unlike that of *Nightmare Abbey*, would approximate the object to be parodied.

The author of *Waverley* admitted that he strove for originality in his treatment of *Ivanhoe*, hoping to 'obtain an interest for the traditions and manners of Old England, similar to that which has been excited in behalf of those of our poorer and less celebrated neighbours'.[2] Determined to give his narrative the credibility of history by the use of authentic-sounding detail,

Scott develops, enlarges, transforms whatever he borrows from his sources. He tells his story from that particularly self-assured vantage-point: as though he were an all-knowing and benevolent uncle. Peacock, quite unconcerned with originality of material, shares with Scott a detached point of view, but he is not content with Scott's gentle humour of character and situation. Compare these two analogous passages. In the first, from *Ivanhoe*, the fool Wamba answers the worldly Prior Aymer:

> 'It is true,' replied Wamba, 'that I, being but an ass, am, nevertheless, honoured to bear the bells of servitude as well as your reverence's mule; notwithstanding, I did conceive that the charity of Mother Church and her servants might be said, with other charity, to begin at home.'[3]

Even at his most ironic—and most hackneyed—Scott is easy and mild. But listen to Peacock's Friar Tuck in a typically explosive vein:

> 'Punnest thou?' said the friar. 'A heinous anti-christian offence. Why anti-christian? Because anti-catholic. Why anti-catholic? Because anti-roman. Why anti-roman? Because Carthaginian. Is not pun from Punic? *punica fides*: the very quint-essential quiddity of bad faith: double visaged: double tongued. He that will make a pun will—I say no more. Fie on it' (III, 105-6).

The satiric Dr. Folliott of *Crotchet Castle*, insisting that Scott's works 'contain nothing worth quoting' (IV, 121)—and no doubt forgetting 'by my halidome', which, if it is not actually worth quoting, is at least repeated often enough to stay in the memory—helps to identify his author's approach to romance. Peacock strives, not for historical authenticity, but for a witty portrayal. As usual in his novels, the *how* becomes more important than the *what*. 'I am writing', he tells Shelley in November 1818, 'a comic Romance of the Twelfth Century, which I shall make the vehicle of much oblique satire on all the oppressions that are done under the sun' (VIII, 209). For Peacock the twelfth century represents a vague time in the distant past, when people would drink Canary—before the islands were rediscovered—and when any sort of anachronistic thing might happen without the author worrying about credibility. If it is true, as Peacock writes in 'French Comic Romances', that 'fiction should regard probability even in trifles' (IX, 36), then *Maid Marian* is sloppy fiction indeed. A man with genuine appreciation of the Middle Ages could have thrashed Peacock for inattentions in *Maid Marian* as Peacock himself was to thrash Moore for the flaws in the *Epicurean*. He was neither thorough in his researches nor concerned about being thorough. His diary of 1818 reads: 'Could not read or write for scheming my romance. Rivers castles abbies monks maids kings and banditti dancing before me like a masked ball' (VIII, 440). The Rabelaisian list is not inappropriate for a novel that occasionally echoes Rabelais and that offers at least one character who approximates a character in *Gargantua*. Friar Tuck clearly belongs to the same family as Frère Jean, and is capable of a comparable torrent of words. Yet the manner of Peacock's book is not really Rabelaisian at all.[4] It *is* that of the masked ball— the characters are largely featureless, their actions conventional; and the list of 'monks maids kings and banditti' augurs for roles and types rather than for individuated characters or Peacock's usual spokesmen.

II

The opening chapter makes clear the masked ball qualities and illustrates some of the faults with the narrative. The narrator begins with purportedly factual description of his scene, where all is in readiness for the wedding of the Earl of Huntingdon— Robin Hood to be—and Matilda Fitzwater—Marian to be. There stands the waiting bride; there her father; there the abbot; and—a possible source of suspense—the groom has not arrived. However, Peacock is not interested in suspense. Already in the second sentence he runs off at a tangent: 'The abbey of Rubygill', says the narrator, 'stood in a picturesque valley, at a little distance from the western boundary of Sherwood Forest, in a spot which seemed adapted by nature to be the retreat of monastic mortification, being on the banks of a fine trout stream . . .' (III, 1). When he moves his scene into the chapel and focuses on the galloping approach of the groom, he is

observing the characters but as though from a distance. Significantly, as the ceremony gets under way, the narrator swings
up to the organ-loft, and watches through the eyes of the organ-
blower and organist. The perspective is similar to Stendhal's as
Fabrizio looks down from the church tower:

> The organ-blower, who was working his musical air pump
> with one hand, and with two fingers and a thumb of the
> other insinuating a peeping place through the curtain of
> the organ gallery, was struck motionless by the double
> operation of curiosity and fear; while the organist, intent
> only on his performance, and spreading all his fingers to
> strike a swell of magnificent chords, felt his harmonic spirit
> ready to depart his body on being answered by the ghastly
> rattle of empty keys . . . (III, 3).

Sir Ralph Montfaucon, acting as bad Prince John's ineffectual
and not very hateful agent, interrupts the ceremony—which of
course has to be completed at the novel's close—and occasions
a brawl. Peacock calls the fight a 'desperate skirmish', but
records it, however, in this tangential way:

> Some of the women screamed, but none of them fainted;
> for fainting was not so much the fashion in those days,
> when the ladies breakfasted on brawn and ale at sunrise,
> as in our more refined age of green tea and muffins at
> noon. . . . The earl's bowmen at the door sent in among
> the assailants a volley of arrows, one of which whizzed past
> the ear of the abbot, who, in mortal fear of being suddenly
> translated from ghostly friar into a friarly ghost, began to
> roll out of the chapel as fast as his bulk and his holy robes
> would permit . . . (III, 5–6).

Clearly Peacock is not much interested in his story, in the progression of events. The wedding ceremony, like the other
episodes to follow, is a complete account of one incident—from
the viewpoint of a puppeteer—which stands more or less independently. What it establishes above all is that however many
arrows fly and however many difficulties the hero and heroine
might have, all will be well.

Although the scene offers a certain amount of humour, the fact remains that it represents easy writing. The wit of the opening of *Nightmare Abbey* makes the writing here seem both inflated and pat. The translation of the 'ghostly friar into a friarly ghost' is not a very new turn of phrase and never was a very good one, but Peacock will repeat it later in the book. He will repeat other things too that were better left unsaid, such as the old nugget 'deemed it expedient'. He is not only repetitious, he greatly over-uses the semi-pompous, semi-antique language that was the stock-in-trade of dozens of minor writers. The laxity in the writing, not endemic to the whole book, touches most sections, and makes the narrative unsure. And there is more narrative in this than in the earlier stories, more narrative, and correspondingly less dialogue—and for this reason perhaps, less tension, less genuine wit.

Peacock's difficulties in the handling of the story may have arisen from his peculiar use of the Ritson material. Often his tone approximates Ritson's, and his story is in part a mere re-telling of Ritson's accounts. To borrow in this way is no fault in itself, but the new work must be made self-sufficient or independent of the sources. Jean-Jacques Mayoux shows how Peacock's narrative often becomes a simple paraphrase of the old ballads, or even of Ritson's notes.[5] And the effect is of a loose assembly of scenes, a procession of characters and events that never quite come into proper focus.

After the interrupted wedding, the story continues in this way : Robin Hood, intent on killing the king's deer and avoiding the king's agents—and quite incidentally in robbing and giving to the poor—retires with companions to the sanctity of the forest. Marian soon joins him. Her father, a Falstaffian quaffer and a hearty eater, is Baron of Arlingford, and for his own stubbornness and his daughter's beauty he too must finally go into exile. Prince John, resembling Lord Achthar of *Melincourt*, lays siege to his castle, forcing father and daughter to escape to Sherwood. Robin and Marian then escort the Baron to Yorkshire, engage in a skirmish or two, and return to their forest retreat. In disguise at his homecoming, Robin cracks skulls with Friar Tuck, who has left the forest gang and is posing as a ferryman. Then all meet King Richard—Robin's anti-Jacobin counterpart in the 'real' world—who unaccountably appears alone in Sherwood. There follows the recognition scene, the forgiveness; and all live splendidly ever after.

III

The direction of Peacock's satire, like his story, may have taken its clue from Ritson, who was quite a remarkable man and, as David Garnett puts it, 'an oddly Peacockian character'. Ritson's notes and introduction suggest that he used the Robin Hood material, at least partly, to express his own political convictions, the most important of which called for the distribution of wealth to those responsible for its creation. As an outlaw, a man rebelling against established order and established abuses, Robin Hood represented both a venerable literary personage and an ideal spokesman for old virtues; and Ritson was both an antiquarian and a confirmed Jacobin. Like Cobbett, he worried about the decline in English yeomanry and the increase of urban ills. A man who could speak of Holcroft as being 'one of the persons who had the honour to be indicted for high treason in 1794',[6] Ritson expresses what in him as in Cobbett, and to some extent in Peacock, becomes a kind of conservative radicalism, or what I have earlier called radical agrarianism. Defending Robin Hood's supposed reasons for robbing the rich and giving to the poor, Ritson says: 'In a word, every man who has the power has also the authority to pursue the ends of justice; to regulate the gifts of fortune, by transferring the superfluities of the rich to the necessities of the poor . . . even, when necessary, destroying the oppressor.'[7] In short, yeomen of the nation ought to unite. But Ritson's opinions and allegiances, much as they might ring of revolution, really look backward to imagined better times. In Marxist terms, he is lamenting the debasement of ideals, indeed the disruption of the nation, by the new capitalist hegemony. Yet his analysis remains a purview of isolated or at most indicative symptoms, and his Robin Hood offers a simple-minded alternative to illiberal political tendencies or unwelcome social change. Ritson even suggests that a current lack in the practice of archery bespeaks a general moral bankruptcy. Sharing with Peacock a reverence for Epicurus, the 'great master', and with Monboddo a faith in apes, he writes in praise of vegetarian regimen that the orang-outang 'never meddles with animal flesh'.[8] One wonders what, excepting turnips, Ritson would have had his archers shoot.

Both Scott and Peacock apparently take from Ritson the conclusion that Robin Hood rules *legitimately* as king of Sherwood. What better right 'King Richard could pretend to the territory and the people of England than Robin Hood had to the dominion of Barnsdale or Sherwood', Ritson says with his characteristic heavy irony, 'is a question humbly submitted to the consideration of the political philosopher'.[9] Whereas *Ivanhoe* works quietly on such an assumption, *Maid Marian* contains detailed and often intentionally absurd elaborations of the point. Friar Tuck, who seems to laugh in anticipation of Carlyle's 'hero worship', expounds it in this way:[10]

> Robin Hood is king of the forest both by dignity of birth and by virtue of his standing army: to say nothing of the free choice of his people, which he has indeed, but I pass it by as an illegitimate basis of power. He holds his dominion over the forest, and its horned multitude of citizen-deer, and its swinish multitude or peasantry of wild boars, by right of conquest and force of arms. He levies contributions among them by the free consent of his archers, their virtual representatives (III, 100).[11]

So Peacock parallels Scott and out-Ritsons Ritson. Yet the passage above, while it might be read as parody of either Scott or Ritson, is clearly reminiscent of another voice in another context. In the *Beggar's Opera*, Jemmy Twitcher says:

> But the present time is ours, and nobody alive hath more. Why are the laws levelled at us? Are we more dishonest than the rest of mankind? What we win, gentlemen, is our own, by the law of arms and the right of conquest.[12]

Granted Peacock may have found the stock phrases 'right of conquest and force of arms' elsewhere, but the supporting passage, the mock-righteousness of the speaker, the topsy-turvy satire on the establishment—these are all reminiscent of Gay's story of Polly and Macheath.

Peacock wanted to make his work 'a vehicle of much oblique satire', but most of his satire is no more oblique than Friar Tuck's lambasting of legitimacy. Whereas Gay levelled his charges at the political and social conditions under Robert Walpole, Peacock levels his at the post-Waterloo reactionism. His thrusts are at the Holy Alliance—the foresters live theoretically, on the 'principles of Legitimacy, Equity, Hospitality, Chivalry, Chastity, and Courtesy'—at the English fear of the 'swinish multitudes', as well as at the concept of 'legitimate', by which he understands 'powerful', rule. Except that the targets are different in details, or in the forms they take, they are the same targets that Gay had aimed at a century before.

Mat the Mint excuses the activities of Macheath's gang by arguing:

> We retrench the superfluities of mankind. The world is avaricious, and I hate avarice. A covetous fellow . . . steals what he was never meant to enjoy. . . . These are the robbers of mankind; for money was made for the free hearted and generous: and where is the injury of taking from another what he hath not the heart to make use of.[13]

One of the foresters' 'Laws of Equity' in *Maid Marian* states:

> The balance of power . . . being very much deranged, by one having too much and another nothing, we hereby resolve ourselves into a congress or court of equity, to restore as far as in us lies the said natural balance of power, by taking from all who have too much as much of the said too much as we can lay our hands on; and giving to those who have nothing such a portion thereof as it may seem to us expedient to part with (III, 111–12).

Like Gay, and unlike Ritson, Peacock is laughing at the theories of might, of wealth, of justice, by making his 'outlaws' spokesmen for reapplied, but not therefore legitimate, laws; laws that in fact are unjustifiable whether defended by a Walpole, a Castlereagh, or a Robin Hood. Peacock's real standards, again like Gay's, involve another way of life entirely. Gay hints, in the London setting and in the specifically London occupations of his characters, at values he had already espoused in his *Pastorals*. Peacock projects his idyllic, his alternative life, quite directly. Not London but the idyllic world of Sherwood is their habitat. Towards the end of the story Robin and Marian must live at court, but on the death of Richard they can return to the haven of Sherwood, to their forest retreat. The setting bears on the kind of satire *Maid Marian* finally offers.

After the laughter about obscure metaphysics and Byronic heroes in *Nightmare Abbey*, one would have expected Peacock to have used the opportunities provided by Sherwood and its inhabitants for more literary burlesque. Except in incidental ways, the book offers nothing of this sort. Yet the possibilities were enormous. William Empson, in his brilliant comments on the *Beggar's Opera*, suggests that Lord Byron was in a sense 'almost consciously the poet as Macheath'.[14] The 'mixture of aristocracy and democracy', of the 'heroic and the pastoral' gives Byronism some of its appeal, and also helps to explain Byron's own readiness to laugh at his poses. Robin Hood as Macheath, Peacock creates in *Maid Marian*, though Robin Hood who more nearly approximates a traditional hero of romance. But Robin Hood as poetic Macheath—surrounded by Friar Tuck, as Scott?—or Maid Marian, as a blue-stocking in green? With this sort of thing he does nothing. And because he creates for his characters a world without care, without real challenge and without real debate, the book remains 'romance' with sprinklings of satire, but with no consistent satiric focus. Indeed, the satire is mitigated throughout, if not forgotten. No one could mistake Sherwood for a real alternative; it is the pastoral world of romantic comedy.

'The world is a stage', says Friar Tuck, 'and life is a farce, and he that laughs most has most profit of the performance' (III, 159). He seems to comment for his author about the literary, and probably about the temperamental, provenance of the novel. The friar's opinion, coming from *As You Like It*, suggests the 'golden world' of Shakespeare's play: 'Where will the old duke live?' asks Oliver. 'They say he is already in the forest of Arden, and many a merry men with him; and there they live like the old Robin Hood of England. They say many young gentlemen flock to him every day, and fleet the time carelessly, as they did in the golden world.' Sherwood, too, is a

golden world, if a farcial one, where men fleet the time carelessly.

IV

It is fitting that *Maid Marian* begins and ends with a wedding
ceremony, and that these are by no means the only festivities
within the novel. Peacock has presented Christmas balls, farewell banquets, chess dances, and weddings in the earlier works:
but *Maid Marian* introduces celebrations from first to last. We
learn with little surprise that Peacock loved festivities. After
retiring from the India House to Halliford, he apparently
sponsored such festivals as May Day, inviting children of the
village to dance around the may-pole, and crowning the Queen
of May. Like Leigh Hunt and Hazlitt, who similarly found it a
pity that the old feast days were falling into neglect, Peacock
enjoyed such occasions and bemoaned their passing. But Peacock in writing about Robin and Marian is boisterous in his
defence of the old customs. EAT, DRINK, AND BE MERRY is
inscribed—after the manner of Rabelais' Abbey of Thélême—
over a door of the Gamwell house where Peacock sets his May
Day festivities. Characters are known in this novel, not by their
fruits, but by the way they eat and drink. There is, then, a
pronounced festive quality in this comedy, in part because the
novel ends with marriage and contains forest celebrations, but
also because of a related gaiety, an insistence on lighthearted-
ness, throughout.

The songs in *Maid Marian*, which add to the air of festival,
are more important to this novel than songs in the preceding
works. In one chapter, by way of example, musical harmony
acts upon Marian and Friar Tuck, still called Brother Michael,
so that the two are compelled to sing. When Marian begins a
song—she breaks into it as the best means of placating a dis-
obedient father—her melody 'acted irresistibly on the harmonious propensities of the friar, who accordingly sang in his turn'.
Marian's father, the baron, at once delighted with the music
and angry at the pair's disrespect, is finally 'put out of all
patience'. 'So,' he exclaimed, 'this is the way you teach my
daughter to renounce the devil, is it? A hunting friar, truly!
Who ever heard before of a hunting friar? A profane, roaring,

bawling, bumper-bibbing, neck-breaking, catch-singing friar.'
His outburst is cut short by Michael's good spirits, for, 'warm
with canary, and in his singing vein', he can only respond with
yet another song:

> Little I recked of the matin bell,
>> But drowned its toll with my clanging horn:
> And the only beads I loved to tell
>> Were the beads of dew on the spangled thorn.

And Marian similarly must respond in song, until, after another
duet, the two close with: 'Yoicks! hark away! and tally ho!'
Because the baron is only partly mollified by music, Marian
sheds a few tears, allowing the chapter to end in harmony. The
baron, who in other respects might be a second Squire Western,
cannot withstand his daughter's tears: 'Sing on, in God's name,'
he says, 'and crack away the flasks till your voice swims in
canary' (III, 38–43). The tendency to break into song, especially
in moments of apparent crises, helps to maintain the spirit of un-
broken comedy. At one point Friar Tuck explains how Robin's
men have emptied the pockets of the Abbot of Doubleflask:

> Marry, we turned his cloak to further account, and thereby
> hangs a tale that may either be said or sung; for in truth I
> am minstrel here as well as chaplain; I pray for good
> success to our just and necessary warfare, and sing thanks-
> giving odes when our foresters bring in booty:

>> Bold Robin has robed him in ghostly attire,
>> And forth he is gone like a holy friar,
>>> Singing, hey down, ho down, down, derry
>>>> down . . . (III, 119–20).

Peacock might be speaking of his own way of story-telling when
he describes Friar Tuck later in the novel:

> 'There is a tradition of a damsel who was drowned here
> some years ago. The tradition is——'
>> But the friar could not narrate a plain tale: he therefore
> cleared his throat, and sang with due solemnity, in a
> ghostly voice:

A damsel came in midnight rain,
And called across the ferry:
The weary wight she called in vain,
Whose senses sleep did bury . . . (III, 156).

The narrator also wants to sing rather than 'narrate a plain tale'. It is not true, as Carl van Doren suggested, that Peacock's songs are 'only intensified prose'. While he can rarely continue long poems without 'the loss of his singing garments', most of these brief pieces from the novels are clearly melodic;[15] they may speak directly and without much subtlety of association, but they are nevertheless far from prose, even from prose as polished as Peacock's own. His early reviewers quite rightly appreciated Peacock's skill with metres. (His difficulties are nearly always those of diction rather than rhythm.) Swinburne also praised his songs, and Thackeray called him an accomplished lyric poet. The following song is reminiscent of Burns's 'Ye flow'ry banks'—Peacock does quote Burns in *Maid Marian*—though it has echoes, and approximates the formality of the pastorals of Pope. It is Friar Tuck's final song, almost the last passage in the novel:

Ye woods, that oft at sultry noon
    Have o'er me spread your massy shade:
Ye gushing streams, whose murmured tune
    Has in my ear sweet music made,
While, where the dancing pebbles show
    Deep in the restless fountain-pool
The gelid water's upward flow,
    My second flask was laid to cool:

Ye pleasant sights of leaf and flower:
    Ye pleasant sounds of bird and bee:
Ye sports of deer in sylvan bower:
    Ye feasts beneath the greenwood tree:
Ye baskings in the vernal sun:
    Ye slumbers in the summer dell:
Ye trophies that this arm has won:
    And must ye hear your friar's farewell? (III, 177–8).)[16]

About another of the friar's songs, one more in character, 'The bramble, the bramble, the bonny forest bramble' (III, 12), Thackeray was to write in *The History of Samuel Titmarsh* that it was 'one of Charles Kemble's famous songs in *Maid Marian*, a play that was all the rage then, taken from a famous story-book by one Peacock, a clerk in the India House, and a precious good place he has too'.[17] Charles Kemble was a well-known actor of the time. He recognized in *Maid Marian* possibilities for the operatic stage—immediately, no doubt, conceiving himself in the role of Friar Tuck. With music by Henry Bishop—remembered for the tune of 'Home, Sweet Home'—the story was adapted by James Robinson Planché, who added to it, as well as 'lyrical and other matter', 'two or three situations from *Ivanhoe* . . . Mr. Peacock's story being too slight. . . .'[18] The new *Maid Marian* was produced at Covent Garden twenty-eight times within fourteen months—a success that must have delighted the opera-loving Peacock.

One would expect most of Peacock's novels to lend themselves to stage adaptation; their format has the appearance of a scenario, complete with dialogue and song.[19] Unquestionably, like *Maid Marian*, they could be adapted. (*Nightmare Abbey* has in fact been adapted—as a 'frolic'—and evidently played with some success just a few years ago.) The secret of Peacock's talent is, nevertheless, not the dialogues or the songs or the separate, self-sufficient scenes; it is rather these in combination with the manipulating and ironic narrator. *Maid Marian*—besides its 'romantic' subject and its head-cracking slapstick—lent itself so naturally to adaptation largely because the narrative itself, shifting with the various scenes, lacks the controlling wit and the ironic consistency of the other stories. Planché could adapt it so easily because the story was too easily put together.

There is enough in *Maid Marian* to make it pleasant reading: brilliant patches of narrative, of dialogue, or farcical combinations of the two that climax in the songs. The conception of the inverse satiric world, though only partly developed, offers intriguing associations and possibilities. Indeed, for some of Peacock's readers, especially the late Victorians and Edwardians, *Maid Marian* has proved the most delightful—a word often invoked—of the seven novels. (It was also soon translated into French and German.) Richard Garnett praised its idyllic quality, George Saintsbury its urbanity. The book offers both, yet not always at the same time or with the same intent. *Maid Marian* remains, as I suspect Peacock's delayed completion and publication imply, a book with significantly unresolved problems, a book not fully conceived.

6

The Misfortunes of Elphin:
a Lord of Misrule and the Magic
of Bards

> I see, methinks, as I sit on Snowdon, some glimpse of Mona
> and her haunted shades, and hope we shall be very good
> neighbours. Any Druidical anecdotes that I can meet with, I
> will be sure to send you . . . but I cannot pretend to be
> learned without books, or to know the Druids from modern
> Bishops at this distance.
>
> THOMAS GRAY, in a letter to Mason.

I

Between publication of *Maid Marian* (in 1822) and *The Misfortunes of Elphin* (in 1829), Peacock completed no extended work except *Paper Money Lyrics*, and he began only one other project, 'The Pilgrim of Provence' (1826?), a sketch based on a work by Fontenelle, which took first a dramatic and later a narrative format, but remained in either case unfinished. The few pages of narrative suggest a hastily begun chivalric romance, with burlesque or comic overtones similar to those in *Maid Marian*. The whole episode could have been written in a morning.

After August 1822 Peacock was kept busy as Shelley's executor; presumably, too, he had his share of duties at the India House. Yet he was clearly in no hurry to write another novel. *Elphin* is the leisurely creation of a man writing at his ease, perhaps as relaxation from work or from private cares, for the novel takes place as far from the realm of personal suffering as from the tedium of public service. No reference to the novel has been found in Peacock's papers, no indication when it was begun, nor suggestion as to his intent. The fifth of his novels, it is clearly related to the earlier ones, but it does have qualities all of its own.

Like *Maid Marian, Elphin* offers a humorous treatment of the past, but it substitutes for the rowdy burlesque in the earlier work a restrained irony and an ease of movement: Rabelaisian tumbling and head-walloping occur only sporadically. Historical Sherwood Forest is supplanted by prehistoric Cambria; Friar Tuck is superseded by Prince Seithenyn—whose love of wine leads to the inundation of the kingdom; and the talkative Maid Marian gives way to quiet, almost featureless heroines, not dissimilar from some of Scott's. The two books have nevertheless much in common, and they are certainly closer to each other than to Peacock's other novels. There is, for example, little more of devout romance and of the supernatural in *Elphin* than there is in the tale of Robin Hood.

Edith Nicolls wrote about *Elphin* that her grandfather conceived of it merely as a frame for his songs. One can imagine Peacock, in a characteristic gesture of ironic self-depreciation, brushing off his work in this way. (It is in any case the typical mock-humility of the satirist.) Whether or not he said anything of the sort, his comment seems much more applicable to *Maid Marian*. One point of contrast between *Maid Marian* and *Elphin* is the evident care Peacock took with the later story, his solicitude about including transitions, his insistence on what for him is a new kind of story completeness. If he does not go into great detail, he goes into enough detail to make his attention noticeable.

In another way, too, he took pains with *Elphin* that he did not take with *Maid Marian*. *Maid Marian* had been a light-hearted garner from Ritson's *Robin Hood*. *Elphin* represented years of reading, if not actual research, into the literature of the Welsh, of King Arthur, of the poet Taliesin, and of the history and legends associated with ancient Britain. The book is related to the Welsh revival, begun in the eighteenth century and associated with a new interest in antiquities and remote landscapes. Ritson himself, in an attempt to correct other antiquaries, had edited metrical romances and therefore touched on the activities of Arthur; Scott had also dabbled with the surrounding literature. But for *Elphin*, Peacock's reading went much farther afield.

His attitude towards Wales was always a little ambiguous.

As early as 1810 he praises Welsh scenery in his letters to
Edward Hookham:

I resolved to devote the whole interval to exploring the
vicinity, and have been climbing about the rocks and
mountains, by the rivers and the sea, with indefatigable
zeal, carrying in my mind the bardic triad, that a poet
should have an eye that can see nature, a heart that can
feel nature, and a resolution that dares follow nature [the
triad appears as an epigraph for a chapter in *Elphin*]; in
obedience to which latter injunction I have nearly broken
my neck (VIII, 181).

In *The Philosophy of Melancholy* and 'Farewell to Meirion' (1812)
he waxes rapturous about Welsh scenery and implies that
Welsh women are beautiful, while expressing contempt for a
backward and superstitious people. He was, however, fascinated
by the superstitions. If at the time he wrote *Headlong Hall*
(1815) he merely set his story in Wales because Wales offered a
secluded and isolated scene, he was already by that time
familiar with some of the literature of the revival. In *Melancholy*
he refers to a recent edition of Giraldus Cambrensis. He was
soon after to invoke King Arthur in 'Calidore' (1816) and in
'The Round Table' (also 1816). Much of Peacock's learning
remained that of the interested dilettante whose grasp of a
subject was appreciably less than he cared to admit. This is not
the case with his Welsh studies. At some time—probably after
he married Jane Gryffydh—he learned the language, and this
enabled him to read, not only the secondary literature or
literature in translation, but also some of the original. Thus in
addition to the work of antiquarians like Edward Jones
and Edward Davies, and the *Cambro-Briton*, a new 'Welsh'
periodical, he also read the *Myvyrian Archaiology of Wales* and
the *Mabinogian*, a collection of Welsh tales not then available
in English.[2] Although it may be a trifle absurd to suggest, as
David Garnett does, that the time delay between *Maid Marian*
and *Elphin* was caused by the extent of Peacock's researches,
nevertheless Peacock prepared himself for this story as he manifestly had not for *Maid Marian*.[3] One realizes why, in 1827, he
was so harsh on Moore's *Epicurean*, despite the obvious grounds

for compassion in the fact that his own earlier romance had
been no less lax about matters of authenticity.

The book that resulted from Peacock's archaeological labours
was not wholly free of academic paraphernalia or a lecturing
tone. (There are in *Elphin*, as in *Palmyra* and *Rhododaphne* obtrud-
ing traces of the learned amateur.) But it was an imaginative
re-creation of the old legends. The *Cambrian Quarterly* called it
'the most entertaining book, if not the best, that has yet been
published on the ancient customs and traditions of Wales'.[4]
Such an accolade recalls the rosebud that Byron sent to Peacock
to express his delight with *Nightmare Abbey* and to imply that
he recognized its satire as partly tongue-in-cheek. Peacock may
have taken his researches in earnest. Sir Edward Strachey
recalled that he boasted about his 'accuracy': 'I heard him say
that he had great difficulty in getting at the true story of
Taliesin's birth . . . and he was proud of the fact that Welsh
archaeologists treated his book as a serious and valuable addition to Welsh history.'[5] But if he had earnest intentions, or if
he saw the story as fictionalized research—and it seems to me
unlikely—the little book that resulted rarely betrays his
zeal. Its tone is that of a supercilious Walter Scott, who
makes his re-created world into something half-nostalgic, half
burlesque.

Scott was interested in the times he depicted as important or
representative historical stages, and while he ignores current
social or political issues, he charges such issues with meaning in
the times he describes. Whether he writes middle-class epics in
the historical novels—as Georg Lukács and others argue—is
debatable,[6] but Scott creates a vast and detailed canvas on
which his 'ordinary' heroes tread between great forces. However one judges Scott's stature or his grasp of historical meaning,
his descriptions of historical events always seems vivid and real
—even when padded to undue length. Lukács is right in arguing Scott's indebtedness to the social realists, the Fieldings and
the Smolletts, of the preceding century.)

Peacock's reading may indeed have led him into a search for
historical fact, yet his story makes no pretence to authenticity of
experience, no gesture towards a historical conditioning of the
characters. A loose screen of experience surrounds his characters,
but it does not in fact matter much whether they live in a

moderately accurate representation of sixth-century Wales or whether the whole historical setting is mere spoof, an allegorical frame for the satire. Characters may do what people with their names reportedly did at a certain point in time, but there is no illusion that they are living in the time, or even that they are really living. Without inner thoughts or moral dimensions, they act out a number of historical scenes. Peacock is not writing a historical novel in *Elphin*, but a historical romance. And hence, although most of his characters are colourless and mediocre, two are of preternatural stature. In such a book Peacock can take liberties with psychology as much as with history.

Peacock's understanding of history is not drawn from Scott, in spite of his having read and, to an extent, having appreciated what Scott attempted. The boy who was introduced to Gibbon and Hume at his mother's knee retained throughout his life an eighteenth-century or Enlightenment view of history. For Peacock, human nature remains the same; it is only conditions that change. If he is interested like Voltaire, in the 'pageant of the past', he has a related conception of historical determinism. His intent is not re-creation but illustration, and therefore he looks at the past irreverently, never quite taking it seriously, and largely uses it as a means of satirizing his own times. Undeterred by thoughts of genuine illusion, he often interrupts his narrative with tangential satiric asides, as in the following passage, where the poet Taliesin arrives at King Arthur's court at Caer Lleon:

The city, which had been so long the centre of the Roman supremacy, which was now the seat of the most illustrious sovereign that had yet held the sceptre of Britain, could not be approached by the youthful bard, whose genius was destined to eclipse that of all his countrymen, without feelings and reflections of deep interest. The sentimental tourist, (who, perching himself on an old wall, works himself up into a soliloquy of philosophical pathos, on the vicissitudes of empire and the mutability of all sublunary things, interrupted only by an occasional peep at his watch, to ensure his not overstaying the minute at which his fowl . . . has been promised to be ready,) has, no doubt, many fine thoughts well worth recording in a dapper volume;

but Taliesin had an interest in the objects before him too
deep to have a thought to spare, even for his dinner
(IV, 101–2).

The all-too-busy narrator here, whose overwrought joke finally
robs the reader's interest in the ostensible subject, clearly offers
no impression of discovery. Taliesin's feelings are illustrated by
an inverse comparison with the negative response of the
picturesque tourist—who might be a portrait of Peacock himself as he sat down to compose *Palmyra* and *The Genius of the
Thames*.

II

The events of *Elphin*, while covering more time and offering
more variety than the other novels, are still fairly straightforward. Even in a work based on legends and myth, Peacock
does not concern himself with intricacies of plot, although he
introduces background information about the times and some
of the characters. Nor, on the other hand, does he seem to be
entirely consistent. Herbert Wright indicates that Peacock's
emphasis in the first part of the book, nominally about Elphin,
is upon Seithenyn. And that in the second part it is on the poet
Taliesin.[7] The reasons for the apparent shift can be ascribed to
the material itself, since Peacock interweaves three otherwise
unrelated, or only loosely related, strands of legend. The
narrator manages, however, to give a unity to his story by
gradually focusing on the deeds and powers of Taliesin, for
which the early chapters provide a necessary introduction.

Elphin's father, King Gwythno—as the story opens—has left
his prosperous little kingdom to the supervision of lieutenants.
'Glorious in feasting', as he is glorious in hunting and in the
writing of poetry, Gwythno submits himself to the pleasures of
life. Elphin's misfortunes begin as a result of his father's temperament, for the kingdom is lost. An old sea-wall, holding back
the waters of what we know as Cardigan Bay, has been super-
vised by Seithenyn, a Gargantuan drinker and a therefore
careless overseer. Representative of those who oppose any and
all reform—perhaps specifically based on the Duke of Welling-
ton, perhaps on Canning or Burke—he advocates letting things

stand as they are. His arguments parallel those of the apologists for the Constitution prior to the 1832 reform. What has proved itself useful, he argues must still be useful, and he acts upon his theory.

One night, predictably, the sea-wall collapses, inundating the land. Seithenyn, leaping with raised sword into the swirling waters, is presumed to be drowned. Elphin marries Angharad, Seithenyn's daughter, and inherits the mountainous strip of wasteland that remains of the kingdom. He becomes a fisherman, logically enough, and the royal family subsists quietly and industriously. One night Elphin finds a floating basket trapped in his weir, in which the baby Taliesin, Moses fashion, has miraculously survived. As the years go by and Elphin's daughter, Melenghel, grows up, Taliesin falls in love with her. But though a bard and taught his lore by the ageing King Gwythno, Taliesin dares not ask for her hand. Peacock dispenses cursorily with the passing of time, being interested after the first events in the older Taliesin. This is the way he bridges the years: 'Taliesin', he says, 'drew in the draughts of inspiration among the mountain forests and the mountain streams, and grew up under the roof of Elphin, in the perfection of genius and beauty.' And he continues directly in the next chapter:

> Gwythno slept, not with his fathers, for they were under
> the sea, but as near to them as was found convenient. . . .
> Elphin was now king of Caredigion, and was lord of a
> large but thinly-peopled tract of rock, mountain, forest, and
> bog. He held his sovereignty, however, not, as Gwythno
> had done during the days of the glory of Gwaelod, by that
> most indisputable sort of right which consists in might, but
> by the more precarious tenure of the absence of inclination
> in any of his brother kings to take away anything he had.
> Uther Pendragon, like Gwythno, went the way of all
> flesh, and Arthur reigned in Caer Lleon, as king of the
> kings of Britain. Maelgon Gwyneth was then king of that
> part of North Wales which bordered on the kingdom of
> Caredigion (IV, 61–2).

In a short passage Peacock has matured Taliesin, described Elphin's predicament, and accounted for some necessary facts.

Finally, the story will end at Arthur's Court, and, more immediately, Maelgon Gwyneth will upset the 'precarious tenure' of Elphin's kingdom. Maelgon, an uncivilized equivalent of Squire Headlong, chances into Elphin's tract on a hunting expedition. Because he has the 'sort of right which consists in might', he insists that Elphin accompany him back to his kingdom—to partake of his hospitality. Elphin, who has more honesty than tact, will not admit that Maelgon's wife is more beautiful than his own. For his honesty he finds himself in a dungeon.[8]

After an exchange of flytings with Maelgon's bards, whom he demolishes, Taliesin commits himself to freeing Elphin. The remainder of the story concerns his adventures on Elphin's behalf. Arriving finally at Arthur's stronghold, Caer Lleon—and here Peacock draws on various accounts in the *Mabinogion* —Taliesin makes himself useful to the troubled King of kings. King Melvas, as hasty as Maelgon, and more powerful, has abducted Queen Gwenyvar, and, believing zealously in the 'right of might' and the 'right of possession'—again the same phrases, the same satiric thrusts as in *Maid Marian*—simply refuses to give her back. Taliesin has learned, in the Castle of Dinas Vawr and from no other person than the resuscitated Prince Seithenyn, the Queen's whereabouts. He manages the return of the Queen and saves Britain from civil war. His reward is the release of Elphin, for which Elphin gives him the hand of his daughter Melanghel. Seithenyn becomes second butler to King Arthur; Elphin returns to his family; and Taliesin, after winning his lady, additionally wins the title of Chief of the Bards. All, of course, live happily ever after.

III

Like *Maid Marian, Elphin* is full of banquets and drinking parties, as well as of eaters and drinkers. The most remarkable of Peacock's imbibers and, according to a bardic triad, one of 'the three immortal drunkards of the isle of Britain' (IV, 10), is the prodigiously thirsty and endlessly drinking Seithenyn ap Seithyn Saidi, High Commissioner of the Royal Embankment. Like Falstaff—with whom it is hard to avoid the comparison— Seithenyn is ponderous on his feet, and, were he to step upon it, would probably lard the earth like Shakespeare's Knight. He also has a comparable disdain for points of honour. Peacock introduces Seithenyn when Elphin enters his castle to complain about the embankment. Seithenyn's followers are singing 'a song in his praise' entitled 'The Circling of the Mead Horns':

> But Seithenyn ap Seithyn, the generous, the bold,
> Drinks the bright-flowing wine from the far-gleaming gold:
> The wine, in the bowl by his lip that is worn,
> Shall be glorious as mead in the buffalo horn (iv, 11).

Elphin and his companion stand waiting for a moment before Seithenyn notices them and roars:

> 'You are welcome all four.'
>   Elphin answered, 'We thank you: we are but two.'
>   'Two or four,' said Seithenyn, 'all is one. You are welcome all' (iv, 12).

When he realizes that he speaks with King Gwythno's son, Seithenyn attempts to stand; first teetering on inadequate, because relatively unused, ankles, he ends by sprawling on the floor. (Peacock typically closes the scene by creating general, and in this case bacchanalian, confusion.) Unwieldy he may be, but, like Falstaff, Seithenyn proves agile of tongue. His great illogicalities, punctuated by 'Cupbearer fill!' or 'wine from gold', and rolling on a great flood of language, are as winning as they are foolish. 'Decay', said Seithenyn, 'is one thing, and danger is another. Everything that is old must decay. That the embankment is old, I am free to confess; that it is somewhat rotten in parts, I will not altogether deny . . .' (iv, 15). He embodies the twin capacities for pure rodomontade and eternal drinking; he is a great, amoral hulk. Peacock is interested enough in Seithenyn to describe him, for we see his movements and gestures in a way that is rare in Peacock's stories. J. B. Priestley calls Seithenyn one of the great English comic characters.[9] And so he is. If Peacock creates in his novels any single figure deserving of immortality, it is this bibulous lord in *Elphin*.

The novel depicts another character who, if not quite so

overwhelming, nor ever so clearly drawn, contrasts with Seithenyn as the spirit with the flesh. The poet Taliesin—his name means 'bright brow'—is central to the novel both as a character and as a poetic agent. Not merely a gifted singer, ready to do immediate justice to any topic, he acts as a wordly equivalent for music. He entices, he soothes, he convinces. His almost magical workings restore to Arthur the abducted Queen, because he can draw out information, thwart dastardly acts, and charm irate kings. The novel might more appropriately have been called the *Fortunes of Taliesin*. It is his career and his adventures that provide coherence for the story. But, again, Taliesin is not merely a character; Peacock describes his actions more than the man himself. Like Thomas Mann's 'spirit of story-telling' in the *Holy Sinner*, Taliesin represents the author's means of narrative.

Mann appreciated among the English novelists the writings of Sterne, whose pacing and irony he perhaps emulates in his own work. He might as legitimately have praised Peacock's novels, particularly *Elphin*, with which Mann's story of Gregory has much in common. Peacock has taken old legends and semi-historical figures and made of them pure fiction. He can refer to current happenings—such as the development of 'steam-engines, with fires as eternal as those of the nether world' (iv, 51)—draw historical parallels: in short, he can and does play with time. His story is told with an elevated point of view that makes tragedy possible only by implication and with a verbal irony that circumvents pathos. Shortly after the sea-wall has collapsed, for example, Peacock describes the escape of his characters from Seithenyn's fortress in a way that effectually curtails any thoughts of suffering or danger:

> Teithrin led the way, striking the point of his spear
> firmly into the earth, and leaning from it on the wind:
> Angharad [Seithenyn's daughter] followed in the same
> manner: Elphin followed Angharad, looking as earnestly
> to her safety as was compatible with moderate care of his
> own: the attendant maidens followed Elphin; and the bard,
> whom the result of his first experiment had rendered
> unambitious of the van, followed the female train. Behind
> them went the cup-bearers, whom the accident of sobriety

had qualified to march: and behind them reeled and roared those of the bacchanal rout who were able and willing to move; those more especially who had wives or daughters to support their tottering steps (IV, 33).

Mann allows himself pathos, because his story-teller, ostensibly a likeable and reclusive monk, insists that the reader suffer from time to time. Behind the monk, however, is the 'spirit of story-telling', a device which enables the author to tell a story that is known, to make the telling itself noticeable, and to maintain a slyly ironic and unhurried account. Implicit in both stories is the assumption that the narrative itself can either soothe wrongs and hardships or laugh them out of existence. Mann creates a spirit of the narrative; Peacock creates a Taliesin, his equivalent for such a spirit.

Representing for Peacock a device for the unfolding of story, Taliesin also provides a poetic ideal. The portrait makes clear that Peacock understood the historical function of the old Celtic poets, with their powers of prophecy, of destroying enemies, of punishing false poets. Taliesin is a part-humorous, part-nostalgic creation, who in the words of the bardic triad, has the 'eye that can see nature; a heart that can feel nature; and a resolution that dares follow nature' (IV, 50). He represents, significantly, the old bards—for Peacock was at one in his nostalgia with Gray and Beattie and other singers of poetic dirges in the last century, when poets were at least magicians, if not out-and-out legislators. The implications of the contrast between Taliesin and modern poets are comparable with Peacock's use of the 'four ages' scheme in the earlier essay.

Peacock is not content to call Taliesin a poet without intro-ducing his verse. The songs in *Elphin*, though not as numerous as those in *Maid Marian*, are important to the narrative. Unlike those in *Maid Marian*, they are for the most part based on actual legendary material or on original Welsh songs ascribed to the poets whom Peacock introduces. His translations of Welsh poems are better than his translation from the Greek—which sometimes reads like A. E. Housman's parodic 'Fragment of a Greek Tragedy'. But Peacock was not a gifted translator, and the most successful poems in *Elphin* are those related to the Welsh material, but of his own creation. One, a love duet

between Melanghel and Taliesin, includes this gentle and
well-turned stanza:

> Not yet; not yet: let nightdews fall,
> And stars be bright above,
> Ere to her long deserted hall
> I guide my gentle love.
> When torchlight flashes on the roof,
> No foe will near thee stray:
> Even now his parting couser's hoof
> Rings from the rocky way (IV, 85).

Taliesin overhears, but he does not himself sing 'The War Song
of Dinas Vawr', which is Peacock's finest lyric lampoon. It
follows a characteristically ironic preamble:

> The hall of Melvas was full of magnanimous heroes, who
> were celebrating their own exploits in sundry choruses,
> especially in that which follows, which is here put upon
> record as being the quintessence of all the war songs that
> ever were written, and the sum and substance of all the
> appetencies, tendencies, and consequences of military
> glory:[10]

> THE WAR SONG OF DINAS VAWR
> The mountain sheep are sweeter,
> But the valley sheep are fatter;
> We therefore deemed it meeter
> To carry off the latter.
> We made an expedition;
> We met host and quelled it;
> We forced a strong position,
> And killed the men who held it.
>
> We brought away from battle,
> And much their land bemoaned them,
> Two thousand head of cattle,
> And the head of him who owned them . . . (IV, 89–90).[11]

The war song, evidently parodying such poems as Gray's 'Bard'
and Scott's 'Hail to the Chief', also involves self-parody, bur-

lesque of Peacock's own early poems in the 'heroic' tradition of Ossian. Nor was this the first of Peacock's comments on such verse. In *Melincourt* Mr. Fax comments on Robert Southey's praise of heroic verse, saying:

> As to the 'Scald's strong verse', I must say I have never seen any specimens of it, that I did not think mere trash. It is little more than a rhapsody of rejoicing in carnage, a ringing of changes on the biting sword and the flowing of blood . . . and fulsome flattery of the chieftain, of whom the said Scald was the abject slave . . . (III, 387–8).

Like the travesty of Byron's poems in *Nightmare Abbey*, the war song remains one of the great parodies in the language.

Elphin closes—as do most of Peacock's novels—with a 'magnificent festival', wherein, as with an easy jigsaw, various parts of the narrative are fitted together. But in the penultimate scene Peacock offers 'The Circle of the Bards', a kind of bardic congress, where 'each bard . . . was subjected to a number of interrogatories, metrical and mystical . . .' and where 'many bards sang many songs' (IV, 135), according to the historical practice of the Celtic poets. At the bardic congress Taliesin culminates his triumphs by winning, not unexpectedly, 'the highest honours of the sitting'. His song, a part of the *Hanes Taliesin* (the history of Taliesin), is more formal and restrained than 'Dinas Vawr', and in telling his own story Taliesin incorporates much of the paraphernalia of metric romance. Here is a typical stanza:

> But from the cauldron rose a smoke
> That filled with darkness all the air:
> When through its folds the torchlight broke,
> Nor Gwion, nor the boy, was there.
> The fire was dead, the cauldron cold,
> And in it lay, in sleep uprolled,
> Fair as the morning-star, a child,
> That woke, and stretched its arms, and smiled (IV, 143).

Taliesin's relating his own story, while perfectly appropriate to the novel, remains Peacock's rendering of Welsh material rather than his own independent creation. Yet only someone intimate with the old literature could differentiate the Welsh from the Peacockian in this novel. The charm of the work is that they are so well blended, and perhaps for this reason Herbert Wright called *Elphin* 'one of the few masterpieces in English which sprang from the eighteenth-century Celtic revival'.[12] Never a slave to his material, Peacock does admit an affection for it.

Elphin was well received by critics of the time, drawing praise from the established journals as well as the almost professionally Welsh *Cambrian Quarterly*. Among the notices was one in the *Westminster*, for whom Peacock had reviewed the *Epicurean* and for whom he was shortly to review the *Letters and Journals* of Byron. The *Westminster* was generous to *Elphin*, but with reservations that appear less relevant for the novel than illustrative of their own critical ambitions. 'It is not for the genuine satirist', they wrote, 'either directly or indirectly, to insinuate the superiority of half-barbaric states of existence, by partially adverting to the evils consequent on higher stages of civilization. . . .'[13] One could argue of course that it is precisely the job of a satirist to make such insinuations, and preferably 'indirectly', whatever his actual view of 'half-barbaric states of existence'. The aesthetic positions of the *Westminster*, as Hazlitt rightly pointed out, were those of disguised Puritans with a faith in mechanical progress. They were shortly to write in a review of Tennyson's poems that it would be unthinkable to have no progress in poetry commensurate with that in mechanics.

But lurking behind the *Westminster*'s response is a legitimate critical point. Peacock's 'insinuations' and 'adversions' are not unfitting commentary on the idols of philistinism, but they are often enough gratuitous asides from the narrative. When Peacock describes the environment of Taliesin's youth, his method is consistently one of inverse analogy—as suggested earlier about the description of Caer Lleon. The ancient Britons lacked, he writes, 'some of our light and also some of our prisons'. 'We may well boast of the progress of light, when we turn . . . to the statutes at large, and the Court of Chancery.' So much for law. Of medicine he writes:

Medicine was cultivated by the Druids, and it was just
as much a science with them as it is with us; but they had
not the wit or the means to make it a flourishing trade; the
principal means to that end being women with nothing to
do, articles which especially belong to a high state of
civilization (IV, 53).

Whatever its charms, a work of historical fiction tends—somewhat paradoxically—to limit its appeal to its own or to an
immediately following generation. Even Scott's novels, despite
their incredible popularity in the nineteenth century, are read
today only by the patient few. One possible reason for the
brevity of appeal is that successful reshaping of the past demands
the investing of it with specifically current and local parallels. As
Scott wrote in the Preface to *Ivanhoe*, 'It is necessary, for exciting
interest of any kind, that the subject assumed should be, as it
were, translated, into the manners as well as the language, of
the age we live in . . .'.[14] With his usual modesty and self-
criticism, Scott probably guessed that he was writing for his own
century—although of course his methods were instrumental in
changing entire conceptions of the past that have lasted longer
than the fame of his novels. In short, Peacock's 'adversions' or
'insinuations'—his own way of 'translating' his subject into
modern terms—made *Elphin* as relevant to his times as it is
dated now. *Elphin* is a type of novel that has to be rewritten for
each generation. Its equivalent in our own day is perhaps
T. H. White's *The Once and Future King*.

But criticizing a genre may be to evade specific criticism
of the book, and *Elphin*, like *Maid Marian*, has its problems.
Peacock's excessive references to civilization of his own day, his
unwillingness, or inability, to sustain the historical illusion,
his difficulties with extended narrative, all suggest that his real
talents were not for this sort of fiction. This is not to deny that
Elphin tells a readable story, offering witty interludes—and at
least two intriguing characters. But its entertainment is limited
in a way that is not true of *Nightmare Abbey* and *Crotchet Castle*,
whose characters—despite their genesis in contemporary fads
or problems and their elegant turns of phrase—still talk in a
lively idiom about things that matter.

7

Crotchet Castle:
the Modern Athenians

Each one of them is something of a stylist and a wit. . . .
They explain themselves, as it were, only too well.

J. B. PRIESTLEY, *Thomas Love Peacock.*

I

In *Crotchet Castle* Peacock returns from the world of romance to
the world of talk. After two works named for principal characters, two ventures into the historic past, he creates once again an
eccentric host surrounded by single-minded guests in a country
retreat. Some qualities of romance do, however, carry over. The
world of Squire Crotchet's villa is not much less remote from
ordinary life than that of *Maid Marian* or *Elphin.* If the setting is
a recognizable locality along the Thames in the immediate past,
the time by which the characters live is the suspended duration
of romance. The clock ticks only towards the dinner hour; the
calendar ends with weddings.

Peacock evidently wrote a large part of the new novel shortly
after the completion of *Elphin*, in 1828, and added to it, as a
current reference makes clear, as late as December 1830. It
appeared finally in February 1831.[1]

Among Peacock's readers, *Crotchet Castle* seems to elicit the
most energetic of responses. It is either 'unquestionably his best
novel' or a clear case of 'drying up'; either the happiest combination of eccentric talk or a cantankerous diatribe against
ideas and innovations. The two reactions have been sharply
opposed from the beginning. 'Were we to be asked', wrote the
reviewer for the *Literary Gazette*, 'as to who is the wittiest writer
in England, we should say, Mr. Peacock.'[2] And William
Maginn of the recently established *Fraser's Magazine*—for
which Peacock was later to write—in a commentary so vitriolic
as to read like a pure spoof, had this to say: 'Peacock is one of

the people "marked with the indelible d——d cockney blot;"
... an ignorant, stupid, poor devil, who has no fun, little
learning, no facility, no *easiness*—a fellow whose style and
thought is in the very contrary vein of the Rabelaisian. . . .'[3]
Maginn's spleen may have arisen for reasons of politics—he
may also have recognized in Peacock a rival, too adept at
'impaling our pigmy foes'—yet his comments about style and
tone have been echoed by several later critics, who have found
Crotchet Castle just as unsatisfactory. Maginn's boorish outburst,
raises legitimate questions about a book that is easily and often
misunderstood. Is this, for example, a novel without 'ease' or
'fun'? Or, conversely, is it a piece of earnest propaganda in the
guise of fiction? Is it, in some damaging way, 'in the very
contrary vein of the Rabelaisian', and if so, why did Maginn
bother to make the comparison?

Rabelais, according to Peacock, 'put on the robe of the all-
licensed fool, that he might, like the court jester, convey bitter
truths under the semblance of simple buffoonery' (IX, 258–9).
For the most part, this is not Peacock's own method. In comparison with what Pope had aptly characterized as Rabelais'
'easy chair' story-telling, Peacock tends to be circumspect and,
as I have said before, ironic as much at the readers' as at the
characters' expense. In this respect Maginn was quite right.
Peacock's is a contrary vein from that of Rabelais, who lets his
narrator, as if awed and delighted by all he recounts, play the
traditional role of innocent teller. Maginn may have reacted to
what he thought intellectual smugness, misconceiving Peacock's
narrative restraint—and its pointed sallies—as a sign of literary
as well as personal inadequacy.

Yet as Maginn tacitly acknowledges, there are qualities of
Rabelais in *Crotchet Castle*, the signs of which are more than the
few quotations used as mottoes. Peacock introduces absurd,
Gargantuan, polyglot lists; he insists on large quantities of food
and drink; he derides false rhetoric; and he creates in Crotchet
Castle itself the antidote to the characters and institutions that
he satirizes, making it into a kind of small-scale Abbey of
Thélême. He also indulges, Maginn and certain later critics
notwithstanding, in easy 'fun'. Still, it remains true that the tone
of this novel is rather more astringent than that of *Headlong Hall*
and *Nightmare Abbey*, as well as of the later *Gryll Grange*. What

seems unaccountably to be overlooked about the book is that
the militant tone occurs almost wholly at the beginning.[4] As the
story progresses, the 'easiness' and good-nature that Maginn
found wanting are clearly in evidence. One wonders indeed
whether Maginn and those who follow his judgments ever read
the entire story. Even more than Peacock's other novels,
Crotchet Castle undergoes a change in the course of narrative:
not an arbitrary change, but one closely linked with the irony
of the narration and the structure that the irony controls.

J. B. Priestley speaks about 'two men at work in these novels:
one is a humorist, . . . laughing at life itself; the other is a
satirist, a man who wrote only for his contemporaries and with
the purpose of advancing one set of opinions and denouncing
. . . another set of opinions'.[5] But again, there is not simply an
unresolved tension so much as a progression from satire to
humour, from the militant to the tolerant. Humour and satire,
moreover, are part of the larger comic whole, which determines
the role of both. It is better to speak of two tones or two voices
at work within the comedy, one of which finally dominates.

Crotchet Castle opens in a way that reflects the two voices.
Possibly thinking of Dr. Johnson's 'happy valley' in *Rasselas*,
Peacock writes:

> In one of those beautiful vallies, through which the Thames
> (not yet polluted by the tide, the scouring of cities, or even
> the minor defilement of the sandy streams of Surrey,) rolls
> a clear flood through flowery meadows, under the shade of
> old beech woods, and the smooth mossy greensward of the
> chalk hills . . . stood the castellated villa of a retired
> citizen (IV, 1–2).

A satiric thrust affects the description—in the phrase 'scouring
of cities'—and the parenthesis admits of humour, as a gram-
matical aside. But the tone is actually that of pastoral. Here
Peacock is at his descriptive best, and his pictures of Wales,
later in the novel, like that of the 'beautiful valley', are un-
equalled in the other novels. (Peacock will also introduce
characters, like the 'medievalist' Mr. Chainmail, who are outspoken apologists for rural beauty. Chainmail's feeling is that
modern poets, largely 'civic' or Cockney poets, know 'no nature,

no simplicity, no picturesqueness'. 'The cowslip of a civic poet', he says, 'is always in blossom' [IV, 125].)

Within one or two sentences of his mention of 'mossy greens-ward', the narrator introduces an entirely different remark—again perhaps with an echo of Dr. Johnson. 'It is not so much to be lamented', Johnson had said, 'that old England is lost as that the Scots have found it.' *Crotchet Castle* begins on a similar note and with the same kind of humour. Squire Crotchet is really no squire at all, but a rich merchant whose actual name is Ebenezer MacCrotchet. Desirous of ridding himself of both the Ebenezer and the Mac, he disingenuously calls himself E. M. Crotchet. He is the

London-born offspring of a worthy native of the 'north countrie', who had walked up to London on a commercial adventure, with all his surplus capital, not very neatly tied up in a not very clean handkerchief, suspended over his shoulder from the end of a hooked stick, extracted from the first hedge on his pilgrimage; and who, after having worked himself a step or two up the ladder of life, had won the virgin heart of the only daughter of a highly respectable merchant of Duke's Place, with whom he inherited the honest fruits of a long series of ingenuous dealings (IV, 2).

Peacock had exploited the anti-Jew, anti-Scot humour in earlier verse, especially in *Paper Money Lyrics*, and his including more at the beginning of his novel helps to explain the touch of acerbity that critics have rightly pointed out and that hardly fits with the description of the surrounds. But Crotchet does not remain a typical commercial adventurer of unscrupulous methods. He becomes, if the most preposterous, in some ways the most interesting of Peacock's hosts. His demands on the guests are anything but modest.

The sentimental against the rational, the intuitive against the inductive, the ornamental against the useful, the intense against the tranquil, the romantic against the classical; these are great and interesting controversies, which I should like, before I die, to see satisfactorily settled (IV, 22).

To which David Garnett appends, 'What an awful way to pay for one's dinner! What a prize bore!'[6] True enough, but Crotchet redeems himself, not only by having a cellar stocked with Hermitage and Madeira, but also by condemning what we might call respectable morality. Like a man of the Enlightenment, he says: 'Where the Greeks had . . . any thing that exalts, delights or adorns humanity, we have nothing but cant, cant, cant' (IV, 96–7).

In short, he recognizes, or comes to recognize, the limitations in the system, which, as 'foreigner' on two counts he has heretofore energetically supported. Peacock may begin by finding Crotchet an intruder in the rural scene, a Trimalchio, a bore, and a *parvenu*, who represents commercialized society. Having made Crotchet choose the country life, however, Peacock is led to mitigate the original attack and to find in the self-made squire the man who, like the Greeks themselves, knew how to use their wealth for hospitality. (Crotchet remains a kind of boundlessly improvident Timon of Athens.)

The treatment of the squire is paralleled in the treatment of his guests, who, as the story opens, congregate at the Villa as an honest group of parasites, each with his own crotchet or humour. Again one thinks of Trimalchio's guests or of Lucian's sketch, the *Sales of Lives*, wherein 'philosophers' are sold for whatever they may fetch on the open slave-market. In Peacock's story the philosophers begin by selling themselves, descending on the Villa in the hope of rich entertainment.

Peacock introduces the Squire's guests in two separate ways, one fairly conventional, the other with intriguing literary associations. After telling about Crotchet and setting the stage for the talk, he uses the second chapter, 'The March of Mind', for a brief, prefatory skirmish in a manner he had exploited earlier:

'God bless my soul, sir!' exclaimed the Reverend Dr. Folliott, bursting, one fine May morning, into the breakfast room at Crotchet Castle, 'I am out of all patience with this march of mind. Here has my house been nearly burned down, by my cook taking it into her head to study hydrostatics, in a sixpenny tract, published by the Steam Intellect Society, and written by a learned friend. . . . My cook must read his rubbish in bed; and as might naturally be expected, she dropped suddenly fast asleep, overturned the candle, and set the curtains in a blaze. Luckily the footman went into the room at the moment . . . (IV, 13–14).[7]

Dr. Folliott's outburst is directed against the activities of Henry Brougham, who, in 1825, founded the Society for the Diffusion of Useful Knowledge. (Carlyle was to call it the Society for 'Useless Knowledge'.) Folliott's tirade is characteristic: he fails to see that Crotchet has other guests and, dispensing with all preliminaries, simply speaks his mind. His comments are then taken up by Squire Crotchet and Crotchet Junior, by Mr. Skionar, a poetic metaphysician, again based on Coleridge, by Mr. MacQuedy, a Scottish political economist, spokesman for the 'Modern Athens' and 'the son of a demonstration', by Mr. Firedamp, for whom 'water is death to the soul', and by Lord Bossnowl, a fop after the manner of Mr. Listless of *Nightmare Abbey*.[8] Bossnowl, whose main contribution to the debate is a 'He! He!' does have wit enough to ask Folliott why the footman happened—'very providential to be sure'—to enter the cook's room, so that Folliott can conclude the anticipated joke. 'Sir,' he says—he always sounds a little like Boswell's recording of Dr. Johnson—'as good came of it, I shut my eyes. . . . I suppose he was going to study hydrostatics, and he found himself under the necessity of practising hydraulics' (IV, 14). Folliott also gets the last word in the debate. When Mr. MacQuedy, already Folliott's adversary, concludes an argument with 'The savage never laughs', the Doctor adds: 'No, sir, he has nothing to laugh at. Give him Modern Athens, the "learned friend", and the Steam Intellect Society. They will develop his muscles' (IV, 26).

The Squire's group continues to grow. Captain Fitzchrome, a suitor for Lady Clarinda—Peacock's wittiest lady, and his closest equivalent to Congreve's Millamant—arrives at the Villa, disguised as a picturesque painter. He is invited[i] to stay and manages at the evening 'Party' to sit next to Clarinda. Peacock interrupts the free-wheeling conversation with a chapter called 'Characters', in which Clarinda comments for her lover on the diverse assembly. Robert Bage lets a character do this in *Barham Downs*; Isaac Disraeli lets one of his characters do it in

Vaurien; but Peacock's more likely models were Petronius's *Satyricon* and Molière's *Le Misanthrope*.

At Trimalchio's massive banquet Encolpius's neighbour describes in crude dialect and with limited awareness some of the people present, including the incomparably boorish host himself. In *Le Misanthrope*, Célimène comments on the assembled characters, fixing, as Robert Elliott writes, 'an essential characteristic' that can be 'grasped, turned, elaborated upon'.[9] Molière and Petronius both add irony and humour to their accounts of the strange companies by the device, which offers a performance within the performance and an extension of the satiric irony.

Peacock's scene more closely resembles Molière's than Petronius's, in that Clarinda, like Célimène, is conscious of her role. Her depictions are precisely of the 'essential characteristic' of each guest; and she moves round the table as though herself a satirist of note. 'I will describe the company to you', she says. 'First, there is the old gentleman on my left hand [Squire Crotchet]. . . . He is a good-tempered, half-informed person, very unreasonably fond of reasoning, and of reasoning people; people that talk nonsense logically. . . .' She moves round to Lord Bossnowl, her brother, who 'has finished his education'; to Miss Crotchet, who is 'tolerably accomplished . . . and is extremely desirous to be called "my lady"'.

In addition to Mr. MacQuedy, Mr. Firedamp, and Mr. Skionar, whom she sums up better than the narrator has in the earlier chapter, Clarinda introduces Mr. Eavesdrop, 'a sort of bookseller's tool [who] coins all his acquaintance in . . . sketches of character'—Thomas Moore or Hazlitt seems to be intended; Mr. Henbane, 'the toxicologist, I think he calls himself. . . . The first thing he did . . . was to kill the cat'; Mr. Trillo— originally O'Trill—'the dilettante composer', who might be based on Victor Novello;[10] Dr. Morbific, 'who has been all over the world to prove there is no such thing as contagion; and has inoculated himself with plague, yellow fever . . .'; Mr. Chainmail, 'with very antiquated tastes'; Mr. Toogood, 'the co-operationist'—based on Robert Owen; Mr. Philpot, 'the geographer'; and Sir Simon Steeltrap, 'Member for Crouching-Curtown, Justice of the Peace . . . and . . . a great preserver of game and public morals' (IV, 55–69).

The list is long, even in Clarinda's witty account, longer in fact than any of the earlier *dramatis personae* excepting that of *Melincourt*. But a comparison with *Melincourt* works immediately in favour of the later story. What develops here and what conspicuously does not develop in the earlier story is the social unit, the group within the larger group that manages by the novel's close to surpass their limitations of crotchets and humours. Peacock actually forgets Sir Simon Steeltrap, for example. Steeltrap is a man capable of inflicting real suffering, a man with vices. The other characters, with varying degrees of malice or stridency, are victims of intellectual waywardness, mere perpetrators of folly. They can be redeemed.

II

The story of *Crotchet Castle* centres on tested, disappointed, and fulfilled love. As in *Melincourt*, the characters take an extensive journey, though with a different purpose. Peacock lets Crotchet and his guests talk their way—by boat—to Wales, where, under idyllic conditions, part of the love stories takes place.[11] At the opening of the novel there are complications between two of the lovers. Captain Fitzchrome loves Lady Clarinda, who returns his love, though she refuses to admit it, but who feels the need to marry into money. She speaks much as Dickens's Bella was to speak in *Our Mutual Friend*, insisting 'that I am a commodity in the market, and . . . ought to set myself at a high price' (IV, 58). Susannah Touchandgo loves, or at least has loved, Crotchet Junior; Crochet Junior loves money, and because Susannah's father has absconded to America—there to blow the economic bubbles that have burst in England[12]— Crotchet has automatically shifted his attentions to Clarinda. As the story begins, Susannah lives in semi-retirement in the mountains of Wales, where Mr. Chainmail is to discover her and to bring her, Alcestis-like, back to civilized life. Although Chainmail himself loves the twelfth century, when he meets Susannah he is willing to divide his attentions.

Peacock plays with the various love complications, laughing now with Clarinda at Fitzchrome's abjectness, now at Chainmail for his medieval expectations. He also plays with the means of story-telling itself. We have seen instances of this in the earlier novels.

To some extent, especially in *Headlong Hall*, Peacock seems to be adapting a Restoration or eighteenth-century comedy into semi-narrative, reserving a large role for the narrator as a kind of stage manager who sits in the wings.[13] We laugh in *Headlong Hall* at the Chaplinesque movements, at the witty thrusts, and at the farce, too, where the author reaches over and topples Mr. Cranium into the pond, or sends the love-lorn Mr. Escot peripatetically into a graveyard. In *Headlong Hall* and *Nightmare Abbey* the narrator is unobtrusive, though upon his stage omnipotent. Whereas in *Melincourt* and *Elphin* the narrator, far more intimate with the reader, takes advantage of the intimacy to moralize, in *Headlong Hall* and *Nightmare Abbey* he retains the ironic anonymity.

Crotchet Castle offers a rather less slapstick narrator than the one in *Headlong Hall*, a rather less anonymous narrator than the one in *Nightmare Abbey*. While still fairly circumspect, the speaker is also more cavalier. In the tradition of Fielding, Richard Graves, and other eighteenth-century novelists who speak about the 'provision' of their novels, he introduces a number of culinary metaphors. Folliott, for example, acknowledges the spring with 'lobster is, indeed, matter for a May morning', just as Graves, in *The Spiritual Quixote*, had written, 'Lamb and sallad ceased to be a Sunday's dinner. . . . In other words the spring was far advanced.'[14] The whole gustatory vocabulary—as emblem of season, character, subject matter— represents an 'easiness' of story handling and a pose on the narrator's part of amiable, disengaged bonhomie.

When Lady Clarinda has retailed her observations for Captain Fitzchrome, she pretends that her powers of observation have been sharpened due to her having been writing a novel. 'A novel!' exclaims her bewildered lover—as though nothing quite that deplorable could have been associated with Clarinda—and she, calmly as ever, replies: 'Yes, a novel. And I shall get a little finery by it. . . . You must know I have been reading several fashionable novels, the fashionable this, and the fashionable that; and I thought to myself, why I can do better than any of these myself' (IV, 68). Peacock is laughing here specifically at novels of the silver-fork variety; but he has made the same kind of satiric thrust before. In *Headlong Hall* the only novelist represented on Squire Headlong's estate had been Mrs. Opie in the guise of Miss Philomena Poppyseed. There as here, Peacock laughs at novel-writing with a wide-swinging guilt by association, and in a way not very flattering to his own readers : readers, that is, of the 'fashionable this and that'. He lets the narrator interrupt an argument at one point with : 'We would print these dialogues if we thought anyone would read them : but the world is not yet ripe for this *haute sagesse Pantagrueline*' (IV, 127).

The narrator in *Crotchet Castle* plays with his material in other ways, too. He uses the nonce word 'veridicous', for instance, in the following context :

> This veridicous history began in May, and the occurrences already narrated have carried it on to the middle of autumn [in other words, time is of no importance here, except as a counter to be shuffled at random]. Stepping over the interval to Christmas, we find ourselves in our first locality, among the chalk hills of the Thames . . . (IV, 185).

The return to the chalk hills, to Squire Crotcher's estate, is prelude to the final summing up of the various love stories. Susannah Touchandgo has in the meantime, and after an idyllic courtship, happily married Mr. Chainmail and has adopted the necessary twelfth-century traits, chiefly that of hospitality. Lady Clarinda finally admits what she has known all along : that she prefers love in a cottage with Fitzchrome to life in a castle with Crotchet. In one sense she has no choice, since Crotchet's career as bubble-blower has taken the same ill-fated course as that of the elder Touchandgo. For good measure, Peacock adds a third marriage, giving Miss Crotchet, the Squire's daughter, to Lord Bossnowl. So the narrator pulls all strings together. The novel ends with the ringing of bells, the tinkling of plates and glasses, and harmony ascendant. The guests gather together at Chainmail Hall for the Christmas celebrations.

The love affairs offer a continuity, possibly also an excuse for

festivities, but they comprise only one of the two stories of
Crotchet Castle. The sustaining action is not the substratum of
romance so much as the conversation of the Squire's friends and
the changes they undergo. Just as Chainmail wins his lady—by
marrying her for 'what she is'—so he, Dr. Folliott, Mr. Mac-
Quedy, and most of the others talk their way to a point of
unanticipated rationality. They develop from the almost mob-
debators of the beginning to something resembling an intellectual *élite*, 'a choice philosophical party', in the younger
Crotchet's words.

Not all the discussions contribute to the progression. There
are several tangential or too purely local interludes, including a
scene in which Dr. Folliott defends himself, after the manner of
some of Fielding's characters, from a pair of thieves, and
another in which he is interrogated by foolish members of a
charity commission. According to Ian Jack, all of *Crotchet Castle*
is local; he calls it a book that belongs to a particular moment
in time.[15] It is quite true that, like *Melincourt*, *Crotchet Castle*
contains a great number of allusions to the England of its day,
among them a hypothetical attack by 'Captain Swing' and his
incendiaries, who were historically symptoms of a turbulent
political climate prior to the 1832 reforms. Also the topical
allusions occur throughout the novel—'Captain Swing' himself
makes an entry so late as to seem gratuitous. Yet the relative
importance of outside reference diminishes. The emphasis shifts
from the specifically satiric to wide-ranging dialogue that is
finally local in little more than origin.

This is not to suggest that Peacock keeps, or for that matter
ever entirely makes, the discussions sober. The issues are generally larger than the men who discuss them. During the scene in
which Squire Crotchet defends his collection of undraped
statuary—specifically Venuses—against a shocked Dr. Folliott,
and launches into his diatribe against 'cant, cant, cant',
Crotchet does to an extent surpass himself, becoming a sympathetic exploder of prudery and sham. But his grasp of the
topic remains obviously limited, and it is not so much that he
wins the argument as that his opponent loses it. When Folliott
gathers up his largely fictitious wrath and desires to end the
argument dramatically, he merely ends it with a bang. 'Sir', he
addresses his host,

'I shall take the liberty to employ, on this occasion, the *argumentum ad hominem*. Would you have allowed Miss Crotchet to sit for a model to Canova?'

MR. CROTCHET. 'Yes, sir.'

'God bless my soul, sir!' exclaimed the Reverend Dr. FOLLIOTT, throwing himself back into a chair, and flinging up his heels, with the premeditated design of giving emphasis to his exclamation: but by miscalculating his *impetus*, he overbalanced his chair, and laid himself on the carpet in a right angle, of which his back was the base (IV, 101).

'When Peacock feels that his strain is growing monotonous', writes David Worcester, 'he makes his characters crack their skulls or fall downstairs or meet with some other violent bodily mishap.'[16] He might have added that, despite the incidence of such mishaps, astonishingly few people ever get hurt. Peacock relies on physical upsets, but he often does so less when the 'strain is growing monotonous' than when his characters are at the height of an argument, at the precise instant when they have farthest to fall or can look the most ridiculous. Many of the bathetic descents work as emblems of deflating intellectual pride.

Despite Dr. Folliott's indecorous, if emphatic, fall, he has often been cited as Peacock's first real mouthpiece for his own ideas. Henry Cole reported that Peacock 'used to say that this character was intended to make the *amende honorable* to the clergy for the satires of them in the Reverend Dr. Gaster, the Reverend Dr. Portpipe, and others in previous tales'.[17] If this is the case, the clergy might still have lodged a vigorous complaint, for Folliott is far more the epicurean gentleman than he is the good pastor. Indeed, he rarely participates in any but the most secular of roles.

If Folliott makes poor amends to the clergy, he does make a suitable spokesman for many of Peacock's opinions. Again, Folliott scoffs at Lord Brougham, whom he nicknames 'Sir Guy de Vaux'—and whom *Punch* was shortly to censure for moving with 'uncanny velocity from Whiggism to Toryism';[18] and he comments on Oxford in a way that singularly lacks ambiguity. For political economists and Scotsmen, both embodied in Mr. MacQuedy, he registers no patience, and he shows anger like Peacock himself for such things as 'the march of mind' and the decline in classical learning. Then, too, he is both 'learned and jolly', can spout Athenaeus and Chaucer, and admires Rabelais. Above all, he loves his food. But in fact Folliott is little more of a mouthpiece for his author than a number of earlier characters. In *Headlong Hall* Mr. Escot had spoken lines that later recurred in 'Fashionable Literature'. In *Melincourt*, Mr. Forester had, like Peacock, been a lover of poetry, an enemy to reactionary politics, and an abstainer from sugar because an opponent of slavery. In *Nightmare Abbey*, Mr. Hilary had shown a capacity for a considered epicurean cheerfulness and tolerance. None of these is appreciably less a spokesman than the witty cleric.

Folliott is another of Peacock's characters who are more nearly right than wrong but who are never entirely either. Folliott consistently defeats MacQuedy, but he yields to Squire Crotchet, to Mr. Chainmail, and, at the time of the mishap, to his own humbug. The point is that he participates in debates in which no individual is finally victorious. These are, to repeat, mock Socratic dialogues without a guiding Socrates, without a clear direction, though with some form of inverse climax, such as a fall, a drinking song, 'a summons to tea and coffee'.[19]

Typical of the dialogues is a chapter entitled 'Theories', in which Crotchet senior and junior, Mr. Skionar, the Reverend Dr. Folliott, Mr. MacQuedy, Mr. Toogood, Mr. Trillo and others play on a theme established by the younger Crotchet: 'There is one point in which philosophers of all classes seem to be agreed; that they only want money to regenerate the world' (IV, 70). Peacock's having prefaced the chapter with a motto from Butler—

> But when they came to shape the model,
> Not one could at the other's noddle—

ensures that no one can possibly win. Dr. Folliott scoffs at MacQuedy's political economy. Mr. Skionar speaks a language comprehensible to none of the others. Mr. Toogood explains his 'diagram' of a 'co-operative parallelogram, with a steam-engine in the middle'. Mr. Trillo pleads for the resuscitation of the

Athenian theatre: 'regenerate the lyrical drama!' No one really listens, or can listen. All are set in motion by a spare word, by a cue. And, apparently in the middle of their talk, they interrupt themselves with a drinking song:

> If I drink water while this doth last,
>   May I never again drink wine:
> For how can a man, in his life of a span,
>   Do anything better than dine?

After the song the narrator simply appends: 'The schemes for the world's regeneration evaporated in a tumult of voices' (IV, 85).

The 'tumult of voices' recurs throughout the novel, as though to alternate with the dialogues of the various lovers. But in a more central way the dialogue parallels the love stories, and fittingly ends with them. The party at Chainmail Hall, complete with harper and wassail—it might be a burlesque of scenes in Scott's *Lay of the Last Minstrel*—includes only part of the original guests who congregated at the Villa:

> Three of that party were wanting. Dr. Morbific, by inoculating himself once too often with non-contagious matter, had explained himself out of the world. Mr. Henbane had also departed, on the wings of an infallible antidote. Mr. Eavesdrop, having printed in a magazine some of the after-dinner conversations of the castle, had had sentence of exclusion passed upon him . . . (IV, 185–6).

Not only, in short, has Crotchet Junior been punished for half-hearted courting, his plight has been matched by the less desirable 'humours'. They have either passed on with a fitting death or, in Eavesdrop's case, been scapegoated by the remaining group. Side by side with the love stories, then, Peacock shows the maturing of the other characters, who, though still objects of laughter, somehow triumph over their intellectual limitations and create an internal and not wholly absurd norm of behaviour. In a sense Peacock may be said to vacillate between that kind of humour identified by Bergson, whereby characters are laughable in so far as they are mechanical and their humanity restricted—which is specifically the realm of satire—and that kind of humour which demands geniality and good-natured laughter, the final end of which is not militant at all.[20]

Because he presents humours and belittles forms of intellectual arrogance, Peacock has been accused of an anti-rational streak, a charge that is partly legitimate, though no more for him than for Rabelais, Petronius, Swift, Juvenal, Aristophanes, Ben Jonson. All the great rational satirists, as Robert Elliott writes, create anti-intellectual satire.[21] Yet if Peacock at times transgresses the line that separates satire of certain fraudulent kinds of intellection from that of real rationality, he is in a sense far less guilty than, say, Swift or Aristophanes. One can argue like Walter Raleigh that Peacock was not a rebel against ideas, a mere spokesman for common sense, and that 'he had deep down in him a great love of ideas'.[22] The point is rather that the genre itself, while depending on the traditional laughter against pedants and cranks, in fact concludes by an implicit apology for what they represent.

The ending of *Crotchet Castle* differs from that of the earlier novels of talk in a peculiar way. As the 'twelfth-century feast' progresses, cries are heard without. They are those of Captain Swing and his incendiaries, demanding weapons. The response of those within the castle is as varied as their points of view. The arch-conservative Folliott says: 'What was Jacquerie in the dark ages, is the march of mind in this very enlightened one—very enlightened one.' Mr. Chainmail, with sentiments of Cobbett and Ritson behind him, replies: 'The cause is the same in both: poverty in despair.' And the apostle of new Athenian light, Mr. MacQuedy adds: 'Very likely, but the effect is extremely disagreeable' (IV, 199). Peacock's own response to such movements as Chartism was ambivalent. The election scene in *Melincourt* shows that, as the advocate of reform, he had nothing but contempt for the vote-controlling Mr. Corporate. At the same time he makes the crowd who would chair Sir Oran, and who need to elect their own representatives, into mindless numbers. He feared, as he told the India House Committee, nothing more than the mob. Essentially his dilemma was that while he could not approve plans for universal education, as sponsored by such men as Brougham, he felt the necessity of distributing power partly into the hands of those who were still incapable of its proper use. The problem was—and is—no trivial one, yet Peacock's vacillations and doubts remain peculiarly incidental to the novels that reveal them. In both the scene of Sir Oran's election and the siege of Chainmail Hall, external forces or issues merely act to unite the central group of actors. With cavalier unconcern, Dr. Folliott takes arms against the yelling incendiaries, routing them from the castle and banishing them from the story. At this point in the novel, outside politics, whatever their urgency in the ordinary scheme of things, must be kept outside. They bow to the demands of comedy.

8

Later Fragments and *Gryll Grange*: a Nod to Aristophanes

Oh for a breath of Aristophanes, Rabelais, Voltaire, Cervantes, Fielding, Molière.

GEORGE MEREDITH, 'An Essay on Comedy.'

I

The years between publication of *Crotchet Castle* and *Gryll Grange* were for Peacock a time of public responsibilities and personal cares. For the India House he served on various committees, advising and representing the Company; his discussion of Steam Communication for the India routes appeared in the *Edinburgh Review* (1835), testifying to his competence as public official. After the final illness of James Mill, Peacock succeeded in the mid-1830's to Mill's position as Examiner, in which capacity he served for twenty years. He then retired, not only from work, but from London, moving permanently to Lower Halliford and his house fronting on the Thames.

His personal life in these years, though there are a few records, remains as ever somewhat obscure. But unquestionably, and however little it may show in his writings, Peacock had his share of troubles. Troubles with a chronically ill wife, who never recovered from the shock of the early death of one of their daughters; troubles with his favourite daughter, Mary Ellen, who lost her first husband after a few months of marriage, and whose second marriage to George Meredith ended in a pathetic elopement with the painter Henry Wallis. (One wonders about Peacock's role in the marriages of his children. Evidently he was opposed to all their marriages for one reason or another.) In 1833 Peacock's mother died, leaving him to find professional outsiders to look after his children and his ill wife, and leaving him, too, without his closest literary associate. 'I passed many of my best years with my mother', he was to write to Thomas L'Estrange, 'taking more pleasure in reading than in society' (VIII, 259). He is reported to have 'read all his writings to her, consulting her judgment, and seeking her criticism; he often said that, after his mother's death, he wrote with no interest, as his heart was not in his work'.[1]

It was not only that he wrote with no interest—if that was the case—but that he wrote hardly at all. As Brett-Smith puts it. 'The effect of his mother's death and his domestic affairs is evident in any list of Peacock's writings; he published little from 1834 to 1838, nothing from 1838 to 1850' (I, clxxxii). He managed to do a few poems and essays before 1838 and after 1850, and, though he was to complete only *Gryll Grange*, he also began several new novels.

Shortly before James Mill's death and the acceptance of the Examinership, Peacock toyed with a story that reads like Dr. Johnson's rendering of material by Mrs. Radcliffe. Set in the mountains of Bohemia, it introduces a party of garrulous travellers, who speak inquisitively about 'The Lord of the Hills'. This of course was the folklore character Rübezahl, or Herr der Berge, legends about which the German Musäus had collected in the previous century, and which Peacock evidently met in translation. Rübezahl is a supernatural figure, a good-natured giant—the Bohemian cousin of Robin Hood.

In Peacock's only attempt to make extensive use of the supernatural, it is amusing to see how unlike Mrs. Radcliffe he becomes. Elements for mystery are present in 'The Lord of the Hills': there are mountains, swift-falling darkness, a young lady, the local superstition. But the conversation, occupied with the mundane, precludes horror, and the tone of the story resembles the quietly facetious tone of *Elphin*. Peacock's conception of Rübezahl is fairly traditional: he is the mocking spirit, scoffing at illusions with loud, derisive laughter. But one wonders whether he might not, for example, have emerged as Voltaire's ghost. One of the characters speaks for him by saying: ' "It will be enough to say . . . that man cannot live without illusions. His life is nothing else. The echo that laughs at illusions will laugh as heartily as ever at the idea of a featherless biped without them" ' (VIII, 361). Whereas Mrs. Radcliffe explains her supernatural after the event, Peacock accounts for his beforehand. 'The Lord of the Hills'—containing French phrases, French characters, and a potentially 'romantic' voyage, actually comes closer, not to Mrs. Radcliffe, but to a writer like Marmontel. More than any other of Peacock's writings, it resembles an eighteenth-century French *conte*.

During these later years between *Crotchet Castle* and *Gryll Grange*, spent either in London or on Lower Halliford, Peacock played at various times with different topics. 'Julia Procula', another venture into historical fiction, he laid aside in 1848—presumably without loss to his readers, since the surviving fragments offer only a few dull dialogues set in ancient Rome. A reader is apt to be, in the words of the narrator, 'much perplexed as to how far he was in earnest' (VIII, 379).

In 'A Story Opening at Chertsey' and 'A Story of a Mansion Among the Chiltern Hills', Peacock introduces material that he was to exploit in *Gryll Grange*. Both of these brief sketches (the first written about 1851, the other shortly before *Gryll Grange* in 1859) are experiments, though along familiar lines. 'Chertsey' presents three friends: a 'classicist' and two 'medievalists', who were probably to have become a trio similar to that of Escot, Foster, and Jenkison. But here, as in the forthcoming novel, Peacock is thinking less of types than of predominant interests:

> An early breakfast, an early dinner, a long walk and a supper imply that these were old-fashioned young gentlemen. And so indeed they were: their habits and their tastes were all antique. One was devoted to Greece and Rome: one to medieval art and manners: one to legends of chivalry and romance: not so exclusively that each did not enter pretty largely into the domains of the others . . . (VIII, 384).

The 'Mansion' fragment introduces, in its few pages of narrative, Catherine of Alexandria, the saint with unmatched powers of persuasion, whom Peacock—and perhaps for her verbal powers as much as for her religious convictions—admired in later life, and who in *Gryll Grange* dominates a whole chapter of conversation, being Algernon Falconer's ascetic ideal. In

Peacock's account, Mario Praz might call her a *biedermeierliche femme fatale*.

Two other fragments were either contemporary with or slightly later than *Gryll Grange* (probably, that is, 1859 and 1860). 'Boozabowt Abbey', much the rowdiest of the later sketches, explains itself fully in the title. 'Boozabowt' becomes little more than a sophisticated, and rather less farcical, version of 'The Monks of St. Mark', but it also has specific echoes of *Elphin*. Brother John, even more indebted than Friar Tuck to Frère Jean of Rabelais, indicates that Peacock was to play once more with the stock humour of monkery. This is Peacock at his closest to the genial but glib and inconsequential narrative of the *Ingoldsby Legends*.

In 'Cotswold Chace', last of the incomplete stories, Peacock offers less boisterous conversation. He returns to the format of *Melincourt*, although the story lacks *Melincourt*'s immediate political bias, by presenting a reclusive, wealthy, and beautiful young spinster, around whom the story was evidently to have revolved.

II

During the thirty years that elapsed before Peacock completed another novel, England found a whole generation of novelists. Scott and Jane Austen gave way to Dickens, to the Brontës, to Thackeray, to Trollope, to George Eliot. In view of Peacock's penchant for assimilating, it would seem reasonable for him to have drawn on the younger writers, especially on Dickens, whom he read and admired. Yet his reported comment on Dickens, the tenor of which is predictable, makes clear that the provenance of the last novel differs little, if at all, from that of the earlier stories. 'Dickens,' he is supposed to have said, 'is very comic, but—not *so* comic as Aristophanes.'[2] The phrasing here is probably not Peacock's, but the sentiment clearly is. The scenario for 'Aristophanes in London', a play produced by the guests at Gryll Grange, occurs towards the high point in the story. But of Dickens there is neither mention nor echo. Excepting its satiric references, *Gryll Grange* deferred to its times only by appearing serially in *Fraser's Magazine*.

Peacock may be said to have borrowed for this novel from

his own earlier works. The characters and setting are new, the targets of his censure are in part also new, yet 'the author of *Headlong Hall*' is as readily identifiable in this his final novel as in his first, written over forty years before. *Gryll Grange* and *Headlong Hall* actually share qualities that are to a degree absent from the intervening novels. Although *Gryll Grange* comes close to *Melincourt* in its size and in its type of story and registers, like *Crotchet Castle*, some grave doubts about the Victorian temper, it approximates more nearly the other-worldly quality of *Headlong Hall*. Squire Gryll proves a less impetuous host than Squire Headlong; Dr. Opimian emerges a far more rational, if equally conservative, clergyman than Dr. Gaster; acute apologists for rural retreat supplant diverse philosophers; still, there is a familiar atmosphere with the same detached and stylized comedy of ideas.

Except for the official side of his life, most of what had occupied Peacock during his seventy years emerges in one way or another in *Gryll Grange*, so that the novel becomes a kind of last manifesto. It treats of good fellowship, good food and wine, and of classical literature. Opimian receives an invitation to visit Mr. Falconer only because, on stopping to admire 'The Folly' —Falconer's residence—he mutters to himself some lines from Homer, which Falconer overhears. Elsewhere Opimian says: 'Consider how much instruction has been conveyed to us in the form of conversations at banquets, by Plato and Xenophon and Plutarch. I read nothing with more pleasure than their *Symposia*: to say nothing of Athenaeus, whose work is one long banquet' (v, 197). This is the usual provision of Peacock's works; but he also yokes together comments on land enclosure, vestal virgins, St. Catherine, competitive examinations, America, public lectures, ice-skating, and knighthoods.

Thackeray, who met Peacock at Erle Stoke, home of Lord Broughton (John Cam Hobhouse), in 1850, described the 'small select party' gathered together by the host, 'a most polite and good natured [man], with a very winning simplicity of manner'. Not knowing that Peacock was still to write *Gryll Grange* and continued to write poems, Thackeray says:

—Peacock—did you ever read *Headlong Hall* and *Maid Marian*?—a charming lyrical poet and Horatian satirist he was when a writer; now he is a white-headed jolly old worldling, and Secretary [*sic*] to the E. India House, full of information about India and everything else in the world.[3]

The narrator of *Gryll Grange* speaks like 'a jolly old worldling' and, excepting India, seems to introduce the range of information that had impressed Thackeray. The *Saturday Review*, delighting in Peacock's learning, also praised his 'quaint, hearty, unostentatious Paganism'. 'The volume reads', they suggested,

> like a few numbers of *Notes and Queries* jumbled up with a funny love story, and pervaded by a fine Pagan morality. The greatest tribute to its merits that can be paid is to say what may be said with perfect truth—that all this queer mixture flows easily along, and that we never feel we have been delivered over to a learned bore.[4]

Goethe, who himself wrote far into old age, remarked that the greatest of the arts was that of self-limitation. And, tacitly, Peacock seems to have worked by a similar maxim. The queer mixture or medley—which somehow, as the *Saturday Review* pointed out, manages to move along without difficulties in the narrative or without the notes and queries seeming like the intrusion of pedantry—offers a description that is as true of the earlier works as much as of *Gryll Grange* itself. To say that the book deserved all of the *Saturday Review*'s praise is not, then, to imply that Peacock as an old man became an inventive novelist, striking out in a new direction. This is not the case at all. But the novel seldom flags from limited incident or meagre story. It repeats, but it is not redundant, while offering the wisdom that too rarely comes with age and the wit that all too often disappears.

As in *Melincourt*, Peacock once again builds two neighbouring estates, the one conveniently housing the hero, the other the heroine. Algernon Falconer and Morgana Gryll are less Rousseauistic and less priggish versions of Forester and Anthelia. They are also more fully presented as people. Of the various characters who visit the country estate of Squire Gryll, few resemble the crotcheteers of the earlier works. Unlike Squire

Crotchet, Gryll is a relaxed gentleman, particular about his guests. The guests include such people as Miss Ilex, Peacock's one pleasant old lady, and Miss Niphet and Lord Curryfin, who, while not complex characters, have a certain emotional range—and a capacity to listen. Curryfin, Peacock's first portrait of a lord that is not damning—and who perhaps reflects his later friendship with Lord Broughton—actually develops during the course of the story by learning something about himself and by acting according to the knowledge. He begins as a fashionable public lecturer, telling fishermen about fish, but at the close of the story he puts aside childish things and deserves the inscrutable Miss Niphet. In short, Peacock seems to make amends here for the not very agreeable family of the Crotchets and for their sometimes poor taste in guests. The people in *Gryll Grange* spout opinions and disagree, but Peacock clearly approves of host and guests alike.

Entitled 'Misnomers'—it might have been called 'Farrago' in Juvenal's sense—the first chapter of *Gryll Grange* not only introduces the work and three of its important characters, it reveals Peacock's entire method in miniature. Consider Dr. Opimian's opening conversational gambit:

> 'Palestine soup!' said the Reverend Dr. Opimian, dining with his friend Squire Gryll; 'a curiously complicated misnomer. We have an excellent old vegetable, the artichoke, of which we eat the head; we have another of subsequent introduction, of which we eat the root, and which we also call artichoke, because it resembles the first in flavour, although, *me judice*, a very inferior affair. This last is a species of helianthus, or sunflower genus of the *Syngenesia frustranea* class of plants. It is therefore a girasol, or turn-to-the-sun. From this girasol we have made Jerusalem, and from the Jersualem artichoke we make Palestine Soup.'

Apart from offering a witty gastronomic *jeu d'esprit* and a textbook example of chiasmus, the doctor's words serve as a cue to Squire Gryll. He replies, 'A very good thing, Doctor'; and when Opimian responds that it is 'A very good thing; but a palpable misnomer', Squire Gryll can launch into an almost equally

epigrammatic and well-turned speech on 'a world of misnomers'. Each provides the other with a mounting-block; each
is ready to discuss any subject. For when the squire closes his
polished tirade, he invites the Doctor to continue: 'While we
are on the subject of misnomers, what say you to the wisdom of
Parliament?' And Opimian, needing but the slightest prompt,
bounds after the new topic. He then accedes to the Squire's
contention that 'Palestine soup is not more remote from the true
Jerusalem than many an honourable friend from public
honesty', and cheerfully agrees to a glass of Madeira.

At this point Morgana Gryll, lovely niece of the Squire,
enters the conversation and epitomizes what has transpired:
'You and my uncle, Doctor, get up a discussion on everything
that presents itself; dealing with your theme like a series of
variations in music.' She both speaks to the point, and prompts
the talk once more: 'You have run half round the world *àpropos*
of the soup. What say you to the fish?' Dr. Opimian, like
Athenaeus's characters, is an authority on fish, and speaks
accordingly. After a list of various species and their merits—
Opimian prefers the taste of the fish with one-syllabic names—
the subject moves to Lord Curryfin, a lecturer on fish, to lectures
in general, to *tensons* and their possible use in conversation, and
finally to the desirability of producing an Aristophanic comedy
—for passing judgment on the times. Miss Gryll suggests that
the comedy be presented at Christmas, and that suitable roles
might include 'Homer, and Dante, and Shakespeare, and
Richard the First, and Oliver Cromwell'—in addition to the
original and ancestral Gryllus, who, the narrator says, 'maintained against Ulysses the superior happiness of the life of other
animals' (v, 1–12), specifically that of pigs.[5] The narrator
finally interrupts the conversation: 'Before we proceed further,
we will give some account of our interlocutors', and the chapter
closes (v, 1–12).

Several things become clear from this chapter. Every sentence
is at once carefully developed and seemingly spontaneous.
Because of their turns of phrase, many of the sentences are self-
contained, standing as prose epigrams. Miss Gryll's desire for a
formal *tenson* is, as the narrator implies, gratuitous, since the
kind of *tenson* she envisions is taking place as she speaks. The
'series of variations in music', as she describes it, is a matter of

balance and interplay between the speakers and their themes.[6] Just as each sentence is complete in itself, so is the whole episode. The pause to give 'account of our interlocutors' offers the same sort of cue that Opimian gives to Gryll, for the chapters, discreet like the sentences, proceed from one conversational episode to another.

In range of subject the chapter is broad indeed: a few pages treat of many topics. Yet this is the lightest of conversation, delicate, mannered, and intellectual. It takes place, after all, over the span of two courses at dinner: and the dinner provides the stimulus for the talk. Whatever will arise in the next chapter, it is clear that the characters will return to table before long, and that whatever thunderclouds may develop within the course of the story, such an opening calls for such an end.

The story itself follows the pattern of the earlier novels, though it presents a new complication. Morgana Gryll, only relative of the Squire, remains unmarried, not having encountered her ideal young man. Through the quaintly Pandaric activities of Dr. Opimian, she is introduced to the Gryll's reclusive neighbour, Algernon Falconer. Falconer resembles Molière's Alceste, except that he has a little self-knowledge. Peacock laughs at him, sympathizes with him, reforms him. Unfortunately for Morgana, as the story opens, Algernon has committed himself to a life of retirement, boasting the service of a group of seven sisters, 'seven vestals', who look after his household while he occupies his mind with Homer and his spirit with St. Catherine. Unlikely as all this seems—and Mrs. Opimian's comment is: 'I don't trust young men'—the story nonetheless depends upon it. For Morgana, an emancipated young lady, admits her love for Falconer by leaving open a revealing page of the poet Boiardo, so that the resolution of the novel depends upon his descent from a tower, in which he actually does live. Falconer, then, plays his own *senex* in this comedy, and of course his younger self finally triumphs.

Falconer has a temporary rival in Lord Curryfin, who veers towards Morgana before falling in love with the quieter and, it turns out, more suitable Miss Niphet. But all is finally resolved. Algernon asks for Morgana, thereby giving Squire Gryll hope for an heir. The seven 'vestals' marry seven fortuitously suitable local farmers, and Lord Curryfin asks for Miss Niphet. There is a mathematical coupling, outstripping even that of *Headlong Hall*. After performing the Aristophanic comedy, everyone joins in celebrations, which, like those of *Headlong Hall* and *Crotchet Castle*, take place at Christmas.

Peacock introduces few songs in *Gryll Grange*. One guest sings a gentle song of 'Love and Age':

> I played with you 'mid cowslips blowing,
> When I was six and you were four;
> When garlands weaving, flower-balls throwing,
> Were pleasures soon to please no more.
> Through groves and meads, o'er grass and heather,
> With little playmates, to and fro,
> We wandered hand in hand together;
> But that was sixty years ago ... (v, 146)

and Dr. Opimian recites a rather cantankerous poem called 'A New Order of Chivalry' (probably written earlier and inserted into the novel). But the songs are proportionately fewer and usually weaker than those in the earlier novels. Instead of songs, Peacock offers the play within a play, 'Aristophanes in London'. As might be imagined, Aristophanes, with Circe and Gryll as his main characters, finds even more to condemn in modern England than he had in ancient Athens. He speaks, as a matter of fact, with a distinctly English intonation. Circe can sum up his indictment in a few lines:

> Three thousand years ago,
> This land was forest, and a bright pure river
> Ran through it to and from the Ocean stream.
> Now, through a wilderness of human forms,
> And human dwellings, a polluted flood
> Rolls up and down, charged with all earthly poisons.
>
> Houses, and ships,
> And boats, and chimneys vomiting black smoke,
> Horses, and carriages of every form,
> And restless bipeds, rushing here and there
> For profit or for pleasure, as they phrase it (v, 279).

Industry is, in short, the major villain. But Peacock also levels some of the traditional charges of Aristophanes, indicting political demagoguery, misleading rhetoric, and idle theoretical speculation.

Peacock suggests by his play, and by the conversation generally, that in an age given over to absurdities, when people travel without purpose and live without enjoyment, some things may be offered as fingers for the dike. What one cannot change, one can by music, conviviality, and natural surroundings avoid. Falconer says to Opimian shortly after they meet: 'The world will never suppose a good motive, where it can suppose a bad one. I would not willingly offend any of its prejudices. I would not affect eccentricity. At the same time, I do not feel disposed to be put out of my way because it is not the way of the world . . .' (v, 30). So he, like the other characters, does go his own way, and the world may go to the devil.

Such an attitude necessarily reflects on the Aristophanic comedy, which is really more of a tribute to Aristophanes than a re-creation of his method; it is, to use the phrase of Meredith, 'a breath of Aristophanes'. Carl Van Doren has called *Gryll Grange* 'New Comedy', as opposed to the 'Old Comedy' of *Maid Marian*, and though the distinction is useful, it is not wholly apt, for even *Maid Marian* has little of Aristophanes—and its plot, like that of the other stories, is essentially 'new comedy'.[7] Van Doren's point calls attention, however, to some differences between *Gryll Grange* and the earlier novels. Peacock has dispensed in his final novel with characters who are merely 'embodied classifications'; he has substituted more or less normal movements for the farcical tumbling of, say, *Headlong Hall*; he has become less harsh in his censure of humours, and somewhat more preoccupied with effecting the traditional happy ending.

In *Melincourt* Peacock had spoken of the type of writer convinced of his powers to set the world right, perhaps with his earlier self in mind. The course of his novels, slight as the changes may be, culminates in *Gryll Grange*, for, aware and acute as he is, Peacock has accepted another role. One way to appreciate his attitude is to consider the author's note preceding the novel, where he says: 'In the following pages, the New Forest is always mentioned as if it were still unenclosed. This is the only state in which the author has been acquainted with it. Since its enclosure, he has never seen it, and purposes never to do so.' The 'as if it were' epitomizes the underlying attitude of the work. Not bitterly muttering his *vanitas vanitatum*, or bemoaning everything like his own Mr. Toobad, Peacock is rather talking eloquently in the world's despite.

In addition to Aristophanes, Peacock pays tribute in *Gryll Grange* to Petronius, whom he quotes extensively and cites with approval. Dr. Opimian owes his name, ultimately, to the famous wine produced during the rule of Opimian, but Peacock no doubt borrows the name directly from Petronius. In the *Satyricon* Trimalchio serves his guests 'Opimian wine 100 years old'—and therefore, presumably, unpalatable. Peacock has often referred to Petronius, often laughed with him. He delights in the anecdote about the German scholar who, informed that a 'complete Petronius' had been discovered, raced down to Italy to find the mere corporeal remains of the Catholic saint (IX, 361). In Petronius, as in Lucian, he found an enviable blend: here was a satirist, a versifier, and a man, like himself, with antipathy towards his age. The *Satyricon*, mixing prose and verse, and revolving around Trimalchio's incredible feast, understandably became one of Peacock's favourite works. His own fiction, similarly oriented around dinner tables, similarly mixing prose and verse—a practice already waning in the late-eighteenth-century novel—might be considered a modern equivalent for Petronius's type of Menippean satire. What qualifies such a view is Peacock's restraint. There is little in his novels, and particularly little in *Gryll Grange*, of Petronius's gross burlesque of social customs, certainly none of the explorations of sexual oddities. If Peacock could admire Petronius's energetic descriptions and the range of his comments—unlike Smollett, who found the *Satyricon* unfit reading for an English gentleman, but whose 'realism' seems occasionally indebted to Petronius—Peacock borrows only a general method of narrative. He has been said to have the amused curiosity of Lucian rather than the fierce mockery of Swift. Petronius substituted for Swift would affect the justice of the observation little. But it might be better to say, as Thackeray did, that he has the tolerant laughter of Horace rather than the—partly assumed—anger of Juvenal. And Dr. Opimian, that broad-ranging student of classics, devotee of Athenaeus, and connoisseur of lobster, Dr. Opimian himself embodies Peacock's amiable satiric tone. His name stems from a Falernian wine, but his real genesis is the good-humoured eighteenth-century eccentric, in Addison, Fielding, or Sterne.

III

The qualities of Peacock's comedy are reflected throughout in the various houses and country settings, wherein he creates 'all this queer mixture' of 'funny love story', 'Pagan morality', and talk. Peacock began at least one story after *Gryll Grange*, but he completed none;[8] and the Gryll mansion is the last of his comic settings. It is worth a few more comments.

Houses, of course, play an important part in so much mid-nineteenth-century fiction. One has only to think of such titles as *Bleak House* and *Wuthering Heights*; or to remember the drama enacted in the Casaubon library in *Middlemarch*, in Miss Haversham's unlit room, where Pip enters upon his illusions as well as his expectations, and in Mowbray Castle, in Disraeli's *Sybil*, where 'the two nations' finally meet in symbolic battle.[9] Thackeray, in *Vanity Fair*, creates an entire satiric stage in Becky and Rawdon's house in Curzon Street and in 'the house on Russell Square'. Wilkie Collins makes Blackwater Park, its name suggestive enough, into a place of villainy and intrigue in *The Woman in White*.

Peacock's houses, by comparison, suggest another muse and another world, with entirely different rules and possibilities. As in those of Jane Austen, there is no hunger in his houses, no echo of guns; there is also no treachery, no lasting affliction, no real pathos. Whereas the Brontës, Dickens, and George Eliot use their houses as emblems of a world in emotional or social turmoil, Peacock's remain at an apparently safe remove. Even Meredith, in the houses of the Feverils and Sir Willoughby Patterne, describes places of dark corners, and his comic spirit, whatever its indebtedness to Peacock, casts intermittent shadows down below. In *Melincourt*, Peacock moved briefly in the direction of the great Victorian realists; but in that novel, too, comedy raises its voice at the expense of pathos. More usual in Peacock is the situation of Headlong Hall and Nightmare

Abbey, separated from 'civilization' by narrow and almost impassable roads.

The final novelistic setting, Gryll Grange, epitomizes these isolated and carefree houses; it is as enclosed and self-contained as Windsor Forest itself. There can be no doubt, I think, that the Gryll residence reflects a more genial comedy than that in *Crochet Castle* and the earlier novels. More genial because more isolated, more consciously separated from satanic mills, dark city streets, and the conditions that Marx and Owen, Carlyle and Mill had been crying out against.

And hence the houses of Peacock's younger novelistic contemporaries seem not only more involved with contemporary life, but also more committed to life itself. In our own time, when literature is often associated with political ends, when realism has become the accepted norm for fiction, when a writer's sincerity seems more important than his artifice, when 'serious' grappling with moral issues has been offered as the hallmark of the *real* English novel, of the great tradition, works like Peacock's may seem like unimportant escapism. The charge has occasionally been made, and it is one that ought to be met.

Let me begin by twisting the meaning of a comment by Northrop Frye, who argues—with a view to the ritual elements of comedy—that comedy contains within itself potential tragedy.[10] This is evidently true of *Measure for Measure*, say, or *Volpone*, as it was of the more immediately ritualistic comedies of Aristophanes, Menander, or Plautus. Is it also perhaps true of Peacock's comedy? My point throughout has been that Peacock places his characters in an intact world, where they have little to do but talk; and that, whatever the import of their talk, the characters enact traditional comic roles. In *Melincourt* and in parts of *Crotchet Castle*, Peacock draws in the outside world, either by extensive allusion, or by letting his characters confront suffering. Elsewhere his characters are remote from suffering. And they seem especially remote in *Gryll Grange*.

The point to be made about *Gryll Grange* is not that the book contains potential tragedy; rather that tragedy is the assumed daily condition—beyond the bounds of Gryll's estate. The more isolated Peacock makes his setting, the more he suggests tragedy by implication. For the setting, the intact social world, is as precarious as it is desirable. There is the same sort of parallel at work in *Gryll Grange* as in Shakespeare's *As You Like It*. However idyllic the forest and unscathed the foresters, we know that Arden is a good, a green or 'golden' world only by inverse reflection on the usurped dukedom. (Some of Peacock's characters, Scythrop and Toobad among them, sound like Jacques: professional malcontents in idyllic surroundings.) To speak about 'romantic comedy' may be a way of calling Peacock's books anachronistic modes in an age of literary realism, a way of saying that they are, after all, escapist literature. The question to be asked is whether such description automatically implies censure or whether it merely offers a useful means of classification.

To Mario Praz, among the harshest but most persuasive of Peacock's commentators, and normally one of the acutest critics, Peacock's retreats, and generally his type of fiction, represent stagnant eddies in the nineteenth-century mainstream. I have mentioned before Mr. Praz's dislike of Peacock's songs. To such an opinion he is clearly entitled; it matters little whether one critic likes a song and another does not. But arguing on the basis of a thorough misconception of Peacock's art, Mr. Praz allows himself almost incredible obtuseness when he speaks about the novels. He can say, for example, 'Peacock is bourgeois in every paragraph'.[11] Does he mean by this that Peacock's houses and the characters they contain represent a middle-class ideal: the pot of aspidistra writ large? So that Gryll's estate might be anticipatory of the suburban house, his banquets the Sunday dinners after Sunday papers? Whatever charge is intended, it is of dubious application. For in one sense or another all the important nineteenth-century writers— and probably most of the eighteenth-century writers—are *bourgeois*: of, for, and about the middle class. Jane Austen presumably is. So is Dickens; so is George Eliot. The Marxist critic Georg Lukács calls Walter Scott great largely because he could depict historical periods in terms of *bourgeois* ideals. To label a writer *bourgeois* is, without careful definition, to misuse an already overused word, to avoid the issue. The term is poor censure because it is inaccurate description.

If, however, Mr. Praz intends by the term the loose associations of easy optimism or faith in progress or the smugness consequent on newly-acquired wealth, then one can say categorically that he could not be more wrong. As much as Arnold, Newman, Thackeray, and George Eliot, Peacock censured the philistinism of his time. He hated the Bounderbys, the Podsnaps, the Pumblechooks, and the Pecksniffs as much as Dickens did. And if, like Dickens, his conception of economic forces left much to be desired, that makes him no less a responsible observer of how men thought and lived. One has only to compare him with Trollope to see how critical, how iconoclastic he was. In short, the implications of Peacock's isolated comic dialogues do not have to be negative at all. Peacock *chose* a particular art form, or, rather, created one to suit his needs. He was not necessarily incapable of feeling, callous to suffering, insensitive to tragedy—or hopelessly middle-class. But even if Peacock had these and other limitations as a man; even if his novels reflect a certain temperament, the statement made in the novels is of a different order entirely. Peacock, like many great comic novelists, illustrates that fiction takes the form of self-criticism and self-parody almost as easily as it does self-apology.

There may indeed be escapism in his novels. No doubt Peacock would have applauded Matthew Arnold's comment in *Popular Education in France* (published a little more than a year later than *Gryll Grange*): 'For anyone but a pedant . . . a handful of Athenians of two thousand years ago are more interesting than the mills of most nations of our contemporaries.' But as 'Aristophanes in London' makes clear, an interest in Greece had implications for Peacock comparable with those it had for Arnold. 'Now', Arnold writes, 'all the liberty and industry in the world will not ensure these two things: a high reason and a fine culture.'[12] For Peacock as for Arnold, culture itself was not only the end, it was also a means to a further end, for 'culture begets a dissatisfaction, which is of the highest possible value in stemming the common tide of men's thoughts in a wealthy and industrial community.'[13] Arnold's use of culture in this passage from *Culture and Anarchy* has not quite the same meaning as in the lines from *Education in France*. What is important, however, is not the definition but the overwhelming concern with quality of life or civilization in Crystal Palace England.

It is worth repeating that Peacock's characteristic mode of criticism was not Arnold's and that the medium itself inevitably modifies the terms of criticism. Nonetheless, Peacock's fictional worlds do two things that Arnold is calling for. They offer critical debate, and they offer an alternative vision, based upon 'the spectacle of ancient Athens'. His appeal is for intelligent scrutiny, for order, beauty, art. He does not defend the *status quo*, nor is he an easy reactionary. Like Arnold, he concerns himself with a whole state of mind, which he rightfully associates with the state of literature and the state of politics.[14] Arnold spoke of Peacock, appropriately, as 'a man of keen and cultivated mind'.[15]

Peacock's houses are the setting for a singular type of comedy, full of exuberant intellectual gaiety and, whatever the satiric or critical basis, full of music, dance, and the ritual ingredients of older comedy. Where Arnold points soberly towards an ideal, Peacock brings his to life. Like Walter Landor, he creates in his imaginary conversations glimpses of the best that has been thought and said. In a setting where dialogue is as much a staple as the dinners and the port, he lets his characters talk their way to a kind of absurd rationality. At the least he lets them pass judgment on the 'crazy fabric' of the world outside. His worlds are not Biedemeier worlds, not the stuffy retreats of an abject middle class. Their ideals are as old as Plato's.

NOTES

1 Introduction

1. The search was also of course for the appropriate 'voice' or style. Could one use the 'high' style for poems that were not strictly speaking epic? For two informative discussions of this problem see Geoffrey H. Hartman's *Wordsworth's Poetry, 1787–1814* (London, 1964) and Herbert Lindenberger's *On Wordsworth's Poetry* (Princeton, 1963).

2. See Robert Langbaum's remarks on 'local poetry' and its relation to the work of the great nineteenth-century English poets in *The Poetry of Experience* (London, 1957), Chapter II.

3. Geoffrey Tillotson, 'Eighteenth-Century Poetic Diction', in *Eighteenth-century English Literature*, ed. James L. Clifford (N.Y., 1959), p. 218.

4. Stopping to lecture in a footnote to his satiric ballad, 'Sir Proteus', Peacock says: 'This undistinguished passion for literary novelty seems to involve nothing less than a total extinction of everything like discrimination in taste. . . .' He considers Wordsworth a prime offender. *The Works of Thomas Love Peacock* [the Halliford Edition], ed. H. F. B. Brett-Smith and C. E. Jones (London, 1924–34), Vol. VI, 209. Future references to Peacock, except as noted, are from the Halliford Edition and will appear in the text according to volume and page numbers.

5. See Lord Houghton's preface to Peacock's *Works*, ed. Henry Cole (London, 1875), Vol. I, xxii.

6. Edith Nicolls, in the 'Biographical Notice' to the Cole Edition, Vol. I, xxix.

2 Boyhood Verse and *Palmyra*

1. Clive Bell, *Pot Boilers* (London, 1918), 67.

2. Frances Winwar, *The Romantic Rebels* (Boston, 1935), 131.

3. Compare Dr. Johnson's letter to Mrs. Thrale in July, 1771: 'Dear Madam, Last Saturday I came to Ashbourne; the dangers or the pleasures of the journey I have at present no disposition to recount. Else might I paint the beauties of my native plain, might I tell of "the smiles of Nature and the charms of art", else might I relate how I crossed the Staffordshire Canal one of the great efforts

of human labour and human contrivance, which from the bridge on which I viewed it, passed away on either side. . . . I might tell how these reflections fermented in my mind till the chaise stopped at Ashbourne, at Ashbourne in the Peak.' *Letters*, ed. R. W. Chapman (Oxford, 1952), Vol. I, 257–8.

4. 'It is not given to everyone', writes J. B. Priestley, 'to make acquaintance with Epicureanism and irony at his mother's knee.' *Thomas Love Peacock* [*English Men of Letters Series*] (London and N.Y., 1927), 5.

5. Clive Bell, *Pot Boilers* (London, 1918), 67. Quoted in I, xxiii.

6. Peacock's reading included the Bible, Ossian, and Gibbon, but the two main sources for *Palmyra* were *Travels in Syria* (1787), by Volney (Constantin François Chasse-Boef), and *The Ruins of Palmyra, otherwise Tedmor in the desert*, by Robert Wood. Wood was, like Peacock, a self-taught classicist; he was also a politician and archaeologist. His work on *Palmyra* was translated into French and reissued several times in the century after its publication; it drew praise from the Abbé Barthélémy, from Horace Walpole, and from the many archaeologists who were to follow Wood's example.

7. *Critical Review*, CXVI (February, 1806), 210–11.

8. [Christopher Moody], review of 'Palmyra', *Monthly Review*, XLIX (March, 1806), 323. As late as 1831 a collection of *Oxford Prize Poems* contained at least one poem on Palmyra among its several 'ruin' poems. Palmyra, like Pompeii and Rome, long served as a topic for verse.

9. Shelley, *Letters*, ed. Frederick L. Jones (Oxford, 1964), Vol. I, 325. Shelley's later assessment of Peacock's verse was less generous. He was a 'nursling', Shelley wrote in 1819, 'of the exact & superficial school in poetry'. Vol. II, 126. Peacock may also have borrowed from *Thalaba*, a kind of Spenserian *Arabian Nights* ode, wherein he could have found such phrases as 'the everlasting Now of solitude' and 'the circling waste'. Perhaps Shelley appreciated in *Palmyra* treatment of a similar motive. Mary Shelley, in a later note to *Queen Mab*, was to suggest that the poem was indebted to 'the wild fantastic machinery' of Southey's poems.

10. Peacock later termed *Palmyra* a 'juvenile production'. For a discussion of his revisions see VI, v.

11. Hazlitt, *Works*, ed. P. P. Howe (London, 1930), Vol. V, 118.

3 Earnest Tidings: *The Genius of the Thames* and *The Philosophy of Melancholy*

1. Characteristic of his tributes are the lines about James Thomson:

> The airy lyre of Thomson sighs,
> And whispers to the hills and meads
> IN YONDER GRAVE A DRUID LIES! (VI, 147).

Readers would be expected to recognize the final verse as a quotation from William Collins's 'Ode on the Death of Mr. Thomson'.

2. See Robert Aubin's chapter on river poems in *Topographical Poetry in XVIII-century England* (N.Y., 1936). Aubin suggests that the English poets turned to Horace, Ausonius, and, especially, to Virgil for their models. Peacock quotes Virgil in *The Genius of the Thames*.

3. 'Teisa' (1788), quoted in Aubin, 235. The *Anti-Jacobin* poets were to write, in burlesque of a whole tired genre:

> Let HYDROSTATICS, simpering as they go,
> Lead the light Naiads on fantastic toe.

The Poetry of the 'Anti-Jacobin' (London, 1898), 152.

4. Wordsworth himself was not averse to 'local poetry', as his praise of William Crowe's mediocre poems would indicate.

5. Shelley, *Letters*, I, 325. For Shelley's reasons see the diatribe against 'commerce' in *Queen Mab*, canto IV:

> Hence commerce springs, the venal interchange
> Of all that human art or nature yield.
>
> .   .   .   .   .
>
> Commerce! beneath whose poison-breathing shade
> No solitary virtue dares to spring.

6. What Shelley disliked, the two reviews relished. The *British Critic* accorded the poem 'almost unqualified applause', XXXV (August, 1810), 18, while the *Anti-Jacobin* discovered 'a vein of pleasing melancholy, an affecting pathos', which bespoke 'a man of good religious and moral principle', XXXVII (September, 1810), 82. A man of good principle in the eyes of the *Anti-Jacobin* is, one would suspect, a man of questionable virtue indeed. But again, if we are to believe Peacock's letter to Hookham, Peacock expressed certain ideas because he thought they belonged to the poetic tradition or were a necessary part of the genre.

7. Langbaum, *The Poetry of Experience*, Chapter II, *passim*.

8. *The Shelley Correspondence in the Bodleian Library*, ed. R. H. Hill (1926), 3. Cited in I, xliv.

9. In 1800, when Peacock was fifteen—and De Quincey, who had similar adventures and the same love of Wales, was the same age—Mrs. Piozzi was writing about her Welsh estate: 'Brynbella is the fashion. We have people coming to take views from it, and

travellers out of number,—*Tourists*, as the silly word is.' Cited in B. Sprague-Allen, *Tides in Taste* (Cambridge, Mass., 1937), 204. Jane Austen was to have her fun with devotees of the picturesque in *Northanger Abbey*. Peacock probably knew the satires of Richard Graves (*Columella*) and Isaac Disraeli (*Flim-Flams*), two of Miss Austen's witty predecessors.

10. Jean Hagstrum, *The Sister Arts* (Chicago, 1958), 234.

11. *Eclectic Review*, XVI (October 1812), 1030–5. *Melancholy* almost won for Peacock more influential reviews. One enterprising admirer promised to 'recommend it to Mr. Gifford with all possible earnestness, and endeavour to set it down upon the list of publications to be reviewed' [in the *Quarterly*]. Nor did he think that enough. 'If Mr. Jeffrey comes to London, I shall be glad to recommend it to his fostering patronage. From what I know of his mind, I think him likely to admire this poem extremely.' Cited in VI, 343. Perhaps we owe the satire on Jeffrey, Gifford, and other reviewers in Peacock's later works to their lack of response. In any case, their 'fostering patronage' was not forthcoming.

12. By the time he wrote *Melancholy*, Peacock had abandoned the older type of spelling ('emblemed', for example, rather than 'emblem'd') and of capitalization ('doom' rather than 'Doom'). The iambic couplets bespeak even more than the mixed verse of the Thames poem a love of neo-classical idiom.

13. Eleanor Sickels, *The Gloomy Egoist* (N.Y., 1932), 218. Miss Sickels calls it one of the best of these poems.

4 From *The Dilettanti* to *Rhododaphne*

1. Shelley, *Letters*, I, 325.

2. Shelley, *Letters*, I, 392.

3. 'A Note on Shelley and Peacock', *MLN*, XXXVI (June 1921), 373. Perhaps the best discussion of the friendship is that by O. W. Campbell in her short but often very perceptive study, *Thomas Love Peacock* (London and N.Y., 1953).

4. 'A lengthy return in those years for money spent at the box office' is Allardyce Nicoll's explanation for the 'truly enormous number of short plays, of which melodramas, farces, comic operas, and pantomimes formed by far the largest part', written in the early nineteenth century: *A History of English Drama* (Cambridge, 1955), Vol. IV, 120. Peacock probably hammered out his two farces with a lengthy return in mind—he was short of money at the time. There is some indication that *The Three Doctors* was read by a director. Neither work was published before this century, and they appeared

not for any intrinsic worth but because they indicate something about the apprenticeship of the author.

5. Shelley, *Letters*, I, 380.

6. Byron, *Letters and Journals*, ed. Prothero (London, 1899), Vol. III, 90. Cited in I, lvi.

7. Peacock is parodying William Collins's 'The Passions, An Ode for Music':

> They would have thought who heard the Strain,
> They saw in *Tempe's* Vale her native Maids, . . .

8. It was not merely a matter of years that occasioned Peacock's humorous treatment of Shelley's friends. The Halliford editors make a good case for Peacock's having written a letter to the *Monthly Review* in 1811, responding to articles by Newton in that publication. The writer scoffs at zodiacal systems and vegetable diets: 'If Mr. Newton's plans were generally adopted', he concludes, 'I think the apothecaries would have to thank him, although the butchers would not' (VII, 421).

9. Peck suggests ('A Note on Shelley and Peacock', 373) that *Rhododaphne* occasionally echoes *The Revolt of Islam* (*Laon and Cythna*). He also points out lines in Shelley's later poems that echo *Rhododaphne*.

10. Shelley, *Letters*, I, 569.

11. Shelley, *Letters*, I, 569.

12. Byron's statement was first recorded in 1866 and may be fictitious. See I, lxxviii.

13. *Literary Gazette*, No. 57 (February 21, 1818), 115.

14. Douglas Bush, *Mythology and the Romantic Tradition* (N.Y., 1937), 180. While I disagree with Mr. Bush's interpretation, his essay still offers both a fine commentary and the best 'placing' of *Rhododaphne* in the poetry of the time.

15. J. B. Priestley, *Thomas Love Peacock*, 11.

16. Edward B. Hungerford, *Shores of Darkness* (N.Y. 1941), 33. See also Alex Zwerdling's more recent 'The Mythographers and the Romantic Revival of Greek Myth', *PMLA*, LXXIX (1964), 447–56. Neither Mr. Hungerford nor Mr. Zwerdling mentions *Rhododaphne*.

17. According to Douglas Bush (*Mythology*, 184), *Rhododaphne* 'may owe something to the *Dionysiaca*'. Perhaps a few passages echo Nonnus's poem, but Peacock certainly does not write the same kind of rambling, amorphous story, whatever his affection for Nonnus.

18. James A. Notopolous generally overstates Peacock's neo-Platonic (or should it be Platonic?) allegiances, in *The Platonism of*

Shelley (Durham, N.C., 1949), but his comments on *Rhododaphne*, 52–4, are apt and informative.

19. *Monthly Review*, LXXXVIII (February, 1819), 178.

20. E. A. Poe, *Works* (London, 1899), Vol. III, 443. Poe called the poem 'brimful of music'.

21. For some of Keats s indebtedness to *Rhododaphne* see Bush, 111. There are also a number of verbal echoes.

5 Later Verse

1. Shelley, *Letters*, II, 29.

2. Cited in Shelley, *Letters*, II, 29.

3. As a young man, Peacock still thought of himself among the 'inspired'. In a letter to Hookham (quoted earlier), in which he speaks about poets tending to extremes of high and low spirits, he writes: 'Cratinus, Democritus, Horace, and others, have opined that a certain degree of *noncomposity* is essential to the poetical character: and I am inclined to think there is considerable justice in the observation' (VIII, 184). And he describes himself as being noncomposed.

4. He seems not to have thought of the new employment as interrupting his writing, for in a letter to Shelley (in November) he speaks of old and new projects. After mentioning *Maid Marian*, he says: 'I have suspended the Essay [on Fashionable Literature] till the completion of the Romance. The Political Pamphlet [?] I shall publish about the meeting of Parliament. I have thought of an historical work, which would be more useful than any I have yet planned' (VIII, 209). But whatever he may have intended, nothing was written.

5. Leigh Hunt, *Autobiography* (London, 1850), Vol. II, 194. Ironically, Hunt himself was a far worse offender, borrowing substantial amounts from Shelley. This fact seems not to have mitigated Hunt's assessment of Peacock.

6. In her reply to Peacock's offer of marriage, Miss Gryffydh said that she thought herself his intellectual inferior and doubted whether the eight years had added to their mutual interests. Except that the two shared an interest in Wales, they probably had rather little in common. A comment on the marriage may be Peacock's unfinished 'Dialogue on Friendship After Marriage' (written in 1859, some years after his wife's death), wherein 'Galatea' laments the fact that she needs a friend who is not her husband—only, she says, for conversation. 'Amaryllis' and 'Aegle' insist that marital constancy is necessary for a happy relationship. They seem to be winning the argument.

7. John Stuart Mill wrote in his *Autobiography* (London, 1874),

82: 'I do not know any of the occupations . . . more suitable . . . to any one who . . . desires to devote a part of the twenty-four hours to private intellectual pursuits.'

8. When 'Newark Abbey' was finally published (*in Fraser's Magazine* for November 1860) it won the immediate praise of Tennyson, who, having found the lines 'so beautiful', sent a copy to friends. See I, cci. Perhaps Tennyson had 'Newark Abbey' in mind when he wrote his own comparable 'Roses on the Terrace' (1889).

9. In its almost arid simplicity, this, with other of his poems of the time, is comparable with John Gay's 'Airs' in the *Beggar's Opera* (e.g. xxviii). See the later mention of Gay in the section on *Maid Marian*.

10. Theodore Hook wrote a comparably ironic, pattering series of poems on the 'Bubbles of 1825', which includes the lines:

Run neighbours run, you're just in time to get a share
In all the famous projects that amuse John Bull. . . .

Elsewhere Hook's wit is more acerbic—he could be a virulent Tory —but in these poems both writers seem to preclude any desire for reformative satire by the insistence on light, rapid verse.

11. Peacock also includes this poem in a note in *Crotchet Castle*.

12. Compare Peacock's final couplet with the following by Hookham Frere in 'The Bubble Year': 'Sinking the sister isle/At least a statute mile/With a low, subsiding motion/Beneath the level of the German Ocean.' See the later mention of Frere in relation to 'Calidore' and *Nightmare Abbey*.

13. Peacock also wrote a satirical poem about the new London University, which he, like Wordsworth and others, opposed on the basis of its practical or scientific curriculum.

See George Kitchin, *Burlesque and Parody in English* (London, 1931), 194–5. Elsewhere Kitchin writes: 'As a ballad lyrist Peacock had few to match him', 201.

14. Leigh Hunt, *Literary Criticism*, ed. Houtchens (N.Y., 1956), 532. For evidence of Peacock's authorship, see p. 693. There is no mention of the poem in the Halliford Edition.

15. Hunt, *Literary Criticism*, 533–4.

PART 2

1 Peacock and the Informal Essay: Introductory

1. Edward Strachey, 'Recollections of Thomas Love Peacock', in *Calidore and Miscellanea*, ed. Garnett (London, 1891), 21.

2. Hazlitt, *Works*, Vol. VIII, 242.

2 'The Four Ages of Poetry' and Peacock's Literary Criticism

1. There is some debate as to who wrote the *Edinburgh* article, and the Halliford editors are silent on the matter. It was perhaps a piece by Hazlitt, doctored by Francis Jeffrey. Peacock himself seems to have been unaware of the writer's identity. See Hazlitt, *Works*, Vol. X, 411.

2. Johnson had also levelled his guns at the 'ignorant' and mischievious periodical critics. Compare *Idler*, 60: 'Criticism is a study by which men grow important and formidable at very small expense.' By Peacock's time the reviews had grown far more powerful and were considered dangerous by many writers. Hazlitt and Keats were both outraged at the power of the *Edinburgh* and *Quarterly*.

3. M. H. Abrams, *The Mirror and the Lamp* (Oxford, 1953), 126.

4. Shelley, *Letters*, II, 244.

5. Shelley, *Letters*, II, 261.

6. Milton Wilson, *Shelley's Later Poetry* (N.Y., 1959), 13.

7. For a discussion of the relationship of the two texts, see especially John E. Jordan's edition, *A Defence of Poetry and The Four Ages of Poetry* (N.Y., 1965).

8. Shelley, *Letters*, II, 261. Yet he could also write: 'You will see that I have taken a more general view of what is poetry than you have, and will perhaps agree with several of my positions without considering your own touched', *Letters*, II, 275.

9. Shelley, *Letters*, II, 273.

10. Shelley, *Letters*, II, 275.

11. Joseph E. Baker, in *Shelley's Platonic Answer to a Platonic Attack on Poetry* (Iowa City, 1963), offers some interesting observations about both essays; but he makes only the vaguest case for Peacock's argument being 'Platonic'.

12. Vico had, according to René Wellek [in *A History of Modern Criticism, the Later Eighteenth Century* (New Haven, 1955), 135], a minimal influence on later eighteenth-century Italian critics and absolutely none on the English. Coleridge, one of the first English critics introduced to Vico, read his work in 1825. There is no evidence to suggest that Peacock was the exception, that he might have read Vico before writing 'The Four Ages', even though his thesis is remarkably similar to Vico's. If the application of the four-ages scheme to poetry was not his own, he might have found it in David Hartley's *Observations*. Dr. Johnson had already poked fun

(*Idler*, 60) at critics who glibly say 'genius decays as judgment decreases'. See the later comments on Hazlitt's *Lectures*.

13. One small irony within 'The Four Ages' helps to clarify Peacock's altered opinion: at one point he quotes, almost word for word, a sentence taken from a patronizing review of *The Genius of the Thames*.

14. Compare Pope's related parody in *Peri Bathous*, Chapter VIII : 'The circumstances which are not natural are obvious, therefore not astonishing or peculiar. But those that are far-fetched or unexpected or hardly compatible will surprise prodigiously. These therefore we must principally hunt out', *Literary Criticism*, ed. B. Goldgar (Lincoln, Nebraska, 1965), 58.

15. Peacock evidently did not care for Mill as a man. Sir Edward Strachey recorded several anecdotes Peacock told at Mill's expense. His response to one of Mill's disquisitions was : 'Yes; but, as usual, all the reason is on your side, and all the proof on mine.' Cited in I, cxxx.

16. Jeremy Bentham, *Rationale of Reward*, *Works* (London, 1843), Vol. II, 253.

17. Shelley, *Letters*, II, 276.

18. Frederick Jones, in 'Macaulay's Theory of Poetry in "Milton" ', *M.L.Q.*, XII (December 1952), 356–62, argues that Macaulay's thesis was probably drawn, almost *in toto*, from Peacock. It may have been, but Peacock himself was using something that was in the air.

19. Hazlitt, *Lectures on the English Poets*, *Works*, Vol. V, 9.

20. Keats, *Letters*, ed. Hyder E. Rollins (Cambridge, 1958), Vol. I, 252. But the letter (to Haydon) is only half-serious.

21. Robert Buchanan, *A Poet's Sketchbook* (London, 1883), 107. There is, probably, little truth in the comment ascribed by Edward Clodd to Meredith : 'Keats is a greater poet than Shelley; in this Peacock agreed.' Cited in Augustus H. Able, *George Meredith and Thomas Love Peacock* (Philadelphia, 1933), 11.

In a late novelistic fragment, 'Cotswold Chace', Peacock quotes the opening lines of *Endymion*, but if this was a sign of his approval, it seems to have been the only one.

22. Keats, ironically, would probably have agreed. His cryptic assessment of one of Moore's works had been : 'A new work of Moores . . . nothing in it', *Letters*, II, 73.

23. Peacock's judgment on the work proved almost identical with Leigh Hunt's. Compare the passage above with this by Hunt : 'In short, Mr. Moore is no real biographer, no prose-writer, no thinker; there is not one original reflection in all his remarks, nor one that

has not been made in a better manner before him. . . . . His world is the little world of fashion; his notions of liberty those of a Whig-Aristocrat, without the excuse; and the whole secret of his deification of Lord Byron is that their intercourse was one of flattery and convenience', *Literary Criticism*, 304.

24. James Sutherland, *On English Prose* (Toronto, 1957), 96.

25. The Sotheby Catalogue of Peacock's library can be found in the British Museum [S.-C.S. 567. (3)]. Most of his books were editions of Greek and Latin authors.

26. S. T. Coleridge, *Essays and Lectures* [Everyman] (London, 1907), 324–5.

27. H. C. Robinson, *On Books and Their Writers*, ed. E. J. Morley (1938), Vol. I, 82. In our own time, Georg Lukács (*The Historical Novel* [Boston, 1963]) has found in Scott's middle-class 'concensus' views a source of his greatness.

28. Peacock wrote two related pieces during the same years: an appreciative essay on Demetrius Galanus, a modern Greek and a scholar who left his native Athens to study in India (*Fraser's Magazine*, November 1858) and a laudatory review of Müller and Donaldson's classic *History of Greek Literature* (*Fraser's*, March 1859).

29. G. O. Trevelyan, *Life and Letters of Lord Macaulay* (London, 1876), Vol. II, 300. Cited in I, clxxiv.

30. J. A. Roebuck, *Letters* (London, 1897), 8–9. Cited in I, liii–liv.

31. The verse translations in this essay are among Peacock's best —supple and idiomatic, and clearly superior to the work between 1810 and 1814 discussed in Part I. See, for example:

> The dawn scarce glitters o'er the hills:
> The nightingale, where trees embower,
> Still sits in thickest shade, and fills
> The air with song of gentlest power,
> Pouring the soft, sad, tuneful strain,
> For It is, It is, mourned in vain.
> The reed makes music from the rocks,
> As shepherds upland drive their flocks (X, 46).

32. Peacock's first known poem appropriately contains the line: 'And I, if a poet, must drink like a gypsy . . .' (VII, 153).

33. Peacock perhaps alludes to Wordsworth's comments in 'Of Literary Biography': 'The poet, treating of primary instincts, luxuriates among the felicities of love and wine. . . .' Cited in

Hugh Walker, *The English Essay and Essayists* (London, 1915), 216.

3 Politics of Scepticism and Faith

1. Lord Houghton, Preface to the Cole Edition, Vol. I, xvii–xviii. Several critics, including George Saintsbury and Douglas Bush, have insisted that Peacock was a Tory; but, apart from overwhelming general evidence to the contrary, he himself specifically denies the possibility. See his letter to Thomas L'Estrange (VIII, 254), where he calls Tories as 'extinct as Mammoths' and not even worth his criticism.

2. In January 1835 the *Edinburgh Review* published the essay as *Report from the Select Committee* [of the East India Company] *on Steam Navigation to India*. Brett-Smith writes that Peacock 'never claimed its authorship, but it is proved to be his work by letters preserved among the records of the India House' (I, clxv).

3. Kingsley Martin, *French Liberal Thought in the Eighteenth Century*, new ed. (London, 1962), 278.

4. He speaks in the same letter—to Shelley—of 'a gang of ruffians [the French] prepared and determined to do all the mischief in their power to the happy and liberal institutions of the United States'. The sentiment was not uncommon, of course. Cf. Coleridge's 'Fears in Solitude', where he speaks of 'an Impious foe,/Impious and false, a light yet cruel race', etc. There is, curiously, no discussion of French politicians in Peacock—Napoleon included—despite his intimacy with French literature.

5. *The Great Tradition* (N.Y., 1935), 3. Robert Buchanan maintained in his reminiscence of Peacock in *A Poet's Sketchbook* (London, 1833), 103, that Peacock was not anti-American in his later years. While it is true that Opimian is not Peacock himself and that all the characters get caught up in their own rhetoric, the animus is still evident. One has only to contrast the positions of the speakers in *Gryll Grange* with those in *Melincourt* to see how much shift in attitude there must have been.

6. Leigh Hunt also wrote appreciatively about Locke. It is likely that Peacock's political views were influenced by Hunt, whom he knew personally, and by the *Examiner*, which he read as a young man and wrote for as an older man.

7. He objected to Brougham's plan on two grounds: (1) he feared State control—which at the time necessitated Church administration —of a delicate problem, and (2) he recognized that Brougham interested himself primarily in 'technological' training (witness the

founding of the Mechanics Institutes, which Peacock burlesques in *Crotchet Castle*). Education to Peacock meant primarily a study of the arts. In attacking Brougham, Peacock allied himself with the *Westminster*, one of whose favourite themes was a contrast between Bentham's ideas and Brougham's. Like Peacock, the *Westminster* reviewers considered Brougham selfish and unpredictable.

8. Crane Brinton, *The Political Ideas of the English Romanticists* (London, 1926), 26. The distinction is that between what Professor Lovejoy calls 'historical' and 'cultural' primitivism. For a discussion of Peacock's satiric treatment of primitivism, especially in *Headlong Hall*, see Lois Whitney's *Primitivism and the Idea of Progress in Popular Literature of the Eighteenth Century* (Baltimore, 1934).

9. Again, Peacock himself once flirted with the idea of moving to Canada. In 1818 he wrote about Morris Birkbeck's *Notes on America* that 'the temptation to agriculturalists with a small capital must be irresistible; and the picture he presents of the march of population and cultivation beyond the Ohio is one of the most wonderful spectacles ever yet presented to the mind's eye of philosophy' (VIII, 205). The last phrase is vile, but the sentiment clearly genuine. Actually, Birkbeck's own settlement, as George Keats—the poet's brother—found to his dismay, was untouched virgin forest: a place to eat up 'a small capital' and break hearts.

10. The terms 'liberal' and 'conservative' are, admittedly, vague and adulterated. Lionel Trilling, in *The Portable Matthew Arnold* (N.Y., 1949), 434, speaks about the difficulties facing a modern reader who finds, e.g., 'liberal' nineteenth-century thinkers opposed to State-administered universal education and 'conservatives' supporting factory legislation. I use the term 'conservative' not as synonymous with 'Tory', but in its literal sense.

11. His dilemma must have caused him difficulties professionally. In *Paper Money Lyrics* he pokes fun at the Establishment, including the views of his superiors, James Mill among them. But as a witness for the East India Company during its fight for charter renewal in the early 1830's, Peacock was called to defend a reactionary position. See Ralph E. Turner's *The Relation of James Silk Buckingham with the East India Company* (Pittsburgh, 1930) in which Peacock is cited for his reactionism and even—with not a great deal of evidence—for duplicity on his employers' behalf.

4 Music Reviewer for the *Examiner*

1. Hazlitt, 'The Utilitarian Controversy', cited in IX, 402–3.
2. In Vol. IX, 402–45.

3. I have been anticipated in this and in a number of observations by E. E. Mackerness, 'Thomas Love Peacock's Musical Criticism', *Wind and Rain*, IV (Winter, 1948), 177–88. See also his *A Social History of English Music* (London, 1964), which does not touch on Peacock but which is generally relevant.

4. Unsigned review by Peacock in the *Examiner* (London, June 6, 1831), 389. Those passages not available in Vol. IX of the Halliford Edition will be cited below in text by date and *Examiner* page number. Peacock could be scathing in his comments on bad criticism, 'which he assailed with a formidable conciseness; when *The Times* critic professed to have seen the whole of Rossini's *Tancredi* (though only the first act had been played) without hearing a word that was spoken by Laporte (though Peacock, at the very back of the pit, had heard every syllable most distinctly), the comment is merely that "Hearing nothing may be a fair set off against seeing double" ' (IX, 412–13).

5. The humorous portrait of Mr. Trillo in *Crotchet Castle* may be based upon Novello. See Part III, Chapter 7.

6. Alfred Einstein, *Music in the Romantic Era* (N.Y., 1947), 122.

7. Leigh Hunt, *Dramatic Criticism*, ed. Houtchens (N.Y., 1949), 107.

8. Hunt, 141.

9. Arthur Quiller-Couch, *Studies in Literature*, Third Series (Cambridge, 1930), 217ff.

10. Hunt, *Dramatic Criticism*, 270. Mackerness compares Hunt and Peacock on Paganini, but comes to a different conclusion.

11. As late as 1895 Henry Davey described Mount-Edgcumbe's book as 'one of the best ever written upon musical matters by an English amateur', *History of English Music* (London, 1895), 410. But see Cyrus Redding—in the *D.N.B.*, s.v. Mount-Edgcumbe—who called him 'a mere fribble, exhibiting little above the calibre of an opera connoisseur, with something of the mimic'. Peacock approved of Mount-Edgcumbe's unprofessional manner and enjoyed his enthusiasm.

12. George Hogarth, *Memoirs of the Musical Drama* (London, 1838), Vol. II, 412.

13. Carl Van Doren, *The Life of Thomas Love Peacock* (N.Y. and London, 1911), 202–3.

14. *Shaw on Music*, ed. Eric Bentley (N.Y., 1956), 68.

15. Shaw, 69–70.

16. Edmund Wilson, 'Musical Glasses of Peacock', *Classics and Commercials* (N.Y., 1951), 407.

5 Personal Writings and a Theory of Biography

1. Thomas Carlyle, review of *Lockhart's Life of Scott*, in James L. Clifford, *Biography as an Art* (London, 1962), 84.

2. Carlyle, *Critical and Miscellaneous Essays* (London, 1928), Vol. I, 56.

3. Coleridge, 'A Prefatory Observation on Modern Biography', in Clifford, 57. But Peacock's views were hardly unusual for the time. Arnold's response to Dowden's *Life of Shelley* was to repeat all of Peacock's objections. 'Shelley', *Essays in Criticism*, Second Series, (London 1888).

4. Richard Garnett, intro. *Headlong Hall* (London, 1891), 18.

5. Ian Jack, *English Literature, 1815–32* (Oxford 1963), 363.

6. In addition to the letters in the Halliford Edition (Vol. VIII), see especially *New Shelley Letters*, ed. W. S. Scott (London, 1948). This collection includes a number of letters from Peacock to Thomas Jefferson Hogg which suggest a fairly close relationship.

7. Shelley considered the letters to Peacock from Italy a substitute journal: 'The only records of my voyage will be the letters I send you', *Letters*, II, 70.

8. Shelley, *Letters*, II, 6.

9. Shelley, *Letters*, II, 29.

10. Richard Garnett, in the *National Review* (1887). Cited in VIII, 504.

11. Robert Buchanan, *A Poet's Sketchbook*, 96–7.

12. Jean-Jacques Mayoux, *Un Epicurien anglais: Thomas Love Peacock* (Paris, 1933), 2.

13. Buchanan, *A Poet's Sketchbook*, 105–8.

6 An English Gastronome

1. For a description of eighteenth-century cookery handbooks, see, e.g., Esther B. Aresty, *The Delectable Past* (N.Y., 1964).

2. Boswell, *Life of Johnson*, ed. Hill (Oxford, 1934), Vol. III, 285. Johnson, of course, was quite wrong about lady authors. Women had begun and continued to write most of the best cookery books.

3. For a discussion of the authorship see IX, 446–7.

4. J. W. Duff, *A Literary History of Rome* (N.Y., 1909), 153.

5. One of the curious historical paradoxes of the nineteenth century is the fact that while gastronomy interested a great number of people, many children of *wealthy* families were actually starving. Rickets was very common in girls' schools, where diet was often wholly inadequate. Boys were almost consciously starved to keep

them out of—mainly sexual—mischief. See Steven Marcus's illuminating discussion of William Acton's medical theories in Chapter I of *The Other Victorians* (New York, 1964). For a useful and often fascinating survey, see also J. C. Drummond and Anne Wilbraham, *The Englishman's Food* (London, 1939).

6. Boswell, *Life*, Vol. I, 467.

7. Actually Steele: and as usual, Peacock misquotes slightly. He refers to *Tatler*, 148, where Steele speaks about the need for 'good-natured, cheerful . . . friends' and 'exhorts' his readers to 'return to the food of their Forefathers', by which he means good, simple repast.

8. Henry Fielding, 'An Essay on Conversation', *Works*, ed. G. Saintsbury, Vol. XII, 186.

9. C. B. Gulick, ed., *The Deipnosophists* (London, 1927), Vol. I, x.

10. See the discussion of 'The Horrible Party' in Gilbert Highet's *The Anatomy of Satire* (Princeton, 1962), 221–3. Among the modern absurd parties, Mr. Highet mentions those in Francesco Berni, Mathurin Régnier, and Boileau, with all of which Peacock was likely to have been familiar.

PART 3
1 Backgrounds for Peacock's Comedy

1. Carlos Baker, *Shelley's Major Poetry* (Princeton, 1948), 8.

2. In Boccaccio—as in Chaucer—the introductory narrator partially gives way to the narrators of the various stories, but the frame itself is a device for creating intimacy, since it has the effect of drawing the reader into the group. Peacock may conceivably have seen his own imaginary rural retreats in an analogous sense; certainly there develops an analogous effect. But, of course, he substitutes dialogue for the stories, or anecdotes, in the *Decameron*.

3. Wayne Booth, *The Rhetoric of Fiction* (Chicago, 1961), *passim*. Mr. Booth does not discuss Peacock, but many of his observations about 'implied author', 'reliable' and 'unreliable narrator', etc., offer useful insights.

4. Frances Russell, *Satire in the Victorian Novel* (N.Y., 1920), 65.

5. Lord Houghton, Preface to the Cole edition, Vol. I, xxiii.

6. Richard Hurd, *Moral and Political Dialogues* (London, 1788), xviii. Peacock himself wrote no formal dialogues, saving the incomplete 'Dialogue on Friendship After Marriage' (see earlier note, p. 292), written at least as late as 1859, which uses conventional pastoral names and setting and looks back to the Theocritan tradition. A century earlier it would have been a very common sort of literary exercise.

7. Jean-François Marmontel, *Moral Tales*, Eng. trans. (London, 1813), iii.

8. George Saintsbury, *Prefaces and Essays* (London, 1933), 222. For a discussion of Peacock's relationship to the French *conte* see Jean-Jacques Mayoux, 605–8. Mayoux says that it is 'pure fantasy' to link Peacock with Marmontel, but he thinks that Peacock resembles writers of the *conte philosophique*, particularly Diderot. Peacock and Diderot are, he writes, '*deux épicuriens . . . deux intellectuels vigoureux, deux esprits dialectique, incapables de se tenir à une position sans apercevoir la force de la position inverse, et donc incapable d'orthodoxie*', 606.

9. Ian Watt contrasts the 'elegant concentration' of most pre- and some post-eighteenth-century narratives with the 'exhaustive presentation' of Richardson, Defoe, and even Fielding, with whom in this respect Peacock clearly differs, *The Rise of the Novel, Studies in Defoe, Richardson, and Fielding* (London, 1960), 30.

10. Cited in J. M. S. Tompkins, *The Popular Novel in England* (London, 1932), 332.

11. C. B. A. Proper, *Social Elements in English Prose Fiction* (Amsterdam, 1929). See also Allene Gregory, *The French Revolution and the English Novel* (N.Y., 1915), 190, who calls Peacock's 'revolutionism' 'the echo of an echo'.

12. Crane Brinton, *Political Ideas*, 32.

13. G. K. Chesterton, *Charles Dickens* (London, 1906), 114. The *Literary Gazette*, whose comment on *Nightmare Abbey* heads this chapter, also wrote aptly about *Melincourt*: 'We should not . . . be surprised if it led the way to a new species of humorous writing; which, taking the novel for its foundation, and the drama for its subject matter, should superadd to both, the learning and inquiry of the Essay.' Quoted in Bill Read, *The Critical Reputation of Thomas Love Peacock* (Xerox Book, University of Michigan, 1959), 142. Among those writers attempting the 'new species' was W. H. Mallock, who called his main source 'the so-called novels of Thomas Love Peacock', *Memoirs of Life and Literature* (N.Y. and London, 1920), 87.

14. Northrop Frye, *The Anatomy of Criticism* (Princeton, 1957), 309. Needless to add, it is not with the general validity of Mr. Frye's argument that I am concerned here, but only with the difficulties involved in its application to Peacock.

In *The Great Tradition* (London, 1948), 19. Mr. Leavis also compares Peacock with Jane Austen and his praise is as high as Mr. Frye's. Appropriately, however, his remarks are to be found in a footnote.

15. This point is not intended to explain away or defend Peacock's obvious limitations as a writer. And to some extent the type of

narrative he chose invites a related type of fault. Kingsley Amis exaggerates when he speaks of Peacock's 'inordinate capacity for simple diffuseness and repetition' as well as his 'wild disparity' and narrative 'uncertainty' (in 'Laugh When You Can', *Spectator*, CXCIV [April 1, 1955], 403). But without the adjectives the charges are apt, as I shall point out, for several of the novels. Mr. Amis concludes, in spite of his criticism, that Peacock was 'somebody far more energetically original' than is generally acknowledged.

16. Alvin Kernan, *The Cankered Muse* (New Haven, Conn., 1959), Chapter I. See also the more recent *The Plot of Satire* (1965).

17. The posthumous catalogue of Peacock's library (a Sotheby catalogue) is available in the British Museum, shelf no. B.M.S.— C.S. 567 (3).

2 *Headlong Hall*: 'the Wand of Enchantment'

1. See the discussion of *The Dilettanti* and *The Three Doctors* in Part I. The actions in *Headlong Hall* are closer to pure farce than those in the later novels (except in parts of *Melincourt* and *Maid Marian*), and the pace of the work is much faster.

2. *Critical Review* (January 1816), 69. Cited in I, lxiv.

3. Charles Clairmont, in *Shelley and Mary* (London, 1882), Vol. I, 84–5. Cited in I, lxiii.

4. See Newman Ivey White, *Shelley* (London, 1947), Vol. I, 192, 213, 591.

5. Sir Walter Scott, *Waverley*, ed. Lang (Boston, 1893), Chapter 16. Such description was also the stock-in-trade of novelists of sensibility. See, e.g., Chapter XXXIV of Henry Mackenzie's *Man of Feeling* (1771). The Welsh pass also suggests picturesque travel. Mr. Escot's comment on the scene described is: 'These are indeed . . . *confracti mundi rudera*. . . .' It may be coincidental, but Lord Lyttelton's *Journey into Wales* (*Works*, London, 1776) contains similar descriptions of the same region, and arrives at the same conclusion: 'The view of the said sands is terrible, as they are hemmed in on each side with very high hills, but broken into a thousand irregular shapes. At one end is the ocean, at the other the formidable mountains of Snowdon, black and naked rocks. . . . They do altogether strongly excite the idea of Burnet, of their being the fragment of a demolished world', 340. Later in the novel Peacock satirizes Marmaduke Milestone's plans for Lord Littlebrain's estate, presumably thinking of Lyttelton's Hagley.

6. W. L. Renwick suggests that Peacock writes the same kind of

fiction as Hannah More—and implicitly that he might have borrowed from her works: *English Literature, 1789–1815* (Oxford, 1963), 67. In *Coelebs in Search of a Wife* More creates a novel out of a series of moralistic essays, and the work is naturally episodic. Since Peacock's novels are also episodic, and since both writers indulge in the essay, there may be some grounds for comparison; but the two writers are generally as unlike as Dr. Johnson and John Gay.

7. David Garnett, 8. As a satiric portrait, Mr. Escot clearly incorporates more than Shelley. His deteriorationist views and his allusion to Thomas Burnet and the '*confracti mundi rudera*' (see p. 303) also suggest that Peacock used him to burlesque Burnet and Burnet's followers in the eighteenth century, who interpreted landscape in terms of a fanciful cosmogony.

8. W. H. Smith, *Architecture in English Fiction* (New Haven, 1934), 213. Smith calls attention to the curious fact that, despite the importance of Headlong Hall and the other houses, Peacock has little to say about specifically architectural matters. Even Nightmare Abbey is described in detail that is purely literary—with its 'ruined wing', etc.—since it burlesques the dark abbeys of so many Gothic romances.

9. Headlong's conversations with Milestone and O'Prism are probably lampoons of 'dialogues' about landscape and the picturesque by Payne-Knight, Price, Gilpin, and other landscape gardeners. Gilpin wrote a piece 'On Picturesque Beauty', in which six 'philosophers' share their views.

10. George Kitchin points out, in *Burlesque and Parody in English* (London, 1931), 260, that landscape gardening—particularly the desire to 'shave and polish'—had been laughed at in the *Anti-Jacobin*; and he suggests that Peacock's 'extensive use of the comic footnote again betrays the *Anti-Jacobin*'. But if Peacock was familiar with Richard Graves and Isaac Disreali, among others, he would have found novelistic precedent for both his choice of satiric target and for this particular satiric method.

11. *Literary Beacon*, No. I (June 18, 1831), 26. See also Mario Praz, who makes an almost concerted effort to misunderstand Peacock: 'Amongst the expedients for achieving comic effect, the least convincing is perhaps the very ancient one of giving characters names which crystallize the characteristics that the author intends to parody', *The Hero in Eclipse in Victorian Fiction*, trans. Angus Davidson (London, 1956), 101.

12. When, in the 1790's, Elizabeth Hamilton wrote her *Memoirs of Modern Philosophers* she was in some ways anticipating Peacock's laughter at the expense of intellectual folly. Disgusted with theorists

of the day, particularly French ones, Mrs. Hamilton used the novel as a cane to thrash naughty thinkers. While parodying ideas and scoffing at eccentrics is fairly easy, keeping the reader's interest in belittled characters can be difficult. That Peacock maintains the reader's interest is perhaps attributable to his sympathy for the characters or his final tolerance of their views.

13. William Beckford, Preface to *Azemia* (London, 1797).

14. A. Martin Freeman, *Thomas Love Peacock: a Critical Study* (London, 1911), 233.

15. Leigh Hunt called the song 'the masterpiece of its class'. *Literary Criticism*, 550.

16. While there is direct evidence that Peacock read Dickens, there is none that Dickens read Peacock. But Dickens edited *Bentley's Miscellany* during the late 1830's (see Part I, p. 66), one of the contributors to which was 'the author of *Headlong Hall*'. My own guess is that Dickens knew Peacock's novels and that he adapted a number of scenes and situations. For instance, Dickens's Eatanswill episode in *Pickwick*, though more crowded, more busy, than any-thing in Peacock, might be indebted to the pre-1832 election scene 'Onevote' in *Melincourt*.

3 'Calidore' and *Melincourt*: Hints from Spenser and Voltaire

1. According to the Halliford editors, 'At some earlier date [1813? 1815?], moved to satiric merriment by the misadventures of the South Pacific missionary ship *Duff* and the apostasy of an evangelist named George Vason, Peacock had begun the tale of "Satyrane: or The Stranger in England". In this he described the landing on *terra incognita* of a solitary surviving "chosen vessel" from the wrecked Australasian "missionary ship *Puff*", but the fragment comes to an untimely end at the point where this "long-faced gentleman" has heard, and is about to disturb, the revelry of the local heathen. In "Calidore" Peacock made a new beginning, but treated the same subject' (I, lxvii).

2. Hookham Frere, of *Anti-Jacobin* fame, also wrote his mock heroic 'King Arthur and His Round Table', or 'The Monks and the Giants', at about the same time. Frere's interests often seem to coincide with Peacock's, and it is likely that Peacock knew Frere's writings in the *Anti-Jacobin*. There was, however, a flurry of interest in King Arthur at the time.

3. 'Calidore' offers another indication of Peacock's interest in

syncretic mythology and, more generally, in antiquarianism (see Part I, Chapter 4). His interests had already taken him to the Orient in *Palmyra*, and the whole field of study opened up by Wood and Sir William Jones. *The Philosophy of Melancholy* shows signs of interest in Welsh antiquities. Later to read such authors as Edward Davies—the scholar, antiquarian, mythographer, and expert on Wales—for his Welsh studies, he seems already by 1816 to have interested himself in a variety of related fields.

4. Oliver Elton, *A Survey of English Literature, 1780–1880* 4 vols. (London and N.Y., 1920), Vol. I, 381.

5. Not all of Peacock's readers have responded positively to Sir Oran. Herbert Paul could write that an orang-outang 'getting drunk, falling in love, and being returned to the House of Commons, is . . . purely grotesque, and an insult to the intelligence of the reader'! 'The Novels of Peacock', *Nineteenth Century*, LIII (April 1903), 654–5.

6. Isaac Disraeli, *Flim-Flams* (London, 1806), 71. Disraeli's *Vaurien*, with its satire on many other aspects of eighteenth-century intellectual life, is similarly pertinent.

7. Hamilton, according to George Saintsbury, may have provided a model for Peacock's stories (*Essays and Prefaces* [London, 1913], 222). Except for a few sentiments that the two writers held in common, there seems to be little connection between them.

8. Leigh Hunt, *Literary Criticism*, 550.

9. Peacock's laughter at neologisms and his love of lengthy lists are reminiscent of Rabelais, whom he often quotes with approval, and of such Elizabethans as Nashe. One wonders, too, if Peacock knew Urquart of Cromarty, the seventeenth-century translator of Rabelais, himself a kind of Scottish Rabelais. Peacock actually added several words of his own to the language: 'By the testimony of the *New English Dictionary* the list includes mastigophoric, noometry, antithalian, inficete, excubant, kakistocracy, hylactic, adoperation. The *Century* gives veridicious, titubancy, titubant. To these half-whimsical pedantries may be added the ungarnered Aristophanic mintages, jeremytaylorically, tethrippharmatelasipedioploctypophilous, etc . . .', Van Doren, 247.

10. Mr. Mystic has one unmistakeable characteristic of the real Coleridge: his power of interminable monologue, or what H. M. Margoliouth aptly calls his 'oneversations'. Peacock's satiric account is not too far from Keats's and Hazlitt's of actual meetings with Coleridge, but it is closer to the descriptions in Carlyle's *Life of Sterling*, where Carlyle records the dismay of Coleridge's auditors, who listened for hours in the hope of one substantial point.

11. A. E. Dyson, *The Crazy Fabric* (London, 1965), 57–71. The title is a phrase from *Nightmare Abbey*.

12. Albert Cook, 'The Nature of Comedy and Tragedy', in *The Dark Voyage and the Golden Mean* (N.Y., 1966), 49.

13. Ian Jack, *English Literature, 1815–1832*, 215–17.

14. A. E. Dyson, *passim*, attacks Peacock's attitudes. He suggests that Peacock's sanctioning of charity involves an implicit apology both for class distinctions and the *status quo*. The argument is a telling one (and I can neither do it full justice here nor counter it with complete satisfaction). I suspect, however, that Peacock was, despite his hammerings at politics, essentially a non-political man and that his novels—as Dyson himself agrees—are not intended to be answers for the world's ills. In other words it is likely that Peacock very often missed the implications of his own arguments, largely because his interests lay elsewhere. It is also possible, of course, that Dyson himself is mistaken: perhaps charity, in the sense of spontaneous generosity to those in need, may be an ethical question, independent of politics. But let us consider this matter in its relevance to Peacock's fiction. Very often Peacock's irony is at his own expense; if he does concur with Mr. Forester on many points, he also makes him into a sympathetic fool. In short, his irony protects him by anticipating such objections. A reader is concerned less with Forester's idealism than with his conversation with other eccentrics. Peacock may not—but again the point is debatable—present liberal views about the peasantry, but after all his main interest is not the peasants; he is not at his most typical or at his best a social novelist. To put this another way, the failure of individual sections of *Melincourt* —or even of the entire work—need not imply failure of the writer.

15. Satire usually offers an alternative set of values to the targets of its attack, tending, as Gilbert Highet writes (in *The Anatomy of Satire*), to be protreptic. Though whether 'all satirists are at heart idealists' (p. 243) is another matter. Peacock's dialogues can, as I have pointed out earlier, be compared with the methods of formal satire. See Mary C. Randolph, 'The Structural Design of Formal Verse Satire', *P.Q.*, XXI (1942), 368–84.

4 *Nightmare Abbey:* 'a Little Daylight on the Atrabilarious'

1. Cited in I, lxxxiv.

2. Whether Peacock knew earlier satires on romance, such as those by Charlotte Lennox (*The Female Quixote*), William Beckford (*Azemia* and *Mahogany Castle*), and George Walker (*The Vagabond*),

would be difficult to say. He was, of course, familiar with the earlier and better-known burlesques of Voltaire and of Fielding, some of whose works will be relevant in a later context. Again, the satires of Richard Graves and Isaac Disraeli often seem to anticipate Peacock's. But there is no obvious model for *Nightmare Abbey* in earlier fiction.

3. Shelley, *Letters*, II, 6.

4. Shelley, *Letters*, II, 27.

5. See the passage from Coleridge's lecture quoted above, p. 105.

6. Shelley had used the same sort of consoling argument after the publication of *Queen Mab*. Echoing Milton and Wordsworth, he committed himself to writing for the 'few'.

7. I am indebted here as for several 'identifications' to David Garnett's notes to Peacock's novels.

8. One could quote parallel lines *ad infinitum*. Those above are taken from Vol. I, 48–9, 100–6, of the first edition (Edinburgh, 1817).

9. Almost twenty years before *Nightmare Abbey*, the *Anti-Jacobin* had parodied Goethe's *Stella* and related works with 'The Rovers', written by Gifford, Ellis, Canning, and Frere. Although Peacock does not appear to echo the earlier burlesque, he again follows the *Anti-Jacobin* in the direction of his literary satire—while taking an exactly contrary political position—and, like the Anti-Jacobins, has fun with the 'double arrangement'. His story follows Goethe's much more loosely than 'The Rovers' does, and he was probably burlesquing something that he hadn't read but that was in the air. One is reminded of Jefferson Hogg's statement that Shelley was 'fascinated' by *Werther*. 'At the same time his opinion was not unqualified; Albert, he thought, played an undignified part, and he projected and partially wrote an amplification of the novel. . . .' Quoted in F. W. Stokoe, *German Influence in the English Romantic Period* (London, 1926), 151.

10. There is no space here to follow out a comparison between *Nightmare Abbey* and *Don Juan* that almost invites itself to be made. Byron wrote his satiric dedication to Southey at about the same time that Peacock finished his novel, but he knew Peacock's work when he wrote the later cantos. The likelihood that Celinda's ghostly form lent itself to 'her frolic grace' is enhanced by the reminder that Marionetta sings a song about the 'grey friar', who is a friar in love:

> But breathe not thy vows to me, grey friar,
> Oh, breathe them not, I pray;
> For ill beseems in a reverend friar,
> The love of a mortal may;
> And I needs must say thee nay (III, 54).

11. At one point Peacock alludes to Henry Carey's mock-tragedy *Chrononhotonthologos, The Most Tragical Tragedy, etc.* Scythrop's call for Madeira recalls the burlesque finale of Carey's work:

> Instead of sad Solemnity, and Black
> Our Hearts shall swim in Claret, and in Sack.

12. J. B. Priestley argues (*Thomas Love Peacock*, 165–6) that Peacock's characters always speak in the same way. Certainly they vary little in comparison with Dickens's characters, but they have different voices none the less.

13. Cf. Alvin Kernan, *The Cankered Muse*, 14: 'Somewhere in the midst of the satiric scene or standing before it directing our attention to instances of folly and vulgarity . . . we usually find a satirist. In some cases he remains completely anonymous, merely a speaking voice who tells us nothing directly of himself, e.g. the narrator in *Nightmare Abbey* or in most satiric novels.'

14. Shelley, *Letters*, II, 98. The periodical Press shared the applause for Peacock's gentle humour. In a belated but appreciative notice, the *Monthly Review* [XC (November 1819), 328] cited Peacock as an alternative to bitter journalists and doctrinaire novelists.

15. David Garnett, *The Novels of Peacock*, 353.

16. John Draper, 'The Social Satires of Thomas Love Peacock', *MLN*, XXXIII (December 1918), 463; and Part Two, XXXIV (January 1919), 28. See also the Dyson essay mentioned in the last chapter and later comments on Mario Praz, who argues similarly.

17. Louis Kronenberger, 'Peacock', *Nation*, CLV (August 15, 1942), 135. 'The witty novels go on being read', says Mr. Kronenberger, 'far oftener than they are written about', 134.

18. See Edmund Wilson, 'Peacock's Musical Glasses', 406: 'It was a godsend that in the early nineteenth century, with its seraphic utopianisms and its cannibalistic materialisms, one man who had the intelligence to understand and the aesthetic sensibility to appreciate the new movements and the new techniques . . . should have been able to apply to their extravagances a kind of classical common sense.' The times may not have been quite so out of joint, nor Peacock quite so able to set them right, but Peacock—particularly in regard to *Nightmare Abbey*—would no doubt have been flattered.

19. Humphry House, 'The Works of Peacock', *Listener*, XLII (December 8, 1949), 998.

5 *Maid Marian:* the 'Masked Ball'

1. In *Studies in Green and Gray* (London, 1926), 162–92, Sir Henry Newbolt discusses possible relationships between *Ivanhoe* and *Maid*

Marian and cites a number of parallels; his essay is illuminating, but it fails to emphasize the common source in Ritson, and seems to overstate the importance of certain probable coincidences.

2. Scott's Preface to *Ivanhoe*, ed. A. Lang (Boston, 1893).

3. Scott, *Ivanhoe*, 22.

4. The best discussion of Peacock's indebtedness to Rabelais is Jean-Jacques Mayoux's '. . . *c'est le maitre de Peacock dans le genre de la comédie d'idées; et son pantagruelisme profile une silhouette colossale derrière l'épicurisme du disciple* . . .', 596. But Mayoux rightly points out the temperamental and stylistic differences between the two.

5. Mayoux, 344–7. The full title of Ritson's work is *Robin Hood, a Collection of all the Ancient Poems, Songs, and Ballads now Extant Relative to That Celebrated Outlaw*. Evidently Peacock did not turn to the main earlier sources in Anthony Munday and Henry Chettle —especially *The Downfall and Death of Robert, Earl of Huntington*—but read selections from their work in Ritson.

6. Cited in Bertrand Bronson, *Joseph Ritson, Scholar at Arms* (Berkeley, Calif., 1938), Vol. I, 220.

7. Cited in Bronson, *Joseph Ritson*, 59.

8. Joseph Ritson, *An Essay on Abstinence from Animal Food* (London, 1802), 44.

9. Cited in Bronson, *Joseph Ritson*, 219.

10. Some of Peacock's laughter at the expense of 'might and right' and of 'legitimate' power involves recognition of the ideas that Carlyle was to draw upon—as I have mentioned in other contexts. But, of course, there were individual spokesmen at the time whom he may have been satirizing. (Ritson, after all, had written a generation earlier.) In his discussions of French Literature, Peacock does not talk about *René* or any other works by Chateaubriand. His spoof on legitimacy, on the medieval Church, and generally on the political ideal of the Middle Ages, might be laughter at Chateaubriand's expense, though Chateaubriand's views represented a generally reactionary climate—in literature as in politics—at the time of the 'Holy Alliance'.

11. John Gay, *Beggar's Opera*, ed. John Hampden [Everyman's Library] (London, 1964), 127. See also Peacham's 'air':

> Through all the employments of Life,
> Each neighbour abuses his brother;
>
> .   .   .   .   .
>
> And the statesman, because he's so great,
> Thinks his trade as honest as mine (p. 112).

12. Gay, *The Beggar's Opera*, 127. This thesis became something of

a commonplace in later eighteenth-century fiction. See, for example the robber-gang and its defences in Godwin's *Caleb Williams*.

13. Gay, *Beggar's Opera*, 127.

14. William Empson, *Some Versions of Pastoral* (London, 1935), 208. F. W. Bateson writes (in *English Comic Drama* [London, 1926], 101) that Gay, as a prose writer, 'is nearer to Peacock than any other English writer'. Some of Peacock's prose is similar to Gay's, especially in *Maid Marian*, for he can be comparably light and clear and tends to use rapid, uncomplicated sentences. But Peacock's range is much broader than Gay's. He often writes rhetorically complex syntax or introduces new and unfamiliar words, and generally his style adapts to the specific needs. Sometimes, Bateson notwithstanding, there *are* 'undertones of irony' and implication, and sometimes he sounds more like Congreve or Fielding than Gay, sometimes more like Dr. Johnson.

15. Van Doren, *Life*, 279.

16. Cf. Pope's 'Autumn', lines 27–9:

> Ye Flowers that droop, forsaken by the Spring,
> Ye Birds, that left by Summer, cease to sing,
> Ye Trees that fade when Autumn-Heats remove,
> Say, is not Absence Death to those who love?

17. W. M. Thackeray, *The History of Samuel Titmarsh* (London, 1849), 12. Cited in I, cxxi, from which the following information is taken.

18. James R. Planché, *Recollections and Reflections* (London, 1872), Vol. I, 46.

19. See Edmund Wilson, 'Peacock's Musical Glasses', 407 (and Part II, Chapter 4): 'His books are more like light operas than novels'. Pauline Salz, in 'Peacock's Use of Music in his Novels', *J.E.G.P.*, LIV (July 1955), 370–9, develops the idea and compares Peacock's novels to the movements of Mozart's operas. Some of her observations are excellent, but the analogy is pushed too far. *Don Giovanni*, Peacock's favourite Mozart opera, can only by great stretch of imagination seem analogous in form to, say, *Nightmare Abbey* (where Peacock refers to it).

6 *The Misfortunes of Elphin*: a Lord of Misrule and the Magic of Bards

1. Edith Nicolls, in the Cole ed., Vol. I, xl.

2. Peacock did not know the *Mabinogion* in its present collective sense. 'The title "Mabinogion" is a modern one. It was used by Lady

Charlotte Guest as the title of her translations from the *Red Book of Hergest* and of the *Hanes Taliesin* [1838–49]. . . . The word *mabynnogyon* occurs once only in the manuscripts.' *The Mabinogion*, ed. and trans. G. Jones and T. Jones (London, 1949) [Everyman's Library], ix.

3. David Garnett, *The Novels of Peacock*, 550. What makes Peacock's unabated diligence even less likely is his having owned (according to the posthumous Sotheby catalogue of his library) no books on Wales dated later than 1823. It is hard to think of him working continually on the subject without keeping abreast of new books.

4. *The Cambrian Quarterly Magazine*, I (April 1829), 231.

5. Sir Edward Strachey, in *Calidore and Miscellanea*, ed. Richard Garnett (London, 1891), 19–20. For a full account of Peacock's interest in things Welsh, see Herbert Wright, 'The Associations of Thomas Love Peacock with Wales', *Essays and Studies by Members of the English Association* (Oxford, 1926). See also the discussion of *Elphin* in R. W. Barber's little survey, *Arthur of Albion* (London, 1961).

6. See Georg Lukács, *The Historical Novel* (Eng. trans., Boston, 1963). Despite its Marxist bias, Mr. Lukács' book offers one of the best discussions of Scott as a historical novelist and one of the best discussions of historical fiction generally.

7. Herbert Wright, 'The Associations of Peacock', 42.

8. Some of the absurd rhetoric in these scenes is reminiscent of Fielding's travesty, *Tom Thumb the Great*, which is concerned with King Arthur if not with Wales and contains related burlesque of heroics.

9. Priestley devotes a chapter to Peacock in *English Comic Characters* (London, 1925).

10. Cf. *Poetry of the Anti-Jacobin*, 41. 'Being the quintessence of all the Bactylics that ever were, or ever will be written.' One of many echoes.

11. Peacock's song looks forward to Aytoun's 'The Massacre of the Macpherson' (published in 1844 and part of the *Bon Gaultier Ballads*), a Scottish version of Peacock's bantering lines:

> Fhairshon swore a feud
>   Against the clan M'Tavish;
> Marched into their land
>   To murder and to rafish;
> For he did resolve
>   To extirpate the vipers,
> With four-and-twenty men
>   And five-and-thirty pipers. . . .

T. H. White, who borrows from Peacock, adapts the 'War Song' in *The Once and Future King*.

12. Herbert Wright, 'The Associations of Peacock', 46.

13. *Westminster Review*, X (April 1829), 434. One of Peacock's recent critics has made the same kind of critical mistake, that of defining the limits of satire and prescribing what is proper, or improper as a means of treatment. Joseph Percy Smith (*A Critical Study of Thomas Love Peacock* [unpublished dissertation, Berkeley, 1949], iii) maintains that Peacock was 'not a genuine satirist', because he 'had no clear or useful course'.

14. Scott, *Ivanhoe*, xlviii.

7 *Crotchet Castle*: 'the Modern Athenians'

1. For details see I, cxiv.

2. *Literary Gazette*, XV, No. 735 (February 1831), 115.

3. *Fraser's Magazine*, IV (August 1831), 17. Miriam Thrall writes (in *Rebellious Fraser's* [New York, 1934], 87) that 'Maginn's scornful critique of Peacock's *Crotchet Castle*' proved 'almost the only instance, though a conspicuous one, in which their [Fraser's] critical judgment was thrown hopelessly awry by political hostility.'

4. A. E. Dyson, for example, calls *Crotchet Castle* 'altogether the harshest and least pleasing of Peacock's novels', perhaps without considering this change in tone and the resulting lighter humour of the final chapters, *The Crazy Fabric*, 67.

5. Priestley, *Thomas Love Peacock*, 32.

6. David Garnett, *The Novels of Peacock*, 645.

7. Peacock's turns of phrase here are his own, but the joke itself—as to the ill-effects of 'philosophical' or 'scientific' education on servants—was already rather old. Elizabeth Hamilton's *Letter From a Hindu Rajah* (1796) uses it in a similar context. See the earlier reference to Miss Hamilton's *Memoirs of Modern Philosophers* in the chapter on *Headlong Hall* (p. 304).

8. MacQuedy is probably based specifically on John Ramsay McCulloch, an *Edinburgh* reviewer, professor of economics, and official in the India House. But he represents the entire profession of political economists. The *Westminster* was to suggest that it was unfitting that a political economist should cast doubt on the science of political economy (cf. I, cli). If Peacock considered himself a political economist, he evidently did not associate himself with the MacQuedys. There is, nevertheless, a great deal of self-parody in the novel. Peacock laughs, for example, at 'steam communication', though at the time he was occupied with the subject for the India

House. In short, he burlesques his own skills and humours in this novel, as though to reinforce one of the book's two mottoes:

> *Le monde est plein de fous, et qui n'en veut pas voir,*
> *Doit se tenir tout seul, et casser son miroir.*

The lines are his own adaptation from the Marquis de Sade.

9. Robert Elliott, *The Power of Satire* (Princeton, 1960), 176.

10. David Garnett identifies Trillo as Thomas Moore. He need be no one in particular, but excepting his ability to get up a song and his possible Irish background, he has more in common with the opera-loving Novello, who devoted his life to publications and performances of old as well as modern music. One music critic of the time did call himself 'The Dilettante'. But in Trillo's portrait, too, there is self-parody, for Peacock at the time *Crotchet Castle* appeared was already established as a music reviewer.

11. Peacock and Shelley, with others of Shelley's acquaintance, planned such a trip themselves. Not having Squire Crotchet's means, they were unable to afford the canal tolls and had to abandon the project.

12. See the discussion of *Paper Money Lyrics* in Part I, Chapter 5.

13. Jean-Jacques Mayoux goes into some detail about possible relationships between Peacock's novels and Restoration and eighteenth-century comedy. He suggests, e.g., that one of Bossnowl's lines in *Crotchet Castle* comes from Congreve's *Double Dealer*. See expecially pp. 596ff.

14. Richard Graves, *The Spiritual Quixote* (new edition, London, 1926), 17.

15. Ian Jack, *English Literature, 1815–1832*, 220.

16. David Worcester, *The Art of Satire* (London, 1938), 55.

17. Edith Nicolls in the Cole Edition, Vol. I, xli.

18. *Punch*, VI (January 1846). But Brougham—especially as an older man—was a common target of satire, one of those men, who, however talented, invite ridicule and distrust.

19. An excellent description of Peacock's method of presenting the debates is Augustus Able's, who writes: 'As the line of argument passes from one to the other of them . . . their contradictory points of view are shown to be complementary, for each is a segment of truth made contributary to a rounded whole. Truth is discovered on all sides, although the wranglers themselves are unaware of it; all parties are justified, while none is accredited. . . . The characters themselves are really the threads of argument . . .', *The Influence of Thomas Love Peacock on George Meredith* (Philadelphia, 1933), 102.

20. Stuart Tave does not discuss Peacock—Leigh Hunt is his favourite early nineteenth-century example—in *The Amiable Humorist, a Study of the Comic Theory and Criticism of the Eighteenth and Early Nineteenth Centuries*. But Peacock's 'ridicule' usually mellows to 'raillery', and the final character portraits are 'amiable' in the sense of the *Spectator* tradition that Tave describes.

21. Robert Elliott, *The Power of Satire*, 109.

22. Walter Raleigh, 'Lecture Notes on Thomas Love Peacock', *On Writing and Writers* (London, 1926), 151.

8 Later Fragments and *Gryll Grange*

1. Edith Nicolls in the Cole Edition, Vol. I, xxvi.

2. Buchanan, *A Poet's Sketchbook*, 105.

3. *A Collection of Letters of W. M. Thackeray*, ed. Brookfield (London, 1887), 100. Quoted in I, clxxviii.

4. *Saturday Review*, XL (March 16, 1861), 222. Of all Peacock's stories, *Gryll Grange* contains the most classical references and quotations, but, as the *Saturday Review* suggests, they do not intrude. The response of the magazine was evidently typical, for *Gryll Grange* seems to have been well received. Tennyson, e.g., whose portrait of Cleopatra is likened to the 'Queen of Bambo', is supposed to have ranked himself among Peacock's 'most devoted admirers'. Cited in I, cci.

5. In a lengthy footnote Peacock alludes to the dialogue in Plutarch where 'Gryllus maintained against Ulysses', as well as to Book II of the *Faerie Queene*, in which there is the 'hog' 'hight Grylle by name'.

6. Part of Peacock's brief introductory note to *Gryll Grange* casts light on both the *tensons*—the formalized, spontaneous debates—and the form of the chapters themselves. 'The mottoes', he writes, 'are sometimes specially apposite to the chapters to which they are prefixed; but more frequently to the general scope, or to borrow a musical term, the *motivo* of the *operetta*.' See the references to Pauline Salz and Edmund Wilson (p. 311).

7. Van Doren, *Life*, 233.

8. 'Cotswold Chace.' Peacock's last published work was a partial translation of the Italian play *Gl Ingannati* (1862), which 'with numerous verbal changes is reprinted in the Appendix to Furness's "New Variorum" edition of *Twelfth Night*' (I, cciii).

9. According to one account, Disraeli 'was much delighted with Peacock, and surprised to find in him the author of *Headlong Hall*, and calling him [*sic*] his "master"; but, says Peacock to me, "I did

not know he was my pupil." ' Hobhouse, *Recollections of a Long Life*, quoted in I, clxxvii. Disraeli was not the only statesman to enjoy Peacock. Gladstone, too, owned and read the Cole Edition. See J. L. Maddon, 'Gladstone's Reading of Thomas Love Peacock', *Notes and Queries*, N.S., XIV, No. 10 (October 1967), 384.

10. 'The Argument of Comedy', in *Theories of Comedy*, ed. Paul Lauter (Garden City, 1964), 454.

11. Mario Praz, *The Hero in Eclipse in Victorian Fiction* (London, 1956), 100.

12. In Trilling, *The Portable Matthew Arnold*, 462.

13. Trilling, Ibid., 477.

14. Compare F. R. Leavis's remarks on Peacock, included, as I have mentioned, as a footnote to Jane Austen in *The Great Tradition*, 19: 'In his [Peacock's] ironical treatment of contemporary society and civilization he is seriously applying serious standards, so that his books, which are obviously not novels in the same sense as Jane Austen's, have a permanent life as light reading—indefinitely re-readable for minds with mature interests.' One would not have expected Mr. Leavis to subscribe to this estimate of Peacock, and of course he cannot do so without a certain twisting of the word 'serious' and an appeal to that dubious category of 'light reading'. Implicitly Mr. Leavis suggests that a 'great tradition' can and should be more incorporative than his own rhetoric would lead one to believe.

15. Arnold, *Essays in Criticism*, Second Series, 224.

BIBLIOGRAPHICAL NOTE

Most of Peacock's writings are available in the Halliford Edition, ed. H. F. B. Brett-Smith and C. E. Jones, 10 vols. (London and N.Y., 1924–34; reprinted 1968), a very careful and valuable compilation, which includes bibliographical and textual material. All my references, excluding those to 'A Can of Cream from Devon' and to some of Peacock's music criticism, are based on the Halliford *Works*. The music notices from the *Globe* and *Examiner* appear in selected but representative form in Vol. IX of the *Works*; otherwise they remain uncollected. Also uncollected are a few fragments of stories, some of Peacock's official writings for the India House, and the essay on steam navigation for the *Edinburgh Review*. Letters crop up occasionally. The largest selection outside Vol. VIII of the *Works* may be found in *New Shelley Letters*, ed. W. S. Scott (London, 1948). Additional material is available in *Shelley and His Circle, 1773-1822*, 2 vols., ed. K. N. Cameron (Cambridge, Mass., 1961). Contributing editor for Vol. I, which contains biographical and critical information, is Eleanor L. Nicholes.

There are several editions of Peacock's novels; best is David Garnett's (London, 1947; Harvest Books, 1963). I have relied, as any reader of Peacock must rely, on Mr. Garnett's notes. Older editions of Peacock's works—all incomplete—by Henry Cole (3 vols., London, 1875), Richard Garnett (10 vols., London, 1891), and George Saintsbury (5 vols., London, 1895–7), have been supplanted by the fuller and more reliable Halliford Edition.

There have been several book-length studies of Peacock, though no major work in recent years. The most thorough discussion of his ideas and intellectual background is J. J. Mayoux's *Un Epicurien anglais: Thomas Love Peacock* (Paris, 1933). A. B. Young's pioneer study, *The Life and Novels of Thomas Love Peacock* (Norwich, 1904), now offers little of value. Better is A. Martin Freeman's *Thomas Love Peacock: A Critical Study* (London, 1911). J. B. Priestley's *Thomas Love Peacock* (London, 1927, reprinted 1967) [English Men of Letters Series] includes brilliant insights in its brief survey. Also useful is Olwen Campbell's short commentary, *Thomas Love Peacock* (London and N.Y., 1953), which offers perhaps the most understanding account of Peacock's relationship with Shelley. Other full-length studies include Benvenuto Cellini's untranslated and somewhat derivative *Thomas Love Peacock* (Rome, 1937), and several unpublished dissertations, among them J. B. Ludwig's informative *The Peacock Tradition in English Prose Fiction* (U.C.L.A., 1953). References to some of the many essays and chapters devoted to Peacock may be found in the text and notes. Ian Jack's remarks on Peacock in *English Literature, 1815–1832* (Oxford, 1963), seem to me unquestionably the fairest by a historian of the period.

The standard life remains that by Carl Van Doren (London and N.Y., 1911; reprinted 1966), but Vol. I of the Halliford Edition provides a long biographical introduction, much of which is corrective. Neither is entirely satisfactory as biography.

Bill Read has compiled an invaluable annotated bibliography of works by and about Peacock: *The Critical Reputation of Thomas Love Peacock* (doctoral dissertation at Boston University, 1959), which is available only as a Xerox book (from the University of Michigan). Mr. Read has issued a check list without annotation in the *Bulletin of Bibliography*. Part I, 'Works by Thomas Love Peacock', appears in Vol. XXIV, No. 2, pp. 32–4; Part II, 'Works About Thomas Love Peacock', appears in Vol. XXIV, No. 3, pp. 70–2 and No. 4, pp. 88–91. Little critical attention has been paid to Peacock since Mr. Read published his check-list (in 1964), and any further listing here would be superfluous.

INDEX

Abercrombie, Sir Ralph, 23
Able, Augustus H., 295, 314
Abrams, M. H., 83, 294
Acton, John, Lord, 114
Acton, William, 300
Addison, Joseph, 138, 153, 168, 282
Aeschylus, 49, 107
Aesop, 194
Alfieri, 31
Amis, Kingsley, 302-3
Amory, Thomas, 164, 196
Anderson, Sherwood, 193
Anti-Jacobin Review, The, 13, 29, 289, 304, 305, 308, 312
Apuleius, 46, 49, 51
Aresty, Esther B., 300
Ariosto, 87
Aristophanes, 105, 109, 163, 166, 172, 268, 273, 274, 279-81
Aristotle, 108
Arnold, Matthew, 19, 79-80, 91, 111, 113, 114, 119, 285-6, 300, 316
Athenaeus, 108, 148, 152, 154-5, 167, 189, 166, 277, 282
Atlas, The, 121
Aubin, Robert, 289
Ausonius, 289
Austen, Jane, 136, 179, 187, 189, 210, 273, 284, 290, 302, 316
Aytoun, William, 312

Babbitt, Irving, 91
Bacon, Sir Francis, 143
Bage, Robert, 164-70, 198, 202, 259
Bailey, Benjamin, 78
Baker, Carlos, 160, 301
Baker, Joseph, 294
Barbauld, Mrs. Anna, 169

Barber, R. W., 313
Barthélemy, Abbé, 288
Bateson, F. W., 311
Beattie, James, 4, 249
Beckford, William, 164, 184, 305, 307
Beethoven, Ludwig von, 123, 132, 133, 134
Bell, Clive, 9, 287-8
Bellini, Vincenzo, 53, 124, 126, 131-3, 134
Bentham, Jeremy, xi, xv, 88, 92-5, 112, 118, 120, 121, 146, 295, 298
Bentley, Eric, 299
Bentley's Ballads, 66
Bentley's Miscellany, x, xv, xvi, 66, 142, 305
Berg, Alban, 133
Bergson, Henri, 267
Berkeley, George, 168
Berlioz, Hector, 123
Berni, Francesco, 301
Bible, 10, 288
Birkbeck, Morris, 298
Bishop, Henry, 123, 135, 237
Blake, William, 41, 50, 187-8
Boccaccio, 51, 161, 301
Boiardo, 278
Boileau, 87, 96, 301
Bononcini, 133
Booth, Wayne, 162, 301
Boswell, James, 100, 136, 137, 138, 150, 300, 301
Bowring, John, 113
Bradley, F. H., 120
Brett-Smith, H. F. B., xi, 24, 44, 201, 271, 287, 297, 317
Brillat-Savarin, 151
Brinton, Crane, 117, 298, 302
British Critic, The, 29, 289
Bronson, Bertrand, 310

319

INDEX

Godwin, William, 211–12, 311
Goethe, Johann Wolfgang von, 50,
   83, 109, 212–13, 275, 308
Goldsmith, Oliver, 143, 192, 203
Gosson, Stephen, 87–8
Grainger, James, 20
Graves, Richard, 148, 164–5, 179,
   262, 290, 304, 308, 314
Gray, Thomas, vi, 16, 22, 23–4, 26,
   30, 31, 36, 53, 57, 239, 249,
   250
Green, Matthew, 190
Gregory, Allene, 302
Grisi, Mme. Guiditta, 134
Grosse, Marquis of, 212
Gryffydh, Jane (Mrs. Peacock),
   xiii, xv, 31, 59, 141, 241, 292
Guarini, G. B., 10
Guest, Charlotte, 312

Hagstrum, Jean, 34, 290
Hamilton, Anthony, 198, 306
Hamilton, Elizabeth, 304, 313
Handel, George F., 123, 133
Harmonicon, The, 122
Hartley, David, 294
Hartman, Geoffrey H., 287
Hawkins, Sir John, 123
Haydn, Franz Joseph, 123, 133
Haydon, Benjamin, 295
Hayward, Abraham, 151–2
Hazlitt, William,
   Amory, Thomas, appreciation
      of, 164
   caricatured, 260
   Cobbett, his style, 145
   Coleridge, attack on, ascribed
      to H., 81–2, 294
   Godwin, admiration for, 211
   Lectures on the English Poets, 23,
      95
   Letter to William Gifford, 42
   Liber Amoris, 221
   'My First Acquaintance with
      Poets', 23, 74, 306
   'On Gusto', 104
   Peacock, attack on, 121, 134
   personal essay, writer of, 221
   Pindaric Odes, comments on, 23
   political views, 119
   prose style, theories of, 73–6, 125
   Spirit of the Age, 221

'The Utilitarian Controversy',
   121, 298
   mentioned, 22, 78, 96, 97, 99,
      234, 288, 295
Hegel, George W., 90
Heine, Heinrich, 61, 114, 129–30
Hermann, Johann Gottfried, 103,
   109
Herrick, Robert, 26
Heyne, Christian Gottlieb, 103
Hicks, Granville, 114
Highet, Gilbert, 301, 307
Hill, Dr. John, 149
Hoare, Sir Richard, 311
Hobhouse, John Cam, Lord
   Broughton, xi, xvi, 61, 146,
   274, 276
Hogarth, George, 122, 123, 131,
   299
Hogarth, William, 66
Hogg, Thomas Jefferson, xiv, 37,
   41, 46, 175, 180, 300, 308
Holbach, Baron, 115, 180
Holcroft, Thomas, 169, 175
Holmes, Edward, 122
Homer, 22, 49, 92, 108, 113, 274,
   278
Hooke, Theodore, 66, 293
Hookham, Edward, xiii, 16–17, 25,
   29, 33, 46, 92, 110, 174, 289,
   292
Hookham, Thomas, xiii, 37–8
Horace, 68, 78, 89, 155, 192, 289,
   292
House, Humphry, 220–1, 309
Housman, A. E., 259
Hume, David, 152–3, 243
Hungerford, Edward, 50, 291
Hunt, Leigh,
   Autobiography, 58, 292
   Dramatic Criticism, 299
   Literary Criticism, 293, 306
   Moore, Thomas, criticism of,
      295–6
   music criticism, 122, 125–6, 129–
      130
   Peacock, acquaintance with, 16,
      146
   Peacock, attack on, 58
   Peacock's poetry, praise of, 68,
      70, 199, 222, 305
   poetry, receptivity to, 79
   political views, 119, 297

322